MW00795405

A General Doctrine
of the Sacraments
and
The Mystery of the
Eucharist

Johann Auer
Joseph Ratzinger

Dogmatic Theology

Johann Auer

A General Doctrine
of the Sacraments
and The Mystery of
The Eucharist

Translated by Erasmo Leiva-Merikakis
Translation edited by Hugh M. Riley

The Catholic University of America Press
Washington, D.C.

Originally published in German under the title *Allgemeine Sakramenten-lehre* und *Das Mysterium der Eucharistie*, copyright © 1971 Friedrich Pustet Verlag, Regensburg. English translation from the third revised and enlarged edition, 1980.

The paper used in this publication meets the minimum requirements of American National Standards for Information Science—Permanence of Paper for Printed Library materials, ANSI Z39.48-1984.
∞

LIBRARY OF CONGRESS CATALOGING-IN-PUBLICATION DATA

Auer, Johann, 1910–1989
   [Allgemeine Sakramentenlehre und das Mysterium der Eucharistie.
English]
   A general doctrine of the Sacraments and the mystery of the Eucharist
/ Johann Auer ; translated by Erasmo Leiva-Merikakis ; translation edited
by Hugh M. Riley.
      p.   cm. — (Dogmatic theology / Johann Auer, Joseph Ratzinger ; 6)
   Translation of : Allgemeine Sakramentelehre und das Mysterium der
Eucharistie. 1980.
   Includes bibliographical references (p.   ) and indexes.
   1.   Sacraments—Catholic   Church.   2. Lord's   Supper—Catholic
Church.   3. Catholic Church—Doctrines.   I. Riley, Hugh M.   II. Title.
III. Title: Mystery of the Eucharist.   IV. Series: Auer, Johann, 1910–1989
Kleine katholische Dogmatik.   English ; 6.
BX2200.A7213   1995
234'.16—dc20
94-35606
ISBN 0-8132-0824-6 (cl). — ISBN 0-8132-0825-4 (pa)

Dedicated with gratitude and devotion to my friends and colleagues Dominikus Lindner and Albert Lang for their eightieth birthday

Contents

Preface to the Original German Series

Dogmatic Theology is intended to be a series of textbooks for theology students—in brief compass. It has come out in a pocket book format because it is meant to accompany the student, not just in the classroom but on his or her meditative walks as well. Anyone who has had the task of preparing a three-year dogmatics course will know how impossible it is to achieve for each and every area of dogma that scientific presentation which can be expected from a multi-authored, collaborative work such as *Mysterium Salutis.* By way of compensation, textbooks which are concise, through their selectivity and inner coherence, may illustrate certain points more clearly than is the case in such team products.

We have decided to publish this series of concise textbooks because we believe they fill a gap. They are intended to provide a foundation which appropriate lectures can extend and build upon. In this way they will offer a basis for theological discussion, something which is meaningful in dogmatics only if it can presuppose a certain knowledge of the subject matter.

We have tried to pay special attention to three dimensions which are important for dogmatics today:

1. The biblical foundation of doctrine. This is why we cite biblical texts so frequently. The quotations are there in order to communicate not simply the doctrinal truths themselves but also their spirit.

2. The history of individual doctrines. The historian of doctrine is well placed to show the many facets of the underlying problem as well as the multiplicity of human answers.

3. The systematic inner coherence of doctrine. Doctrinal formulations always tell us about some part of the whole, but the whole is more than the sum of its parts. In the exposition of the individual parts, it is vital to preserve the whole and keep it in view at all times. The main problem in teaching dogmatics is really this: by means of a large number of statements scattered through three or more years of the student's academic life, dogmatics must unfold before the learner's eyes a single reality and a single truth. This fundamentally single whole can stand before the student in its greatness and profundity only to the extent that he or she is able to absorb it in its unity at a single glance.

It is our hope that this series will be used not just as a series of textbooks but also as a collection of materials capable of enriching theological thinking, reflection and meditation. We hope, moreover, that the series may thus stimulate that attitude which all true theologizing requires. That attitude may be summed up under five heads: respect for the uniqueness of the object of theology; sensitivity to the various methods that object demands, and a readiness to employ them; the realization that faith must accompany knowledge, and that both life and action flow from this knowledge of faith; awareness that an individual's theological endeavor needs for its completion the achievement of others both past and present and will thus take its place in the noble history of theology in our Church and find its orientation there—and finally, the awareness that all theology, as reflection on the Church's teaching, shares in the "historicity" both of the Church itself and of the individual theologian within it.

It is our wish that this series, which in the spirit of the

Gospels attempts to present "old and new" (Matt 13,52), may be of service to theology and theologians in a time of widespread and rapid change.

JOHANN AUER

JOSEPH RATZINGER

Preface to the English Edition
of the Series

Dogmatic Theology of Johann Auer and Joseph Ratzinger is now being offered to an English-speaking public in the belief that the three characteristic emphases of the series mentioned in the German preface—informedness by Scripture, attention to the history of doctrine, concern with the systematic coherence of theological teaching—are as desirable in the Anglophone world, far-flung and diverse as that now is, as in the Bavaria which is the author's home. Both men belong to the milieu of South German Catholic theology which has produced, over the last hundred and fifty years, several great schools or centers. In each of these, a rigorously academic theology, concerned to rise to the challenges of documentary accuracy and conceptual orderliness set by universities, was placed at the service of the Church—bishops, clergy and people—and hence obliged to meet the differing but no less exigent requirements of doctrinal orthodoxy and pastoral good sense. It is typical of German Catholic theological work in this inheritance that it is simultaneously open to biblical scholarship, to Church tradition in all its phases and monuments, and to the philosophical culture of its day which, however, it sifts critically, bearing in mind the Johannine dictum, "Test the spirits, to see if they come from God" (I John 4, 1).

Students of dogmatic theology are frequently to be heard making three complaints about the state of the subject. First, they find it difficult to employ contemporary biblical criticism in a constructive fashion in the sphere of doctrine. This Dogmatic Theology, while showing no hostility to historical-critical tools as such, which occupy a limited but legitimate place in its enquiry, seeks to penetrate beyond the historical-critical problems to the revelatory witness that shines forth from the Scriptures. Secondly, students lament the sheer quantity of detailed monographs now available on the history of doctrine. Sinking as one may well do beneath this weight of erudition, the main contours of doctrinal development are easily lost to view. In the Dogmatic Theology, by a judicious selection of *topoi*, an attempt is made to point out the lie of the land to those who cannot see the wood for the trees. Or, to change the metaphor once again, theologically acute historical highlighting illuminates what is of lasting significance for the Church's sensibility, teaching and practice. Thirdly, students do not always find it easy to see how the different facets of doctrinal believing belong together as a unitary whole. Dogmatic Theology addresses itself to this problem in a conscious effort to lead back all the ways of doctrinal reflection to their living center, the Gospel of grace.

Although the series is aimed in the first place at the theological student, whether in university or seminary, the needs it tries to meet are felt much more widely by clergy and laity alike. May that "quest for understanding," to which all Christians are summoned by the gift of faith itself, be stimulated, assisted and brought closer to its goal in the vision of God by the contemplative study of these pages.

AIDAN NICHOLS, O.P.
Blackfriars, Cambridge
Memorial day of St. Isidore,
bishop and doctor of the Church,
1987

Preface to This Volume

A General Doctrine of the Sacraments and The Mystery of the Eucharist (volume 6) is the second volume in the order of publication in the Dogmatic Theology series, coming after *The Gospel of Grace* (volume 5). It will soon be followed by *The Sacraments of the Church* (volume 7), which treats the other six sacraments. For technical as well as intrinsic reasons, as will soon be apparent, we are publishing the sacramental doctrine of the Church in two volumes. It is our hope that these will contribute some clarification precisely today, at a time when, as a result of a liturgical revival full of fruitful promise, the sacramental mystery itself and especially the mystery of the Eucharist have become the object of intense theological discussion.

The following presentation will attempt to bring some equilibrium to the imbalance between theological concept and believed reality which becomes particularly obvious in sacramental doctrine, and we will attempt to close the gap both by the language we use and the method of exposition we apply. Our natural speech is not capable of translating into unambiguous language even the mysteries of personality, and even less the realities and events which only faith can comprehend; this is why language, when speaking of the mysterious, must resort to images, analogies, the construction of adequate models, and the use of often paradoxical statements. This is the origin in theological language of the gap between indicative word and indicated reality. Such a situation has often given rise to the danger of a nefarious dichotomy between a "conceptual theology" in the official schools and a "realistic theology" in the practice of the spiritual life and in mysticism. Especially in the doctrine on the Eucharist the theology of the Church has tried to bridge this dichotomy through deep philosophical convictions which will occupy relatively more space in this present volume because of the importance of the subject.

I would not want to send this book to press without first thanking my dear colleague, Profesor Georg Englhardt, for valuable bibliographical references; my assistants, Father Hermann Josef May and Dr. Heribert Rossmann, for their technical collaboration; my secretary, Frau Ruth Hapke, and the editorial readers, Herr Gerhard Kukofka and Fräulein Monika Bock, for all their kind efforts.

JOHANN AUER
Regensburg
Feast of St. Athanasius, 1970

Preface to the Second Edition

The second edition of this volume makes it possible to discuss three subjects much in prominence today. First, the "Word of God" has been more greatly focused in its sacramental character especially by the entire orientation of Vatican II's Constitution on Divine Revelation. An entire chapter will be devoted to this subject in its relation to the General Doctrine of the Sacraments. Likewise, the question of the meaning and form of "concelebration" and the far-reaching subject of "intercommunion" will be discussed here at least in its dogmatic ramifications.

I offer this second edition to my readers in the hope that this little volume, with its additions, will serve the needs of all those interested in the questions of theology in our time, and may it help them to deepen and clarify their personal faith and knowledge.

JOHANN AUER
Regensburg
April, 1974

Preface to the Third Edition

A few additions have been made to the third edition, especially in view of being useful to ecumenical dialogue, which has gained new insights and perspectives since the appearance of the fist edition. May this small volume, particularly through its bibliographical references, be a guide and a help to in-depth study.

JOHANN AUER
Regensburg
Feast of St. Augustine, 1979

Editor's Note on This Volume

The present volume is the English translation of the third revised and enlarged edition of volume 6 of the Dogmatic Theology of Johann Auer and Joseph Ratzinger. After *Es chatology* (volume 9) and *The Church* (volume 8), this volume becomes the third of the original German series, *Kleine Katholische Dogmatik*, to be offered to the English-speaking public. The popularity of this volume is indicated by the fact that in nine years subsequent to its original publication a third edition was necessary. Renewed interest in the Eucharist as center of the Church's life following Vatican II gave rise to a discussion that laid bare the layers of unfinished business in regard to the theology of the sacraments and particularly of the Sacrifice of the Mass and the relationship between the Eucharist as sacrificial meal and as sacramental sacrifice. When the hardened fronts began to yield to the spring thaw of ecumenism the unresolved dichotomy between word and sacrament reappeared and it soon became evident that the understanding of the Eucharist would be fundamental to Church re-union and that intercommunion and goodwill alone could not achieve this.

In the midst of this theological and religious ferment Johann Auer, the author of this present volume *The Mystery of the Eucharist*, saw the necessity of a wide-sweeping review of the Church's teaching that would take into account biblical, historical, and theological aspects and provide all concerned with Church renewal with a useful compendium, an attempt, as he himself says in his own preface to this volume, "to bring some equilibrium to the imbalance between theological concept and believed reality," in regard to the heart of the Church's life, the Eucharist.

Most useful for those concerned with the ongoing renewal of the Church and a help to those discouraged at the apparent slowness of pace is the thoroughly up-to-date and extensive Select Bibliography produced for this English translation by my friend and colleague Michael A. Fahey, S.J., Professor and Dean of Theology at the University of St. Michael's College, Toronto. This makes accessible to the English-speaking reader the further development undergone in recent years in all the topics treated in Johann Auer's German original.

HUGH M. RILEY, EDITOR
Munich
Holy Thursday 1994

An Introduction to the Work of Johann Auer

Johann Auer was a Bavarian theologian who, throughout a long life of literary production dating back to before World War II, took as his chief interest the theology of grace, placed now at the service of an entire dogmatics which moves from the triune God, through creation, to the person and work of Jesus Christ and the sacramental life of the Church. On his sixty-fifth birthday the editors of a volume of essays in his honor described his work as a celebration of theology as *Heilswissenschaft*, the knowledge and study of salvation.[1] For grace, as Heribert Rossmann and Joseph Ratzinger pointed out, does not merely bring human beings to a knowledge of their true selves, but, as understood by Auer, grants them a share in God's own divine life. If the Catholic Church, at the Second Vatican Council, understood itself as empowered to create unity and peace in the world, this can only be because it is, in Christ, a sign and instrument of the most inward community with god, which Jesus Christ brings us through his life and teaching, death and resurrection. God's gracious action for our re-formation serves to lead human beings, through the Church's community of salvation, to the Uncreated Grace which is the triune God himself.

Who, then, was the theologian of whose ideas this is the leit-motif? Johann Auer was born on May 15, 1910, near Regensburg.[2] He completed his secondary education at the *Humanistisches Gymnasium* in Straubing and went on to study theology at the University of Munich. Ordained a priest at Regensburg (whose cathedral city was one of the

cultural centers of southern Germany in the Middle Ages),
Auer continued his studies after ordination by specializing
in medieval philosophy and theology. His philosophical
dissertation on the freedom of the human will in Thomas
Aquinas and Duns Scotus was published at Munich in
1938.[3] Auer's study of human freedom, in the company of
these two masters, centers on two questions. First, what
must the freedom of the will be like if it is truly human
freedom and not a meaningless, blind arbitrariness unworthy of us? Second, how can the will so be determined as to
constitute meaningful striving, without doing damage to
its freedom? With a care to allow each author his particular approach within the ample space of Catholic thought,
Auer's study highlights the significant differences between
Thomas and Scotus on these issues. Thus, for Thomas
the will is free insofar as it is *rational* appetite, simply;
Thomas is interested, above all, in the meaningfulness of
human striving. For Scotus, on the other hand, the will is,
first and foremost, free with the primordial freedom of its
own nature, from the superabundance of its power; his interest lies in the experienceable *freedom* of a will that is,
to his mind, identical with the soul itself. Thomas' will is
moved by something actual beyond itself, Scotus' by its
own inner force. To Thomas, the object of the will is the
good in general, the ground of value—and ultimately beatitude, which in the last analysis is an act of the speculative
intellect, the vision of God. To Scotus, the will's object is,
rather, being in general, its last goal felicity, attained by
love, necessitated by no object but finding in God an object
with a due proportion to its own infinite striving. Auer
concludes his comparison of the two medieval thinkers by
throwing light on the grounds of their difference. Thomas'
approach is by way of creation as nature, an analogical family of realities of different kinds, and he sets out to present
experienced totalities in terms of thinkable relationships
and laws; Scotus, by contrast, approaches creation as existence—seeking what is particular, singular, concentrating

on the phenomenon in its independence and individual wholeness. The entire human being philosophizes and, in the contrast between Thomism and Scotism, two types of scholar-saint are in play. Thus the mystery of the will's freedom (the subject of Auer's book) takes us back to the mystery of human personality itself.[4]

From this largely philosophical study, Auer then turned to theology proper, under the guidance of the great religious historian of the Middle Ages, Martin Grabmann, and of the dogmatician Michael Schmaus. A certain preference for the Franciscan school issued in his next book, a study of the development of the doctrine of grace in high medieval Scholasticism, with special reference to the teaching of the Franciscan cardinal Matthew of Acquasparta.[5] Here a philosophy of the human will draw from Augustinian and Franciscan sources, and a theology of grace as supernatural love, are joined together. Matthew of Acquasparta, an Umbrian who lived from 1240 to 1302, had been almost forgotten until the late nineteenth century, but as teacher, minister-general of the Friars Minor, cardinal, and reformer he turned out to have been a major figure, outstanding among the young Bonaventurians of his generation. His interest for Auer lies in his combining a fundamental allegiance to the Franciscan tradition, largely Augustinian as this was, with an openness to Thomism. Like all the Franciscans from Alexander of Hales to Bonaventure, he asserted the primacy of will (love) over intellect (understanding), of experience over thought, of the person over the *res*: yet he accepted more of Thomas' theory of knowledge, and metaphysics, than had his predecessors.[6]

In Matthew we see an attempt to appropriate Aristotelian thought in a Franciscan spirit. The starting point was the teaching of the Masters of the Sentences, Peter Lombard, that charity is the direct action of the Holy Spirit. Owing to the distinction between Creator and creature, however, such uncreated Charity must be received by a human being. Some kind of accidental form is needful if it

is to belong to the created realm, however directly it may
be ordered to the divine. Earlier Franciscans had tried to
speak of this, in the imagistic language inherited from Augustine, by a metaphysics of light. Matthew, however, saw
the importance of the new Aristotelian conceptual language of form. Though Matthew was not a particularly
original thinker, Auer evidently admires him for holding
together the Bonaventurian stress on the role of grace in
our moral and religious existence, with the developing
Thomist inquiry into the metaphysical ground of the supernatural order. Now less optimistic about the benefits of
Scotist thought, Auer saw the strains in such Aristotelian-
izing Franciscanism as leading, however, to a tearing apart
of Creator and creature, a separation of faith and knowledge, and finally, a devaluation of the idea of the supernatural in post-Scotist nominalism, since the basis for a human
understanding of the supernatural order is lost. Auer drew
two lessons from this research.[7] First, though theological
pluralism within the Church's communion may well help
to preserve a desirable multiplicity of illuminating perspective, not all the aspects of each and every theology can
be underwritten without further ado. Second, he saw the
possibility of a dogmatics that would take grace as its center, since from grace one may move, as the history of theology could show, through the doctrine of justification to
an account of Christology and the sacraments (and so the
Church), while at the same time, by way of the doctrine of
election (and its shadow, reprobation), one can move to an
account of *theo*-logy proper, the doctrine of God.[8]

After the years of wartime military service, which the
editors of Auer's *Festschrift* describe as "bitter" for him
and filled with extraordinary experience, he was enabled,
by the publication of his *Habilitationsschrift*, to become a
university professor at Munich in 1947, lecturing also
from 1947 to 1950 at the *Philosophische-Theologische
Hochschule* at Freising, the former primatial see of Bavaria
whose name is still incorporated in the title of the arch-

diocese of Munich and Freising. From 1950 until 1968 Auer
was professor of dogmatics and the history of dogma at the
University of Bonn, where his pastoral activities and contribution to the formation of the clergy were notable. In
1968, however, with the creation of the University of Regensburg, he was able to return to Bavaria and to his native
city. After that his name would be linked with the series
Kleine Katholische Dogmatik, although the manysided-
ness of his interests in the history of doctrine and in contemporary theology was also manifested in a constant flow
of articles on particular themes.[9] Johann Auer died in Regensburg on March 17, 1989.

What are the principal features of Auer's mature theological work? They are, in the first place, the holding together of the contributions of Scripture, the history of tradition, and systematic theology, a capacity for synthesis to
which this *Dogmatics* amply testifies. And, in the second
place, in the centrality of the topic of grace to which his
earlier studies had directed him, whereby the Holy Spirit
draws us to himself through faith, hope and charity, in contemplation and *askēsis*.

AIDAN NICHOLS, O.P.

Abbreviations

AAS	*Acta Apostolicae Sedis* (Vatican City, 1900ff.)
ALW	*Archiv für Liturgiewissenschaft* (Regensburg, 1950ff.)
BKV	*Bibliothek der Kirchenväter* (Kempten, 1911ff.)
BL	*Bibel-Lexikon*, 2d ed., ed. H. Haag (Einsiedeln, 1968)
BThW	*Bibeltheologisches Wörterbuch*, 3d ed., ed. Bauer, 2 vols. (Graz, 1967)
CChr	*Corpus Christianorum* (Turnhout, 1953ff.)
CSCO	*Corpus Scriptorum Christianorum Orientalium* (Paris, 1903ff.)
CSEL	*Corpus Scriptorum Ecclesiasticorum Latinorum* (Vienna, 1886ff.)
D	H. Denzinger, *Enchiridion Symbolorum, Definitionum et Declarationum de rebus fidei et morum*, 31st ed. (Freiburg im Breisgau, 1957)
DACL	*Dictionnaire d'Archéologie Chrétienne et de Liturgie*, 15 vols. and 2 supplements (Paris, 1924–1953)
DBS	*Dictionnaire de la Bible, Supplément* (Paris, 1923ff.)
DHGE	*Dictionnaire d'Histoire et de Géographie Ecclésiastique* (Paris, 1912ff.)
DS	H. Denzinger and A. Schönmetzer, *Enchiridion Symbolorum, Definitionum et Declarationum de rebus fidei et morum*, 34th ed. (Freiburg im Breisgau, 1967)
DSAM	*Dictionnaire de la Spiritualité Ascétique et Mystique* (Paris, 1932ff.)

xxviii   Abbreviations

DThC	*Dictionnaire de Théologie Catholique*, 15 vols. and 2 supplements (Paris, 1903–1950)
EC	*Enciclopedia Cattolica*, 12 vols. (Vatican City, 1949–1961)
EKL	*Evangelisches Kirchenlexikon*, 4 vols. (Göttingen, 1956–1961)
Funk	*Didascalia et Constitutiones Apostolicae* I, ed. F. X. Funk (Paderborn, 1905)
GuL	*Geist und Leben* (Würzburg, 1947ff.)
HDG	*Handbuch der Dogmengeschichte*, ed. M. Schmaus, J. R. Geiselmann, and A. Grillmeier (Freiburg im Breisgau, 1951ff.)
HThG	*Handbuch theologischer Grundbegriffe*, 3d ed., ed. H. Fries, 2 vols. (1962–1963)
JLW	*Jahrbuch für Liturgiewissenschaft* (Fulda, 1921–1941.)
KKD	J. Auer and J. Ratzinger, *Kleine Katholische Dogmatik*, 9 vols. (Regensburg, 1970ff.)
Landgraf	A. M. Landgraf, *Dogmengeschichte der Früh-scholastik*, 8 vols in 4 parts (Regensburg, 1952–1956)
LThK	*Lexikon für Theologie und Kirche*, 2d ed., ed. J. Höfer and K. Rahner (Freiburg im Breisgau, 1957–1967)
Mansi	*Sacrorum conciliorum nova et amplissima collectio*, ed. J. D. Mansi, rev. ed., 60 vols. (Paris, 1899–1927)
Meyer K	H. A. Meyer, *Kritisch-exegetischer Kommentar über das Neue Testament* (Göttingen, various editions)
MS	*Mysterium Salutis, Grundriss Heilsgeschicht-licher Dogmatik*, 5 vols. (Einsiedeln and Cologne, 1965–1976)
NCE	*New Catholic Encyclopedia* (New York, 1967)
PG	*Patrologia Graeca*, ed. J. P. Migne (Paris, 1857–1866)
PhJ	*Philosophisches Jahrbuch* (Fulda, 1888ff.)

PL   *Patrologia Latina*, ed. J. P. Migne (Paris, 1844–1855)
RAC   *Reallexikon für Antike und Christentum*, ed. Th. Klausen (Stuttgart, 1950ff.)
RAM   *Revue d'ascétique et de mystique* (Toulouse, 1920ff.)
RGG   *Die Religion in Geschichte und Gegenwart*, 3d ed., 7 vols. (Tübingen, 1957–1965)
RNT   *Regensburger Neues Testament*, ed. J. Eckert and O. Knoch (Regensburg, 1938ff.)
Sacr.M   *Sacramentum Mundi*, 5 vols. (Freiburg im Breisgau, 1966ff.)
TDNT   *Theological Dictionary of the New Testament* [ET of TWNT], trans. and ed. G. W. Bromily (Grand Rapids, 1964–1974)
ThQ   Theologische Quartalschrift (Tübingen, 1819ff.)
TWNT   *Theologisches Wörterbuch zum Neuen Testament*, ed. G. Kittel and G. Friedrich (Stuttgart, 1933–1974)
WA   Martin Luther, *Werke. Kritische Gesamtausgabe* [= Weimarer Ausgabe] (Weimar, 1883ff.)
WdB   *Wörterbuch zur biblischen Botschaft*, ed. X. Léon-Dufour (Freiburg im Breisgau, 1964)
ZAM   *Zeitschrift für Aszese und Mystik* (Würzburg, 1926–1947.)
ZKTh   *Zeitschrift für Katholische Theologie* (Innsbruck, 1877ff.)

ABBREVIATIONS FOR THE TEXTS OF VATICAN II

AA   *Apostolicam Actuositatem*   Decree on the Apostolate of the Laity
AG   *Ad Gentes*   Decree on the Church's Missionary Activity
CD   *Christus Dominus*   Decree on the Bishops' Pastoral Office

DH	*Dignitatis Humanae*	Declaration on Religious Freedom
DV	*Dei Verbum*	Dogmatic Constitution on Divine Revelation
GE	*Gravissimum Educationis*	Decree on Christian Education
GS	*Gaudium et Spes*	Pastoral Constitution on the Church in the Modern World
IM	*Inter Mirifica*	Decree on the Instruments of Social Communication
LG	*Lumen Gentium*	Dogmatic Constitution on the Church
NA	*Nostra Aetate*	Declaration on the Relationship of the Church to Non-Christian Religions
OE	*Orientalium Ecclesiarum*	Decree on the Eastern Catholic Churches
OT	*Optatam Totius*	Decree on Priestly Formation
PC	*Perfectae Caritatis*	Decree on the Appropriate Renewal of the Religious Life
PO	*Presbyterorum Ordinis*	Decree on the Ministry and Life of Priests
SC	*Sacrosanctum Concilium*	Constitution on the Sacred Liturgy
UR	*Unitatis Redintegratio*	Decree on Ecumenism

General Introduction

Christian existence is not possible without the reality that the theology of our Church has called "sacrament" in a general sense since the third and in a strict sense since the twelfth century. Great objections were time and again raised against this reality not only by the Gnostics of the second and third centuries, but also by the Messalians of the fifth century, the Spirituals of the Middle Ages, the Reformation doctrines of Luther and Calvin, and most pointedly since the Enlightenment. Since the Enlightenment the sacramental reality has been accused of dealing in unspiritual "magic" and for this reason it has been rejected as unworthy of the Christian worldview. In most recent times "sacrament" has either been pitted against the "Word of God" or identified with it—that Word that since the First World War has attained to greater importance even in the Catholic sphere as a result of both the biblical movement and the ecumenical movement.

Independently of all these "trends" and tendencies, which are both conditioned by a given epoch and determined by the subject itself, we must affirm that the reality of sacrament remains an essential component of Christian existence, just as much as prayer and the Word of God, just as much as living an active life of grace and following Christ by bearing the cross.

A rapid sketch of four fundamental problems of human existence will now clarify, and perhaps provide a basis for, these affirmations.

The first fundamental problem of human existence is certainly *the distinction of body and soul.* This question has as its object the differentiation and relative autonomy of both these realms of being to which humans belong (the material-corporeal and the spiritual-personal), but also the fact that these realms are oriented toward one another, possess their own dignity vis-à-vis one another, and have a specific valuable service to perform for one another.

Closely linked to this first problem is the second, the *social problem*, which examines the ontological and moral relationship of the individual to the community and of the community to the individual. Just as the individual person bears certain essential social structures within himself or herself, so too every human community is essentially oriented toward autonomous persons.

Against the background of these two questions there emerge two further problems that reach even more deeply into humankind's being and existence so as to probe and illuminate these. The first of these, our third problem, is the distinction and order of *the intellect and the will* as root forces of the human spirit. If the intellect is ordered to the necessary order of things, the will for its part is the bearer of the mystery of the human being's personal freedom. To be sure, more than just the intellect is involved in knowing, and more than just the will is involved in being free; but in our traditional terminology it is precisely these two spiritual faculties that we address as the bases for all human knowing and willing. Many questions that arise from our human existence (intellectualism/voluntarism, contemplation/action) have their origin in this distinction and reciprocal ordering.

Linked to these questions there is a final fourth problem that is defined by the relationship of *being and acting* and that unfolds its specific problematic not so much in the material world of objective causality as in the spiritual world of the person. Even though the person is indeed the highest step on the ladder of being, we must nevertheless affirm that this particular sort of being fulfills itself only by a kind of "self-realization." It is a being that must always become what it is by realizing itself. As the doctrine concerning God shows us, in its highest perfection being as person would be simply "actuality," *actus purus.* It may be that in human "creaturely being" this full "personal being" can never become reality in this world, because of human corporeality and mortality, which result from both human creatureliness and sinfulness. But in human "creaturely being as person" this tension also becomes evident when we humans come to recognize "ideas and values" that become concrete reality only through our own action, when we develop concepts that in spite of their intrinsic greatness nevertheless remain sterile and worthless within the sphere of actual facts, and when we do not creatively and by our deeds realize such concepts in the objective world and turn them into real accomplishments. And yet it is only such facts resulting from deeds [*Tatsachen*] that are of significance for our human and Christian existence.

In various ways these fundamental problems of existence become significant in human life, especially in the religious life of human beings, because the religious life compels the whole person to make the ultimate decision. The problems we have here enumerated come to the fore in the context of the tensions between faith and love, between contemplative and active life, between visible cult and a religion of the spirit, between individual piety and the living worshiping community—and these are problems that arise in all religions.

In the case of *religions founded by human beings,* these tensions have been variously resolved. Starting from great ideas, these religions have in a first period become concretized in a rich external cult, and later on they have developed more spiritualized forms. But this evolution had to be paid for with the dissolution of the cultic community and, therefore, with the dissolution of religion as such. (Take, for instance, the dissection of Greek folk religion by Greek philosophy, and the subsequent attempt to introduce a state religion or Oriental mystery religions in order to make good the loss incurred by the individual Greek.)

The *revealed religion of the Old Testament* preserved the tensions we have mentioned by virtue of God's continued intervention, and this until the destruction of the temple in 70 A.D. By pointing to Israel's past history, the great prophets (Amos, Isaiah) kept alive the revealed image of God. They inveighed against the externalization of piety, urging obedience rather than sacrifice (1 Kgs 15,22; Hos 6,6; Amos 5,21–24; Mal 1,6–10; Ps 50); they exhorted to conversion of the heart (Isa 45,22; Ezek 18,30; Jer 35,15) and to social action (Isa 11,17; Jer 7,6; 22,3; Zech 7,10); and whenever the people experienced a plight, they were the ones to fan high the flame of their faith in Yahweh's promises of salvation. And when Christ himself had to fight against the externalized legalistic piety of the Pharisees and doctors of the law, even in his time he found truly pious individuals in Israel who welcomed his message (Mary, the Apostles).

The creator God himself created a *new order* when he sent his only-begotten Son into the world in the fullness of time (Gal 4, 4f.), that he might become man—*et verbum caro factum est* (John 1,14)—and redeem all human beings from the disorder of sin by his obedience unto death (Phil 2,8). By his Incarnation and the redemption he effected, Christ the God-Man assumed the whole of humanity—*et habitavit in nobis* (John 1,14)—and remained with us by his Word and by his Sacrament (Matt 28,19f.; John 6,56f; 17,22), by the mission that he entrusted to the Apostles, and by his divine Spirit, which he sent into his Church at Pentecost (John 14,15–17; Acts 2).

In keeping with God's plan of salvation, Christ's divine and human being became the real solution of all the problems of human existence. *Christ is the primordial sacrament,* for in him the divine mercy became visible and the divine love became efficacious reality.

"There was a time when we too were ignorant, disobedient and misled and enslaved by different passions and lusts; we lived then in wickedness and ill-will, hating each other and hateful ourselves. But when the kindness and love for mankind of God our savior (ἡ χρηστότης καὶ φιλανθρωπία . . . τοῦ σωτῆρος ἡμῶν θεοῦ) were revealed, it was not because he was concerned with any righteous actions we might have done ourselves; it was for no reason except his own compassion that he saved us, by means of the cleansing water of rebirth and by renewing us with the Holy Spirit which he has so generously poured over us through Jesus Christ our savior. He did this so that we should be justified by his grace, to become heirs looking forward to inheriting eternal life" (Titus 3,3–7). The space in which Christ is present and operative in his Spirit, especially since Pentecost, is *his Church,* which like him possesses a sacramental character and may therefore be called the *universal sacrament.* It is "the people of God, the body of Christ, the temple of the Holy Spirit," and as such it continues to bear the three offices proper to Christ (those of teacher, priest, and shepherd) in the name and by the power of Christ. This is why the Church is the proper locus of all the sacraments, which, as visible signs, communicate invisible grace—"the participation in his own life of glory"—in accordance with Christ's own mandate and by virtue of his power. The encyclical *Mystici Corporis Christi* (1943) therefore describes the sacraments as adequate "instruments" for the life, health, and growth of the mystical Body of Christ and its members.

It is the task of the present inquiry into the sacraments to come to understand more deeply the inner structure of the sacraments as well as the structure of our Christian existence as it is determined by the structure of the sacraments. We want to penetrate more deeply into the significance of the sacraments and the manner in which these have their effect, for the glory of God and the salvation of the individual.

There is great difference in the meaning and operation of

the individual sacraments, and for a whole millennium this difference prevented a systematically unified and comprehensive doctrine of the sacraments from developing. Nevertheless, all the sacraments have something in common, and in the first part of this volume, A General Doctrine of the Sacraments, we will survey and discuss this element as it has emerged at least since the thirteenth century. This will free us from having to repeat our discussion of fundamental questions in the second part of the volume, The Mystery of the Eucharist, where we will examine this sacrament and present a particularized sacramental doctrine.

A General Doctrine of the Sacraments

The most important questions of a general doctrine of the sacraments will be discussed here in eight chapters. After examining (I) the concept and nature of sacrament, we will discuss the three constitutive elements of a sacrament, namely (II) the essential structure of the sacramental sign, (III) the saving reality and saving effects of the sacraments, as well as (IV) their origin, their number, and the order among them. The two subsequent chapters present the most important aspects of (V) the minister and (VI) the recipient of the sacraments. A further chapter (VII) deals with the world as sacrament and with the sacramental existence of human beings, and (VIII) a final meditation on "God's sacramental Word" will conclude our reflections.

I

Concept and Nature of Sacrament

The following four sections will attempt to provide a preliminary outline on the concept and nature of sacrament.
After discussing the word itself (1), we will consider the reality itself—the significance and structure of a sacrament—more closely and try to provide some sort of definition (2). A look at certain sacramental analogies, both
pre-Christian (among the Jews) and non-Christian (especially among the Greeks), will perhaps make our findings
even more clear (3). A short history of the general doctrine
of the sacraments will finally exhibit all the elements that
remain to be examined in the second part of this work (4);
this section is intended as well to give us some insight into
the development of these theological doctrines as they
have grown from the ground of Scripture and evangeliza-
tion, from the very nature of the sacraments themselves,
and from religious life, since all of these developments
have their origin in the sacramental rites themselves.

1. The Meaning of the Word "Sacrament"

Sacred Scripture speaks in many places of the seven distinct rites of salvation that are today called "sacraments."
But in Scripture the theological concept of "sacrament" for
the totality of these rites and for each one of them is still
not in use. In the original Greek text of the New Testament
the word μυστήριον appears in Eph 5,32 in connection with

marriage; here it does not mean what we call the "sacrament of matrimony," however, but rather the mystery of love between man and woman that is elucidated in the light of the "mystery of faith" existing between Christ and the Church. In the other places where it occurs (the word appears twenty-seven times in the New Testament, of which twenty are in Paul) it means the hidden plan of God, which has been revealed especially in Christ's saving work and which is called the "mystery of the kingdom of God" by the Synoptics (three times: see Mark 4,11 and par.). In the Apocalypse (four times) mysterious visions are referred to with the word *mysterium.* Ignatius of Antioch uses the word in *Ad Magn.* 9.1 still in the sense of St. Paul, while in *Trall.* 2.3 it designates the service performed by deacons in connection with the mysteries of Christ in the Church. At least since the third century, μυστήριον became in the Greek-speaking Eastern Church (Clement of Alexandria, Origen) the term for holy doctrines and ministries, for holy things and rites in the Church, and thus also for the sacraments (Cyril of Jerusalem, Denis the Areopagite).

In the oldest Latin translations of Scripture (the *Itala*), μυστήριον was rendered as *sacramentum* (cf. 1 Cor 13,2; Eph 5,32), and the Roman province of Africa retained this word *sacramentum* (used 134 times by Tertullian and 64 times by Cyprian). Tertullian, who is of particular importance for the development of ecclesiastical Latin, used this word in many different senses: in a general sense, like the Greek μυστήριον, for initiation rites and the celebrations of the mysteries of the gods; for sacrifices, signs, and gestures of the cults; for faith and the doctrines of faith; for secret teachings and for the divine plan; but especially in the specifically Latin sense of "oath formula" ("pledge of allegiance" in military language) and, as a legal term, it refers to the sum of money deposited as a security in a temple at the time of entering into a contract. In the sense of a "pledge of allegiance" Tertullian applied *sacramentum* especially to the promises of baptism[1] and thereby he lay the foundation for the theological term "sacrament" in the current sense. In the European parts of the Roman Empire it was the Greek neologism *mysterium* that was favored. Thus, in the two Latin words for sacrament there were combined the Greek sense (God's hidden workings) and the Roman sense (human assent and moral duty toward the deity). This word *sacramentum* was supposed to express not only the fact that what had heretofore remained hidden ("mystery") has now been revealed (as Karl Prümm would have it), but much more the reality that our salvation consists of living, acting, and having our existence in Christ. Various other words derived from the language of the ancient mysteries were also used ("to put on Christ," "to die and rise with Christ," etc.[2]). Above all the cult celebrated at Christ's command (Eucharist: Luke 22,19 and par.) was called *mysterium* insofar as it encompassed all at once doctrine, mysterious action and event, symbol and reality. This wide understanding of the interchangeable pair *mysterium* and *sacramentum* persisted until about the middle of the twelfth century, when the word was more closely defined and limited to the seven rites that even today we still call "sacraments." This narrower definition referred especially to the objective manner in which the sacraments have their effect, and also to the institution of these rites by Christ himself. These two elements (effect and institution) were henceforth not to be attributed to other rites, signs, and holy things that had until now been likewise called *sacramentum* and *mysterium* (for instance, the sign of the cross, the Our Father, the rite of burial).

2. The Objective Meaning of Sacrament: Definition of Sacrament

In the Church of the West, as we have seen, Tertullian (d. after 220) contributed considerably to the clarification of the reality of sacrament by borrowing the term *sacramentum* from the language of legal and military Latin. But it is above all Augustine (d. 430) who by his apposite distinctions deserves to be called the founder of sacramental theology. Conditioned by his Platonism in philosophy, and also by his Christian struggle against the Donatists, he introduced the distinction between visible rite and invisible effect, and he termed the visible rite *signum:* "sacramentum, id est sacrum signum" (*De civ. Dei*, 10.5: PL 41,282). What the sacrament effects he termed *res sacramenti:* "signa, quae, cum ad res divinas pertinent, sacramenta appellantur" (*Ep.* 138.7: PL 33,527). "Ideo dicuntur sacramenta, quia in eis aliud videtur, aliud intelligitur" (*Sermo* 272: PL 38,1247). Finally, in the sacramental sign itself Augustine distinguishes the *element* from the *word*, when concerning baptism he teaches: "Accedit verbum [the baptismal formula] ad elementum [the water] et fit sacramentum" (*In Joh.* 80.3: PL 35,1840). In Isidore of Seville (d. 636) it already becomes evident that the decisive element in the sacrament is its efficacy: "Ob id sacramenta dicuntur, quia sub tegumento corporalium rerum virtus divina" (spiritus sanctus) secretius salutem eorundem sacramentorum operatur" (*Etym.* VI 19.40: PL 82,255). Hugh of St. Victor (d. 1141), finally, highlights the element of *institution* in the sacrament, when he defines it as follows: "Sacramentum est corporale vel materiale elementum foris sensibiliter propositum, ex similitudine repræsentans et ex institutione significans et ex sanctificatione continens aliquam invisibilem et spiritalem gratiam": "Sacrament is a corporeal or material thing or event, exhibited in the visible world, which makes present by virtue of its symbolic character, points to something by virtue of its institution, and contains some measure of invisible grace, conferred by the Spirit, by virtue of its having been sanctified" (*De sacramentis chr. fidei*, I 9.2: PL 176,317).

The first complete definition of sacrament is found in Duns Scotus (d. 1308): "Sacramentum est signum sensibile

gratiam dei vel effectum dei gratuitum ex institutione divina efficaciter significans, ordinatum ad salutem hominis
viatoris" (*Ox.* IV d 1 q 2 n 9). In earlier theologians
(Bonaventure, Thomas Aquinas) we find these individual
elements, but not yet in one comprehensive definition.
"Sacrament," then, is an event or a reality or a rite, perceptible to the senses, that was instituted by Christ in
order to signify the saving graces merited by him, to contain them, and to communicate them to human beings
through human beings whenever a sacrament is performed
by both its minister and its recipient.

We see, then, that the structure of a sacrament is determined by four elements: (1) the external sign perceptible to
the senses, which we will deal with in Chapter II; (2) the
interior reality of grace and efficacy, which we will examine in Chapter III; (3) the institution by Jesus Christ, to be
discussed in Chapter IV; and (4) the "location" of a sacrament between the minister and the recipient, something
that points to the ecclesial dimension of sacrament and
that we will discuss in Chapter V.

Let us start by making the following generalizations
with regard to these four points:

1. In a sacrament there is always involved an external reality perceptible to the senses, an event or an action that
can be experienced. Without this external element that
can be experienced by the senses there is no sacrament. A
purely interior, spiritual event cannot be the basis for a
sacrament. Just as a historical human existence is a necessary part of Christ, so too this visible reality is indispens-
able for a sacrament as a *sign of Christ.* This reality also is
the basis for the particular social effect of the sacraments
as authentic *signs of the Church,* insofar as they contribute as instruments of the mystical Body of Christ to
the building up of this Body and to the forming of the People of God—to the glory of the compassionate God and for
the salvation of sinful humanity, which has been redeemed
in Christ. The visibility of the sacramental event makes

possible also a certain control exercised by the community over the rightful uses of the sacrament in the Church (for instance, one is affiliated to the Church through baptism).

2. This aspect of sacrament as *ecclesial sign* is further expressed in the fact that a sacrament is not only in itself a symbol or image for holy things and events (as with the symbolic sign of the cross, for instance, or the symbol of the fish); rather, a sacrament receives its specific *character as sign* precisely through human action in deed and word. Further, it is only through action that human community arises and exists. At the same time, this character of sign further implies that sacraments, as *signs of faith*, are practical efficacious signs for the application of the salvation wrought by Christ to the receiver: "Signum sensibile practicum . . . certum, nisi indispositio suscipientis impedit" (J. Duns Scotus, *Ox.* IV d 1 q n 3).

The certainty of the perceptible reality of the sacrament as sign is a guarantee for the certainty of the salvation communicated, insofar as this sign can be understood and accomplished in an attitude of faith. Simon Magister (1140/50) had already made the internal connection between the sign-character and the efficacy of a sacrament (*sacrum signatum*).

The meaning of this sacramental event or action as a sign is oriented above all to the individual's personal sanctification, so that these sensually perceptible rites exhibit themselves as authentic *signs of grace.* This enables Thomas Aquinas to write: "Sicut antiqui patres salvati sunt per fidem Christi venturi, ita et nos salvamur per fidem Christi iam nati et passi. Sunt autem sacramenta quædam signa protestantia fidem, qua iustificatur homo" (*Summa Theol.* III, q.61, a.4, c). Thus, sacraments are not only signs of the "divine promise," as Calvin and Luther would have it, or signs for the awakening of faith, as Melanchthon taught: "Fides sacramenti, non sacramentum iustificat" (*Apol.* CA XIII 23). At the Council of Trent, given the program of the Counter-Reformation, the Church had had to clarify expressly the fact that the sacraments had not been instituted solely for the strengthening of faith ("propter solam fidem nutriendam" [D 848, cf. 851—DS 1605, 1608]). But at the Second Vatican Council the Church expressly declared the following as its own doctrine: "Sacraments are ordered to the sanctification of human beings, the building up of the Body of Christ, and finally the glory owed to God. As signs they also have the task of instructing us. Not only do they presume faith, but through word and substance they nourish, strengthen and exhibit faith. This is why they are called *sacraments of faith*" (SC 59). This meaning of sacraments as efficacious signs is corroborated by the fact that the sacramental signs are emphatically *natural signs* (immersion, washing, anointing, eating, confessing in word and deed) and not merely conventional signs. Natural signs are endowed with a certain permanence, something that is necessary for the sacraments (as Bonaventure would have it: "significant semper et universaliter" [*Breviloquium* VI c 4 n 3]).

Because of the *historical structure* of both human existence and the human being's interrelated state of grace, the sacramental sign participates in the three dimensions of the human consciousness of time. In this way the New Testament not only is the perfection of the Old Testament but is in itself still incomplete, as Ambrose once keenly exposed in his commentary on the Psalms: "Umbra in lege, imago vero in evangelio, veritas in cœlestibus" (*In Ps.* 38, n. 25: PL 14,1051). And Thomas Aquinas writes concerning the Eucharist: "Sacramentum proprie dicitur quod ordinatur ad significandam nostram sanctificationem, in qua tria possunt considerari: videlicet ipsa causa sanctificationis nostræ, quæ est passio Christi; et forma nostræ sanctificationis, quæ consistit in gratia et virtutibus; et ultimus finis sanctificationis nostræ, qui est vita æterna. Unde sacramentum est et *signum rememorativum* . . . passionis Christi, *et demonstrativum* . . . gratiæ, *et prognosticum*, id est prænuntiativum futuræ gloriæ":

"It is named a 'sacrament' (i.e., a means of salvation) in the proper sense because it is ordered to showing forth our sanctification, in which we must distinguish three elements: the efficacious cause of our sanctification in the Passion of Christ, the formal cause of our santification in grace and the virtues, and the final goal of our sanctification in eternal life. Consequently, a sacrament is a sign of remembrance of the Passion of Christ, a sign that indicates the presence of grace, and a sign that points to the future and promises the glory to come"(*Summa theol.* III, q.60, a.3, c).

This multiplicity of aspects exhibited by the meaning of a sign allows us to understand why the notion of sacrament has found such a wide variety of interpretations in theology. While Greek theology built on its *understanding of ancient symbols,* the Middle Ages looked upon sacrament from the standpoint of the Aristotelian *principle of final end or entelechy* as an "instrumental cause" of salvation. The mystery theology of O. Casel sought the meaning of sacrament by developing, on the basis of the Greek Fathers, a *framework of salvation-history* within which to integrate the sacraments. More recent explorations, by J. Betz and K. Rahner, strive to understand the sacramental sign more closely as a *verbal sign.*

3. That for the Christian such a supernatural and invisible effect can be attributed to this natural visible sign is comprehensible only in terms of the historical fact that these sacraments have been *instituted by Christ.* This is why the Council of Trent declared as follows: "Si quis dixerit sacramenta novæ legis non fuisse omnia a Jesu Christo Domino nostro instituta, . . . anathema sit." (D844—DS 1601). From his own philosophical and theological standpoint, Augustine had spoken only of *Christ as the cause of the sacraments:* "Quando de latere Christi sacramenta ecclesiæ profluxerunt? Cum dormiret in cruce" (*In Ps.* 40 n 10: PL 36,461, cf. 668). It was only the twelfth century, with its juridical mentality, that raised the

question concerning the historical institution of the sacraments by Christ. Thomas Aquinas emphatically answers the question in the affirmative for all the sacraments. In contemporary theological thought we witness many attempts again to seek the *causality* of the sacraments in Christ and in this way to introduce the sphere of the Church into the question concerning the institution of the sacraments; such a direction is desirable since exegetical findings on this question otherwise raise difficulties for some of the sacraments. We will consider these things more closely in Chapter IV.

4. For modern people we have to add, to these three specifications of medieval theology, that it is necessary for each sacrament to be received and not merely instituted, and that it has to be *dispensed* by another person if it is to be *received.* With their feudal understanding of society, medieval people accepted this fact unreflectedly; but if modern people are to understand the structure of a sacrament in all its totality, they will consciously have to ponder the fact. These questions will be further discussed in Chapter V.

5. The evolution in the understanding of the sacrament's character as sign becomes particularly evident in the way *sacraments are portrayed in the arts.* Until the fourteenth century graphic portrayals of the individual rites are *typological representations:* events from the Old and New Testaments are expected to illuminate the effects of baptism, the Eucharist, and penance. This already holds for the images in the catacombs and is even more evident in the portal sculpture of Romanesque churches, especially in Burgundy, in Provence, and in Languedoc.[3] For the most part the Eucharist, baptism, and penance are seen as parts of one whole. In the early Gothic period textual evidence variously illustrates these typologies, for instance in the pairs *exterius/interius* and *sub lege/sub gratia.* Toward the end of the thirteenth century the *liturgical perspective* takes the place of the typological perspective, and at the beginning of the fourteenth century we encounter the portrayal

of the *cycle of the seven sacraments.*[4] Often these seven sacraments are seen in conjunction with other sevensomes (the virtues, the vices, the gifts of the Spirit, the works of mercy). The late Gothic period then contributes the great painted screens (for instance, Roger van der Weyden's of 1450 in Antwerp, and the 1457 Cambrai altar in Madrid).

Parallel to the typological and liturgical perspectives, the sacraments are often interpreted in their connection to the Church as growing from the sacraments, as Augustine would have it: "Domino, cum dormiret in cruce, latus eius lancea percussum est (John 19,34), et sacramenta profluxerunt, unde facta est ecclesia. Ecclesia enim coniux Domini facta est de latere, quomodo Eva facta est de latere [Adam]": [When the Lord was asleep (i.e., dead) on the cross, his side was pierced with the lance, and then the sacraments flowed out, from which the Church was made. For the Church was made as a bride from the Lord's side, just as Eve had been made from Adam's side] (*In Ps.* 126, n. 7: PL 37,1672). Because since 1150 the term "mystical Body" no longer refers so much to the Church as to the Eucharist, the portrayal of the sacraments in connection with the Eucharist becomes more frequent.

In the beginning of the sixteenth century we observe in England (Norfolk, Suffolk) the development of octagonal columns (corresponding to the octagonal form of ancient baptismal chapels) that portray the crucified Christ and the seven sacraments on the eight side surfaces, and this obviously intends to emphasize the connection between the sacraments and the cross of Christ. After the seventeenth century, according to Toussaint, there develop whole series of works representing the individual sacraments, and this surely occurs because of the contemporary interest in particular liturgical forms and in the kind of society that the liturgy shapes.

3. Pre-Christian and Non-Christian Sacramental Analogies

Since the New Testament is the fulfillment of the Old, we may ask to what extent the sacraments of the New Covenant have their prefigurements or analogies in the Old Covenant. And, further, since "natural signification" is a characteristic of the signs and rites of the sacraments, we may ask whether analogies for our sacraments are likewise to be found in non-Christian religions. This question is specified in the New Testament by the fact that the proclamation by the Apostles was primarily addressed to the Graeco-Roman world. Therefore, at least the possibility must remain open that the Apostles, for the sake of the proclamation itself, sought to explain the Christian message to the people of that time partly with the help of the rites and thought-patterns even of this pagan culture.

A. THE RITES OF THE OLD COVENANT

From the perspective of "salvation-history," according to revelation (and independent of speculation from the perspective of "world-history" concerning a paradisal state), we distinguish three stages in the history of humankind before Christ: (1) the primeval paradisal state of grace, (2) humankind under sin and under the natural law (which is the proper locus until today of all people who have heard nothing of the Judaeo-Christian revelation), and (3) the people of the Old Testament that arose when Abraham entered into the covenant and reached its total development and fulfillment in the Mosaic law.

(1) For the paradisal state Augustine could still recognize two sacraments: the *lignum vitæ* and marriage, since by "sacrament" he still understood a type of the New Testament sacrament: "Nec sine mysteriis rerum spiritualium corporaliter præsentatis voluit hominem deus in paradiso vivere. Erat ei ergo in illo [ligno vitæ] . . . sacramen-

tum" (*De Gen. ad lit.* VIII 4.8; likewise on marriage, IX 19.36: PL 34,375,408). Thomas Aquinas, on the other hand, taught that there were still no sacraments in paradise, since no means of salvation was yet needed for sin and the soul already possessed its perfection (*Summa Theol.* III, q.61, a.2). This argumentation is not convincing, because a sacrament is not only a saving means against sin but also a sign of salvation. Sacraments are, indeed, not "things" or non-human realities; rather, their specific reason for being is the human person and their interior form is a "rite," which is to say an event that includes a human action. The significant aspect of this rite, however, is the fact that, unlike other human actions, it is not personal plans and goals. Rather, it is a human activity that a human as a social being (cf. research on human relational behavior) accomplishes in fulfillment of a "mandate," and he or she does this in order to reach the aim intended by this social sphere or the good implied or promised by this mandate. The sacramental rite, then, is not to be compared with the artisan's activity that produces an object, nor with the child's aimless playing, the purposes of which are only self-development and self-expression. The sacramental act, rather, is comparable to social behavior or artistic creation that seeks to embody and realize in a corporeal and historical world artistic ideas that had been "inspired" in a privileged hour. In a similar way the sacramental rite seeks to "realize" the promise by accomplishing the human work connected with this promise of God's. When artistic creation cannot realize the fullness of its ideas, the reason for it is human incapacity and weakness. When the liturgical action in a rite does not realize the fullness of its promises, the reason for it is a lack of radical human self-surrender. Understood in this way sacrament belongs to humankind, which from the outset exists within God's salvation-history, and sacrament can therefore not be wholly absent even in paradise, as Augustine has affirmed.

(2) For the *period under sin and the natural law* (from Adam to Abraham and Moses) we say the following: The natural law had been written in human hearts (Rom 2,14f.) and the grace of redemption had retroactive power at least as far back as the proto-gospel (Gen 3,15). To make any affirmations about this period we must bear in mind two truths of revelation: Just as important as God's general will to save is the fact of the uniqueness and greatness of God's self-revelation in the Incarnation of Christ. For this reason the "sacramental" path to salvation that most clearly is inaugurated when Christ became man is therefore also exemplary for the earlier epochs. Especially since the scholastic age, this earlier period is divided into two parts, the first *from Adam to Abraham* and the second *from Abraham to Moses.* For the first of these what is known as a *natural sacrament* is posited by the theologians that was to free humankind from original sin and reconcile it to God. This seems to be an exigency resulting from God's general will to save as well as from the lack of a specific visible sacrament in this period. Thomas ponders an active faith in salvation that looks forward to the coming Redeemer: "Oportebat ante Christi adventum esse quædam signa visibilia, quibus homo fidem suam protestaretur de futuro salvatoris adventu" (*Summa Theol.* III, q. 61, a.3). As a basis for this Thomas quotes Rom 3,25f. (cf. 22–26): "It is the same justification by God that comes through faith for all and over all . . . who believe in Jesus Christ. . . . Him has God appointed as a sacrifice in his blood to win reconciliation through faith. In this way God makes his justice known. For in his divine forbearance God let sins in the past go unpunished, in order to show his justice in the present time; for he wanted to show at the same time that he is just and that he justifies every one who believes in Jesus Christ."[5] One could equally think of Gal 5,6, where the Apostle simply demands a faith that is active in love, beside which neither circumcision nor noncircumcision amounts to anything.

For the time *between Abraham and Moses* the sign of
the covenant in force is circumcision (Gen 17,9–14), without which a man does not belong to the people of the
covenant, to whom alone salvation has been promised. According to the account for its institution, we are dealing
here with a genuine visible sign for an invisible salvation.
This is also emphasized by Thomas (*Summa Theol.* III, q.
70, a.4), and Innocent III taught as follows in 1201: "Etsi
originalis culpa remittebatur per circumcisionis mysterium, et damnationis periculum vitabatur, non tamen
perveniebatur ad regnum cœlorum, quod usque ad mortem
Christi fuit omnibus obseratum" (D410–DS780). This is
the general persuasion, the opposite opinion of Vásquez
and Bellarmine notwithstanding. It is a theological problem to explain the precise manner of this sacrament's effect. Duns Scotus (*Ox.* IV d 1 q 6) and his disciples attributed to circumcision, like baptism, an effect from itself (*ex
opere operato*), but this is contradicted by St. Paul's many
minimalizing remarks (cf. Heb 7,18: "The previous dispensation [of circumcision] is abolished because of its
weakness and uselessness" [Cf. Gal 5, 2–5; Rom 3,20; 4,15;
7,6]). Even less tenable appears to us Calvin's view (*Institutio* IV 16.10ff.) that in circumcision we are to see only an
external sign of the covenant with no intrinsic efficacy. We
must agree with Thomas (*Summa Theol.* III, q. 70, a.4) in
attributing to circumcision the effect of eradicating original sin, not because of an intrinsic necessity but rather as
an effect that God extrinsically associates with it. In this
case we would not be dealing with a *signum demonstrativum* but only with a *signum prognosticum* (hope in the
Redeemer). This is the same as taught both by the *Decretum pro Armeniis* (D695–DS1310) and the Council of
Trent (D845–DS1602).

But the salvific significance of circumcision ought not to
be exaggerated, since up to the time of the Mosaic law the
only sign given for women and girls was the natural sacrament of an active faith in salvation.

(3) Under the Mosaic law we encounter a whole series of rites that are to be regarded as *Old Testament sacraments*. Thomas organizes them into four groups (*Summa Theol.* III, q. 102, a.5): (1) circumcision (baptism); (2) the eating of the Easter lamb (Exod 12,26), and perhaps the bread of exposition (Lev 24,9: Eucharist); (3) various rites of purification and expiation (Lev 12f.; Num 19f. [penance], cf. Heb 8,5); (4) rites of consecration for the priests (Exod 29; Lev 8), which, however, were dispensed only for Aaron and his sons (priestly orders). Thomas then discusses why confirmation, anointing of the sick, and matrimony find no analogy in the Old Testament (*Summa Theol.* III, q.102, a.5, ad 3).

B. THE PAGAN MYSTERIES

The rites of the Old Testament have an exemplary character for the sacraments of the New Testament. *Pagan mysteries possess no direct significance for the Christian sacraments,* since they are not based on the true reality of God. Beyond this we ought to say the following about the mysteries: (1) In the mysteries people variously sought rather to acquire power of the deity than to submit themselves to the grace of the deity; (2) the myths are consequently atemporal, not determined by Christ's sacrificial death as is the Christian mystery; (3) their intrinsic value consists mostly in a certain moral effort and not really in their quality as religious event. To be sure, even as we say this we must remember that God, in his general will to save, can always bestow his grace on this natural moral striving of human beings. The attempt by liberal religious science to derive the Christian sacraments causally from the non-Christian pagan mysteries must be regarded as a failure.[6] The *mystery theology* inaugurated by O. Casel,[7] however, readily admits the connection between the language of Pauline mysticism and the language of the contemporary pagan mysteries. "It would be quite incomprehensible if the mystery language of the primitive Church

. . . had developed without any relationship to the ancient language of the mysteries," as K. Prümm had contended.[8] Even as it struggled against the pagan mysteries the young Church could not overlook this fact (cf. Clement of Alexandria). In this respect it is possible that Paul built on the preliminary bases of the primitive Hellenistic communities.[9]

The most important mysteries we should mention here are the Greek mysteries at *Eleusis* and the mysteries in honor of the gods Demeter, Persephone, and Bacchus. It is a matter of controversy to what extent historical realities from the ancient time of the kings are here involved or perhaps only a deification of natural forces. The great feast was celebrated for nine days in September–October. High moral demands were made of the initiates, and this is why these mysteries in particular preserved a great importance in Greece until their final decline.

There was probably a greater influence on the language of early Christian theology by the mysteries of *Isis and Osiris* in Egypt. Here too a myth from the ancient time of the kings seems to be originally involved, which was then raised to the status of a nature myth in historical times. One prayer from these mysteries runs as follows: "Thou art father and mother to humankind. They live from thy spirit and must nourish themselves from the flesh of thy body." All questions concerning death and life, fertility and birth, found their answer in these mysteries.

Even more important for the language of early Christianity seem to have been the Persian *Mithras mysteries.* Mithras was the chief Persian deity under Artaxerxes II (359 B.C.): war god, sun god, and judge of the dead all in one. His cult spread in Greece beginning with Alexander the Great. His mysteries were popular in Rome especially under Commodus (180–192 A.D.) and as late as 308 under Diocletian. The Mithraic religion proposed a high moral standard, led to a deep spirituality, and was emphatically based on a doctrine of redemption. The candidate received initiation into the mysteries by a baptism during which he was purified by the blood of a sacrificial bull. The Mithraic cult had seven stages of initiation and a sacred meal with wine, water, and bread. Its principal feast, especially in Rome, was celebrated on December 25.[10]

4. Short History of General Sacramental Doctrine

What we have before us today in the form of a general doctrine of the sacraments developed only in the Middle Ages with respect to its philosophical underpinnings, its theological basis, and its systematic organization. (See Appendix to the text, p. 365.) In the patristic period, as in the Gospel, the language for discussing the sacraments dealt with the *individual rites* mandated by Christ in connection with which he left us particular effects of grace: namely, baptism, which was still developed along the model of John the Baptist, and the Eucharist, which developed on the basis of the event of the Last Supper on the model of the Jewish *pascha* and other rites.

A. FROM THE PATRISTIC PERIOD TO THE MIDDLE AGES

In order to develop a general doctrine of the sacraments it was first of all necessary to establish the terminology for this reality as well as the names for the individual rites. To denote these different holy rites the Greek Church gradually settled upon the word μυστήριον, which Paul used only once for "marriage" (Eph 5,32) but which otherwise referred to the christological event of salvation-history. This choice guaranteed that these rites would forever be incorporated into the sphere of salvation-history and of sacred "mysteries."

In the Western Church, especially in North Africa, the word *sacramentum* became the name for these rites. Tertullian (d. after 220) uses *sacramentum* 134 times. He applied the word in its specifically Latin sense to baptism (pledge of allegiance = baptismal promises) and to the Eucharist. Cyprian (d. 258) uses the word 64 times; he too understands *sacramentum* in the context of military language. In the European part of the Roman Empire, on the other hand, the neologism *mysterium* became the preferred term, and this usage united the Greek sense of "secret teaching" with the Roman connotation of "sacred thing" and "sacred action." Like Cyril of Jerusalem (John of Jerusalem? d. 386) before him in his *Five Mystagogical Catecheses* (preached in 348) and Theodore of Mopsuestia in his *Catechetical Sermons* (composed between 388 and 392), in his book *De mysteriis* (similar to the six books *De sacramentis,* which originated in the same region), Ambrose of Milan (d. 397) provides an introduction to the rites of baptism, confirmation, and the Eucharist. Western Latin theology explained the rites mostly in an allegorical and symbolic fashion.

On the Greek side, Pseudo-Dionysius the Areopagite (about 520) gives in his *De ecclesiastica hierarchia* (Chaps. 2–7: PG 3, 391–584) a more mystical-typological introduction to baptism, confirmation, the Eucharist, and priestly orders set in the context of salvation-history. His work is significantly continued in the late Middle Ages by Nicholas Cabasilas (1320–ca. 1390) in his seven books *On Life in Christ* (PG 150, 491–726), and, finally, by Simeon of Thessalonica (d. 1429), who already expressly refers to the number of the sacraments as seven (PG 155, 175–238). Simeon, interestingly, presents confirmation as a sacrament for the forgiveness of sins and penance as monastic penitence.

In the West St. Augustine decisively deepened sacramental theology. Influenced by his Platonic philosophy and inspired by his fight against the Donatists, he introduced as all-encompassing the term *signum* for these holy rites. As well, he taught that to these visible signs there corresponds an invisible reality (*Sermo* 272: PL 38,1247): "Sacramentum, id est sacrum signum" (*De civ. Dei* X 5: PL 41,282). "Signa, quæ, cum ad res divinas pertinent, sacramenta appellantur" (*Ep.* 138.7: PL 33,527). In connection with his doctrine on baptism he explains this sign even more precisely, specifying: "Accedit verbum ad elementum et fit sacramentum, etiam ipsum tamquam visibile verbum" (*In Joh.* 80.3: PL 35,1840). Since it is Christ himself who is always the real dispenser of the sacrament, lack of holiness of the earthly dispenser or minister of the sacrament is without significance for the effect of the sacrament. This Augustine taught time and again over against the Donatists.[11] Already in the time of Ambrose it had been pointed out that the author of all the sacraments (the word was then still understood in the general sense of "holy thing") was Christ, the Redeemer (*De sacram.* IV 4.13: PL 16,439 A). In his explanations of the Psalms, Augustine often uses the word *dormire* to establish an analogy with the emergence of Eve from the sleeping Adam and say that from the side of Christ, sleeping the sleep of death on the cross, there flowed forth the Church and above all the sacraments: "De latere Christi sacramenta ecclesiæ profluxerunt, cum dormiret in cruce."[12] What Augustine taught here was handed down throughout the centuries practically unaltered, especially by the great Spaniard Isidore of Seville (d. 633)[13] and his disciple Ildefonso of Toledo (d. 667), as well as the numerous great theologians of the period from the Carolingian Renaissance to the twelfth century. Still, however, the word "sacrament" was applied to all holy signs: prayers, creeds, the sign of the cross, the rite of burial, and so on. This is why it was still not possible at this time to give a precise number of sacraments. Holy unction is seldom mentioned, while washing of the feet often comes up because of the special manner in which it is described in Scripture (John 13,15): Ambrose expressly calls it a sacrament.

B. THE MIDDLE AGES

The doctrine of the sacraments experienced a decisive development around the middle of the twelfth century. Under the influence of the newly emerging science of canon law in the Church, attention became directed more to the sign and the rite than to the element or the thing itself. With this questions arose concerning the external *institution* and the internal *cause* of the sacrament, as well as the particular manner in which the sacraments have their *effect*. The first significant presentation of a doctrine of the sacraments at this time was given by Hugh of St. Victor (d. 1141) in his work *De sacramentis* (I 9: PL 176, 315–329; I 12: PL 415ff.). Here he defined sacrament as follows: "Sacramentum est corporale vel materiale elementum foris sensibiliter propositum, ex similitudine repræsentans et ex institutione significans et ex sanctificatione continens aliquam invisibilem et spiritalem gratiam." He spoke of a threefold matter in the sacrament: the *res*, the *facta*, and the *verba*. Nonetheless he still conceives the idea of sacrament in more universal terms, so that holy water, the cross of ashes on the forehead, as well as monastic consecration and the rite of burial, are all to be counted among the sacraments. God himself is the author of the sacraments ("quantum ad deum auctorem dispensationis"), and the effects are looked upon mostly in a moral way ("propter humiliationem," "propter eruditionem," "propter exercitationem"). Peter Lombard (d. 1160) hands down the sacramental doctrine of Hugh of St. Victor when he combines the questions concerning the effect and the cause of grace. He explains: "Sacramentum enim proprie dicitur, quod ita signum est gratiæ dei et invisibilis gratiæ forma, ut ipsius imaginem gerat et causa existat" (Sent. IV d 1 n 4). At this time the conceptual pair *opus operantis* and *opus operatum* is developed in the School of Porretans (pseudo-Poitiers gloss) to approach this question concerning "effect." These definitions make it possible around the middle of the twelfth century for the first time to enumerate the sacraments in the sense of our septenary (*Sententiæ divinitatis*). At the same time there is already developed the doctrine concerning the *intention of the minister*, which is given a permanent expression in the formula "intentio faciendi quod facit ecclesia." In order to be able to distinguish the validity of a sacrament from the fruitfulness of the grace it confers, there is at the same time developed, especially by the canon lawyers (Uguccio, Peter Cantor), the doctrine of *sacramental character* in the sense modern theology still understands it.

The thirteenth century, the era of High Scholasticism, further developed the doctrine of the sacraments by application to it of Aristotelian concepts. In the work of Alexander of Hales (d. 1245), whose sacramental doctrine derives for the most part from William of Melitona, the Augustinian formula *elementum et verbum* had still been interpreted in the general sense of *materia et forma*. But it was Hugh of St. Cher (d. 1263) who for the first time used this conceptual pair in the hylomorphic sense of Aristotelian philosophy. The words, seen as form, are for the element and the action, seen as matter, not only a determinant but also the very cause of the reality of the sacrament. J. Duns Scotus (d. 1308) still distinguishes between a *materia remota* (in the sense of *elementum*) and a *materia proxima* (in the sense of the action that occurs with the element). Even though by this time the exact enumeration of the *sacraments as seven* was taken for granted, the question of the sacraments' *institution* by Jesus Christ was still seriously debated. While Bonaventure, for instance, still considers confirmation and the anointing of the sick as having been instituted by the Apostles under the impulse of the Holy Spirit, Thomas Aquinas (d. 1274) declares that all the sacraments were instituted by Jesus Christ. And Thomas clarifies Peter Lombard's teaching that the sacraments are caused by grace by specifying that God is the *causa principalis* of all graces but that a sacra-

ment is a *causa instrumentalis* in God's hand. How seriously the relation of all the sacraments to Christ is taken
is shown by the teaching that, in Christ, the human nature
is an *instrumentum coniunctum* for the Logos, while the
sacraments are *instrumenta separata.*

This already launches the doctrine of the particular
manner in which each sacrament has it is effects. The
Franciscans' more Augustinian manner of considering the
sacraments, stressing their role in salvation-history, basically interpreted the sacraments as having a *moral efficacy,* while the more Aristotelian theology of Thomas
Aquinas and his school spoke rather of a *physical efficacy.*
A good summary of the medieval doctrine of the sacraments is provided by the *Decree for the Armenians* of the
Council of Florence (1439), but this decree did not aim at
definitions (D 695–702, DS 1310–1328).

C. REFORMATION

The fight against late medieval forms of theology and
piety and the isolating of Holy Scripture as the sole source
of theology are the basis for the new understanding of
sacrament which the Reformers exhibit. "The Word—
which proclaims the story of Christ, interprets it and
makes it present—itself effects salvation through a spiritual power willed by God by creating faith" (Pesch, TRLTh,
326). This *theology of the Word* is for Luther the point of
departure for his *sacramental theology.* For Luther a sacrament is the combination of a word of promise with a sign,
that is, primarily a promise that is accompanied by a sign
instituted by God: "Proprie tamen ea sacramenta vocari
visum est, quæ annexis signis promissa sunt. Cetera, quia
signis alligata non sunt, nuda promissa sunt" (WA, 6, 572,
10). From this we can understand why only two sacraments are recognized as authentic: "Quo fit, ut, si rigide
loqui volumus, tantum duo sunt in ecclesia dei sacramenta, baptismus et panis, cum in his solis et institutum

divinitus signum et promissiones remissionis peccatorum videamus" (WA, 6, 572, 11). Especially in the early period of the Reformation Luther emphasized this character of the sacrament as word, while in the 1530s he again stressed the sacraments as signs to offset the views of the enthusiasts. This connection of word and sacrament also means that a sacrament does not have an effect from itself but becomes efficacious only because of our faith in the sacrament: "Inde fit, ut nullus consequatur gratiam, quia absolvitur aut baptizatur aut communicatur aut inungitur, sed qui credit sic absolvendo, baptizando, communicando, inungendo se consequi gratiam. Verum enim est illud vulgatissimum et probatissimum dictum: Non sacramentum, sed fides sacramenti iustificat" (WA, 57 [Hebr], 169, 23). Luther's doctrine, always based on the Word of Scripture, does not expressly consider the necessity of the sacraments or their particular significance in conjunction with the Word; what is established, rather, is the fact of their institution by Christ. Consequently we do not find in Luther's teaching a general doctrine of the sacraments, but only a doctrine of the two rites of baptism and the Lord's Supper.

The reformed teachings of Calvin, on the other hand, do offer a precise general doctrine of the sacraments.[14] He defines sacrament as follows: "A sacrament is an external symbol (*symbolum*) with which the Lord seals for our conscience the promises (*promissiones*) of his friendliness toward us, in order to offer a support to the weakness of our faith. And by means of this symbol, in turn, we witness to our devotion toward him both before his countenance and in the sight of the angels, as well as before men." The "word of promise" and the "sign" (*verbum et symbolum*) belong together. A sacrament is a "sign of the covenant" and, therefore, to be given high esteem, but it is not to be considered magic. And Calvin ascribes the fruit of the sacraments only to the predestined.

According to Zwingli, the sacraments are signs of remembrance that remind us of the salvation effected by

Christ, and also signs of confession that show our belonging to the Church. Thus we see that, especially in Calvin but also in Zwingli, the sacraments occupy an important and necessary place alongside the proclamation of the Word. On the Lutheran side, however, there is no serious attempt to answer the question why God's efficacious Word of salvation reaches humankind not only through the proclamation but also through the sacraments. This is simply accepted as a fact of the Gospel. Only subsequent reflection reaches the following affirmation: In the sacraments, "the following things come to be expressed in a relatively stronger way [note the influence of Calvinistic ideals] than in the proclamation alone: the sweeping continuum and thoroughgoing character of God's saving action; the moment of sealing the pledge of salvation, which holds good in temptations but which is also binding; the manner in which the whole person is claimed by God, even his or her corporeality; finally, the nature of God's saving action as creating community."[15]

Closer to the Catholic position, Article 25 of the *Thirty-Nine Anglican Articles* holds against Calvin as follows: "The sacraments, instituted by Christ, are not only signs (*notæ*) of the Christian confession, but much more so certain witnesses (*testimonia*) and efficacious signs (*signa*) of grace and of God's benevolence toward us, since he himself is active invisibly in us and not only fosters our faith in him but also strengthens (*confirmat*) it."

D. THE COUNCIL OF TRENT AND POST-TRIDENTINE THEOLOGY

From its seventh to its twenty-fourth sessions (1547–1563) the Council of Trent occupied itself mostly with the exposition of sacramental theology. The seventh session speaks of general sacramental doctrine in thirteen canons (D 844–856, DS 1601–1613). The doctrines are presented for the most part in response to the teachings of the Reformers and on the basis of the theology of St. Thomas

Aquinas. Their essence is this: (1) There are seven sacraments, instituted by Christ; (2) these sacraments are different from the sacraments of the Old Testament; (3) there exists a certain hierarchy among the sacraments of the New Testament; (4) the sacraments are signs necessary for salvation; faith alone does not suffice; (5) the sacraments were not instituted only for the awakening of faith; (6) as efficacious signs, they contain the grace of Christ and bestow it *ex opere operato* on all who do not put an obstacle to it; (9) baptism, confirmation, and orders impress upon the soul of the receiver an indelible character and are, therefore, not repeatable; (10) not all have the same power to administer a sacrament; (11) the minister must have the *intentio saltem faciendi quod facit ecclesia*; (12) even those in mortal sin can administer a sacrament validly; (13) the rites established by the Church are obligatory.

Post-Tridentine theology, continuing in the mind of the Council, dealt further especially with two questions. The first of these has to do with the *intention of the minister*. One sector of Tridentine and post-Tridentine theologians (Ambrosius Catharinus, A. Salmerón) had held the view that a "purely extrinsic intention" of the minister sufficed. Against this opinion, the doctrine generally imposed itself that a virtual intrinsic intention was indeed required.

The other question concerned the *manner in which the sacraments have their effect*. Here three theories were further developed: those of so-called physical, moral, and intentional efficacy.

E. RECENT SACRAMENTAL THEOLOGY

Recent theology has again taken up the question of the *fundamental structure of a sacrament*, in order to examine again in the light of the answer to this question the problem of sacramental efficacy and all other questions connected with sacramental theology. Two theological undertakings have here proved to be of particular significance.

First of all there is the project of the Benedictine Odo Casel (d. Easter Sunday 1948). He had first studied the mystery cults of antiquity and the theology of the Greek Fathers. By applying his findings to sacramental theology he came to consider the sacraments once more, in the words of Rom 6,1–12, as the "realization and making present for us of the event of salvation founded upon the death and resurrection of Christ" (*Mysteriengegenwart*). In his response to this theory, G. Söhngen distinguished the real presence of the mystery of salvation as an "interior sacrament" from our enactment of a sacrament as an "external sacrament," and thus he regarded the application of the reality of salvation as occurring more in our enactment of the sacrament. The decisive point is that in both these views "sacrament" is not an autonomous reality between God and humankind; it is, rather, the immediate divine action in us, and in Söhngen "sacrament" appears as co-determined by our own participation in this divine action by our enactment of a sacrament.[16] Even though the different theories proposed by the "mystery theology," and especially that of O. Casel himself, have not found general agreement, still they deeply affected the newer understanding of the liturgy as well as most other areas of theology, and their influence bore fruit in the Second Vatican Council.[17]

A second position, influenced by Heidegger's philosophy of the word and by the ecumenical concerns of our time, recalls Luther in that it approaches sacrament more from the perspective of the Word and within the framework of a rather broad *theology of the symbol.* Concerning this theology K. Rahner writes: "It takes its departure from the universal and primordial nature of the *word.* Thus, it understands this sacramentally efficacious word not as a subsequent indication of something which exists independently of this word or is to be effected by it. Rather, it conceives of this sacramental word as an 'exhibitive understanding' through which and under whose influence what is expressed actually occurs. Therefore, sacrament is here understood as the *most radical case of God's Word being addressed to human beings.* In other words, sacrament is not an external though efficacious *agens* of grace, but rather a constitutive element in the total event of grace itself. Grace occurs precisely by making itself manifest: *gratia se significando se efficit.*[18] With regard to this theological theory, we must indeed ask whether the word of the sacrament is to be simply accepted in faith, as with Luther, or whether, as in G. Söhngen's theory, this word becomes an event in us through our participating enactment of the sacrament. Both the spiritual activity of human beings, which bears an "expressive character," and reality, which bears the "character of sign," are essential elements in the accomplishment of a sacrament; and both of these realities are now up for discussion in a quite new way. The "theology of symbol" has gained particular significance in its application to the doctrine of the sacraments in the works of E. H. Schillebeeckx (especially the doctrine of the Eucharist). This theologian seeks the possibility of making new theological affirmations above all by applying the "phenomenological method" in the sphere of theology.

The search for the possibility of making new affirmations in sacramental theology vis-à-vis the great questions of our time is now becoming as necessary and important as holding to the ancient truths our faith has taught. The believed reality, however, is always greater than whatever theology may be able to express at a given moment. The *Constitution on the Sacred Liturgy* (1963) summarizes the Church's present understanding of the sacraments in Articles 59 and 61.

II

The Essential Structure of the Sacramental Sign (Structural Determinants)

The word *signum*, introduced by Augustine to designate a sacrament, calls for clarification in many respects because, both in its meaning as a word and in its concrete references, it elicits many questions. These will here be briefly considered from two perspectives: first, we will examine the synthetic structure of the sacramental sign (1), then we will inquire concerning the concrete meaning and, thus, the ontological dimensions of this sign (2).

1. The Synthetic Structure of the Sacramental Sign

1. Origen gave to sacraments the general name of *symbola* (PG 13, 1242, nota 72). Individually these "symbols" have for him a *mystical significance* as with baptism (*In Rom.* V, 562: PG 14, 1040f.; *In Gn.* 28: PG 12, 99), or a more *pneumatic significance*, as with the Eucharist (*In Mt.* XI, 498–500: PG 13, 945–952, commenting on Mt 15,15). The christological controversies resulted in the sacramental signs' acquiring particular significance in Eastern theology as emerging in the context of *salvation-history* (cf. the *Mystagogical Catecheses* of Cyril of Jerusalem).

In a wholly different way, Augustine developed the concept of sign for the Church of the West in a *natural-gnoseological sense*. Thus he writes: "Signum est enim res, præter speciem quam ingerit sensibus, aliud aliquid ex se faciens in cogitationem venire" ["A sign is a thing which makes us think of something different from what its own form represents to the senses"] (*De doctr. chr.* 2.1,1: PL 34,35). Building on that he then develops the distinction between natural and artificial or conventional signs. The signs of the sacraments are judged to be *signa naturalia.*

2. Irenæus had already clearly distinguished in these signs between the *material element* and the *spiritual word,* when he wrote as follows concerning his eucharistic doctrine: "The mingled chalice and the broken bread receive the Word of God and become the Eucharist of Christ's Body and Blood" (*Adv. Haer.* V, 2.3: PG 7, 1125). In a similar way Augustine later writes commenting on John 15,3: "Detrahe verbum et quid est aqua nisi aqua. Accedit verbum ad elementum et fit sacramentum, etiam ipsum tamquam visibile verbum" (*In Jo.* 80.3: PL 35, 1840). At the bottom of these dogmatic distinctions there is the witness of Scripture, which in the case of several sacraments expressly distinguishes these two parts, for instance, in the case of Baptism (Eph 5,26: "lavacrum aquæ in verbo vitæ"), of confirmation (Acts 8,15: it is administered by the laying on of hands and prayer), of the Eucharist (Mt 26,26–28), and of holy unction (Jas 5,14: prayer and anointing with oil).

3. Especially after 1150, when "sacrament" in the sense of the seven sacraments became distinguished from what are called "sacramentals," it becomes apparent that a further distinction is needed in what we call the material element, since with many sacraments (baptism, confirmation, holy unction) not only the *material element* is of the essence but, even more so, the *human action* accompanying this element, and since some sacramental signs have no apparent material element at all but only a human action (confession, orders, matrimony). It was J. Duns Scotus

who finally designated this distinction with the terms *materia remota* (the "element") and *materia proxima* (the
human action). This distinction is significant, since all
sacraments (except the Eucharist) become existent only in
the recipient when the sign is accomplished.[19]

4. The Augustinian distinction between *elementum* and
verbum led at the time of early scholasticism to the designation of the material element as *materia* and of the word
as *forma.* At the beginning of the thirteenth century these
words, *materia* and *forma,* still have a general, undefined
meaning in the *Summa* of Alexander of Hales (d. 1245) or
that of William of Auxerre (d. 1230). But after the arrival of
Aristotelian philosophy, and for the first time in the work
of Hugh of St. Cher (d. 1263), they acquire a strict *hylomorphic* sense. Accordingly, the *words* of a sacrament (as
its *forma*) represent for the "element" and the "action" (as
its *materia*) not only a more precise determination of
meaning: rather, the words are seen to exert the *power of
causal effect.* Thomas Aquinas is then quick to suggest
reasons for the appropriateness of this structure of the
sacramental signs as consisting of matter and form, when
he draws the analogy with Christ, who is the primordial
sacrament (*verbum incarnatum*), and the analogy with
human nature as consisting of body and spirit (since the
sacraments were instituted for human salvation). The *Decree for the Armenians* (1439) (D 695–DS 1310) adopts this
terminology, and the *Roman Catechism* of the Council of
Trent rejoins: "Hæc igitur [materia et forma] sunt partes,
quæ ad naturam et substantiam sacramentorum pertinent
et ex quibus unumquodque sacramentum necessario con-
stituitur." Dominic Soto and other theologians conclude
from these explanations that this dogmatic statement on
the hylomorphic nature of the sacramental sign is therefore *de fide* (a doctrine of faith). This does not mean, however, that hylomorphism itself has become dogma; the only
thing it means is that this manner of expression is seen to
convey adequately the understanding of the Church's faith

concerning sacramental signs. When Luther later explains sacraments on the basis of their character as word, and when more recent Catholic theology likewise speaks of the sacraments' character as word, more is meant than simply the sacramental sign: these statements concern the very effect of the sacraments as deriving from their words.

5. To the question of how the material *element*, the human *action*, and the human-spiritual *word* can together constitute but one sign we must respond that this unity is not a physical but rather a *moral unity*. This unity is created by the speaking and acting person, even though the ministering human being is bound to the material element by divine command. As the form of the sacrament, the *word* possesses not merely an instructive or proclamatory character, but a sanctifying and *consecrating character*, as Augustine already expressed it (*In Jo.* 80.3: PL 35, 1840) and St. Thomas taught it (*Summa Theol.* III q. 60, a.7, d. 1). Bellarmine too exposed the same point in his opposition to the doctrines of the Reformation: "Verbum, quod cum elemento sacramentum facit, non est concionale, sed consecratorium."[20] Related to this is the fact that, ever since the High Middle Ages, and especially since the development of Canon Law, *words*, which had been *deprecative* into the thirteenth century because of the divine origin of grace, now begin to be more *indicative* because of the objective efficacy of the sacraments and the mission entrusted to the sacramental minister (cf. especially the sacrament of penance). The minister does not implore God to forgive the sinner; rather, he himself says to the sinner, *Ego te absolvo.*

6. Such an understanding of sign already touches upon the modern concern for *desacralization*. Particularly for Western thought, that appears as determined by the Aristotelian doctrine of final ends, the danger always exists, both from the material and from the personal aspect, to ascribe a "magical effect" to the sacraments. The danger of understanding the sacraments magically in connection

with their material element is banished by the emphasis given to the word as form of the sacrament. Magical tendencies in connection with the aspect of the minister's personal action, and also in connection with words themselves (magical incantations!), are excluded by the fact that the word either derives directly from Christ or is articulated by Christ's Church in Christ's Spirit; by the fact that the minister does not utter the word on his own behalf, but as a delegate of the Church by virtue of the mission entrusted the minister by Christ in the Church; and by the fact that the real minister of all sacraments is the glorified Lord himself, who is served by a human being only as an "instrumental cause" as the dispenser of the sacraments on earth. Magical thinking in connection with the sacraments has been excluded *a limine* above all by the understanding of the sacraments in the context of salvation-history. This understanding has never been displaced even in the Church of the West by Aristotelian thought categories, and in our time it has been vigorously renewed especially by so-called mystery theology (see Chapter III.2) and by the Second Vatican Council.

Nonetheless, we cannot ignore the fact that, to an outsider who does not understand the internal meaning and interior structure of the sacramental sign, the sacramental rites could appear to be "magic," and this is the reason why in the earliest Christian epochs a special "arcane discipline" was observed in connection with these "mysteries." Thus, too, the non-Christian mysteries imposed on their initiates a special "mystical silence" (O. Casel), not with respect to doctrines and the legends connected with the mysteries, but with respect to the "liturgy of the mysteries."

2. The Essential Interior Meaning of Sacrament (The "Inner Sacrament")

1. We have already noted the complex structure of the *external sign,* which combines in itself the three essentially different realities—the natural element, the human realization of the rite, and the word of the Church—and unites them into one fundamental unity. An examination of the *inner nature* of sacrament exhibits an even more complex structure. For, if sacrament is to be realized as "a sign of the Church, a sign of Christ, and a sign of faith," in it there must converge in one single unity—belonging to both temporal and salvation history—the earthly reality of a rite and the action of God: the earthly reality of a rite accomplished in the world, or of an action carried out in the world and involving the spiritual, moral, and religious reality of a human being who, as person and as image of God, has God for his or her eternal goal, and the action of the eternal God himself within this present time for the sake of human salvation.

2. In his explanations of sacramental theology against the Donatists, who understood the sacraments in a naturalistic and juridical manner, Augustine already distinguished in the sacrament the external sign as the *sacramentum* (*tantum*) from the interior reality and effect of the sacrament as the *res sacramenti* or the *virtus sacramenti.* Thus he writes: "Signacula quidem rerum divinarum esse visibilia, sed res ipsas invisibiles in eis honorari" (*De cat. rud.* 26.50: PL 40, 344). Manna—altare dei—(eucharistia) "in signis diversa sunt; in re quæ significatur, paria sunt" (1 Cor 10, 1–4; *In Jo.* 26.6.12: PL 35, 1612). "Since they [the fathers] understood the visible food [manna] spiritually, they hungered for it in a spiritual way and enjoyed it in a spiritual way, in order thus to be satisfied by it spiritually. For we too daily receive visible food [in the Eucharist]: and yet, the sacrament is one thing and the efficacious power of the sacrament is another! How

many receive from the altar [the sacrament of the altar] . . . and they die precisely by receiving it!" (cf. 1 Cor 11,29) (*In Jo.* 26.6.11: PL 35,1612). Augustine had already touched upon the sacrament's interior reality when, over against the Donatists, he had to defend the fact that a true sacrament can be found even when the effect of the sacrament is absent. Thus, on one occasion, he rejects the second baptism of schismatics demanded by the Donatists on the following grounds: "Consider the case of a soldier who out of cowardice refuses to fight and who thus disowns the mark of the warrior which has been burnt into his body. Subsequently he implores the goodness of his ruler and, because of his repentance, he is granted pardon, and this enables him to go back to fighting bravely. Will a new mark be burnt into the flesh of such a man, who has converted and been pardoned, or will not rather the existing mark be acknowledged anew? Could we say that the Christian sacraments leave any less of a mark than this physical mark of our soldier?" (*Contra Parm.* II, 13.29: PL 43,71f). Here Augustine is clearly speaking of what in the High Middle Ages would be called the sacrament's *character indelibilis.* Thomas clearly defines this character variously as that reality in which the *sacramentum tantum* and the *res sacramenti* originate and exist in unity. He writes: "Character sacramentalis est res respectu saramenti exterioris, et est sacramentum respectu ultimi effectus" (*Summa Theol.* III, q. 63, a.3, ad 2). "Licet character sit res et sacramentum, non tamen oportet omne id quod est *res et sacramentum* esse characterem" (*Summa Theol.* III, q. 63, a.6, ad 3; the presence of the Christ who suffered and rose in the Eucharist is also called *res et sacramentum: Summa Theol.* III, q. 73, a.6). This is why L. Billot, in more recent times, rightly put what is called *res et sacramentum* at the very center of each and every sacrament (*De ecclesiae sacramentis,* In III S. *Th.* I, 1924 [6th edition], 104–115: Thesis VI).

   3. The deeper meaning, the profound interior dimension

of the sacraments, will become even clearer when, following the lead of mystery theology (cf. III. 2), we seek to encounter the sacraments where alone their most unique identity can be revealed: namely, in the sphere of the divine *oikonomia,* accessible to faith alone (Eph 1,10; 3, 2–12), within the context of salvation-history, which is realized within the history of the world for the believer who has received grace and within the Church as being the Mystical Body of Christ. In his book G. Söhngen described this reality as being the *inner* sacrament, and concerning it he writes as follows: "The inner sacrament is that reality, unconditionally contained and caused, which designates sacramental grace and sanctification in an interior and spiritually real manner. . . . The inner sacrament is the interior designation of a human being for sacramental grace and sanctification which is unconditionally effected by the exterior sign. . . . *Only the inner sacrament together with the exterior sacrament constitutes the total concept of sacrament.* . . . In the *inner* sacrament, the sacramental reality and the sacramental signification converge. . . . In this manner, the interiorly signified efficacy of grace becomes ordered directly to its first cause, which is Christ in his work of redemption."[21]

Reginald of Piperno, who completed the *Summa theologica* of St. Thomas, already hints at this concept of the "inner sacrament" when he writes, "In omnibus sacramentis est aliqua spiritualis operatio mediante materiali operatione, quæ eam significat" (*Suppl.* q 45 a 1 c).

III

The Sacraments' Saving Reality and Efficacy

We can begin seeing what a sacrament is, what its inner essence consists of, only when we consider the purpose and meaning of a sacrament—its saving reality and efficacy. According to the account of revelation the godless world, left to itself, does nothing but move in the direction of decay and ruination (cf. Gen 1–11.9): "Sinners shall be destroyed altogether, the descendants of the wicked shall be wiped out. The salvation of the virtuous comes from the Lord" (Ps 37,38f). Welfare of soul and body, peace in the world and in the heart, righteousness of mind, and a life full of blessings—all this is meant in connection with the *salvation* (σωτηρία) of human beings in this godless world. This salvation comes from "God" alone, whom Israel had already experienced at the time of the first deliverance from Egyptian captivity (Exod 15,1) as the "horn of salvation" (Ps 18,3), the "shield of salvation" (Ps 18,36), the "rock of salvation" (Deut 32,15), and the "helmet of salvation" (Isa 59,17). It was during the Babylonian Exile, when the chosen people had had all earthly power and all hope in self-reliance wrested from it, that the people of God of the Old Covenant were first in a position to comprehend the "universality of divine salvation" (Isa 49,6): the place of the earlier mediators of divine salvation, the place of the judges and kings, was then taken in the prophetic consciousness of this time by the figure of the "servant of

God," who through his vicarious suffering was meant to become the salvation of many, indeed, of all (Isa 52, 13–53,12). The faith of the early Christian community understood the historical "Jesus of Nazareth" to be the fulfillment of these prophecies concerning the servant of God: God himself had "reconciled the world with himself in Christ" (2 Cor 5,19). "He [God himself] has taken us out of the power of darkness and created a place for us in the kingdom of the Son he loves, and in him we have our redemption by his blood, the forgiveness of sins. . . . It was God's will that the whole fullness [of salvation] should dwell in him, and that all things should be reconciled through him and for him, everything in heaven and everything on earth, when he made peace through his blood by his death on the cross" (Col 1,13–20). "In him [Christ] alone is salvation; for of all the names in the world given to men, this is the only one by which we can be saved" (Acts 4,12: Peter speaking before the Sanhedrin). Just as Christ came as "savior" (Luke 2,11: σωτήρ) and yet left the world and announced his return (John 14,2f., 28), so too "his salvation" that he has brought us is truly our possession, and yet we are exhorted "to work out our salvation with fear and trembling" (Phil 2,12), "to preserve ourselves, through the power of God, in faith for the salvation that will be revealed at the end of time" (1 Pet 1,5). It is the very meaning and essence of the "sacraments" precisely to hold in readiness and to communicate continually this "salvation" to every situation of our Christian life in this godless world.

The task of this most important chapter in our general doctrine of the sacraments ("The Sacraments' Saving Reality and Efficacy") is to think through what it is exactly that the sacraments communicate to us under the name of "salvation" and how they do this. After some brief reflections on the content of this communication of salvation (1), we will have to discuss the doctrine of what is called "mystery theology" to some extent, since this approach

has some decisive things to say to our contemporary understanding of the sacraments (2). Our consideration of the
"character" of specific sacraments as being their particular
effect (3) will then prepare us for the theological and magisterial pronouncements on the objective efficacy of the
sacraments (4) as well as for the theological attempts to determine more precisely the exact manner in which the
sacraments have their effect (5).

1. The Principal Effects of the Sacraments

In its controversy with the doctrines of the Reformation,
the Council of Trent understood the concept of "sacrament," in line with Thomistic doctrine, as a "sign of
grace," and it declared that the first effect of the sacraments of the New Covenant was as follows: "Omnis vera
iustitia vel incipit, vel cœpta augetur, vel amissa reparatur"
(D 843a, cf. 847–850; DS 1600, 1604–1607). The Constitution on the Liturgy of the Second Vatican Council, too, begins with this doctrine and then expands it in a decisive
way: "The sacraments are ordered to the *sanctification of
humankind*, the *building up of the Body of Christ*, and finally the *honor due to God*; as signs they also have the
task to *instruct*. They not only presuppose *faith*, but they
also nourish it by word, action, and matter; they strength-
en it and proclaim it; and this is why they are called 'sacraments of faith.' They confer grace, but their celebration
also enables the faithful in an intense way to receive this
grace fruitfully, to honor God rightly, and to exercise love"
(SC 59). "The effect of the sacramental liturgy and of the
sacramentals is this: when the faithful are rightly prepared, every event of their lives is sanctified by the divine
grace that flows forth from the Paschal Mystery of the
passion, death and resurrection of Christ, the Mystery
from which all the sacraments and sacramentals derive
their power. They also bring it about that every correct

use of material things can be directed to the sanctification of humankind and the praise of God" (SC 61). This statement clarifies the doctrine of Trent in the following three respects:

1. The first effect of all sacraments is a new, a deepened, or a renewed *immersion of the human being in the "Mystery of Christ"* (Col 2,2): by God's eternal design, and within our temporal history, the relationship of the creature to the Creator, of God's servant to his Lord, and of God's child to his Father, is initiated anew, strengthened, and vivified. The religious sense of the sacraments must first be grasped in this new relationship to Christ; only then can we go on to understand how this relationship to Christ becomes fruitful by communicating salvation to humankind. Even if, from the standpoint of God's great love, the "salvation of humankind" is always the first objective, still, for religious man and woman, it is "the love of God," manifested in Jesus Christ (John 3,16), that must be the goal of his and her sacramental piety and hence also the principle of his and her sacramental theology. "God, rich in mercy, for the great love he bore us, brought us to life with Christ even when we were dead in our sins; it is by his grace you are saved. And in union with Christ Jesus he raised us up and enthroned us with him in the heavenly realms, so that he might display in the ages to come how immense are the resources of his grace, and how great his kindness to us in Christ Jesus. For it is by his grace you are saved, by virtue of faith; it is not your own doing, it is God's gift" (Eph 2,4–8).

According to the witness of Scripture, our *Christian faith* begins with *faith in Christ,* and it is in our interior communion with Christ the Lord that are to be found the deepest roots and the living power of our faith in the truths of Christian revelation. This faith, moreover, is at once the condition for and the fruit of the worthy and fruitful reception of the sacraments.

Whenever this fundamental attitude to the sacraments

is lacking, the danger emerges that the sacraments and their efficacious grace will be manipulated egotistically as means to salvation and even misconceived as magical objects. Before anything else the sacraments are signs of encountering the living God, of entering into the mystery of Christ by being united with the glorified Lord who is the foremost dispenser of all sacraments—signs of being filled with the Spirit of God, through whom the "kingdom of God" is already present and active in our midst (Rom 5,5). Already Thomas Aquinas, who conceives of the sacraments as instrumental causes of grace, stresses the fact that all sacraments derive their effect of grace from Christ's redemptive suffering: "The primary cause for the efficacy of grace is God himself, to whom the human nature of Christ relates as an instrument united to him (hypostatic union in Christ), and to whom the sacraments relate as autonomous instruments separated from him. Therefore it seems fitting that the saving power of Christ's divinity flows over through his humanity into just these sacraments" (*Summa theol.* III, q. 62, a.5, c). Through the sacraments we put on the form of Christ: "Per omnia sacramenta ecclesiæ homo Christo conformatur" (*Summa theol.* III, q. 72, a.1, ad 4).

2. On this basis we can understand the doctrine of both Trent and Vatican II that every sacrament serves the *sanctification of the human being* and therefore either bestows or increases sanctifying grace. This doctrine is founded on the proclamation of both Jesus and the Church that *baptism* confers "forgiveness of sins and the gift of the Holy Spirit" (Acts 2,38) and results in the human being's being "born again for the kingdom of God" (John 3,5); that the *Eucharist* bestows the gift of "eternal life" (John 6,54f.) and *confirmation* communicates "the Holy Spirit" (Acts 8,17); that the *anointing of the sick* dispenses the "forgiveness of sins and salvation" (Jas 5,15). Thus it is also with the effect of all the sacraments, as will be seen when we deal with the particular doctrine of the sacraments.

The fundamental meaning of baptism is that it is the "gate into the kingdom of God" and is dispensed to one who is not yet found in the state of grace. Likewise penance is instituted for one who is no longer living in grace but in sin (John 20,23). For this reason baptism and penance are usually termed the *sacraments of the dead*, that is, of those who are still living in the death of sin. The other sacraments, all of which presuppose the state of grace, are called *sacraments of the living.* Of course, the "sacraments of the dead," when they are received by those who are already in the state of grace,[22] can increase grace. Similarly it appears that a "sacrament of the living," when it is received by a sinner who is not sufficiently aware of his or her state of spiritual death through sin, also effects the "forgiveness of sins," as Thomas expressly teaches in connection with confirmation (*Summa theol.* III, q. 72, a. 7, ad 2).

3. Beyond this, every sacrament effects a grace particular to it, the so-called sacramental grace (cf. D 845–DS 1602). This doctrine derives from the following factors:

a) Christ himself instituted the "different sacraments" and in so doing he stressed each one's specific necessity for salvation, as in the case of baptism (John 3,5) and the Eucharist (John 6,53).

b) The different sacraments possess "different signs," and hence also different effects, since the sign points to what it specifically signifies.

c) The sacraments are given to us humans for the "different situations of our life," and consequently they must contain different effects of grace (*Summa theol.* III, q. 62, a.2, c). We will see more in detail how the Eucharist, being the sacrifice of the Church, occupies a very special place. Baptism and confirmation, each in its own way, are in the service of the human being's spiritual, supernatural life. Penance and the anointing of the sick are given as saving means against sin in either the healthy or the sick person. Priestly ordination and marriage have been bestowed by

Christ for both the supernatural and the natural sociological organism of the Church.

Because grace is given by God and is intended to serve
humans in accordance with their particular nature and
their particular situation, we must say that sacramental
and non-sacramental grace cannot be distinguished from
one another on the basis of the sacrament but only on the
basis of the finality of grace. For this reason we must assume that even sacramental graces can consist partly of
sanctifying grace and partly of actual grace. Since actual
graces are often not yet necessary at the moment of a
sacrament's reception, we can assume that they are given
to the recipient of a sacrament with sacramental certainty
when he or she does need them and asks them of God with
reference to the sacrament (for instance, the graces of state
of life relating to ordination and marriage).

Christ has not made his grace dependent on the sacraments (Peter Lombard, *Sent.* IV d 1 c 5): "Ad excellentiam
potestatis Christi pertinet quod ipse potuit effectum sacramentorum sine exteriori sacramento conferre" (*Summa
theol.* III, q. 64, a.3, c). Nonetheless, it would be disastrous
to ignore the very great *importance of the sacramental
path to salvation* in the Church of the incarnate Son of
God. It is for the sake of human beings, consisting of body
and spirit, that this sacramental path to salvation is of
great importance, and at least since the time of Augustine
a *votum sacramenti* (for baptism and penance) has been
spoken of in one way or another as necessary for salvation
(cf. D 796–DS 1524).

Concerning the measure and extent of the communication of these graces, the Council of Trent taught as follows:
"We receive justification within us, each according to his
or her measure, and this measure the Holy Spirit determines for each one in accordance with his divine will and
corresponding to the preparation and cooperation present
in the recipient himself or herself" (cf. D 799–DS 1529).
This doctrine would have to be expanded by saying that

the measure of graces is also determined by the needs of the kingdom of God and the tasks that the individual has to perform in God's kingdom; for God and his kingdom are the *finis ultimus* of justification itself.

For the Eucharist and penance we must affirm that these sacraments, repeatedly received, incorporate humans with renewed power into the supernatural Mystical Body of Christ and thereby make the individual ever more apt for the service of God's kingdom precisely in the place where God has put him or her in keeping with the divine plan of the Mystical Body. In this way the individual member becomes ever more similar to Christ, the Head and Principle of life, the formative principle and the transfigured final principle of the whole Mystical Body. The decisive factor, however, is that the sacraments be received not only physically, *sacramentaliter*, but in the Spirit of Christ, *spiritualiter*, and in the correct manner. We will now speak about this manner of receiving the sacraments as we reflect in what follows on what is known as "mystery theology."

2. Conformity to Christ as Chief Effect of a Sacrament: Basic Theories of Mystery Theology

HISTORICAL OVERVIEW

What is known as *mystery theology* was developed primarily by the Benedictine Odo Casel (monk of Maria Laach, d. 1948 at the nuns' monastery in Herstelle). Already in 1922 he was speaking of "the liturgy as a celebration of mysteries" on the model of the "ancient mysteries," from among which he particularly concentrated on sacramental rites (baths and meals), enthusiastic rituals (ecstasy through dance), and the dramatic reenactment of stories of the gods (death and resurrection of Osiris in Egypt, and so forth). In his work *Das christliche Kultmys-*

terium[23] he further developed and deepened his thought. A very different concept of mystery theology was developed by G. Söhngen in his books *Symbol und Wirklichkeit im Kultmysterium*[24] and *Der Wesensaufbau des Mysteriums*.[25] V. Warnach sharply criticized G. Söhngen in his article "Zum Problem der Mysteriengegenwart,"[26] and this led to a rich and extensive discussion. D. Feuling, a monk of Beuron, sought to develop this new doctrine on a Thomistic basis, but to this the name of mystery theology really no longer applies. The Catholic dogmatics of M. Schmaus from the outset was very sympathetic to the deepest concerns of mystery theology, in spite of Schmaus's critique of the method. After the appearance of the encyclical *Mediator Dei*, Cardinal Marchetti Selvaggiani stated in an interview on November 25, 1948, that this encyclical constituted a rejection of the theory of mystery theology (especially what concerns the "festal mystery").[27] The 1963 Constitution on the Liturgy of Vatican II, however, incorporates the fundamental concerns of mystery theology (SC 59, 60, and 61).

I. When new directions emerge in theology it is worth our while to distinguish the fundamental *concerns* that give rise to them from the *metaphysics* in which such concerns are cast.

1. The religious concern of mystery theology is the same as the religious concern of our epoch. What is being sought is an ontological and personal deepening of our religious existence, parallel to developments in "existential philosophy" at the same time as mystery theology first emerged. This concern is quite justified: (a) first of all with respect to the main theological currents since Trent, which, in their counterreaction against the subjectivism of the Reformation, did not always escape the danger of a certain material "objectification of the religious"—in whole areas theology was equated with metaphysics; (b) but the pedagogical effects of mystery theology also deserve recognition: the disciple's "imitation of Christ" is sought by mystery theology

in its sacramental reality, and this represents a victory over mere moralism and asceticism.

2. Many difficulties do arise, however, from the metaphysical categories that undergird this central concern. Mystery theology requires that the Christian become like Christ through the sacraments, by really appropriating "Christ's saving deeds"—his death and his resurrection—and this further requires that these historical events from Jesus' life attain to a real *presence in the mystery*. Now Odo Casel understood this "presence" in a more Platonic and idealistic manner, while G. Söhngen conceived it more existentially. In this context mystery theology takes kerygmatic expressions from St. Paul and the Fathers and turns them into metaphysical affirmations. Too, this system has almost no place for the events of the Incarnation and the sending of the Holy Spirit, which are certainly just as important for redemption.

II. In order rightly to understand mystery theology, we must first clearly see its basic tenet: mystery theology does not understand the salvation and grace in which we participate through Christ's redemption anthropologically, as a fruit of this redemption in the sense of a "new life" that makes us to be a new creation; rather, for mystery theology, salvation and grace mean a growing "similarity with the Christ who through his sacrificial death attained to glorification." Paul speaks variously of this *conformity with Christ* in the Christian: "God knew his own before ever they were, and also ordained that they should be shaped to the likeness of his Son (συμμόρφους τῆς εἰκόνος τοῦ υἱοῦ), that [Christ] might be the eldest among a large family of brothers" (Rom 8,29). Likewise in Gal 4,17.19: "I am in travail with you over again until you take the shape of Christ (μορφωθῆ Χριστός)." In his mystical theology Paul speaks of his being crucified with Christ (Gal 2,19; cf. 6,14; Rom 6,6), of his bearing the wounds of Christ (Gal 6,17), of his life's no longer being his own, but that "Christ lives in him" (Gal 2,20). "Baptized into union with Christ, you have all put on

Christ as a garment" (Gal 3,27; Rom 13,14). These statements of St. Paul show that what "conformity with Christ"
involves is not merely an ethical task to be done, or merely
learning one's lesson (Matt 11,29), or even following Christ
by carrying one's cross (Matt 16,24); the heart of the matter,
rather, is a "likeness with Christ" (1 John 3,2:ὅμοιοι αὐτῷ
ἐσόμεθα) that transcends the visible and the human and
that will be revealed in the end. What is still hidden from
our earthly understanding is nonetheless a sure possession
because of our hope in God (1 Cor 2,9; Isa 64,3f.), nothing
less than the glory that God will prepare when the Lord returns: "He will transfigure the body belonging to our humble state, and give it a form like that of his own resplendent
body, by the very power which enables him to make all
things subject to himself" (Phil 3,21).

However, it would be one-sided to look for the whole
concept of grace as given by revelation only in this Pauline
mystical doctrine of identification with Christ. Likewise
included in the concept of grace are participation in the divine life (John 15), participation in the divine nature (2 Pet
1,4), a special relationship to the Holy Spirit (Rom 8), and
the supernatural virtues of faith, hope, and love (Rom 5,5).
But the chief problem of mystery theology consists in
showing the way to the attainment of "likeness to Christ."

III. For mystery theology the most important passage for
answering this question is Rom 6,3–11, which contains St.
Paul's *baptismal theology:*

Have you forgotten that when we were baptized into union
with Christ Jesus we were baptized into his death? By baptism we
were buried with him, and lay dead, in order that, as Christ was
raised from the dead in the splendor of the Father, so also we
might set our feet upon the new path of life. For if we have become incorporate with him in a death like his, we shall also be
one with him in a resurrection like his. We know that the man we
once were has been crucified with Christ, for the destruction of
the sinful self, so that we may no longer be the slaves of sin, since
a dead man is no longer answerable for his sin. But if we thus died

with Christ, we believe that we shall also come to life with him. We know that Christ, once raised from the dead, is never to die again: he is no longer under the dominion of death. For in dying as he died, he died to sin, once for all, and in living as he lives, he lives to God. In the same way you must regard yourselves as dead to sin and alive to God, in union with Christ Jesus our Lord.

In what is actually a commentary on the form of the baptismal rite, with its immersion into and emergence from the water, Paul here simultaneously envisages three levels of meaning. The liturgical immersion and emergence during the baptismal rite is an image of the *historical* burial and resurrection of Christ. This in turn is an image of the *ethical* exigency to die to sin and live alone for God, as well as of the *eschatological* fact of our death and eventual permanent resurrection with Christ.

These three concepts of Pauline mysticism—burial with Christ, resurrection with Christ, life with Christ (συνετάφημεν-συζήσομεν: Rom 6,3.8)—can also be found in other passages of Paul's letters: "God, rich in mercy, for the great love he bore us, brought us to life with Christ even when we were dead in our sins; it is by his grace you were saved. And in union with Christ Jesus he raised us up and enthroned us with him in the heavenly realms" (συνεζωοποίησεν-συνήγειρεν-συνεκάθισεν)" (Eph 2,4–6). "In baptism you were buried with [Christ], in baptism also you were raised to life with him through your faith in the active power of God who raised him from the dead. And although you were dead because of your sins and because you were morally uncircumcised, he has made you alive with Christ (συνεζωοποίησεν)" (Col 2,12f.). "If we died with him, we shall live with him; if we endure with him, we shall reign with him (συναπεθάνομεν-συνζήσομεν-συμβασιλεύσομεν)" (2 Tim 2,11–13). To die with, to be buried with, to live with, to be raised up with, to rise with, to be enthroned with, to reign with: all of the expressions of St. Paul emphatically present Christian life and existence as a *being with and living with Christ.*

Mystery theology sees these expressions as pointing to the way in which the Christian comes to partake of Christ's grace. But Paul himself is rather speaking of the fact that Christian existence consists of a personal and mystical union with Christ. This is especially made clear by Paul's continually using in the same text both the *indicative* mood (of mysticism) and the *imperative* mood (of ethical command), as for instance in such verses as Rom 6,8.11; Gal 3,27 = Rom 13,14.[28] And Paul stresses the ethical elements of this mystical transformation particularly when he writes: "All I care for is to know Christ, to experience the power of his resurrection, and to share his sufferings, in growing conformity with his death, if only I may finally arrive at the resurrection from the dead. It is not to be thought that I have already achieved all this. I have not yet reached perfection, but I press on, hoping to take hold of that for which Christ once took hold for me" (Phil 3,10–12).[29]

IV. If thus the interpretation of mystery theology especially for Rom 6,2ff. is shown to be untenable,[30] even less can it be proved from the *tradition* of patristic theology that mystery theology's theory of a "presence of the mysteries" [*Mysterien-gegenwart*] is well founded. In numerous publications Odo Casel gathered a "cloud of witnesses" from patristic literature to substantiate his doctrines.[31] We will here present three short texts as examples.

The first is from Cyril of Jerusalem: "Let no one believe that the purpose of baptism is only the forgiveness of sins and the conferral of adoption, as the baptism of John had effected the forgiveness of sins. One ought carefully to note that baptism not only purifies from sin and bestows the gift of the Holy Spirit, but is also an image of Christ's sufferings. This is why Paul exclaims: 'Or do you not know that all of us who have been baptized into Christ Jesus have been baptized into his death? With him have we been buried through baptism into his death.' He said this to dispel the claim that, while baptism confers forgiveness of sins and the adoption of children, it is not a real participation in the sufferings of Christ by imitation of him."[32] The second is likewise from Cyril: "Since you have been baptized into Christ and have put on Christ, you have taken on the form of the Son of God. Since God had predestined us to occupy a place as his children, he has made us take on the form of the glorified body of his Christ. Now that you have received a part in the Anointed, you may rightly be called 'anointed' yourselves. . . . But you have become anointed because you have received an image of the Spirit. Everything has occurred in you by way of image, because you are images of God."[33] The third text is from Theodore of Mopsuestia: "By this Paul was clearly teaching that we were baptized in order that we might imitate in ourselves the death and resurrection of the Lord, and in order that, by remembering the events that have taken place, our faith in the things to come might be secured."[34]

Odo Casel's interpretation of these texts makes it evident that he distinguishes the cultic mystery from the historical mystery of Christ, and that his thought continually remains rooted in and concerned with the liturgy. Thus, the objections made from a scholastic and metaphysical standpoint by J. B. Umberg in his essays against Odo Casel do not really touch the heart of Casel's concerns.[35] On the other hand it must also be said that Casel's language and whole manner of approach cannot be made to conform with the metaphysical thought-patterns of traditional dogmatics.

V. How, then, does mystery theology conceive of likeness with Christ? How does this likeness come about? Fundamental to the doctrines of mystery theology is the fact that, through the sacraments, human beings do not really come into relation with Christ and receive his grace; rather, they come into relation with "Christ's death and resurrection," that is, with a deed of Christ's, with an event in Christ, or at least into relation with Christ to the extent that Christ is characterized primarily by this dying and rising. The center of concern is *not Christ's theandric nature,* which has been the foundation of the Church's doctrine of redemption ever since the struggle with Gnosticism; the center of concern, rather, is the *theandric activity* of this Christ. For more specifics on the saving deed of Christ, let us now turn to the following explanations concerning the "presence of the mysteries."

A. ODO CASEL

"The mystery (in the sense of the 'cultic mystery') is a holy action, proper to the cult, through which a reality of salvation becomes present by virtue of the rite. By carrying out this rite, the cultic community participates in the deed of salvation and thereby becomes heir to this salvation."[36] The presence of the mystery here still appears to be a supra-temporal and supra-spatial reality that is separate from both the historical and the eternal and glorified Lord; it is in such a reality that believers participate through the sacramental rite. Largely under the influence of the positive criticism of V. Warnach, Casel specified that this participation comes about through the exercise of faith and love and by the power of the Holy Spirit[37]: "The knowledge imparted by faith makes us see in the sacramental image the archetypal Image itself, that is, Christ's work of salvation. We see it in faith and in *gnosis,* which means that we touch it, make it our own: we are given its very form by our participation in it and, thus, we are transformed according to the image of the Crucified and Risen Lord. By the power of Christ's Spirit, therefore, we ourselves traverse the whole gamut of the work of redemption, we participate in Christ's Pasch, which is to say in his mortal passage through the death of sin, a journey leading out of this present æon and into the Kingdom of God and Christ, into new and everlasting life. The sacrament and the original work of redemption are not two separate things but only one and the same thing, which means that the image is so filled with the reality of the original deed that we may quite correctly assert that the image is the presence of the deed. Thus the Eucharist, in a sacramental manner, is the sacrifice of Christ. In the sacraments Christ is really active as the High Priest of his *ecclesia:* through his saving deed he redeems it and leads it to life. For its part the *ecclesia,* filled with the Spirit of its Bridegroom, celebrates by virtue of his power his and its mystery and thereby grows constantly into greater union with Christ, *ut cum frequentatione mysterii crescat salutis effectus.* Here, once again, the *original mystery* and the *cultic mystery* are seen to be one.

This doctrine reaches new depths in the work *Das christliche Kultmysterium,* where the cultic mystery is further defined in terms of mystery theology: "It is the Lord himself who effects this mystery; but he does not bring it about alone, as he had done the original mystery on the Cross, but together with his Bride, the Ecclesia, whom he acquired for himself on the Cross and to whom he has now given all his treasures that it might communicate them to all the children which it has borne by virtue of his power. Whoever would have God as Father must, since the Incarnation, have the Ecclesia as his Mother. Just as in paradise woman was shaped from the side of the first Adam . . . so, too, the Church is shaped from the side of Christ as he sleeps on the Cross. . . . At the same time, however, as the Fathers teach us, in the water and the blood there flowed out the mysteries from the side of the Lord, from out of his pierced heart. The Church, and at the same time the Christian mystery, were born from the blood of Christ's death, so that *church* and *mystery* are henceforth inseparably bound with one another. In the last analysis it is on account of this fact that the *cultic mystery* becomes liturgy."[38]

B. GOTTLIEB SÖHNGEN

"Sacrament is the symbolic and yet real presence of salvation-history both past and future, the presence both of the basis for salvation and of the realization of salvation."[39] Söhngen explains the presence of the mystery in the following manner: "The sacramental imitation of Christ in his work of salvation is not a self-sufficient and autonomous symbol standing between salvation-history's original model (Christ's death on the Cross) and its sacramental effect in the Church. Rather, the internal symbol consists in and is found alongside the sacramental efficacy, which thus is an effect through imitation or con-formation (*effectus per imitationem*), but in such a way that this conformation is the shaping principle in the effect. The sacramental symbol in itself has no essential or substantial being, but only a pneumatic and dogmatic being, that is, the fluid being of an efficacious spiritual power."[40]

In his second work, *Der Wesensaufbau des Mysteriums*,[41] Söhngen juxtaposes his own thesis to that of Casel and that of the Scholastics:

1a) Casel's thesis: In the Church's memorial sacrifice the Lord's death is represented, and this not only figuratively, which is to say through an image that reminds us graphically of Christ's saving deed, but through an image in which what is symbolized becomes actually present. When the Church, in union with her High Priest, Jesus Christ, accomplishes the memorial of his sacrificial death in the mystery, then this saving deed necessarily becomes re-presented here and now so that we might come to live and partake of its reality.

1b) Scholastic counter-thesis: In the Church's memorial sacrifice the Lord's death is represented through a sign or image that graphically reminds us of that saving deed because it makes present the Body and Blood of the Lord separately under the two species (cf. *Summa Theol.* III, q. 83, a.1).

1c) Söhngen's thesis: When the Church, together with its High Priest, Jesus Christ, accomplishes the memorial of his sacrificial death in the mystery, then this saving deed is made present here and now by virtue of the fact that it is at the same time accomplished in us and by us interiorly, which is to say through the Lord's life-creating Spirit.

2a) Casel's thesis: In the Church's memorial sacrifice the Lord's death is made present, not only by virtue of the fact that the saving power of that sacrificial death becomes effective in us, but indeed because the saving deed itself again becomes present. The saving power has its effect in us because the saving deed itself is made present. Just as we come to partake of the Lord's Body because it has previously become present, so too we are introduced into communion with his sacrificial death because this death has first become present in the mystery.

2b) Scholastic counter-thesis: In the Church's memorial sacrifice the Lord's death becomes present in a symbol; moreover, this symbol is an efficacious sign, so that through the symbolic representation the saving power of that sacrificial death takes its effect in us, or, otherwise stated, the fruits of the sacrifice become applied to us (cf. *Summa theol.* III, q. 83, a.1).

2c) Söhngen's thesis: The Lord's flesh and blood are made present under the separate species in order that his sacrificed Body, marked once and for all with the blood of the Cross, may be designated truly as our own sacrificial offering. Thus, through the sacrifice of the Church, who itself both sacrifices and is sacrificed along with its Lord, the Lord's sacrificial death becomes re-presented in it spiritually and in reality.

3a) Casel's thesis: In the Church's memorial sacrifice the Lord's death is re-presented as a saving deed, but a saving deed not in the factuality of its historical occurrence but rather in the spiritual nature of the mystery (*non in facto sed in mysterio*). Just as the Lord's body becomes present not spatially but in the spiritually real manner of an es-

sential state (*secundum modum substantiæ, non tamquam in loco*), so, too, the Lord's sacrificial deed accomplished on the cross is made present in the unbloody and
spiritually real manner of an essential state (*secundum
modum substantiæ, non tamquam in tempore*).

3b) Scholastic counter-thesis: In the Church's memorial
sacrifice the Lord's death is made present symbolically and
yet *efficaciously,* which is to say in all its mysterious saving power; but the saving deed itself is not made really
present since it is a historical fact and, as such, is past. The
saving deed extends into the present solely in its effects (cf.
Thomas *Sent.* IV, d. 4, q.2, a.1, qa 3.c).

3c) Söhngen's thesis: The Lord's body, as an essential
state (*substantia incompleta*), becomes present even with
respect to this essential reality. Nevertheless, the Lord's
sacrificial death, as an action, becomes present by virtue of
the fact that it takes root in us in the mystery, since our activity becomes conformed to Christ's saving deed and
thus, in our actions, the mystery of the Cross is mysteriously imitated.

4a) Casel's thesis: In the Church's memorial sacrifice the
Lord's death is celebrated as a mystery and therefore, because the Christ-mystery is a living whole and has its center of convergence in the mystery of the Cross, the whole
mystery of salvation becomes present when the mystery of
the Lord's death is celebrated. "Mystery" (*mysterium*) is
the concept referring to the manner or form—the cultic
symbol—under whose veil the historical fact of the Passion becomes sacramentally present (*mysterium sacramentaliter repræsentans factum historicum*); and, indeed,
the Mystery stands as the reality-filled symbol occupying
the connecting middle-point between the past fact of the
sacrifice of the Cross and our own mysterious coming-
into-conformity with the Crucified. And this process of
entering into identity with Christ is communicated or effected by the symbolic bringing-into-presence of the historical act of the Passion.

4b) Scholastic counter-thesis: In the Church's memorial sacrifice it is the Lord's death, and that alone, that becomes present through the symbols of our Lord's body and blood. Christ's other saving deeds that are related to the Cross, especially as historical facts, can be contemplated in this context, but only by our memory.

4c) Söhngen's thesis: "Mystery" is above all the concept referring to the re-presented thing itself, namely, the term for the mystery that becomes present or, more precisely, for the Passion, a fact of salvation-history, as this fact is made present through the sacrament in its mystery and its content of divine salvation, and as this occurs in a mysterious and symbolically real manner (*Mysterium repræsentatum seu historicum factum repræsentatum secundum salutis mysterium in facto historico ut opere salutari exercitum*). Indeed, the mystery made present in us is, in its innermost reality, inseparable from the interior and efficacious realization or effect of the sacrament that, in its full reality, is nothing other than a spiritually real imitation of Christ's work of redemption.

C. MICHAEL SCHMAUS

In his *Katholische Dogmatik*[42] M. Schmaus writes as follows concerning the presence of the mystery, against the background of the thought of V. Warnach[43] and T. Hahn[44]: "We could . . . explain participation in Christ's death in such a way that it is not the work of redemption that becomes present to us, but we who become present to the work of redemption. According to Rom 6,2–11 the baptized person becomes conformed to the image of Christ's death. Now this image is a sacramental image. It makes Christ's death accessible to us. It is the bridge to Christ's unique death, accomplished once and for all in history. In the *today* of the mystery the saving deed is present in a supratemporal manner, not as an act that has duration within time but in a pneumatic mode. And then, through the enaction of the sacrament, a change takes place in us. By becoming conformed to the death of Christ, we are drawn into the mystery of his death and of the life that this death effects. We are taken out of a worldly existence and are given a share in the death and in the glory of Christ. In this process neither the work of redemption is lifted out of its historical past and transferred into the present nor are we transposed into the past. Rather are we inserted into the supratemporal mystery of the saving deed that comes into evidence in the symbolic signs of the sacraments when we accomplish the cultic symbol as believers." In a subsequent edition of his *Katholische Dogmatik*[45] Schmaus leans more to the side of Durrwell when he writes: "Following the line of thought proposed by F. X. Durrwell in his work *La résurrection*,[46] we could say that the transfigured and risen Lord unites himself in the Holy Spirit with those who believe in him. Thus, communion with Christ ought no longer to be imagined as occurring in the manner of a horizontal movement leading out of the past and into the present, but rather must be understood as a vertical movement that, so to speak, leads from above to below, that is, from the mysteriously present Lord to the believer. To this we would have to add, however, that in the transfigured Lord there remain present his own earthly past, above all his death and resurrection, indeed not as acts (which could never be repeated and cannot return) but as the realities which determine his whole existence and give it its unique character. Christ forever lives as the one who has gone through death. The transfigured Christ is identical with the historical Christ. Even though Christ himself lives in a glorious state, nonetheless, for his encounter with the person who believes in him, Christ makes use of a world which has not yet been transfigured but is still pilgrimaging on the road to transfiguration. Within such a world he particularly makes use of the *word* of proclamation and the *sign* of the sacraments—makes use of those means, therefore, which the Father had produced in his work of creation and put at the Son's disposal for his work of redemption both in history and in heaven. Even better, these are the means which the Father, on the basis of the creation which he had designed and realized, himself makes use of for the work of redemption accomplished through the Son."

d. After these references to individual positions, and against the background of Vatican II's Constitutions on the Liturgy and on the Church, we can say the following by way of summary on the subject of mystery theology: Even if the different theological attempts at explanation remain limited and insufficient, nevertheless it is a fact that the central concerns of mystery theology are the central concerns of our time when we are aiming at a new understanding in our sacramental theology and, indeed, in the Church's total doctrine of salvation, and at a deepened liturgical practice. If we were to summarize the different aspects that have arisen in the preceding discussions, we would have to emphasize and interrelate the following structural elements for our theological understanding of sacraments:

a) Sacrament is primarily a cultic event in the Church, an event in which all the Church's possibilities and mandates for the salvation of the person who has opened out to faith become present and actualized, to the end that salvation may truly become an event for the individual as a member of the Church.

b) The model for such an understanding of sacrament is the model of "salvation-history" that is the basis of revelation: this is the "mystery of God's eternal will to save," which becomes manifested in "God's economy of salvation" for this world and finds its highest expression in time and its definitive realization in the "mystery of Christ." Through the sacraments as "organs of Christ's Body, the Church," and through all times to the end of the world, this Mystery becomes an efficacious reality in the "cultic mystery" for everyone who, through the accomplishment of this sacramental rite, would have himself or herself inserted into the unfolding of this salvation-history (Eph 1,3–12).

c) The two partners in this sacramental event belonging to salvation-history are, on the one hand, "the living God, the God-Man Jesus Christ," who even in his supra-temporal transfiguration still bears the forms of the redemptive deed he accomplished within time and also exhibits them in the symbol of the rite, and, on the other hand, the human being, who both drastically needs salvation and is capable of receiving it. Humans participate in the rite as images of God and brothers and sisters of Christ, and as such they are made to enter into corporeal likeness to Christ and therefore then become real brothers and sisters of Christ and real children of God. The way to this salvation is the sacramental, symbolic, and real participation in Christ's work of redemption, in his death, and in his resurrection (Rom 6,2–11).

d) For humans, who consist of body and spirit, and precisely because of their corporeality, the medium for this "exchange" or *commercium* (cf. M. Herz, *Sacrum Commercium*, 1958) between the mystery of God and Christ working in salvation-history and the liturgical and sacramental mystery of the cult in the Church is the "visible sign of the sacramental rite" by virtue of its perceivable form. Through this sacramental sign the believing person opens out to God's saving work in history, and also through this sign the eternal God, in Christ and in his symbolically re-presented work of salvation, reaches into our spatial and temporal human world. The believing Christians' enactment of the sacramental rite in the Church is an instrument of salvation in God's hand that people take and use as they accomplish the liturgy. In the hylomorphic understanding of the sacramental sign (matter and form: event and word), the Church is a locus that evokes and incorporates both the natural-supernatural social tension (membership in the Church) and the human being's body-spirit nature. This ecclesial locus, then, becomes the very foundation and medium for the reciprocal exchange, the transfer, and the unity that occur both in the ontological-creaturely and in the personal-dialogic field of relationships between God and humans. Action and happening, event and the believer's understanding of it, giving of self and receiving of that gift—all these things become helps and warrants for the believer's participation in the death and resurrection of Christ, who is the source of the salvation of humankind and, through it, of the world that "impatiently awaits the revelation of the children of God" (Rom 8,19–25). Thus, within the space of temporal history in the Church, the sacramental sign is a *signum memorativum* (for it remembers Christ's work of salvation), a *signum repræsentativum* (for it makes present the advent of grace in Christ), and a *signum prognosticum* (for it anticipates eternal salvation). By virtue of this its triple character, the sacramental sign points to the eternal mystery of God, to the mystery of Christ that has occurred within time, and to the mystery of eternal bliss that is to begin at the end of time.

Thus, the reception of the sacraments is the Christian's realization of his or her existence within the Church: it is an appropriation of the mystery of Christ within the cultic mystery of the Ecclesia. Only within this "locus of Christian mysteries" do we reach and achieve the full meaning of the reception of the sacraments, and it is precisely this that is the fundamental concern of mystery theology.

3. The Sacramental Character as Effect of the Sacrament

Mystery theology has helped us to understand better the fruitful and interior spiritual reception of the sacraments. (See Appendix to the text, p. 367.) This is of particular importance for the Eucharist and for penance, which are frequently received. But mystery theology was especially applied to the doctrine of baptism, which, like holy orders, is received only once in a lifetime. Precisely in connection with these sacraments there arose in the third century new problems for sacramental theology.

1. Historical Background: When many members of heretical groups sought admission to the Church, a debate emerged on the question of whether those baptized by heretics had to be baptized again when received into the Catholic Church. The churches of Africa and Asia Minor normally did re-baptize around the middle of the third century, whereas Rome and Alexandria insisted on the absolute unrepeatability of baptism. When Cyprian of Carthage sought to have the African practice recognized by Rome at the Synod of Carthage in 256,[47] Pope Stephen I responded with the formula *Nihil innovetur* (D 46–DS 110) and ruled that the Roman usage alone was legitimate. This confrontation resulted in great strife and in a temporary separation of the Roman and African churches.

Part of the background for this controversy was not only a different understanding of the nature of sacrament but also a development in the understanding of the Church itself: Rome tended more to a conception of an institutionally centralized church and therefore approached baptism more "juridically" in its objective liturgical form as a sacrament of initiation, whereas the concept of the church in the provinces and in Asia Minor was still more episcopal and therefore more greatly emphasized the "moral" validity of the sacrament as depending on the worthiness of an orthodox minister.

In the fourth century the biblical phrase concerning the "seal of baptism" became more and more developed: "God has established both us and you in Christ and has anointed us. It is he who also has impressed the seal upon us and has given the Spirit into our hearts as a pledge" (2 Cor 1,21f.; cf. Eph 1,13; 4,30). The seal (σφραγίς), in connection with the pledge of the Spirit (ἀρραβὼν τοῦ πνεύματος), may be seen as the early Church's formula for what in the fourth century came to be specified as the sacramental *character*. Decisive for this development was the controversy against the Donatists under Pope Miltiades (311–314), who stressed the validity of ordinations conferred even by the *traditores*, as was also taught by the Synod of Arles.[48]

Ephrem the Syrian (d. 373) interpreted this doctrine as follows: "The Holy Spirit impresses his sign upon his sheep with oil. Just as a signet ring impresses its image upon the wax, so too the secret sign of the Spirit is conferred through the oil upon those persons who are anointed in baptism and thus signed with it."[49] Consequently, Ephrem repeatedly refers to the threefold effect of baptism: (1) the sealing with the oil, (2) the baptism with water (purification), and (3) the admission into Christ's flock.[50] Cyril of Jerusalem (d. 387) writes on the same subject: "The Spirit has given you a heavenly and somehow divine sign (Eph 1,13: σφραγίς), before which the demons tremble. To receive it unworthily entails an irreparable evil (ἀκατόρθωτον κακόν)."[51] And John Chrysostom (d. 407) teaches, "Just as a mark is impressed upon soldiers, so is the Holy Spirit impressed upon believers."[52]

Starting in 393 Augustine more than anyone had taken up the fight against the very strong faction of the Donatists: in 411 at the Carthage debate 286 Catholic bishops confronted 279 Donatist bishops. Now Augustine interpreted the image of the baptismal seal by reference to the Roman practice of burning the image of the emperor or of the general into the skin of soldiers, and thus he taught: "Even if the sacramental sign of Christian baptism is efficacious even when conferred by heretics and suffices for consecration to God, nevertheless it is not sufficient in conferring participation in eternal life. Rather, such consecration makes the heretic guilty of bearing the *mark of the Lord* outside of the Lord's flock and exhorts him, not to have himself consecrated anew, but to let himself be healed by sound doctrine."[53] "A sheep that has gone astray and has received the external mark of the Lord from its deceptive mercenaries, when it comes into the salvation conferred by Christian unity, must be led back from its strayness to the right path, must be freed from its entanglements, must be healed from its wounds; but its mark, that bespeaks its belonging to the Lord, must not be despised."[54]

Accordingly, the *character dominicus* or the seal of baptism is a warrant for the fact that baptism had been conferred validly, regardless of where it was received and how it was received. This doctrine of Augustine's slowly fell into oblivion, so that Hugh of St. Victor and Peter Lombard do not discuss it. Only with Pope Innocent III do we again see the doctrine revived when in 1201 he teaches that whoever has received baptism either *coactus* or *ficte* nonetheless has assumed the *character christianitatis* and is therefore held to fulfill the obligations of the faith. . . . But if someone not only never gives his assent but, what is more, rather rejects [the reception of the sacrament], that person receives neither the grace nor the character of the sacrament; for it is a greater thing expressly to reject than not to assent" (D 411–DS 781). This declaration of the pope against the Waldensians became an occasion — especially beginning with the *Summa* of Alexander of Hales — for this doctrine's being treated in detail by the Scholastics.[55] The doctrine was proclaimed in the Decree for the Armenians in 1439: "Baptismus, confirmatio et ordo, quæ characterem, id est, spirituale quoddam signum a ceteris distinctivum, imprimunt in anima indelebile . . ." (D 695–DS 1310) and in the Canons of the Council of Trent in 1547 (D 852–DS 1609).

2. It is a doctrine of the Church that the three sacraments of *baptism, confirmation, and priestly ordination impress an indelible character* upon the soul of the recipient. Now this "character" or "mark" exhibits four features: (a) it is different and somehow separable from sanctifying grace; (b) it abides inalienably even in the soul of the sinner; (c) it represents the intrinsic reason for the un-

repeatability of these three sacraments; and (d) it is the warrant for the revivifying of sacramental grace when, in the case of these sacraments, the *obex* or "obstacle" has been eliminated that prevented the effect of grace from occurring even when the sacrament had been received validly.

The scriptural proof for this doctrine is usually taken from those passages that deal with the "seal" (σφραγίς) of the Spirit: Eph 1,13, 4,30; 2 Cor 1,22.[56]

3. On the question concerning the *essence of this sacramental character,* Thomas declares (*Summa theol.* III, q. 63, a.2, ad 3) that this character is not merely a relation but *aliquid in anima,* a real potency in a human being upon which rests the relationship with Christ and with the Church that this character confers. In the character the Scotists see a *relatio realis,* in keeping with their metaphysics of the person and of society. Durandus of St. Porcian (d. 1334) saw in the character only a *relatio rationis ex ordinatione vel pactione divina* (*Sent.* IV d 4 q 1), in keeping with his nominalistic metaphysics of person and society.

It is indeed correct not to see the sacramental character as engaging the entire soul (the whole person, which as such is the subject only of sanctifying grace) but only a potency of the soul that can be the bearer of those relations that are determinants for the character. When later theologians (Bellarmine, de Lugo) come to regard the whole substance of the soul as locus of the character, we must conclude that they are articulating character and sanctifying grace much more intimately.

We will probably remain most faithful to the original conception of sacramental character if we regard it as a supernatural, formative reality that bestows upon a human being's personal core an impress corresponding to the purpose of the character.

4. Purpose and Meaning of the Character: We must note that, with the sacraments in question, unworthy reception confers the character without conferring the grace. The person in mortal sin loses the grace but retains the charac-

ter. Baptism of desire confers the grace without the character. The character guarantees a valid reception of the objective sacrament, even when this reception cannot be
fruitful or bestow grace because of the subjective obstacle.
Thus, the character is an expression of and a warrant for
five things: (a) the objective, ontic, and real relation to
Christ the Redeemer and to his Church as his real mystical Body (*character Christi* [*Summa theol.* III, q. 63, a.3]);
(b) God's absolute immutability, with which the human
being enters into relation through the subjective reception
of the objective sacrament; (c) the objective reception of
the sacrament, which does not tolerate any interior reservation and binds unconditionally; (d) the objective possibility of receiving grace as the fulfillment of the signified
relation to Christ; and (e) the capacity of the Christian to
be active within the Kingdom of God, which is the Church,
as both a receiver and a participant according to the particular measure of the character bestowed (cultic faculty).
The character, then, implies above all an *objective consecration*, and not a subjective sanctification.

Thomas Aquinas studies the sacraments especially from
the standpoint of the Eucharist and hence locates the
essence of the character in its being ordered to the cult
(perhaps in some measure there is here detectable an influence of the Benedictines of Monte Cassino, where he
was educated in his youth): "Cum homines per sacramenta deputentur ad aliquid spirituale pertinens ad cul-
tum dei, consequens est quod per ea fideles aliquo spiritu-
ali charactere insigniantur" (*Summa theol.* III, q.63, a.1, c).

To the question of why it is that only these three sacraments confer a character we must first simply say that tradition ascribes the effect of character only to these. A
deeper reason may perhaps be found in the *relation of the
character to the triune God* and to the offices of Christ: (a)
Even though it is true that with all sacraments we enter
through grace into relation with the life of the triune God,

nonetheless it is proper to the meaning of these three signs that each of them brings us into a special and inalienable relation to one particular Person: baptism makes us children of the Father (through brotherhood with Jesus Christ); confirmation makes us temples of the Holy Spirit and witnesses to God's Spirit; priestly ordination brings us in a special way into relation with Christ as the one sent by the Father and as savior of the world. (b) Each of these three sacraments, and these alone, resembles one of *Christ's three offices:* Baptism confers participation in Christ's new priesthood. The baptized person, as child of God, can glorify God and offer him sacrifice in a manner that is fully sufficient and fully pleasing to God, something that the unbaptized cannot do. Confirmation renders the Christian capable of sharing Christ's teaching office—indeed, it enjoins this upon him—and of bearing the kind of witness for God's Kingdom that belonged to the Apostles after Pentecost. Priestly ordination bestows participation in Christ's human and divine office as shepherd and king (not primarily in Christ's own priestly office, since every priest is ordained only for others and not for himself and is incapable of administering any sacrament to himself in the authoritative sense).

5. Formal Function of the Character: On the basis of statements found in Denis the Areopagite (*De eccl. heir.* c II § 4, 17: PG 3, 399) and John Damascene (*De fide orth.* IV c 1: PG 94, 1244 C), Scholasticism, especially since St. Thomas, teaches that *character significat, disponit, distinguit, assimilat.* The character, therefore, is four things: (a) a *signum distinctivum* within the Church, but also before God, for those who in an ontically real manner have been called to be children of God and have been designated as such; (b) a *signum dispositivum* for grace, not in the physical but in the moral sense, and for an office in the physically supernatural sense; (c) a *signum obligativum* that binds to a particular service in the Kingdom of God ac-

cording to the sacrament's specific character; (d) a *signum configurativum*, especially with regard to Christ, but also, through him, with regard to the triune God.[57]

According to a number of theologians, marriage too confers something like a sacramental character by virtue of the fact that in Eph 5,26 marriage is seen to represent a special relation between Christ and the Church, which as such is indissoluble.

With these sacraments, the character is conferred first of all for the Christian's condition of pilgrim on earth (*Summa theol.* III, q. 63, a.1, ad 1), and we are to assume that it will cease to exist in the context of eternal bliss, when the offices of the pilgrim Church will no longer be required. But if this character is considered more in its connection with sanctifying grace, then we must assume that it will perdure even in eternal bliss as a *signum distinctivum.*

4. The Sacraments' Objective Efficacy (*ex opere operato*)

What the doctrine of the hypostatic union is for christology, the affirmation of the "objective efficacy" of the sacraments is for sacramental doctrine.

1. The Catholic doctrine concerning the objective efficacy of the sacraments was developed with particular clarity at the Council of Trent, since the Reformers, starting from their conception of grace (God's own good pleasure) and justification (the overlooking or concealing by grace of human guilt), necessarily explained the effect of the sacraments in a more largely subjective manner, on the basis of God's Word (the promises) and the human being's faith.

The Reformers are fundamentally rooted in nominalism, which sees *God and the human being* as two equal persons dialogically confronting each other; therefore, the effect of the sacraments must be sought in God (*non imputatio*) and in *the human being* (*fides*), and the cause of this effect, once again, is God's promise and the human being's faith. By contrast, the Catholic conception and that of the early Church is based rather on the relationship between *Creator and creature:* God is everything, and human beings are merely capable of giving themselves to God by virtue of *potentia obœdientialis.* But God the Creator brings about grace in human beings and gives to the sacraments that he has bestowed through Christ the power to contain, effect, and communicate this grace. The path that takes us over the visible sign constitutes God's plan of salvation (*potentia ordinata*), begun and realized in Christ and meeting the human being's bodily and spiritual being on its own ground, even if our own human thinking, always open to correction, can conceive the possibility of God's (*potentia absoluta*) having chosen another path of salvation, without the instrumentality of external visible signs.

2. The Council of Trent teaches as follows: "If anyone should say: that the sacraments of the New Law do not contain in themselves the grace they signify (*non continere gratiam, quam significant*), or that they do not bestow this grace on those who do not close themselves off to it (*non ponentibus obicem non conferre*), as if they were only external signs of the grace or justification received through faith [Luther, Calvin] and certain marks of the Christian confession that distinguish the believers from the unbelievers in the sight of human beings [Zwingli], *anathema sit*" (D 849–DS 1606).

3. Proof from Scripture and the Fathers. Especially in its presentation of baptism Sacred Scripture always expresses unequivocally the objective and real effect of the sacrament: Christians are described as purified by the bath of regeneration and sanctified by their renewal in the Holy Spirit (Tit 3,5), and as born again from water and the Holy Spirit (John 3,5). Just as unequivocal is the teaching of Christ's *sermon on the Eucharist* (John 6,48–58, Mark 14,23–25).

To be sure, such effects are also ascribed to *God's Word,*
the Holy Gospel, and in this sense the revealed word itself
(the divine saving truth in the dress of human speech) has
a sacramental character: "You have all been born anew
with an immortal, imperishable birth, through the word of
God which lives and abides for ever" (1 Pet 1,23); "It was
his will to give us birth, through his word of truth" (Jas
1,18); "You, through the word I have preached to you, are
clean already" (John 15,3). Other passages of Scripture
(Rom 1,16; 1 Cor 15,2) ascribe similar saving effects to the
Gospel in conjunction with our faith.

The Fathers speak in great detail of the fruitfulness of
baptismal water, and they call baptism the maternal womb
that births us to life.[58] The baptism of children, widely
practiced at least since the second century, and the reservation of the Eucharistic species for the communion of the
sick are particularly eloquent signs for the Church's faith
in the objective and real efficacy of the sacraments. (Chapter VIII will deal with God's word as sacrament.)

4. Speculative Basis. Since the end of the twelfth century
the conceptual pair *ex opere operato–ex opere operantis*
has been used to describe the efficacy of the sacraments
(first known usage in the Pseudo-Poitiers gloss of Peter of
Poitiers [d. 1205] and in the Bamberg Codex, Patr. 136). The
sacramental action itself is regarded as the instrumental
cause of grace, while the action of the dispenser is at first
termed *opus operantis;* starting with William of Auxerre
(d. 1231 or 1237), however, it is the action of the recipient
that is so termed, in order thus to deny him or her any efficacious causality for grace. Innocent III (d. 1216) still uses
the terms in this sense in work on the Blessed Sacrament,
when he writes: "Quamvis igitur opus operans aliquando sit
immundum, semper tamen opus operatum est mundum"
(III, 5: PL 217, 844). Thomas does not use this conceptual
pair. Only at the time of the Council of Trent (D 851–DS
1608) does the expression *ex opere operato* appear in a magisterial document. The efficacy of grace is ascribed only to

the rite as an objective event; the work of the dispenser and of the recipient has no causality of its own for grace. The expression *operatum*, as the supine of *operari*, here has a passive sense, against all grammatical expectations. This expression is not intended to reject the activity proper to human beings as a necessary condition for the reception of grace; rather, such activity is denied any efficacious or meritorious causality. That this *ex opere operato* cannot be understood in a "magical" way is shown by the dependency of its efficacy upon the *non ponentibus obicem. Obex* (*obiex* = "hindrance"; "bolt") means, in the active sense, "rejection" (positive action against), and, in the passive sense, the lack of necessary "disposition."

The decisive consideration for the understanding of sacrament and its objective efficacy is that it is not regarded as a thing or object, but rather as a sign and a *function within the mystery of God, Christ, and the Church*, as an organ for humans of their encounter with God (Schillebeeckx), as an answer to fundamental questions of human existence (Smulders), and as a "sign" in the comprehensive sphere of the Christian *mysterium.*

Duns Scotus sums up the doctrine on the objective efficacy of the sacraments in the following words: "Sacramentum enim ex virtute operis operati confert gratiam, ita quod sufficit, quod non requiritur ibi bonus motus interior, qui mereatur gratiam, sed [sufficit], quod suscipiens non ponat obicem" (Ox. IV d 1 q 6 n 10 [*Op. om.* XVI, 221 ff.]). If theology has from time to time affirmed the validity of the baptism of children, even against the will of their guardians (D 1490–DS 2562), and also of holy orders dispensed to children even before they could consciously make a choice for this state, what is manifested here is not some kind of "sacramental magic" but rather a one-sided juristic understanding of sacrament.

5. The Manner of the Sacraments' Effect

Whereas the objective efficacy of the sacraments is a defined dogma, the more precise philosophical explanation of this doctrine is a *theologoumenon* that is the subject of different interpretations in the various schools of theology, according to each one's different conceptions of grace and sacrament. As an introduction to these questions, the late Middle Ages elaborated fundamental reflections on the various possibilities of *causality*: causality is indeed an analogous concept and is determined in an essential way by the realities that stand in causal relation to one another. Let us here indicate the following "causal figures": (a) *causa materialis–formalis* (regarded from the standpoint of a material thing or of the sculptor's work); (b) *causa efficiens–finalis* (seen from the standpoint of free or necessary movement); (c) *causa exemplaris–instrumentalis* (seen from the perspective of the technical work); (d) *causa generativa–receptiva* (for the act of reproduction in the realm of living beings; (e) *causa abstractiva–motiva* (for spiritual knowledge and the motivated actions of human beings; (f) *causa physica–moralis* (for events and actions among human beings); (g) *causa in se–causa sine qua non* (cause and condition for every kind of causality); (h) *causa libera particularis–totalis* (for the cooperation between God and human beings in freedom); (i) *causa libera–socialis* (for the manner in which one person is influenced by another or by society); (j) *causa socialis in mysterio* (for the activity of human beings within the salvific sphere of the mystery of Christ or of the Church); (k) *causa instrumentalis socialis in mysterio* (for the interpretation of the efficacy of the sacraments in the spirit of mystery theology).

Early Scholasticism prepares the way for what subsequent Schoolmen will develop. Hugh of St. Victor (d. 1141) sees in the sacraments "vessels and causes" (*vasa et causæ*) of grace. "Ex similitudine repræsentant, ex institutione significant, ex sanctificatione conferunt aliquam spiritalem gratiam" (*De sacramentis christianæ fidei* I, 9 c 2, and 4: PL 176, 317 and 322). Bernard of Clairvaux (d. 1153) teaches: "Verbi gratia, investitur canonicus per librum, abbas per baculum, episcopus per baculum et anulum simul. . . . sic et divisiones gratiarum diversis sunt traditæ sacramentis" (*Sermo in cœna Dom.* 2: PL 183, 272). William of Melitona (d. 1257) proposes the theory that the sacraments effect an *ornatus animæ* or an objective *dispositio* by virtue of which God immediately and with all certainty confers his grace (*Summa Alexandri Hal.* IV q 5 m 3 a 5 § 1).

1. Moral efficacy. This viewpoint looks more to the realization of the sacrament in its reception or actualization; it conceives of grace as the light and power of God himself and further reflects thus: God has bound himself by the promise (*pactione quadam*) to be present to the recipient of the sacrament (*per assistentiam*) and so bestow his grace on him or her. Thus, the sacrament does not contain grace formally but only *per ordinationem et assistentiam Dei,* by virtue of God's ordinance and because he has granted his support to the sacrament. This was the teaching of Bonaventure and of the great Franciscans who came after him, Duns Scotus and the Scotists, and also later on of the Jesuit theologians involved in the Molinist controversy (Vásquez, de Lugo, and Franzelin). Duns Scotus casts his teaching in the following formulation: "The reception of the sacraments is a disposition which necessarily leads to the effect signified by the sacrament, not as by an intrinsic form, however, through which this disposition would attain to its goal or give rise to a preceding disposition, but solely through God's assistance: it is God who calls this effect into being, and not with absolute necessity but only with a necessity that follows from the divine ordinance. This means that God has generally ordered things (and informed His Church of his design) in such a way that He Himself wills to communicate to the recipient of such a sacrament the effect signified [in the sacramental sign]

(*Ox.* IV d 1 q 5: *Op. omn.* XVI, 140). As clarifying examples
Bonaventure offers the king's sealed promissory note (cf.
Bernard of Clairvaux), and Scotus the relationship between
merit and reward, assured by a wage contract. This explanation, however, seems little suited to elucidate baptism
and the Eucharist.

2. Physical efficacy. This viewpoint looks to the sacramental sign in itself, and grace is here seen to be a creaturely quality; those who hold this conception, therefore,
teach as follows: The sacrament contains and communicates grace itself directly and somehow formally; God
alone is the *causa efficiens* of grace, but he communicates
it to us through mediation of the sacrament as a *causa instrumentalis* (*instrumentum separatum*). The effect, to be
sure, does not have a being of its own; it is not, therefore,
a thing but an *esse transiens ex uno* (God) *in aliud* (the
human being) *et incompletum.* The sacrament is not a vessel of grace (as with Hugh of St. Victor) but rather may be
compared with a conductor whose makeup determines the
flowing of the electrical current. In this connection Thomas
affirms that the sign contains grace in the same way as a
word contains its meaning (*Summa theol.* III, q. 62, a.4, ad
1). This doctrine is taken up especially by Thomas (starting with *De ver.* q. 27 a.4 and *Summa theol.* III, q. 62, a.5)
and later Thomists (Cajetan), but also some Jesuits (Bellarmine, Suárez). It found its particular expression in the
Council of Trent and to a large extent corresponds to the
teaching of the Greek Fathers. Still problematic in this explanation is how a sacrament can be valid without having
its effect; as well, it is difficult to apply to penance and
marriage.

3. Intentional efficacy. This approach derives from a
more anthropocentric standpoint within the world as it fo-
cuses upon both the recipient and the reception of the
sacrament. Its logic is as follows: The reception of the
sacrament is the *dispositio necessitans* for God to bestow
his grace, just as the generation of a human child is the *dis-*

positio necessitans for God to create the immortal soul. This theory was developed above all by the Jesuit Louis Billot (d. 1931). It particularly stresses the great significance of human cooperation, just as the Thomistic solution stresses the significance of the sacramental sign, Scotus stresses the freedom of God and the freedom of the human being, and Bonaventure stresses the sublimity of grace. This theory is not really adequate to explain baptism and the Eucharist.

4. Efficacy as symbolic cause. More recent theologians, especially K. Rahner, have attempted (in a way similar to Luther's) to understand "sacrament" as the most radical case of "God's Word" coming to human beings. Consequently, the effect of the sacrament (now by contrast to Luther, who to the Word of God juxtaposes faith on the side of the human being) is not sought in the grace that is effected but rather in the sacrament's "character as word," in which and through which what is expressed itself directly occurs in us. Grace takes place by making itself known in the sacramental symbol (as word).[59] Problematic here is the philosophy on which the argument rests: the sacramental sign emerges as an absolute word (in the Hegelian sense), and this abolishes, in a monistic manner, the scriptural polarities of Creator and creature, material world and spiritual word. This, in turn, necessarily leads either to a theistic-supranaturalistic interpretation of grace or an anthropocentric-naturalistic one. Very rightly Thomas remarks: "Sicut etiam in ipsa voce sensibili est quædam vis spiritualis ad excitandum intellectum hominis, inquantum procedit a conceptione mentis (*Summa theol.* III, q. 62, a.4, ad 1). The sacramental sign is a directly human, inner-worldly reality, and hence only a mediate sign of God.

The value of this theory rests in the seriousness with which it takes the Word and the spiritual reality of the sacramental sign.

5. As concerns the interpretation from the perspective of mystery theology, we point the reader to the conclusion of

Chapter III.2. But by way of summary we can here say the following: Just as grace is a participation in the divine life by existing within the living, Mystical Body of Christ, so too the sacrament is much more than a self-enclosed reality—whether matter or word or human action. The sacrament, above all, is a sign, instituted by Christ and efficacious by virtue of his action and his promise. It is given for the sake of human beings, who themselves are not self-enclosed and absolute, but rather are members of the Mystical Body of Christ and of one another: thus, they are supernaturally and existentially united to Christ; they are ordered to Christ's activity and have already been grasped by him. These signs are administered in keeping with the intention of the Church, which is to say of the Christ who continues to live among us; they are at base facsimiles of Christ, the God-Man, who bears the marks of death and resurrection. These signs are modeled on the Primordial Sacrament of the Church as the Mystical Christ, in whom individuals—both the dispensers and the recipients of the sacraments—are bound to one another with a new responsibility and fruitfulness through their living relationship to Christ, the Head.

Perhaps we can here suggest an image: the sacraments are like a musical "score" written by Christ within the sphere of the Church and that can be performed only within the sphere of the Church. We Christians must make this score come to life in sound through our own personal work, but the thing that resounds is wholly and exclusively a gift of God and Christ's own work, and it can be made to resound only within the sphere of his Church. Thus, to sum up, we may state the following: *The Mystical Body of Christ is that temporal-supratemporal reality within which we, as temporal-historical beings, come to participate through the sacramental, temporal-spatial signs in the saving significance and saving reality of Christ's sacrificial death, and through Christ we gain access to the divine life of God's Holy Trinity.*

IV

Origin, Number, and Organic Structure of the Sacraments

Our survey up to this point has shown us the possibility, reality, and saving efficacy of the sacraments. The question now arises concerning the source from which such powerfully effective signs of salvation derive their efficacy, and, as well, the question concerning the person who is responsible for instituting them (1), the question of how many sacraments there are (2), and, finally, the question concerning the order among them according to both their nature and their efficacy, and concerning the interior system existing among them and what their human and theological adequacy might be in the light of salvation-history (3).

1. The Historical Christ, Author of the Sacraments

1. From the understanding of the sacraments that we have been developing we can only conclude that the living Christ alone can be the author and the meritorious and efficacious cause in all the sacraments for the salvation of humankind. This living Christ, however, can be correctly seen only if we understand him to be at one and the same time the *historical Jesus of Nazareth,* the *transfigured Lord* who abides with the Father, the Church's *first and foremost liturgical celebrant* and the *mystical Head* of the

83

Body of which Christians are the members. And just as Christ here must be understood *historically,* in the context of salvation-history, as the living reality of all the mysteries, and also *mystically* in his significance as Savior of the individual, so too the sacraments are to be regarded as rites that the individual accomplishes within the Church and into which the Church initiates the individual. These are rites that, as organs of the Mystical Body of Christ for the salvation of its members—a salvation effected by God—must ever be actualized anew in Christ, rites that are a reality, a happening, an event, that exists in the Church to the glory of the Father in the Holy Spirit. Understood as an individual rite, a sacrament is not intended to mislead a Christian into an existence as isolated Christian concerned only with his or her own salvation. Rather, a sacrament is intended to lead the individual out of his or her isolation and egotism and into the community of Christ's members—that is, the Church—and, through this, to the "freedom of the children of God" by the power of Christ's cross and in the love of the Spirit, to the praise of the Father for all time and eternity. The basis for this remains the fact that the historical Christ, as founder of the Church, is the sole author of all these sacraments.

Over against the Reformers, who besides baptism and the Eucharist (and also penance with Luther) recognized no other sacrament, the Church declared at Trent: "If anyone should say that the sacraments of the New Law were not all instituted by our Lord Jesus Christ, *anathema sit*" (D 844–DS 1601). And in the decree *Lamentabili* (July 3, 1907) the Church likewise declared against the Modernists: "That affirmation is false which says that the sacraments arose from the Apostles' and their successors' interpreting an idea and intention of Jesus in a way appearing advisable to them in light of the circumstances and events of their time, or indeed enjoined upon them by such circumstances and events" (D 2039–DS 3439f.).

2. The following may be stated as proof for this teaching.

The institution by Christ is clear in Scripture for the sacraments of baptism (Matt 28,19), Eucharist (Luke 22,19), and penance (John 20,23). For the other sacraments we possess at least a clear apostolic tradition, and such a tradition must be traced back to Christ himself inasmuch as the Apostles considered themselves to be no more than "servants of Christ and ministers of the mysteries of God" (1 Cor 4,1). Thus, institution by Christ must be concluded for confirmation from Acts 8,17 and 19,6, for anointing of the sick from Jas 5,14ff., for priestly orders from 2 Tim 1,6, and 2,2, and for marriage from Eph 5,25 and Matt 19,3–9.

The deeper reason for saying that Christ alone can be named the institutor of the sacraments is provided by soteriology, which teaches us that all redemptive grace can come only from Christ, and what the sacraments do is apply such redemptive grace to us. Thomas (*Summa theol.* III, q. 64, a.3) distinguishes in Christ three forms of fullness of power: (a) the *potestas auctoritativa,* which is proper to Christ by virtue of his divine nature and is therefore incommunicable; (b) the *potestas excellentiæ,* which is proper to Christ's human nature because of its union with the Logos and which, according to Thomas, is likewise incommunicable. (Perhaps an aspect of this form of fullness of power may be seen as active in the Church of Jesus Christ—his Mystical Body after all—when, for instance, the Church at the Council of Trent gives a new form to the sacrament of marriage, or when Pope Pius XII recasts the form of priestly ordination, or when in the Church of the seventh century the sacrament of penance receives a new development.) (c) But as God-Man, Christ also properly possesses the *potestas ministerii,* that form of fullness of power that comes to him as a human being by virtue of his being sent by the Father (John 20,21). This is a form of power that was communicated by Christ to the Apostles; thus, by nature it is communicable. The proper power that the dispenser of the sacraments in the Church holds as his own is a participation in the fullness of power deriving from the mission of Jesus Christ. Nevertheless, because the sacraments are all ordered within the sphere of the Church, it is Christ himself who always remains their first and foremost dispenser, as Augustine often explains: "Baptismus autem, quem dedit Petrus, non erat Petri, sed Christi; et quem dedit Paulus, non erat Pauli, sed Christi," and so on (1 Cor 3,6: *Ep.* 93, 11, 47: PL 33, 344). And Ambrose teaches: "Sacramentorum auctor quis est, nisi Dominus Jesus? De cælo ista sacramenta venerunt" (*De Sacr.* IV 4, 1: PL 16, 439).

3. Pope Clement VI had already affirmed in 1351 that the Church, or the Roman pontiff, as may be the case, could tolerate different rites or introduce new ones, "salvis semper illis, quæ sunt de integritate et necessitate sacramentorum (D 570 m–DS 1061). Now the question is: What belongs to the essence or to the integrity of the sacrament, and what rites must therefore the historical Christ himself have established if sacraments are supposed to have been instituted by him? Theologians have attempted to give an answer to this question by making certain distinctions. Bellarmine, de Lugo, and Billot, among others, taught that Christ determined the matter and form of the sacraments at least in general (*in genere*), so that these are in their substance immutable for all time. Suárez, Alphonsus Liguori, and others demanded that Christ should have determined the matter and form of the sacraments in particular (*in individuo*) as well. But this exact determination cannot be tenable considering the difference in form of the sacraments between the Eastern and Western Church, as well as the changes of form that the Church itself has introduced for marriage, penance, and priestly orders in the course of time. Today there is much talk of an institution of the sacraments by Christ *in specie,* that is, that each individual sacrament goes back to an act of Christ's will, even if in the form itself it remains to be determined what was instituted by this act of Christ's will and what has been developed beyond that by necessity in the dispensing of the

sacraments by the Church. It would also suffice for this if we assume that Christ determined the form of individual sacraments by reference to Old Testament rites (for instance, baptism by reference to the baptism of John and completion of the formula of baptism in the missionary mandate of Matt 28,19f.) or by expressly approving a pre-existing form (such as of marriage at the wedding feast of Cana) by his presence with his Apostles and perhaps by pronouncing some specific word.

Just as the individual sacraments owe their efficacy only to the one historical and redemptive sacrifice of Jesus Christ, so too they must go back to a command of the historical Jesus. And the Church itself must clarify the extent to which such a command may be understood as a direct and complete determination or as an indirect one partly handed over to his Church.

The error of Modernism lay not only in its denying the historical institution of the sacraments by Christ; beyond this, it completely misunderstood the essence of the supernatural itself and therefore also tried to explain the supernatural and life-relationship of the Church's Apostles to the living Christ using merely psychological categories of human experience.

The rites prescribed by the Church for dispensing the sacraments, even though always given and changed *salva sacramentorum substantia,* are in each case binding under danger of incurring "nullity of the sacraments."

4. Chapter VII will deal with the way in which the Church determines the changeable rites of both sacraments and "sacramentals."

2. Seven, the Number of the Sacraments

1. The systematization that resulted in the various "sentences" treatises of the twelfth century by application of the dialectical method to salvation-history led to estab-

lishing firmly both the concept of sacrament and their number as seven (the "septenary"), a number that had already been factually given by tradition. (See Appendix to the text, page 368.) The first enumeration of the sacraments as seven comes from the *Sententiæ divinitatis* (written in 1147), a work of the school of Gilbert of Poitiers (d. 1154).[60] This work is followed by the *Sentences* of Peter Lombard (written in 1152–1158), and the *Summa* of Master Simon of Tournai (written in 1165–1170).

At least since the *Summa* of Pseudo-Peter of Poitiers (completed around 1170) (*Sent.* V c 3: PL 211, 1229 CD), the number seven is customarily exposed as such, and this number is justified by the different saving functions of each of the sacraments. For the first five sacraments, which are necessary for every Christian, the following is normally said: Baptism is for the *intrantes*, confirmation for the *progredientes*, the Eucharist for the *pugnantes*, penance for the *redeuntes*, and anointing for the *exeuntes*. Priestly orders and marriage are *voluntaria* for every Christian. The background for these assignations is given by the concept of *militia Christi* as the task of every Christian, as Bonaventure will later expose with great clarity (*Breviloquium* VI 3). In his *Gloss* (written in 1223–1227), Alexander of Hales bases himself on the scriptural passage of 2 Kgs 5,10, in which Elisha says to the leprous Naaman: "Wash yourself seven times in the Jordan, and you will attain to health of body and to purity," when he comments as follows: Against the sevenfold *infectio* that derives from the different kinds of sins, the sacraments perform the following tasks: Baptism is *medicina curatoria*, confirmation is *medicina conservativa*, priestly orders is *medicina meliorativa*, marriage is *medicina præservativa*, anointing of the sick is *medicina mitigativa*, the Eucharist is *medicina conservativa, meliorativa et confortativa*.[61]

Beyond this, Alexander seeks to present the seven sacraments as aids *quæ habilitant ad usus virtutum*, "which make one capable of exercising the virtues," meaning the four cardinal virtues and the three theological virtues: Baptism instills faith, confirmation fortitude, the Eucharist love, penance justice, marriage temperance, priestly orders wisdom, and anointing of the sick hope.

Besides more or less imaginative applications of the seven stars (Rev 1,16), the seven candlestands before God (Rev 1,13), and the seven pillars in the temple of wisdom (Prov 9,1–3), during this same period the theologians of the Eastern Church especially conceive of the *seven gifts of the Holy Spirit* (which derive from the Messiah and which he confers on all who follow him: Isa 11,2) as analogies of the sacraments,[62] and they speak of the *seven eschatological charisms:* the seven sacraments are intended to prepare the Christian for these charisms in the world to come: Orders for *perfecta scientia,* penance for *pax,* marriage for *satietas,* the Eucharist for *immortalitas,* baptism for *agilitas,* anointing of the sick for *subtilitas,* and confirmation for the *veritas gloriosa.* In more recent times H. Schell has interpreted the seven Letters to the Churches (Rev 2–3) in function of the seven sacraments,[63] and others have read the seven petitions of the Our Father in terms of the seven sacraments.

For the Western Church the reflections of Thomas have been of particular importance. In a sober manner he applies the effects of the individual sacraments to the different life situations of human beings: "The sacraments of the Church are ordered to a double purpose: first, to perfect human beings with respect to what belongs to God's service according to the Christian religion, and second, to serve as means of healing the harm caused by sin. Now under both headings it is appropriate that there be seven sacraments. For the life of the spirit exhibits a certain concordance with the life of the body. . . . In their bodily life humans are perfected in a twofold manner: with respect to their own person and then in their relationship to the whole of the human community in which they live. . . . With respect to themselves they are perfected in a twofold manner: first, in themselves, because they attain to a certain perfection of life; and then by virtue of the fact that they overcome restrictions upon their life such as illnesses and the like. In itself, moreover, bodily life is perfected in a threefold manner: (1) By the generation whereby a human being begins to be and to live. Corresponding to this in the life of the spirit we have Baptism, which is a spiritual rebirth (Tit 3,5: λύτρον παλιγγενεσίας καὶ ἀνακαινώσεως πνεύματος ἁγίου). (2) By the growth whereby a human being is brought to perfect stature and power. Corresponding to this in the life of the spirit we have Confirmation, which confers the Holy Spirit so as to communicate his strength (Luke 24,49: ἐξ ὕψους δύναμις). (3) By the nourishment that sustains in human beings life and power. Corresponding to this in the life of the spirit we have the Eucharist (John 6,54: ἄρτος . . . ὑπὲρ τῆς τοῦ κόσμου ζωῆς) that nourishes us for eternal life.

"These three would be sufficient for humans if spiritually and bodily they had a life incapable of suffering. But, since at times they become sick, both in their physical life and in the life of their spirit through sin, humans necessarily need a healing intervention. This process is twofold: (4) First, a means whereby health is restored. Corresponding to this in the life of the spirit we have Penance (Ps 41,5: *sana animam meam quia peccavi tibi*). (5) Another means whereby the pristine power is restored through the right nourishment and exercise. Corresponding to this in the life of the spirit we have Extreme Unction, which does away with the traces of sin and prepares human beings for everlasting glory (Jas 5,15: ἁμαρτίας . . . , ἀφεθήσεται αὐτῷ).

"In their relationship to the community, furthermore, humans are perfected in a twofold manner: (6) First, by receiving the power to lead a great number of people and perform public acts. Corresponding to this in the supernatural life is the Sacrament of Orders (Heb 7,27: θυσίας ἀναφέρειν). (7) Finally, with regard to natural procreation, this occurs through Marriage both in the bodily and in the spiritual life, which makes it to be not only a sacrament but also a service to nature (Eph 5,25: ἑαυτὸν παρέδωκεν ὑπὲρ αὐτῆς).

"In this manner the number of the sacraments also becomes clear in so far as they are directed against the harms caused by sin. Thus, Baptism is directed against the absence of a life of the spirit; Confirmation against the soul's weakness; the Eucharist against our instability with regard to sin; Penance against personal sins committed after Baptism; Extreme Unction against the remainder of sin that has not yet sufficiently erased by Penance; Priestly Orders against the dissolution of the people; Marriage against personal concupiscence and against the disappearance of the people as a result of death's snare.

"Many derive the number of the sacraments from their appropriateness for the virtues and the harms caused by the wounds of guilt and punishment. They say that Baptism corresponds to faith, Extreme Unction corresponds to hope, the Eucharist corresponds to love, Orders corresponds to wisdom, Penance corresponds to justice, Marriage corresponds to temperance, and Confirmation corresponds to courage" (*Summa theol.* III, q. 65, a.1).

These specifications became significant for the Council of Lyons in 1274 (D 465–DS 860) and for the Council of Trent in 1547 (D 844–DS 1601ff.). And J. W. von Gœthe made his own this encomium of the seven sacraments (*Aus meinem Leben,* VII, 2).

In the Latin West, except in Rome, and beginning in the fourth century, the washing of the feet (John 13,1–17) was widely practiced after baptism (with reference to John 13,10). Ambrose taught that through the washing of the feet original sin was forgiven, just as through baptism personal sins were wiped out, and that therefore the washing of the feet, as a sacrament, belonged to baptism.[64] Similarly, Bernard of Clairvaux called the washing of the feet a sacrament for the forgiveness of everyday sins (*Sermo I de cœna:* PL 183, 273). Despite the text of John 13, the Church has from the beginning not recognized the washing of the feet as a sacrament, and has therefore rejected isolated statements to this effect by theologians as not founded in Tradition.[65]

2. The Church firmly states that Christ instituted no more and no fewer than seven sacraments, namely, baptism, confirmation, the Eucharist, penance, anointing of the sick, priestly orders, and marriage. At Trent it emphasized this doctrine in particular over against the Reformers (D 844–DS 1601ff.). From the outset Calvin and Zwingli accepted only baptism and the Eucharist. Early in 1520 Luther was still teaching all seven sacraments; in the autumn of 1520 (in the *De captivitate Babylonica*) he had reduced these to baptism, penance, and the Eucharist; and by 1523 he taught only baptism and the Eucharist. In 1522, in his *Loci theologici*, Melanchthon accepted baptism and the Eucharist, but in 1530, in the *Apology*, he accepts baptism, the Lord's Supper, absolution, and ordination. Article 25 of the *Thirty-Nine Articles* teaches only two sacraments and states that the other five rites "pro sacramentis evangelicis habenda non sunt." Leibniz, who labored for the reunion of separated Christians, accepted seven as the number of the sacraments.

3. As proof for seven as the right number for the sacraments we can today only point to the proof for the authenticity of the individual sacraments that we will present in the discussion on the individual sacraments.[66] But in general it can be said that, since the twelfth century, the Catholic Church has always insisted on this doctrine of seven sacraments. But Tertullian's principle of "prescriptive proof" ("Quod a multis unum invenitur, non est erratum, sed traditium" [*De præscriptione*, c. 28, 3:CChr 1, 209]) would take us much further back: Already at the time of Photius (869) seven sacraments are accepted, and this enables the Eastern Church to defend itself against Crusius (Tübingen, 1573), when he proposes the Protestant doctrine of two sacraments, by appealing to its tradition of seven sacraments. Furthermore, we must note that

the groups that separated themselves from the ancient Church already in the fifth century (Copts, Syrians, Armenians [D 696–DS 1310], Nestorians, and Monophysites [Assemani]) also teach seven sacraments. But we must also remember that in the Eastern Churches from a very early date anointing and penance have been understood differently than in the Western Church.

We have no record, moreover, of any claim of adulteration or falsification in what concerns the sacraments during the first five centuries; there is no question anywhere of a sacramental controversy concerning the recognition of any one of these sacraments. This entitles us to trace the Church's silent tradition on the matter of the seven sacraments back to apostolic times.

The arguments from appropriateness for the sacraments as seven that we have presented previously and that we encounter ever since the Middle Ages are rooted in the medieval understanding of this question. Medieval people did not, in positivist fashion, ask the question concerning the number of the sacraments; what interested them, rather, was the question concerning the specific quality of the seven sacraments. Once the concept of sacrament in the narrower sense had given them a new understanding of the sacraments, medieval people saw themselves compelled to demonstrate in a new way why only one sacrament does not suffice for the Christian life but that seven sacraments are necessary. Reference to the possible sevenfold significance of sacrament for people's lives, as well as reference to God's sevenfold gift, made the number seven especially enlightening for them. Medieval people were led to their reflections not by sheer delight in the number seven, but by the possibility of erecting the doctrine of the necessity that there be seven sacraments upon biblical foundations and at the same time upon the foundations of human reason. Medieval people knew nothing of modern people's purely positivistic and historicistic manner of thought, at least not in matters of faith.

The realities of faith are not the objects of the same positive knowledge with which we approach the world, but realities that can be grasped only when humans—in their innermost being and in their deepest problematic—and God are considered inseparably from one another: God, who, according to our contemporary manner of knowing, is to be comprehended primarily as an anthropological question and not on the basis of an objective apprehension of the non-human world.

3. Order and Necessity of the Seven Sacraments

1. At least beginning with the *Sentences* of Peter Lombard, in the Western Church the sacraments have been ordered in the following series: baptism, confirmation, Eucharist, penance, anointing of the sick, priestly orders, and marriage (IV d. 2, c 1). As the *Sententiæ divinitatis* already stressed, the first five sacraments were instituted for the individual and the last two as social sacraments for the Church. Among the first five sacraments, moreover, the first three are sacraments of life and the other two (penance and anointing of the sick) exist to counter sin. This is the express sense in which Thomas explores the ordering of the sacraments (*Summa theol.* III, q. 65, a.2).

In the sacramental doctrine of the Eastern Church, penance and anointing normally appear as the last two sacraments, the other five coming before them. The reason for this is that both penance and anointing are directed against sin. But these two sacraments, as has been mentioned, take on in the Eastern Churches a somewhat different form from that given them in the Western Church: Penance is monastic penitence, and anointing is an annual sacrament for the forgiveness of sins.

Already Thomas developed at length the idea that the Eucharist is to be seen apart from all the other sacraments

(*Summa theol.* III, q. 65, a.3). He points out that in this sacrament not only is Christ's grace present, but Christ himself; he says that all other sacraments are ordered to the Eucharist as to their goal and that almost all sacraments find their completion in the Eucharist. Our contemporary understanding of the liturgy is quite different from the medieval understanding of liturgy, which in many respects was allegorical. This holds especially for the conception of the Mass and the Eucharist. Our manner of understanding the liturgy views the Eucharist not only as sacrament but also as the sacramental sacrifice of the Church; indeed, the sacrament of the Eucharist is to be understood only as a participation in this sacrifice of the Church. This understanding, then, justifies us in separating the Eucharist from the other six sacraments in order to treat it as a sacramental sacrifice and as the sacrificial meal of the Church. The remaining six sacraments would then constitute *three groups,* the first in the service of supernatural life (baptism and confirmation), the second directed against the sin of human beings (penance and anointing of the sick), and the third as serving the Church as the community of believers and as God's holy people (priestly orders and marriage). Within each of these three groups there is to be noted a further articulation: Baptism bestows the life of God and confirmation brings this divine life to full maturity. Penance abolishes the personal sin of human beings and the anointing of the sick does away with those aberrant inclinations and attitudes that remain in humans as bodily and spiritual beings even after the first abolition of sin. Priestly orders sets a person apart and consecrates him or her to the service of the supernatural life of Christians within the framework of a greater and somehow "ordered" part of the total Church, what we call the liturgical "community" or "assembly"; marriage commissions and consecrates persons for the natural service of the natural "cell" or unit of the People of God—that is, the Christian family—which in both a natural and a su-

pernatural sense is also a primal cell and the natural
"womb" where the individual's Christian life begins to
take shape.

2. All of this leads us to the question concerning the
sacraments' *necessity for salvation.* Peter Lombard already wrote: "Cum igitur absque sacramentis, quibus non
alligavit potentiam suam Deus, homini gratiam donare
posset, . . . sacramenta tamen instituit" (*Sent.* IV d 1 c 5),
and indeed God instituted the sacraments for the sake of
humans, "propter humiliationem, eruditionem, exercitationem" (*Sent.* IV d 1 c 5; echoing Hugh of St. Victor, *De
sacram.* I, 9,3: PL 176, 319ff). Thomas is of the opinion
that the sacraments, with their corporeal elements, are
necessary for the salvation of humans ("Necessaria,"
Summa theol. III, q. 61, a.1) because it is only through
them that humans can again become freed from the material world to which they have subjected themselves
through sin and because it is precisely through the sacraments that humans can confess their faith in Christ, the
Son of God who has become man, the Redeemer. This argument from appropriateness elaborated by Thomas will
then be reinterpreted and accepted in a new way in our
days by the understanding of sacrament developed by
mystery theology. Nonetheless, the question remains
whether each and every sacrament is necessary for the
salvation of each and every Christian. To this Thomas answers (*Summa theol.* III, q. 65, a.4) that baptism is unconditionally necessary to every human being, penance
to the sinner, and priestly orders to the Church so that it
can lead the People of God (Prov 11,14). He adds that the
other sacraments are necessary only to make the acquisition of salvation easier. Consequently Thomas holds that,
in spite of John 6,53 ("If you do not eat the flesh of the
Son of Man . . . you do not have life in you"), the Eucharist is not necessary, just as baptism appears necessary
from John 3,5 ("Whoever is not born again . . . can not
enter the Kingdom of God"); necessary for him is only a

"spiritual communion," which is to say participation in the Mystical Body of Christ, as he explains with reference to Augustine (*In Joh. tr.* 26, 15: PL 35, 1614; *Summa theol.* III, q. 65, a.4 ad 2).

Canon Law has enjoined the reception of confirmation, the Eucharist, and the anointing of the sick—for which no *necessitas medii* can be demonstrated—by express command (Can. 787, 859, 944) (*necessitas præcepti*), so that willful neglect to these three sacraments can be construed as a violation of Church Law.

These questions concerning the necessity of the sacraments must today be thought through anew from the standpoint of our present understanding of the sacraments and of the Church—we mean that understanding that has emerged particularly in the wake of the liturgical movement and of mystery theology, and officially at the Second Vatican Council. This is precisely what we intend to do in this work when we investigate the individual sacraments. But we can now make the following preliminary observations: The answer of Thomas Aquinas is conditioned by his conception of the Church, which is viewed more in the sense of a juridical institution within a feudal society. It is one thing for the Church to be understood as the People of God and as the Mystical Body of Christ and for this Church in the Middle Ages to issue an express commandment on Sunday obligation for the sake of each Christian's salvation and of the Church's own supernatural life; but today we must ask the much deeper question concerning the necessity of receiving the Eucharist as significant participation in the eucharistic sacrifice of the Church.

Likewise we must develop a new conception of the sacrament of marriage on the basis of this new understanding of the Church and answer the question concerning its necessity from this perspective. In the context of a correct understanding of the Church, the necessity of the sacrament of marriage cannot be less than the necessity of the sacrament of orders.

In the last analysis the question concerning the necessity of the individual sacraments for the salvation of the Christian can no longer have the same theological meaning it had in the Middle Ages with its juridical model of the Church and its feudalistic understanding of society. That question today must be answered on the basis of our understanding of both the Church and the sacraments, which recognizes as autonomous realities the ecclesial and social character of the sacraments, their significance for the worship of God in the Church, and their anthropological work of salvation. There can no longer be any question of obligatory reception of the sacraments; the crux of the matter is the gift of salvation offered in them, a gift in which God's creative love, the Redeemer's compassionate love, and the Spirit's healing and sanctifying love become manifest in these signs of the divine saving activity among us humans. Not whether we must receive the sacraments, but rather that we can and may receive them is the question for religious persons, who know and offer thanks for the fact that they owe both themselves and their all to God's gracious favor. [See *Appendix to the text*, page 369.].

V

The Minister of the Sacraments

In the Mystical Body of Christ there are no isolated entities or persons, but only free persons united by symbolic realities and by suprapersonal grace and personal love. For this reason, even salvation is not communicated only through sacramental signs in themselves, but the sacraments themselves are communicated through particular persons. A sacrament must not only be received; it must also be ministered. *Both a recipient and a minister are constitutive of the fundamental structure of the sacraments.*

Medieval feudal society accepted this fact without particular reflection. Modern people, however, must expressly make themselves aware of it in order, by so doing, to come to a full realization of the meaning of sacrament as well as of their Christian existence and of their Church—the reality of the Christian mysteries in its totality—and thus also fully realize their responsibility to this reality. This structural element of a sacrament has great significance for the individual member of the Church. By being referred to a human minister the individual, as recipient of a sacrament, is prevented (a) from indulging in what are the greatest errors for a Christian, namely, self-sufficiency and vainglory; and by the conscientious and active participation of the other he or she is also preserved (b) from his or her own weakness (the kind of absence of conscience that destroys a sacrament or doubts with regard to the external reception); (c) finally, that fundamental function of the person we call *communicatio,* having been elevated to the sphere of the supernatural and the sacramental, becomes a part of the believing consciousness.

Thus, sacrament—and here we must include the "Word of God" when it is proclaimed and heard—is seen to possess a special *function as laying the foundations of the ecclesial principle.*

In the present chapter we will first consider the minister of the sacrament as such, and in the following chapter we will discuss those questions that concern the recipient of the sacrament.

We must here consider the minister from two different aspects: the objective, official aspect in the context of the Mystical Body of the Church (1) and the subjective, personal aspect that concerns the manner in which he exercises his office (2).

1. The Person of the Minister

1. If we take a total look at the sacraments and at the results of our consideration of mystery theology (III.2), we must first of all state the principle that *the primary minister of the sacraments is God (the Father) through Christ in the Holy Spirit.*

This statement shows that a sacrament can be rightly understood only in the context of the whole Mystery, as we saw in III.2. Here we see that God, Christ, and the Spirit are the source and wellspring of all grace. For this truth the Fathers refer us particularly to the following passages of Paul: "The man who plants, the man who waters, count for nothing; God is everything, since it is he who gives the increase" (1 Cor 3,7). "We are only God's fellow-workers" (1 Cor 3,9: συνεργοί). "That is how we ought to be regarded, as Christ's servants, and stewards of God's mysteries" (1 Cor 4,1: ὑπηρέτας Χριστοῦ καὶ οἰκονόμους μυστηρίων Θεοῦ).

The Fathers stressed this truth especially against the Donatists. Thus Pacian (d. before 392) writes: "Whether we baptize or impose penance or forgive guilt, we do it with Christ's authority (*Christo auctore*) (*Ad Sympron.* ep. 3 c 7: PL 13, 1068C). Augustine never tired of pointing this out: "Cum quisque Christi baptismo baptizatur, Christum baptizare fateantur de quo solo dictum est: Hic est, qui baptizat in Spiritu Sancto" (John 1, 33: *Contr. Ep. Parm.* II, 11, 23: CSEL 51, 73; PL 43, 67). "Non baptismum vestrum acceptamus, quia non est baptismus ille schismaticorum vel hæreticorum, sed Dei et ecclesiæ, ubicumque fuerit inventum et quocumque translatum" (*De bapt.* I, 14, 22: CSEL 51, 166; PL 43, 121). The occasion for St. Augustine's answer in this vein is almost always the question concerning the *validity of the baptism of heretics* and schismatics. "Quomodo baptizent, quos damnavit ecclesia? . . ." With reference to Eph 5,24, he then answers: "The Church may not put itself above Christ, for instance by believing that such as have been judged [mortal sinners] by him [God] are able to baptize, but that such as have been judged [heretics] by itself are not able to baptize; for God always judges according to the truth, but ecclesiastical judges can err at times, being human. As far as visible ministry goes, then, both the good and the bad baptize; but through these he invisibly baptizes from whom both visible baptism and invisible grace derive. Both the good and the bad are able to immerse; but only he can cleanse our conscience who is forever good. . . . This is why even those who are outside the Church can baptize" (*Contr. Cresc.* II, c21; PL 484; CSEL 52, 385; cf. ibid. 7f, 24f.).

This truth holds also for the sacrament of marriage, even if in the visible sphere it is the two partners who minister it to themselves. And it is precisely because of this that the natural bond between man and woman becomes a Christian sacrament.

2. *The secondary and sole minister of the sacrament in the sphere of this visible world is man as a minister of Christ.* In Heb 5,1 we read: "Omnis pontifex ex hominibus

assumptus," "every high priest is taken from among men," and this is being said of Christ as primary "human" minister of all sacraments. In this ordering of things we ought to admire God's wisdom and love as well as the deep appropriateness of the sacraments for humans' bodily-spiritual and social structure.

In the lives of the saints and elsewhere "angels" are often called the ministers of the sacraments, in the early Church documents more in the case of baptism and in the Middle Ages more in the case of communion. The reason for this is that since early Christian times the angels appear as the bearers of the great "divine cult" according to their portrayal by Revelation itself[67] In the oldest liturgies angels are present not only in the cult of the Mass but also in each of the other sacraments.[68] On this subject Augustine writes: "Quod pertinet ad baptismi sanctitatem, adest Deus qui det, et homo qui accipiat, sive per se ipsum Deo dante sive per angelum sive per hominem sanctum, . . . sive per hominem iniquum" (*Contr. Ep. Parm.* II, 15, 34: CSEL 51, 88ff.; PL 43, 76). The theme of angels as ministers of the Eucharist perhaps began to develop on the basis of 1 Kgs 19,5ff. (Elijah nourished by an angel from God).

When Luther extravagantly affirms that even the Devil can baptize, ordain, and forgive sins[69] we are to understand his statement only as an expression of his vexation and his rejection of an official priesthood, not as a serious theological proposition.[70]

a) *The minister and the recipient of the sacrament must be two different persons.* No one can minister a sacrament to himself or herself. In 1206 Innocent III expressly declared "self-baptism" invalid, with reference to Matt 28,19, and John 3,5 (D 413–DS 788). The priest's apparent "self-communion" at Holy Mass is to be understood only as the completion of the sacrifice that the priest celebrates for and with the Church (the community), not alone or for himself. The minister of the Eucharist, therefore, is not the person who distributes Communion (in principle any be-

liever can give Holy Communion to himself or herself),
but rather the priest, who in the Holy Sacrifice of the Mass
makes present the reality of the Eucharistic Christ.

b) *Not every person, not even every Christian, can minister every sacrament.* At Trent the Church expressly affirmed this over against the doctrines of the Reformers:
"Whoever says that all Christians have the power to administer the Word of Revelation and the Sacraments of
Christ, *anathema sit*" (D 853–DS 1610). In his own church
Luther abolished the hierarchy and the priestly office by
interpreting Matt 16,18, in the sense that Christ established his Church not upon Peter but upon Peter's faith,
and by claiming that in John 21,15ff. Peter is addressed
only as the representative of the believing community of
all times. Luther further reasoned that the "office" is but
the "ministerial" side of the priesthood equally entrusted
to all Christians. The community appoints to this office or
calls to this office, whose bearers then perform their duties
with full power and as representatives of Christ—thus in
the name of God and by his commission—and not on the
basis of a directive determined by the believers themselves. The priestly office here is not a reality guaranteed
in this world by succession and ordination, but rather a
more idealistically conceived reality that is over and beyond the community and is carried out by the community.

The Catholic Church, by contrast, insists on a special
"priesthood of office" that contrasts and complements the
common "baptismal priesthood" of all the faithful. The reasons for this are (1) the fact that Apostles were appointed not
by the community but only by Christ and his "mission"
(John 20,21; Matt 28,18–20), and (2) that from the very beginning (cf. the Pastoral Epistles) this "mission of Christ" was
conferred by the "laying on of hands," a ceremony taken over
from the cultic practices of Israel (1 Tim 4,14; 2 Tim 1,6).[71]

c) *For the valid ministering of the sacraments, their
minister must possess the faculty (through ordination)
and the full power (through mission) from Christ in the*

Church. Just as in the historical reality of humankind
being and act, faculty and accomplishment, right and exercise of right both are distinct from one another and yet
belong together, so too for the priestly office both *ordination (consecratio)* and *mission (missio)* are necessary. Paul
speaks of the *charisma* that is conferred by the laying on of
hands (ἐπίθεσις τῶν χειρῶν : 1 Tim 4,14; 2 Tim 1,6). Christ
himself was "consecrated" by his becoming man (John
1,14; 1 Tim 3,16; 2 Pet 1,17); to explain his activity he continually referred to his having been sent by his Father (John
8,16.29.42; 13,16; 14,24); and it was he himself who expressly handed his own mission over to his Apostles (John
20,21: "As the Father has sent me, so do I send you"). Paul
therefore calls himself "a servant of Christ and a steward
of the mysteries of God" (1 Cor 4,1), one who can forgive
sins solely *in persona Christi* (2 Cor 2,10) and can exercise
his office only "in Christ's stead" (*pro Christo ergo lega-
tione fungimur:* 2 Cor 5,20).[72]

Baptism can be ministered by any human being (CIC,
can. 742, 1). Even though Christ's command to baptize was
given only to the Apostles (Matt 28,16–20), already in
apostolic times the so-called charity helpers (deacons such
as Philip, Acts 8,4–13) also baptized.

The sacrament of *marriage* is ministered by the bridal
pair themselves by virtue of their common Christian
priesthood, but it can take place only *in facie ecclesiæ*
(CIC, can. 1094), that is, in the Church with Christ as the
primary minister. For the priestly minister of the other
sacraments, see the chapters concerning the individual
sacraments in volume 7, *The Sacraments of the Church.*

2. Subjective Requirements in the Minister of the Sacraments

The objectivity of the sacraments is not based on some
intrinsic "materiality" and especially not on some kind of

"magic"; rather, it means a "reality within the Mystery of Christ and his Church" that does not do violence to or ignore the freedom of person but rather summons a person and leads him or her to a new, supernatural freedom. For this reason the minister of the sacrament, operating within such a mystical-sacramental realm, is not merely some kind of mechanical instrument but a servant of Christ who is offering free and personal cooperation. A sacrament, however, is a free gift of God's grace and as such can never be a work and an achievement of a human being. Consequently the question arises, What must be expected from the minister of the sacrament in order to guarantee, not only its canonical *licitness* and its ascetical *worth*, but above all its dogmatic and objective *validity?* Here we must consider four different aspects in the subjective makeup of the minister: his orthodoxy and state of grace, his intention, his attentiveness, and finally his particular deed in the performance of the sacrament.

1a) Already at the time of the baptismal controversies and the Donatist controversies of the North African Church the clear doctrine of the Church emerged that the *validity of a sacrament is not dependent on the orthodoxy of the minister.* Augustine writes as follows concerning ordination by Donatists: "May those [heretics], then, like Peter weeping over his mendacious fear, feel bitter sorrow over their previous shameful error, and come to the true Church of Christ, that is, to the Catholic Mother [of all]. May they become fruitful within this Church, becoming clerics and even bishops, even though they had once had a hostile attitude toward this [Mother of all]. . . . Only Donatus himself has been condemned . . . and so the bishops of the Roman Church have decided to admit the converted clerics to their proper offices [as clerics and bishops] even if they had been ordained outside of the Church" (*Ep.* 185, *De correct. donat.* c. 10, 46: PL 33, 813).

The Council of Trent declares on this subject: "If anyone should say that the Baptism that has been conferred by heretics in the name of the Father and of the Son and of the Holy Spirit, with the intention of doing what the Church does, is not true, valid Baptism, *anathema sit*" (D 860–DS 1617). The basic requirement for the minister, of course, is the Christian state[73] or the priestly state in the sacramental sense.[74] But even though the baptism of the heterodox (what used to be called "heretical baptism") is valid, nevertheless the Church cannot permit the baptism of a Catholic child to take place in a non-Catholic church, since in the Catholic understanding "Church" implies not only a sacramental community but also a community of faith and common government.

When at certain times the ordinations performed by Arians or Novatianists (fifth to seventh centuries) and even by simoniacal bishops (eleventh century) were repeated when the ordained returned to the true Church, this can be explained by the fact that at those times there was still no adequate distinction between ordination and mission, so that an *ordinatio irrita* was simply regarded an "uncanonical investiture."[75]

1b) *The state of grace is also not a condition for the validity of a sacramental act.* A person in the state of mortal sin can minister the sacraments validly. This truth was expressly emphasized at the time of the Donatist controversy, and in the Middle Ages against the opinion of the Waldensians (Innocent III in 1208: D 424–DS 793) and that of Hus and Wycliffe at the Council of Constance in 1418 (D 169, 488, 584–DS 356, 9914, 1154). The Council of Trent teaches: "If anyone should say that the minister of a sacrament, who is living in the state of mortal sin but fulfills all the essentials necessary to the ministering and accomplishing of the sacrament does not in fact minister and accomplish the sacrament, *anathema sit*" (D 855–DS 1612).

As a proof for this affirmation reference is made to 1 Cor 4,1 ("servants of Christ and stewards of the mysteries of God"), as well as to Matt 7,22 (even those evils ones who did not acknowledge Christ have performed miracles in the Lord's name and driven out demons). Time and again Augustine points out that it is Christ himself who baptizes. Pope Anastasius II (496) taught: "If the rays of the sun do not become tainted by passing through repulsive filth, much less is the power of God working in the sacraments diminished by the unworthiness of their minister" (D 160–DS 356).

The mistaken Donatist doctrine would either have to conceive of sin in a purely exterior manner in order to be able to affirm that the minister of the sacraments is a sinner, or, if it conceived of sin in an interior manner, it would have to lead to absolute uncertainty in the faithful concerning their reception of the sacraments. The human being as human being is the minister of the sacraments, and sin does not belong to the essence of the human but is only an accidental evil.

The independence of the sacraments from the orthodoxy and moral purity of their minister, which we are here discussing, is seen to guarantee (1) the objectivity of the sacraments, (2) the high priesthood of Christ as primary minister, and (3) the moral and sacramental certainty of believers concerning their salvation. Even the sinful minister can nonetheless be of service to another's salvation, even when he is operating to his own condemnation.

2. If sacrament is to be understood, not as a merely material sign or as an extrinsic instrument, but as a "living function in the living Church of Christ," within the mystery of Jesus Christ, then an important aspect of the realization of sacrament as a sign of the minister is not only the sacrament's actual enactment but also the *personal intention* of the minister. In this connection the *Decretum pro Armeniis* (1493) teaches as follows: "Omnia sacramenta tribus perficiuntur, . . . materia, . . . forma, et persona ministri conferentis sacramentum cum intentione faciendi, quod facit ecclesia" (D 695–DS 1312). The Council of Trent declares: "If anyone should say that in the ministers who perform and minister the sacraments there has

not to be found at least the intention to do what the Church does, *anathema sit"* (D 854–1611). Again, as proof for this, reference is made to 1 Cor 4,1 ("servants of Christ and stewards of the mysteries of God"). The servant of Christ must consciously be serving Christ and his Church. The necessity of this intention becomes especially clear in the sacrament of penance, in which the confessor exercises the power of judge (John 20,23); in the sacrament of marriage, which has the form of a contract; and in the Sacrifice of the Mass, in which the priest has not only to recite Christ's words of institution but to utter them in the person of Christ.

The question concerning the intention of the minister has its own history in the Church. It is clear that from the Church's beginning a certain existential clear-headedness and seriousness were demanded of a minister of the sacraments,[76] but, during the controversy concerning heretical baptism and that with the Donatists, there was such necessity to underscore the objectivity of the sacraments that the equal necessity of the minister's intention was lost from sight. Thus, even Augustine could not dare decide concerning the validity of the baptism of the boy Athanasius, which had been performed jokingly and in the manner of a mime; he himself admitted it as valid.[77] It is Hugh of St. Victor who again demands that the minister manifest his unequivocal intention, when he writes: "Vide ergo et considera, quod rationale esse oportet opus ministeriorum Dei, nec propter solam formam præiudicare, ubi intentio agendi nulla est" (*De sacram.* II, 6, 13: PL 176, 459ff.). Beginning with Præpositinus (d. 1210) theologians will henceforth require the *intentio faciendi, quod facit ecclesia.*[78] The term "intention" became controversial in the light of the further development of the understanding of the sacraments, as for instance at the Council of Trent, when Ambrose Catharinus (d. 1553) offered the opinion that it suffices if the minister accomplishes the sacramental form externally with exactitude, even if internally he has the intention *not* to do what the Church does.[79] Salmerón, S.J. (d. 1585), Contenson, S.J. (d. 1674), and many others were in agreement with this opinion in the name of the objectivity of the sacrament and as a reaction against the subjectivism of the Reformers. In 1690, under pressure from the Inquisition, Pope Alexander VIII condemned the doctrine of the Belgian theologian Farvaques that that "baptism is valid which is ministered by a minister who adheres to the whole external rite and external form of Baptism, but interiorly in his heart says to himself: 'Non intendo, quod facit ecclesia'" (D 1318–DS 2328). Many French theologians rejected this decision as not given directly by the pope, and they subscribed to Ambrose Catharinus' doctrine of intention.[80] This doctrine was represented in Germany by Stattler (d. 1797), Dobmayer (d. 1805), Oswald, Glossner, and others.

The background to this entire discussion is important, for indeed it involves the understanding of the sacraments as such. A more *juridical understanding* of the sacraments sees in Catharinus' exterior intention a sufficient guarantee for the validity of the sacramental event; a fuller *understanding from the standpoint of mystery theology* will have to exact from the minister a genuine, interior intention *faciendi, quod ecclesia facit.*

The sacrament is dubious when the recipient of the sacrament can recognize already externally that the minister of the sacrament is only jesting, and here the Council of Trent requires that the recipient of the sacrament search out another minister (D 902–DS 1685). Fiducial faith alone "does not abolish sin, and it would be a bad Christian, *salutis suæ negligentissimus, qui sacerdotem iocose absolventem cognosceret, et non alium serio agentem sedulo requireret."*

A sacrament must be declared invalid when its conferral has involved even a passing alteration of the Church's prescribed form, because this would signal the fact that in the minister of that sacrament there no longer was present an intention corresponding to that of the Church. This becomes even more clear when the minister of the sacrament gives theoretical expression to his denial of the reality of the sacrament to be conferred. It was for this reason that in 1896 Leo XIII declared *Anglican orders* to be invalid, since under Edward VI the form of ordination had been so altered that clearly a denial of the sacramental priestly state was here to be ascertained, all the more in the light of the *Thirty-Nine Articles* of the Anglican High Church. The subsequently restored ancient formula of ordination cannot change the fact that the valid line of succession had been interrupted.[81] In recent times this rejection of Anglican orders by Leo XIII has been contested in the interest of a reunion of the Anglican Church with the Catholic Church and as a reaction against the attempt to see the Anglican Church as but one of the other Protestant churches.[82]

The *intention*, however, does not have to be actual, that is, temporally coexistent with the conferral of the sacrament; a *virtual intention* suffices, that is, one that has been made once and for all in the past and has not been revoked. A habitual intention, that is, an interior inclination that has never become a personal decision or a genuine act of the will, would not correspond to the appointed task of a sacramental minister. The intention does not have to be reflected, that is, one specifically intending the sacrament's special effect; a *direct* intention suffices, one intending the rite prescribed by the Church as a saving sign; but an *indirect* intention would not be sufficient, that is, one involving only the person of the minister but not the work of the minister. As a virtual intention it must be directed to a particular person (or group of persons) and to an individually determined matter.[83]

3. The intention must be directed to the "action of the Church" (*facere, quod facit ecclesia*). To a Modernist and historicist trend of critical thought that would have as its aim *facere, quod fecit Christus*, we would have to reply that it constitutes an illusory attempt that appears con-

trary to the very mandate of Christ himself. What has been revealed to us concerning the sacraments as rites instituted by Christ has been handed down to us by the writers of the New Testament Scriptures, as this has been understood and lived by the Church from the very beginning. Christ himself left no written instructions, nor did he even command that his words and deeds should be recorded. The written documentation came about by mediation of "the Church" out of a human need. Christ sent out his Apostles expressly to accomplish this work of proclamation, and he both promised and gave them the Holy Spirit as a pledge for the existence of the truth in the Church for all times.

Therefore, when the Church subsequently determines the particular form of a sacrament when Scripture itself has not given a precise formulation for this (cf. the formula of absolution since Thomas Aquinas, form of marriage since the Council of Trent, form of ordination since Pius XII), it does not do this arbitrarily but in direct continuity with revelation and tradition. And in so doing, the Church is acting as the continuing presence of the living Christ, and its motivation cannot be other than an active will to save its members, for whose sake she proclaims Christ's Word to each succeeding new age.

The phrase *quod facit ecclesia* refers in the first place to the exterior sign of the sacrament, its matter and form, that the minister must accomplish and, by accomplishing which, he brings into a moral unity. But *quod facit ecclesia* also refers to the minister as a person within the Church and to the mystery of Christ as a whole, which is where the sacrament alone attains to its full meaning.

4. The *attention* or external clear-headedness simply is the care directed to the accomplishment of the prescribed rite, both its matter and its form. Here too we must note that *virtual attention* is sufficient for the validity of the sacrament.

5. A *worthy ministering of the sacrament* requires of the

minister (a) that he be in the state of grace, that is, that he be acting as a living member within the Mystery of Christ; (b) that he carry out his task conscious of his duty, that is, out of love for his office and for the purpose for which he has received his mission and his ordination[84]; (c) that he refuse the sacrament where he is not allowed to minister it (Matt 7,6; 1 Tim 5,22), and that he not evade this obligation by dissembling (D 1179–DS 2129).

VI

The Recipient of the Sacraments

The sacraments are signs of salvation all of which find their proper realization in human beings. For this reason it is necessary now to consider the recipient of the sacraments, both the person (1) and the subjective conditions for reception (2).

1. The Person of the Recipient

As we have seen, a sacrament is nothing other than a "function" of the mystery of God, of the mystery of Christ and his Church; and sacramental grace means nothing other than a participation in these divine mysteries and, hence, at the same time in the divine life and in the divine nature (2 Pet 1,4), which means participation in the creative love of God himself. Consequently, only that being is capable of receiving the saving and grace-bestowing sign of the sacrament who through his or her spiritual and personal nature is open to God (*Dei capax*, in Augustine's phrase) and who at the same time and by existential necessity possesses a body; for the structure of such a being corresponds to the manner in which, in the sacrament, a visible sign, and invisible grace are united. This being can only be *homo in statu viatoris*, "a human being in his or her present state as a wayfarer." Only a human being in this state, therefore, is a *recipient of the sacraments.*

A non-spiritual, apersonal animal has no possible relationship with the sacramental order, as was repeatedly shown in the early Middle Ages especially in connection with the Eucharist, in answer to the question *quid sumit mus* ("What does a mouse eat if it consumes the Eucharist?").[85] Nor can an angel be considered the recipient of a sacrament, since, being a pure spirit, it derives no profit from a thing that is rooted necessarily in a visible sign. In the same way a *dead person*, who as corpse is no longer a person and is no longer capable of performing a personal act, cannot be considered a recipient of the sacraments. This point has been much discussed especially in connection with 1 Cor 15,29, where Paul speaks of a proxy baptism for the dead.[86] The Third Synod of Carthage (397) expressly forbade baptism and Communion of the dead.[87] Perhaps Paul is here speaking of such catechumens as have received baptism in order after the Resurrection to be able to be with Christians who had already died, "for the benefit of these dead."

Not every person can receive all the sacraments: penance, anointing of the sick, and marriage may only be received by those who have attained to the age of reason. The anointing of the sick was instituted for people who are seriously ill, and priestly ordination—if Christ's action is to remain normative here—can be ministered only to male persons as successors to the Apostles. For the two great social sacraments (priestly orders and marriage) the Church has made their reception dependent upon "conditions" that for various reasons are considered important for God's concrete Kingdom on earth.[88] Insofar as these "conditions" may be culturally and socially determined, they stand in need of constant revision.

2. Subjective Requirements for the Recipient of the Sacraments

Although the sacraments find their realization in the recipient—even the Eucharist fulfills its meaning in the recipient—nevertheless they remain objective signs of salvation and means of grace that have their effect *ex opere operato.*

1a) For this reason the *objective orthodoxy of the recipient* is not required for the validity of sacramental reception. From this rule neither penance (as many a dogmatist thinks) nor marriage is an exception; marriage, in particular, is expressly declared by Canon Law to be a valid sacrament among Protestants too. The declaration of the validity of the sacraments of the Eastern Church likewise fully attests to this rule. This does not mean, however, that "religious belief" is not a condition for the reception of the sacraments, if indeed a sacrament is to be understood as a "sign of faith." Thus, Augustine explains: "In the matter of the validity and completeness of a sacrament, it is irrelevant to ask what the recipient of the sacrament believes and with what faith he might be filled (*quid credit et quali fide imbutus sit ille*): this question has great significance for the salvation of human beings, but is irrelevant to the question concerning the sacrament itself. *Fieri enim potest, ut homo integrum habeat sacramentum et perversam fidem"* (*De bapt.* III, 14,19: PL 43, 146). This in no way disputes the fact that the sacrament as a sign of faith presupposes a certain faith in the recipient, even if this faith is not total or dogmatically correct. A person who would be totally ignorant of the meaning of sacrament or wholly an unbeliever cannot receive a sacrament validly, because the sacraments are not "magic."

b) *Likewise, the lack of the necessary disposition* (state of grace or *attritio*) *does not make the reception of the sacrament invalid,* but at most unworthy. From this fact we can then understand the possibility of an "unworthy reception." On this point Augustine says: "Baptismi ergo puritas a puritate vel immunditia conscientiæ, sive dantis sive accipientis, omnino distincta est" (*Contr. lit. Petil.* II, 35, 82: PL 43, 288).

c) The significance of subjective faith and of a will ready

to receive a sacrament becomes particularly clear in the doctrine that a sacrament can be received efficaciously not only through the actual rite and reception of the visible sign but also *ex voto,* when for some reason the external reception is not possible.[89] Such a *sacramentum ex voto* is not regarded absolutely as a valid sacrament because, if the opportunity arises, it has to be ritually performed. Nonetheless its original efficacy is not contested. We encounter this doctrine already in Augustine, when he discusses the salvation of catechumens who died before being baptized (*De civ. Dei* 13, 7: CSEL 40, 622f.; PL 41, 381), and it was extended to the sacrament of penance (contrition that effaces sin before official absolution), to be developed especially by the Canonists of the twelfth century and introduced into theology by Peter Lombard (*Sent.* IV, d 17 c 1 n 167; d 18 c 1 n 178). Elaborating ideas of Cyprian's, Augustine had already said: "Invenio non tantum passionem pro nomine Christi id quod ex baptismo deerat, posse supplere, sed etiam fidem conversionemque cordis, si forte ad celebrandum mysterium baptismi in angustiis temporum succurri non potest": "I find that not only suffering for the name of Christ can substitute for the absence of the baptismal rite, but also faith and conversion of heart as well, when because of the adverse circumstances of the times the rite of baptism is not possible."[90]

2. *A validly received sacrament can nonetheless remain unfruitful* despite its validity if the disposition necessary for the sacrament's fruitfulness is lacking or if there is present in the recipient a disposition that opposes the effect of the sacrament. In the case of sacraments that may be received only once (such as baptism, confirmation, and priestly orders), the question may be asked whether such a sacrament can become fruitful subsequently and confer grace. Theologians here speak of a "reviviscence" of the sacraments (*reviviscentia sacramentorum*).

a) If the obstacle (*obex*) was not known to the recipient of the sacrament, then the sacrament's effect of grace is immediate. In the general opinion of theologians, in such a case a sacrament "of the living" can effect sanctifying grace even in a person in the state of mortal sin.

b) If the obstacle was consciously known to the recipient of the sacrament, then in the case of these unrepeatable sacraments, and because of their "sacramental character," their fruitfulness comes into effect when *the necessary disposition becomes present.* This disposition will mostly consist of repentance (*attritio*), the will to receive the sacrament, and a new openness toward God, Christ, and his service. If since the valid reception of these sacraments a period of serious sin intervened, then either perfect contrition or the sacrament of penance is required. In this connection, Augustine writes as follows speaking of a baptism that had been deceptively received: "In illo, qui fictus accesserat, fit ut non denuo baptizetur, sed ipsa pia correctione et veraci confessione purgetur, quod non posset sine baptismo, ut quod ante datum est, tunc valere incipiat ad salutem, cum illa fictio veraci confessione recesserit": "In the case of one who had come to the baptismal font with pretense, the procedure is that this person cannot be baptized again; what cannot be cleansed away without Baptism will, in this case, be cleansed by pious conversion and a sincere confession of faith. What had been given previously [through the pretended baptism] will begin being efficacious for salvation only when that fiction is removed through a sincere confession of faith" (*De bapt. contr. Donat.* I, 12, 18: PL 43, 119). The same is to be assumed in the case of marriage and the anointing of the sick, as "relatively unrepeatable sacraments." There is no "reviviscence" of sacramental grace in the case of penance and the Eucharist, which are sacraments with no limit on their repetition.

3. Since justification and sanctification as fruits of the sacraments are a matter of the person, a *positive intention* must be required for the valid reception of a sacrament. Refusal or even a neutral attitude (Cajetan) would call a

sacrament's validity into question. Innocent III declared: "Ille vero, qui numquam consentit sed pænitus contradicit, nec rem nec characterem suscipit sacramenti" (D 411–DS 781). The intention must be at least *virtual*, especially in the case of penance, marriage, and priestly orders. For the baptism of infants the intention of the responsible adult who brings the child to the Church for baptism suffices.

4. *For a worthy reception, the state of grace* is required, in the case of the sacraments of the living; and in the case of the sacraments of the dead, *repentance* is required (at least *attritio*). For a living understanding of the sacraments, particularly as contributed by mystery theology, we should keep the following three fundamental attitudes in mind for the reception of the sacraments.

a) Contrasting the concept of a sacrament's "instrumental efficacy of grace" as proposed by Scholastic doctrines, which could be called a kind of "sacramental materialism," more recent theology (K. Rahner, O. Semmelroth) has particularly called for the *personal realization* of a sacrament. This view holds that the heart of the matter is the actualization of the Christ-mystery in the Church and in personal spirituality, a living encounter with Christ, and the personal readiness to be transformed and to be receptive before the living God. The reception of the sacraments must "make us free for God before God." An objectified or "material" view of the reception of the sacraments contains the danger of moral egotism and of the religious bondage that has its roots in it.

b) Particularly by expanding on Augustinian terminology, Scholasticism already demanded a *spiritual reception of the sacraments* (*spiritualiter manducare*), especially for Holy Communion, alongside a merely valid reception of the sacraments (*sacramentaliter manducare*). This means that what was demanded was not only an interior and personal disposition, but also a genuine religious disposition that has become wholly free and selfless by the grace of the

Holy Spirit: the reception of the sacraments must be sought with the longing of one's heart that derives from a faith animated by love (Gal 5,6). About such a reception of the sacraments Augustine says: "Quia visibilem cibum spiritualiter intellexerunt, spiritualiter esurierunt, spiritualiter gustaverunt, ut spiritualiter satiarentur" (*In Joh tr.* 26, cap. 6, 11: PL 35, 1611). In the Eucharistic treatises of the twelfth century the *memoria passionis Christi* especially is given as motive for this longing out of love,[91] and in the spirit of mystery theology we could say that this holds true for every sacrament.

c) On the basis of the new understanding of Church and liturgy as articulated by the Second Vatican Council we would have to consider a new *openness to brotherhood in the Church* (cf. Matt 5, 23f.) and also *to the Christian obligation to the whole world* as one of the goals for the right reception of the sacraments. Just as Christ took his sacrificial death upon himself for the sake of the whole world and all humankind, so too the sacraments must make us free for an ecclesial, Christian, and human service to our brothers and sisters and to God's world. The sacraments ought to lead us out of our "private piety" and into the "ecclesial piety" that consists of the praise of God in the liturgical cult and the practice of living Christian charity (Jas 2, 15f.; 2 Pet 1,5–11). "The division in the mind of many between a faith which is confessed and their daily lives belongs to the grave aberrations of our time. . . . We are to erect no artificial opposition between our professional and social activity, on the one hand, and our religious life, on the other" (GS 43).

VII

The Sacramentals

The Mystery of God—his eternal plan of salvation and its realization in and through and with his creation—has found its fulfillment in the Mystery of Christ; but this Mystery of Christ is not limited to the reality of the sacraments. Into his saving activity God has admitted human beings themselves as partners, "collaborators and stewards" in all phases of his history of salvation. *Thus, the sacraments, which are a gift from Christ, have their continuation in the "sacramentals," which are given by the Church.* These constitute a significant part of the "cult of the Church" and serve for the glorification of God in this world. By prolonging the sacraments, as it were, the sacramentals tend to put the whole earthly world at the service of God and especially to be a stimulus and a help for humans themselves as they in their own person, try to bring the "servant of Christ and the steward of his mysteries" (1 Cor 4,1) in this world more and more to full expansion and maturity.

Throughout the rich history of the liturgy in its first millennium, the Church developed the greater part of these rites and defended their principle against the nominalistic rationalism of a Wycliffe and a Hus in 1418 (D 665–1255), and then against the Reformers, who in these ceremonies saw nothing but the human attempt to make oneself holy by one's own works (D 856, 943, 954, 955–DS 1613, 1746, 1757, 1775). These rites received a more precise theological treatment in the twelfth century, at the time when the doctrine of the seven sacraments itself was clarified.

Peter Lombard already uses the term *sacramentale* (PL 192, 855), and likewise Thomas (*Summa theol.* III, q. 65, a.1, ad 3). in the *Summa* and Suárez in his treatise on the sacraments (PI q 65 disp. 15.). Sacramentals were given a more exhaustive analysis with the development of liturgical studies in the nineteenth century (F. Probst, F. Schmid), and with the breakthrough of the liturgical movement after the First World War they became more and more significant in the general Christian consciousness.[92]

By contrast to the sacraments we can say the following about the sacramentals:

a) They have been instituted by the Church (not by Christ [D 856, 843–DS 1613, 1583]) as signs of its faith and of its love for humankind.

b) It is not the external sign that effects grace in them, but the faith of the Church, the faith that accomplishes the sign, the faith of the minister and of the recipient who fill the sign with their faith and their love.

c) The visibility of the sign is a claim to belonging to the Church's community of faith, in whose prayer and treasury of graces those participate who make use of the sign. For instance, the blessing of the priest is not only his personal blessing like the blessing a father gives his children; it is the blessing of the whole Church, to which the piety of the minister and the recipient gains access.

The discussion of the variety of particular forms the sacramentals can take is the concern of *liturgical science* and will be treated at its proper place. Here, in our more dogmatic considerations, we will limit ourselves to the bases and principles involved insofar as these show the sacramentals to be the continuation and development of what is already given as a "sign" in the sacraments. We will here speak of the sacramentals, then, insofar as they are significant for giving shape to a "sacramental world" (1) and for fostering the complete formation and maturity of the "sacramental existence" of the individual Christian (2). (See Appendix to the text, page 370.)

1. The World as Sacrament

1. HISTORICAL BACKGROUND

1. If we are to speak today concerning the "bases for sacramentals," not only in practical theology but also in dogmatics, it is necessary first to point to several important changes in the development of theology in the past fifty years.

After the First World War there took place a first breakthrough from the side of the dogmatic theology that had developed in the context of nineteenth-century Romanticism in its reaction against the Enlightenment. This breakthrough took the shape of mystery theology and of the liturgical movement, and it led to a new understanding for *the sacred* in the world of the cosmos and of human beings themselves. Works such as Vonier's *Der klassische Katholizismus*[93] (which sees Christianity and the Church as God's new covenant) and J. Pinsk's *Sakramentale Welt*[94] are characteristic of this shift. The spirit of Scheeben's dogmatics had here become effective. The *sacralization of the human world* according to the pattern of the cosmos understood as a creation was the goal of this new Christian understanding of the world and of self. Even within the so-called Third Reich this kind of Christian spirituality was an essential force for the resistance fighters and for those groups within the different churches who were the bearers of authentic Christianity. Out of this spirit, too, emerged the *Church Dogmatics* of Karl Barth, which at that time exerted tremendous influence.

Soon after the Second World War, and as a reaction to the totalitarian power of National Socialism, beginning in the 1950s and attaining a real breakthrough at the Second Vatican Council, there developed a new spiritual movement on whose banner three leading principles were inscribed: (a) *freedom of person* and individual opinion; (b) community established not by violence and edict, but through *free dialogue;* (c) *freedom of the intellect and of science* realized through a free and open critical spirit.

This reaction against a reign of violence and terror was further supported by three other movements that occupied the public arena at this same time: (d) the scientific breakthrough that occurred as a result of splitting the atom and the atomic physics that has developed since, imposing itself on all the natural sciences, have opened up unforeseeable *possibilities and obligations toward humankind and the world* (in biology, for instance); (e) the necessary confrontation with the totalitarian power of world Communism has given much momentum to the interest in the original ideas of K. Marx, an interest at work at least since 1918. This project has sought to enunciate the desirable connections between the Marxist system and the more general attempt to *affirm the world and plan for the future of the world,* a world that has been unified into one social and economic unity. (f) Finally, depth psychology has elaborated insights into the joint activity of the conscious and the individual or the collective unconscious in the psychic life of humans (C. G. Jung), and into the personal pleasure-principle and the socially conditioned reality-principle with its creation of a super-ego (S. Freud, G. Fränkl, L. Szondi)—all of which insights are important for the whole of *social and cultural anthropology.* Now, the convictions of our Christian faith concerning humans and their world must be confronted with these various insights if the permanent truth our faith contains is to be correctly presented to the men and women of our time.

In the face of this new understanding of themselves and their world of today's people, the fundamental attitudes of the preceding Christian movements (which today automatically tend to be termed "integralist") have become questionable. Consequently, the critical thinking of our theology must tackle the task of looking at Christian truths anew within this modern context, in order to express their basis in a new way. The great attempts that have been made since the Council in the direction of a liturgical renewal, a new evaluation of the realities of the world and of real progress made in the most varied realms of human coexistence (economics, society, culture, science), were already called for in the conciliar decrees (especially those On the Liturgy, On the Church, On the Church in the Modern World, and On the Laity). Such attempts have become articulated in the new theology especially in its demand that Christians affirm a secular, *hominized world,* that they work at a *desacralization of the world and of Christian life,* that they come to dominate the world in a new way and establish a new social structure (democracy).

2. Everthing that the Church has developed in its "sacramentals" since the first centuries of its existence must now be seen anew against this modern background. With regard to the non-human world, what is involved above all are the following realities: From revelation the Church has derived its *view of the world,* which sees the world both as God's *creation* and as the realm in which, alongside *nature* with its forces and *humans* with *their* works, there are *spiritual powers* at work, both good and evil. Consequently, on the basis of the power of the keys entrusted to it (Matt 18,18: "Whatever you bind on earth is bound also in heaven, and whatever you loose on earth is loosed also in heaven"), the Church always strives to have an effect upon the course of the life of the world through *conjuring prayers of a deprecatory and imperative nature* (exorcisms), through *imploratory and benedictive prayers* (blessings) that bestow God's favor on things and events, and finally through *constitutive consecrations* that lift the things and persons of this world out of their earthly order ("profaneness") and are intended to set them aside and sanctify them for God's service (the "sacral world").[95] "Sacramentals, therefore, are things and actions which the Church is accustomed to use in a certain imitation of the sacraments, in order, through its prayer, to achieve effects which are above all spiritual" (CIC, can. 1144).

3. If we are to provide a basis for these ecclesial sacramentals from the perspective of the new understanding of the world and self, and also with an eye to the critical and skeptical questioners from today's world, we must articulate in a new way the fundamental elements of the Christian understanding of world and self that we have as believers.

a) In the first place, it is important to assert that the *consecrations* of the Church have nothing to do with "magic," even though at times they may, in their rites and prayer formulas, remind people of more ancient folk formulas and blessings. The Church's blessings and consecrations, rather, are intended to express three things: (1) that the consecrated object or the consecrated person, through his or her free human decision and his or her free human gift of self, is taken out of ordinary worldly availability in order to enter—forever and exclusively—the *service* of the religious activity of humankind *before God and for God.* (2) This freely chosen "exceptional state" that is entered into is not only the doing of a human will; through this consecration the Church also wants to underscore the fact that, through its prayer, it has handed over the object or the person to God through Christ, at whose service the Church always stands—the service of Christ, who is its Lord and the first Celebrant of its liturgy. (3) Finally, the Church confirms this human gift of self on the basis of its participation in Christ's mission (John 20,21); this happens when, on the basis of its power of the keys that is rooted in Christ's mission, the Church declares in the earthly and human sphere that this thing or person has been accepted by God.

Being Christ's body, the Church has the living and transfigured Lord himself as its Head and, therefore, it here acts in Christ's stead and for Christ (2 Cor 5,19f.). Thus, its "word of self-surrender and imploration" in the consecration signifies a participation in the objective effect of the sacraments, which is guaranteed because Christ himself

instituted them. The basis and the guarantee for the efficacy of these consecrations are no longer institution by the
historical Christ, but rather the Church's actions within
the community, within the scope of the mission and mandate given by the transfigured Lord. The "Mystery of
Christ" and the "Mystery of the Church," the Incarnation,
and the divine Mission, are the foundation for this convic-
tion of faith.

b) In the same way we may say concerning *blessings*
that the Church, through its supplication and its intention
to bless "in place of Christ and for Christ," incorporates in
an efficacious manner into the living "Mystery of Christ"
those realities and persons that, as God's creatures, are already to be found in God's power and under God's protec-
tion. It is in this Mystery of Christ that the salvation and
blessing of us all are realized and applied to us in this
world, the Mystery in which and out of which the Church
prays and acts, consecrates and blesses.

c) For today's manner of thinking there are greater difficulties in the matter of *exorcisms,* as we encounter these
in the Church, especially in connection with the sacrament of baptism but also as separate formulas for use apart
from baptism. The chief difficulty here derives first of all
from the fact that the reality of angels—which is part and
parcel of creation—and in connection with it, the reality
of the bad angels, Satan or the Devil, must be thought
through anew theologically in light of the overturning of
the natural view of the world of an older tradition, insofar
as the biblical view of the world is conditioned by the "sci-
entifically false view" of Scripture. The doctrine of the angels (volume 3, *The World: God's Creation*) discusses this
problem in more depth. Here it must suffice to point out
that the "Christ-event," as presented in the revelation of
the New Testament, is decisively marked by this reality of
"Satan,"[96] and that the young Church understood the persecutions to which it was destined as the work of Satan.[97]
Moreover, in its "exorcisms" the Church is only following

in the steps of its Lord Christ when it, in Christ's stead and for Christ, seeks to rebuff Satan as Christ himself did, by invoking his work of redemption in the context of salvation-history, which is continually being accomplished within the history of the world.

4. It is, therefore, decisive for us to see three things with respect to the Church's use of sacramentals.

(1) In using sacramentals the Church is not acting as an inner-worldly, autonomous power over against a world which itself is understood as autonomous (as, for instance, the modern thinking of a M. Heidegger sees the world and humans as standing one over against the other); rather, the Church is acting as a *servant who has been commissioned by Jesus Christ,* a servant, that is, who seeks to accomplish his mystery of redemption in this world by the use of words that are both of imploration and of conjuration, both commanding and apodictic.

(2) In the sacramentals what is involved is not only human rites and experiments but, as with the sacraments, *signs* are involved that are *an indication and a guarantee of a real world* that exists over and beyond the visible world of ordinary experience. That is a world that has not been made by human beings but is activated and borne by God the Creator; it both lies at the foundation of the world we commonly experience and is a reality of salvation-history superimposed upon this world. Just as in this material world of our experience humans are busy constructing their own world of spirit by means of technology, culture, and science, so too over against this human world of our experience, according to revelation, a *history of salvation* has been set into motion by God's initiative with actors (powers and angels) who stand far above our world, and it is within this salvation-history alone that the world of our experience can attain to its full meaning and realization. The significance and the task of the Church's sacramentals, particularly as they relate to the non-human world, are to serve this full meaning that God has established and

this realization that God has bestowed upon the world in Christ's mystery of redemption.

(3) *The center of salvation-history is Christ,* in whom the world was created, in whom the world continues to exist, who has redeemed the world through his death (Col 1,15–20), who will perfect the world as judge (Matt 25,21ff.), and who in the end will bestow the New Heaven and the New Earth (Rev 21). "God has rescued us from the power of darkness, and transferred us to the kingdom of his beloved Son. . . . He is the true likeness of the God we cannot see; his is that first birth which precedes every act of creation. Yes, in him all created things took their being, what is in heaven and what is on earth. . . . They were all created through him and for him; he is the culmination of all things, and in him all things subsist. . . . He is also the beginning, since his was the first birth out of death; thus in every way the primacy was to become his. It was God's good pleasure to make the whole fullness [of God] dwell in him, and through him to win back all things, whether on earth or in heaven, making peace with them through his blood, shed on the cross" (Col 1,13–20). The Church with its sacramentals stands at the service of this *Christ who has become cosmic* by virtue of God's dispensation for salvation-history.[98]

5. In conclusion we would here like to present a few theological reflections on today's exigency for a *desacralization* not only of the cosmic and the human worlds, but also in the sphere of the Church, in our understanding of faith ("demythologization"), and in the liturgical actions of the Church.

a) The demand for desacralization and the manner this is understood today are articulated mostly from the standpoint of the experimental sciences of sociology and psychology. Important as the contributions of these sciences may be for an understanding of that process in the interior of the human being out of which emerged this catchword of "desacralization," nevertheless they can never reach to those depths of being in which the mystery of the spirit (which is more than that of the soul), the mystery of human freedom (which transcends all experiential norms of the individual and of the socially conditioned person), and the mystery of the world as conceived by faith all have their ontological foundation. To be sure, even a theological meditation on the questions of the sacred and desacralization cannot dispense with these modern insights into the workings of a certain mechanism that engages both the individual person and the structures of society, that involves both the objectification of human ideas and the institutionalization of human modes of behavior, and that interrelates the education received by a certain class of society with the formation of myths and legends. Sociological and psychological insights do doubtless make comprehensible certain factual and practical legitimations of generalized value-systems, but the heart of the matter itself and its foundations must be brought to light by cognitive efforts of a far different sort.

b) A valuable aid in this regard is offered us by a consideration of the *history of sacralization and desacralization* of the human worldview at least within the realm of our own culture; in this sphere we may still hope for a certain understanding even of the past if we rely on the real uniformity of ideas and continuity of development that are there. It is far more difficult to apply this manner of historical meditation validly to other cultures.

Within our own cultural sphere there is today general agreement on the fact that ancient pagan culture conceived of the world as sacred: it was a thoroughly divinized world in which all inner-worldly mysteries that could not yet be explained by a natural science or another experimental science were seen as divine manifestations or ways of approaching the gods, who for their part became comprehensible as transcendental objectivations of human ideas and ideals.

With their image of God as the Creator of the world and

the Lord of human history, the *revealed religions*—at least
Judaism, Christianity, and Islam—they demythologized
the ancient world and removed the gods from it. But it
would be a gross error to say that by so doing these revealed religions neutralized, desacralized, and secularized
the world. What occurred is that through the process of
revelation the sacred assumed an essentially different
structure. Just as the God of revelation is but one single
and personal God (over against the numerous gods of Antiquity, who were understood as being more like ideas or
powers), so too the sacred is now no longer only one element that may be experienced in the material world (a *nu-
minosum* or a magical reality) but rather a reality that may
be localized and experienced only in the human historical
world, and this through a believing understanding of both
self and world of the human being's. The sacred has become a reality that exacts a free answer from humans in
their acts—this in place of the pagan sacred, which was a
magical power that compelled human beings to a specific
form of behavior.

  c) On the basis of these affirmations we can now understand why the *neutralization of the world* really begins
when human beings and their world part company from
one another, or when the world no longer finds its center
either in God or in human beings. At bottom we may say
that credit for this enormous deed goes to Copernicus
(1473–1542), who not only lifted the earth out of its al-
leged central position in the universe but who also, more
fundamentally, simply deprived the world of its center.
The world no longer manifests itself as ordered around a
center, but rather as ordered by an internal law that per-
meates the whole. In the measure in which the *Renaissance* then made a *secundus deus* out of the human being
as a creative being,[99] and the *Enlightenment* also made
questionable or denied every connection to the divine in
the human interior being, we may say that the process inaugurated by Copernicus led to an understanding of the

world in which the world may be termed desacralized in the authentic meaning of the word.

Such a development, however, cannot be explained on the basis of Christian faith. On the contrary, today natural science itself has in its research again come up against the internal limits, the internal mystery of nature, and attained to a wholly new domination of the world that makes human beings questionable or even seriously endangers them as a part of nature and in their own higher being. And this situation has made it evident that the world must again have a center. In this world, which has been made transparent by human beings and which in great part is in the process of being shaped more and more by human beings, the center is not given along with the world itself; rather, a new center is being proposed: and *the center of the world as now understood is the human being.* These human beings have been able not only to subject the world to themselves, but—if they do not wish to destroy themselves—must also put the world at the service of their high task of self-realization.

Such a sublime enterprise, however, again points people in the direction of those depths that are the locus where, along with the mystery of freedom and spiritual personhood, there also emerge for humans the mystery of the absolute Thou, the mystery of humankind's absolute future, and finally *the mystery of God.* This necessity again makes us view the world as a sacred world and puts us squarely before a *new structure of the sacred.*

d) In light of the fulfillment of revelation through Jesus Christ, we may say that this process has found its expression in those determinants of human existence and of the human understanding of self and world that today we encapsulate in the words "eschatologization," "pneumatization," and "christologization" (cf. R. Schnackenburg).

Christologization: Through the salvation-historical event of God's Incarnation (which we are not to term "world-historical"), and through the salvation-historical event of the world's redemption through Jesus Christ, a new and real possibility in sacrality has dawned for the whole of human history and, thus, also for the history of the world—a possibility of the sacred that both should and can become an ever-new reality in this world through the believer's life and activity "in Jesus Christ," which means in the grace and mission of Jesus Christ.[100] A person can realize this "Christ-mystery" in this world in various ways through his or her life and actions as a believer: by public confession of Christ, by bearing witness to Christ and proclaiming his Good News, by mutual love in Christ, by personal following of Christ, and by fulfillment of Christ's mandates in the sacraments and in cultic acts centered on Christ, to the glory of the Father in the Holy Spirit. And in this Christ-mystery the "sacralization of the world" is continually being renewed. This is indeed the deeper meaning of *St. Paul's theology of the Body of Christ*, when it is seen in connection with the Christ-hymn from the Letter to the Colossians. Paul also wrote: "He who went down [Christ] is no other than he who has gone up, high above all the heavens, to fill creation with his presence. Some he has appointed to be apostles, others to be prophets, others to be evangelists, or pastors, or teachers. They are to order the lives of the saints for the work of his service, build up the frame of Christ's body, until we all realize our common unity through faith in the Son of God, and fuller knowledge of him. So we shall reach perfect manhood, that maturity which is proportioned to the completed growth of Christ; we are no longer to be children, no longer to be like storm-tossed sailors, driven before the wind of each new doctrine that human subtlety, human skill in fabricating lies, may propound. We are to follow the truth, in a spirit of charity, and so grow up, in everything, into a due proportion with Christ, who is our head. On him all the body depends. Bonded and knit together by every constitutent joint, the whole frame grows through the due activity of each part, and builds itself up in charity" (Eph 4,10–16).

This process at the same time involves a *pneumatization* (not "spiritualization" in the Greek sense), insofar as Christ has not only sent his Pneuma, which is also the Father's Pneuma (John 14,26; 15,26), but which he himself *is* as transfigured Lord (2 Cor 3,17: "The Lord is the Pneuma; now, where the Lord's Pneuma is, there is freedom").

At the same time, this means *eschatologization*, insofar as this human process and activity is characteristic of that human state in the world that signals the Christian end of time, the æon between the first Easter and Pentecost and the last coming of the transfigured Lord as judge of all and perfecter of the world.

It is these specifically Christian determinants that address and put forward the true Christian meaning of the "sacred" for humans and their world and for the cosmos. The church not only encompasses humankind but, as Body of the cosmic Christ, it also encompasses the human world and the cosmos itself; for this reason, therefore, the Church is the sphere of which Paul says: "We are God's co-workers; you are a field of God's tilling, a structure of God's design" (1 Cor 3.9: Θεοῦ γάρ ἐσμεν συνεργοί, Θεοῦ γεώργιον, Θεοῦ οἰκοδομή ἐστε), the sphere within which the Apostle's injunction becomes meaningful: "My brothers, I appeal to you by God's mercies to offer up your bodies [yourselves] as a living and holy sacrifice, pleasing to God. This is the worship due from you as rational creatures" (Rom 12,1: παραστῆσαι τὰ σώματα ὑμῶν θυσίαν ζῶσαν, ἁγίαν, εὐάρεστον τῷ Θεῷ, τὴν λογικὴν λατρείαν ὑμῶν).[101]

2. Human Sacramental Existence and the Sacramentals

1. Just as the sacraments were instituted for each person and become realized in the actions of humans, so too, and to an even greater extent, *the sacramentals become real-*

ized only in the actions of human beings. This is why in
a particular manner they too exist for the sake of human
beings. Just as the world was cursed because of human beings (Gen 3,17–19), so too is it intended again to participate in God's blessing through the actions of human beings. What "Adam" destroyed by his sin, Christ as second
Adam has made new and sanctified through his work of redemption. "If this one man's [Adam's] fault brought death
on a whole multitude, all the more lavish was God's grace,
shown to a whole multitude, that free gift he made us in
the grace brought by one man, Jesus Christ. . . . And if
death began its reign through one man, owing to one
man's fault, more fruitful still is the grace, the gift of justification, which bids men enjoy a reign of life through one
man, Jesus Christ. . . . A multitude will become acceptable
to God through one man's obedience, just as a multitude,
through one man's disobedience, became guilty" (Rom
5,15.17.19). To act with Christ and in Christ and for Christ
is the meaning of the human activity that the sacramentals realize.

2. In this activity human beings are intended to allow
Christ's gift of grace to become an event for themselves.
They direct their spirit and their heart to the sanctification
of the world, which is a fruit of redemption by Christ.
They place the material world, in and of which they live
insofar as they are corporeal, under the sign of Christ's redeeming cross. They offer themselves to Christ the Redeemer as an instrument of redemption, in order that they
themselves may be more and more purified and sanctified
by the service of sanctification they perform for the world
through their gift of themselves, and by the fact that God
in his condescension makes use of them.

3. By this purification and sanctification of their own
being, people create and effect the condition necessary to
ensure that all their works of "culture," all their attempts
at fashioning the world as God has commanded (Gen 1,28:
command to engage in works of "culture"), will occur in

keeping with God's will; for *die Seele der Kultur ist die Kultur der Seele,* "the soul of culture is the culture [or cultivation] of the soul" (Momme Nissen). *The redemption of the material world is dependent on the sanctification of humans.* This is what Paul described in the following words: "Created nature has been condemned to frustration; not for some deliberate fault of its own, but for the sake of him who so condemned it, with a hope to look forward to; namely, that nature in its turn will be set free from the tyranny of corruption, to share in the glorious freedom of God's children. The whole of nature, as we know, groans in a common travail all the while. And not only do we see that, but we ourselves do the same; we ourselves, although we already possess the firstfruits, the Pneuma, we groan in our hearts, waiting for that adoption which is the ransoming of our bodies from their slavery. It must be so, for we are saved through hope and for hope" (Rom 8,20–24).

4. At the same time, in this effort at working for salvation that becomes articulated in the sacramentals, humans take the stance of those who are permanently watchers and workers because in this world they are to serve and come to resemble him who protects them and never sleeps (Ps 121,3f.), him who forever is a vigilant and pure Spirit, *actus purus* (analogy of spirit). Through this alertness of the spirit in the service of the "Kingdom of God," humans seek to preserve that interior center in which they—conscious of their autonomy—gather themselves up and become free to enter on the road to him who, as highest person, is the *ens in se* (analogy of person), and who is to be found only on the path that leads through "interiority," since he is himself "more interior to each being than this being can be to itself."[102] Of course, human watchfulness must continually be engaged against evil just as much as for good, as God has spoken through the prophet: "As I watched over them with intent to pull down and to uproot, to demolish and destroy and harm, so now will I

watch over them to build and to plant" (Jer 31,28). In a similar manner Jesus admonishes us: "Keep watch, then, praying at all times, so that you may be found worthy to come safe through all that lies before you, and stand erect to meet the presence of the Son of Man" (Luke 21,36).

5. In conclusion, we must understand the sacramentals correctly, not only as those variable ceremonies with which the Church has surrounded the conferral of the sacraments in the course of time, but rather as the reality of *benedicere, exorcizare et consecrare* that is practiced from the heart of a Christian attitude toward existence. With this understanding of our Christian activity as a continuation and a completion of our Christian life in the sacraments, we will also be able to understand what Paul was speaking of in these paradoxical words: "You must work at your salvation in fear and trembling. . . . Both the will to do it and the accomplishment of that will are something which God accomplishes in you, to carry out his loving purpose" (Phil 2,12f.). "For we are God's work, created in Christ Jesus for such good works as God has prepared beforehand, that we should walk in them" (Eph 2,10).

Thus, the sacraments and the sacramental life are intended to prepare us for the coming æon, where no longer sense-perceptible signs but the spiritual reality itself will be authoritative; where no longer our human attempts but God's own actions with us will be conclusive, where, as at the confluence of great rivers, faith will flow out and be transformed into vision, hope into possession, and love into union with him who alone "is all in all" (1 Cor 15,28).

VIII

God's Word as Sacrament

New interest in the "Word of God" has been awakened of late by a great number of factors, among which we could name the new approach to the relationship between the word of Scripture and revelation evidenced in the Dogmatic Constitution on Divine Revelation, the introduction of the vernacular as official liturgical language, the new stimuli for theology deriving from the ecumenical movement, and other timely issues such as democratic ideology and personalism. This new understanding of the Word of God is best grasped if we approach it as God's *sacramental* Word in the context of our general doctrine of the sacraments. To do this we will offer some short reflections on the history of our understanding of *word* (1) and on the sacramental sense of God's Word (2).

1. Toward an Understanding of "Word"

1. The *word* is a primal element or component of human language. Human language, in turn, is an expression and an instrument of the human spirit. Now the mystery of the human spirit encompasses both the mysteries of the human reality and the mysteries of the human world, that world that both preexists humans and is a creation of humans. For our present concern, a reflection on the "Word of God," we will confine ourselves to the one problem introduced by Ferdinand de Saussure (d. 1913) by his distin-

guishing *langage, langue,* and *parole,* that is, a distinction between speaking or the ability to speak, on the one hand, and language itself and word, on the other.

De Saussure described speech or language (*langue*) as a social reality (*faite sociale*) and the word (*parole*) as an individual happening (*acte individuelle*). More momentous than this distinction between individual and community as bearer of language is the statement that language is not to be understood merely as a sum of words but as an integrated structure, a whole that, according to the particular linguistic system, may be present either in only one word or in many words of varying construction; moreover, language exhibits at times a more personal relation and at other times a more objectified relation. At times language appears more as an expression of the thinking, feeling, and willing of the speaker, at other times more as a turning to the addressee (in communication or appeal); and at still other times it seems to be more like information or a dialogue about a particular state of affairs that belongs to the world of the speaker or of the addressee or of both.

2. We can see how language can simultaneously bear and fulfill this twofold relationship—to the human being's speaking and to the thing addressed—by reference to the ancient problem posed in Plato's *Cratylus:* whether language is a natural given or a human creation. The answer is that, in the case of living language, both these aspects belong together, so that even proper names and classifying concepts may be seen as an expression of a whole universe of sentences. Only a technical understanding of language that abstracts from the concrete human act of speaking will regard these elements in isolation from each other. The eight parts of speech of Alexandrian grammar (noun, verb, participle, pronoun, preposition, adverb, conjunction, and article—which the Romans replaced with the interjection), as well as the five parts of the sentence (subject, predicate, object, attribute, adverbial phrase) as introduced by K. F. Becker (d. 1854), the ten kinds of words in German linguis-

tics as classified by J. C. Adelung (d. 1806), and the modern attempts to distinguish different "kinds of words" in specific languages—twenty-four in Latin, thirty in Dutch, and so on—all of this complex speculation in the end points to one thing, which is the interplay and interdependency of the elements of *langue* and *parole*. We are brought to the conclusion that language is always a context whose individual elements possess not only specific "meaning" [*Bedeutung*] but also associative "sense" [*Sinn*]. In this we see language to be a permanently open-ended undertaking that participates in the ever-necessary development of the human spirit and of the human world that perforce accompanies it.

3. In Greek thought, at least since Heraclitus, the *word* as *logos* had attained to such autonomy that "logos" was seen to represent the norm and the law of all reality (truth and law); hence, it was considered to be far more than just a bridge of understanding between human beings and the word, between person and person, or, in Late Antiquity, between humans and God. "Logos" as word, thus, is the ever-valid cosmic law, obedience to which is the task of the wise person. In the Neo-Platonism of Late Antiquity, the Logos became a divine being, a god.

By contrast the Sophists (Gorgias, for instance) reduced the Logos, as an element of speech, to a concept belonging to "rhetoric," and they appealed to the human spirit and the human soul (νοῦς and ψυχή) as creators of the word ('έπος or 'ρῆμα) to use their freedom to obey the normative power of the Logos. Plato attempted to bridge over this opposition between Heraclitus and Gorgias[103] by an admonition to reverence before the Logos. Thought and word, thing and deed, existence, essence, and norm are all interconnected in the Greeks' conception of the Logos, particularly as the Stoics understood it. The fact that the spirit operates through words in accordance with the Logos is what, according to Aristotle, distinguishes human beings from the animals.[104] When in the Hellenistic mysteries we see the Logos appear as a secret doctrine and as a revelation of the divine Being, and finally even personified as the god Hermes, what we are witnessing is a very Oriental development of the conception of "word."

4. In Hebraic thought, which always presupposes the Creator God as the beginning of all being, "speech" and "word" are likewise primarily understood in connection with the activity of the self-revealing God. "Word" (*dabar*) is etymologically connected with *debir*, which is the All-Holy, understood against the background of the temple. The dianoetic and the dynamic meanings of "word" belong together: The Word of God has to do with God's saving actions and, hence, it *is* God's revelation in history. The prophet is one who has been grasped by God's Spirit and God's Word (2 Sam 23,1: David), and since Samuel the "Word of the Lord" is the decisive power in the history of Israel. It is in this "Word of God," moreover, that the particular form of "God's Law" becomes expressed (Exod 34,28; 24,4). In the post-Exilic era, the Word-as-creation[105] becomes joined to God's Word-as-revelation and his Word-as-law. In its most dynamic form, "word" emerges in the Old Testament not only as the "Word of God" that we see especially in the Prophets, but also as the "curse and blessing" that different persons utter obedient to God's commands. The power humans possess over things becomes evident in the way they *assign names* (cf. Gen 2,19f.). However, the power of the word can never be understood in Israel in any magical sense, as occurs in the non-biblical world of Egypt or Babylon: in Israel the power of the word is forever rooted in the reality of God.[106]

5. The New Testament contributes wholly new aspects of the biblical view of the "Word of God." Side by side with the texts of the Old Testament we now have, as *Word of God,* the "word of Jesus," the word of witness to Christ, and the missionary preaching of the primitive Church (cf. Acts 4–19). The Apostles are nothing else than "servants of the Word" (Acts 6,2; 1 Cor 14,36), proclaimers of this

new revelation of God in Christ. Even when an Apostle lies in fetters, the Word of God is not bound (cf. 2 Tim 2,9). The "mystery of the Christ" is the actual content of the proclamation (Col 1,25–28; 4.3f.). At its depths what this proclamation is all about is the message of redemption through Christ (cf. 1 Tim 1,15). The proclamation is the word about the Cross (1 Cor 1,18), about reconciliation (2 Cor 5,19), about salvation (Acts 13,26), about grace (Acts 14,3), about life (Phil 2,16), about truth (Eph 1,13). The Gospel concerning Christ has been given by God, and the Apostle is only its servant (cf. 2 Cor 5,19f.). The power of the Apostle's preaching derives only from God (cf. Heb 4,12; 1 Thes 2,13), and in and of itself it effects grace, deliverance, and life. All a person has to do is receive the Word of God (cf. Acts 8,14; 11,1), believe in the Word (1 Thes 2,13), bring the Word to fulfillment (Matt 7,24).

Unlike the Prophets, Christ himself never refers to a word he has received from God; he speaks from the full perfection of his own power.[107] The offer and the efficacious power of the Word of God were proposed by Christ himself in the parable of the sower (cf. Mark 4,13–20 and parallels). This Word of God is a "power of God" (1 Cor 1,18; 2 Cor 6,4–7). As an authentically prophetic book, the Apocalypse always calls its own proclamation "words of God," and these continually prove to be a "witness for Jesus Christ" (cf. Rev 1,2.9; 6,9; 20,4). Finally, the very name of Christ is presented as being *the Word of God* (ὁ Λόγος τοῦ Θεοῦ, cf. Rev 19,13). Here the ancient Jewish meaning of רבד (*dabar*) as a word that is event and reality again imposes itself: the Word of God is the historical Christ-event that has become realized in the person of Christ. Christ is thus termed the Yes and the Amen, the ultimate fulfillment of revelation (cf. 2 Cor 1,19; Rev 3,14). In Christ, consequently, a "new creation, a new commandment, a new covenant," has been given (cf. 2 Cor 5,17; John 13,34; Luke 22,20). In his Sermon on the Mount, Christ presented himself as a new Moses (cf. Matt 5,17,22).

The apostolic proclamation created nothing new of its own: all it did was to take seriously and give witness to this self-understanding of Jesus as he himself proclaimed it in his preaching. This is what in the end entitles John to say that Christ, whom the Apostles "heard and saw and contemplated with their own eyes and touched with their own hands," *is* the Word of Life that was from the beginning (cf. 1 John 1,1). The Hymn to the Logos in the Gospel of John (John 1,1–16) intends nothing else but to trace this belief in *Christ as the "Word of God"* back to God himself as he utters his Word—to God who is identical with this Word—and at the same time to present this Word of God as the Word of creation and of grace in the sense of the New Covenant. In this way Christ appears as the fulfillment of the Old Covenant's Word of the Law and he, being grace, truth and life, is set over against the Pharisees' understanding of the Word of the Law in Jesus' own time. The "Word became flesh" so that the Old Testament's Word of God, which in the context of Phariseeism had become an instrument in the hands of human beings, might become a new divine reality in this world: Emmanuel, which is to say "God with us" (Isa 7,14). This new Word of God may no longer be manipulated and used by us according to our own whims, because it became manifested as *person.* Thus, the history of the Word of God in Christ's person and, through him, in the New Covenant and in the Church of Christ, has led us to contemplate a form of the Word of God that, as eschatological fulfillment of all the old, has made a new "beginning," whose particular form we now intend to clarify as the "sacramental form" of the Word of God.

2. The Sacramental Form the Word of God Assumes in the New Covenant

It is a peculiarity of human faith in the living, personal God as he has revealed himself within Judæo-Christian salvation-history that such faith zealously clings, not only to human accounts of divine deeds, but also to utterances that the believer declares to be the "Word of God," that is, that they represent a message or an instruction or a promise that has God himself as its immediate author. It is hoped that the following reflections will show that here the "Word of God" is to be understood *only* in a sacramental manner and yet in a *truly* sacramental manner.

1. All utterances of Scripture are utterances made by human beings and contained in a human language that is historically unequivocal; such language, therefore, exhibits all the characteristics of human discourse as conditioned by a specific historical moment. This applies as well to those utterances that make a claim to be "word of God" or "words of Christ" or to derive from word-of-mouth or eyewitnesses of events in the salvation-history of either the Old or the New Testament. It is only this human derivation of "God's words" that explains why "God's Word," a divine utterance that can be only one and the same, nevertheless receives various and widely differing expressions in salvation-history: examples of this are the Ten Commandments (Exod 20,1–17 and Deut 5,6–18), the words of institution of the Holy Eucharist (Matt 26,26–29, and Luke 22,15–20), and certain specific events such as Paul's conversion (Acts 9,7 and 22,9). And yet the Prophets always insist that it is not their own doctrine or wisdom that they proclaim, but rather the instructions and promises of the living God in whose service they stand. We find the expression "Word of God" used in this sense twelve times in Samuel, fifty times in the Books of Kings, nine times in Isaiah, sixty times in Ezekiel, and fifty-two times in Jeremiah. In his first letter Paul writes as follows on this point: "This is why we give thanks to God unceasingly that, when we delivered the divine message to you, you recognized it for what it is, God's Word, not a human one; it is God, after all, who manifests his power in you that have learned to believe" (1 Thess 2,13). The human

word is in some way the audible sign, but also the efficacious means, for God's revelation, instruction, and promises. As such, the "Word of God" is pure gift. Paul thus affirms concerning the Jews: "The words of God were entrusted to them [the Jews]" (Rom 3,2). In his farewell
discourses Christ emphasizes this in a similar way: "I have
given them the words which thou gavest to me, and they,
receiving them, recognized it for truth that I came from
thee [Father], and found faith to believe that it was thou
who didst send me" (John 17,8). To be sure, this gift of
God's must be freely "received" and welcomed in faith.
The Letter to the Hebrews makes the point well: "The
message of salvation has been proclaimed to us, just as it
was to them [the Jews]. But the message that came to them
did them no good, because it was not met by belief in what
they heard" (4,2). The Parable of the Sower also stresses
this: "The grain that fell in good soil stands for those who
hear the word, and hold by it with a noble and generous
heart, and endure, and yield a harvest" (Luke 8,15).

2. The Scripture therefore never tires of speaking of the
wonderful effect of the "Word of God," an effect that can
otherwise be attributed only to the sacramental reality.
Thus, the Prophet Isaiah has God himself say: "As the rain
and the snow come down from heaven and do not return
until they have watered the earth, making it blossom and
bear fruit, and give seed for sowing and bread to eat, so
shall the word which comes from my mouth prevail; it
shall not return to me fruitless without accomplishing my
purpose or succeeding in the task I gave it" (Isa 55,10f.; cf.
Ps 147,15–20). Again Isaiah: "I make my servants' prophecies come true and give effect to my messengers' designs"
(Isa 44,26). And Jeremiah: "If a prophet has a dream, let
him tell his dream; if he has my word, let him speak my
word in truth. . . . Word of the Lord! Do not my words
scorch like fire? Are they not like a hammer that splinters
rock?" (Jer 23,28f.). We have only to think of the encomium of the Word of God as instruction in deutero-

nomic literature (cf. Ps 119) and of the glorification of God's creative Word in wisdom literature (cf. Sir 42,15ff.; Ps 33,6.9). The preacher of the Letter to the Hebrews resumes this truth in the following words: "God's Word to us is something alive, full of energy; it can penetrate deeper than any two-edged sword, reaching the very division between soul and spirit, between joints and marrow, quick to distinguish every thought and design in our hearts. From him, no creature can be hidden; everything lies bare, everything is brought face to face with him, this God to whom we must give our account" (Heb 4,12f.). The quasi-sacramental effect of God's Word becomes particularly clear when Christ himself says, in the context of his farewell discourses in John: "You, through the word I have preached to you, are clean already" (John 15,3). And in the First Letter of Peter we read: "You have all been born anew with an immortal, imperishable birth, through the Word of God which lives and abides for ever" (1 Pet 1,2.3). Finally, the Letter of James says: "It was his will to give us birth, through his Word of truth" (Jas 1,18). The Word of God here becomes palpable as a "word that saves."

3. The saving character of the Word of God in revelation comprehensively understood—that is, revelation as including all the biblical accounts of God's saving deeds in the history of humankind—becomes evident whenever human beings open themselves up in faith to God's revelation in the Word of Scripture. Just as with the worthy recipient of a sacrament, so too an act of believing attention directed at Sacred Scripture, which "receives the Word of God with reverence," confers grace and salvation, not only *ex opere operantis*—which is to say in proportion to the intensity of this act of faith—but also *ex opere operato*—which is to say on the basis of a faith-filled listening to the God who reveals himself in Scripture. The Second Vatican Council's Dogmatic Constitution on Divine Revelation (*Dei Verbum*) has this to say on the subject: "In his goodness and wisdom God decided to reveal himself and make

manifest the mystery of his will.[108] that through Christ, the Word become man, and in the Holy Spirit all may have access to the Father and come to partake of the divine nature.[109] In this revelation the invisible God[110] addresses men as his friends because of his overflowing love[111] and has familiar dealings with them[112] in order to invite them and receive them into communion with himself. The event of revelation occurs in both deed and word, and these two things are intimately bound up with one another: that is, the works that God accomplishes in the course of salvation-history reveal and substantiate his teaching and the realities that the words signify; and the words, in turn, proclaim the works and make the mystery that they contain come to light. The depth of the truth that opens out to us through this revelation concerning God and human beings' salvation becomes fully radiant for us in Christ, who is at once the mediator and the fullness of the whole of revelation" (DV 2). "The 'obedience of faith'[113] is the adequate response to God as he reveals himself. By so doing man freely entrusts all of himself over to God; he 'submits fully with both intellect and will to God as God reveals himself to him' and thus man willingly assents to God's revelation" (DV 5).

4. The sacramental character of the "Word of God" likewise becomes evident in that listening with faith to revelation in the Scripture, as in the case of a sacrament, is fully possible only "in the Church," since it is in the Church that the Word of God will be found in the living relationship between "minister and recipient." Tradition and the Magisterium are always necessarily involved if the scriptural revelation is to be rightly pondered, understood, and believed. "With the aid of the Holy Spirit, this apostolic tradition in the Church undergoes a development: the understanding of those things and words which have been handed down grows through the meditation and the study of believers who ponder them in their hearts[114]; it grows through the interior insight which derives from spiritual

experience and through the proclamation of those who have received the sure charism of truth with their succession in the office of bishop" (DV 8). "We can see, then, that Holy Tradition, Sacred Scripture and the Church's Magisterium are so bound up with each other and so conjoined by God's wise design that none of these can perdure without the others and that all of them together, each in its own way, effectively serve the salvation of souls through the activity of the Holy Spirit" (DV 10).

The maxim of the Reformers that the proclamation of the Word of God is itself the Word of God (*prædicatio verbi Dei verbum Dei est*), therefore, can be justified only to the extent that this proclamation takes its ultimate norm from biblical revelation itself and to the extent that the proclaimer participates in the mission of the Apostles or proves, through a holy life in the Church, to be a "prophet," whose particular calling in any case stands in need of being recognized by the Church.[115]

5. What has been said (III.5) on the manner of the sacraments' effect likewise holds for the manner in which the Word of Scripture has its effect. In general we may speak of a moral or an intentional manner of effect. And yet, we may even speak of a physical manner of effect when, for instance, through God's special grace, a single word of Scripture can effect the conversion of a person, as in the case of Augustine, who traces his conversion back to the passage of Rom 13,13f.,[116] or of Anthony, the first hermit, who experienced his conversion on hearing the Parable of the Rich Young Man.[117] This physical manner of effect by the Word of God becomes particularly clear when it is spoken in obedience to Christ's own mandate, as is the case with the baptismal formula (Matt 28,19) in the sacrament of baptism and the words of institution (Luke 22,19) in the celebration of the Eucharist.

Thus, through the sacraments and the sacramentals and through the Word of God as we encounter it in the revelation of Scripture and the proclamation of the Church, the whole world, and above all human history, becomes a "sacred world" by virtue of this activity in faith. In this sacralized world the believer can encounter the living God, *his or her* God, in an ever new way, and in such a world the living God is forever beginning anew his search for humankind, *his* creation, whom he has made in his image and likeness.

The Mystery of the Eucharist

Introduction

1. In revelation God speaks to humankind. And what God says always aims at the whole of reality and the human being's true welfare.[1] Both in human beings and in the world at large these two fundamental questions—the *question of reality* and the *question of salvation*—can no longer be treated as one question insofar as in reality, alongside order and the good, there also exist evil and disorder, which are obstacles and harrassments on the path to salvation and insofar as in humans themselves there is active a longing for happiness that is no longer oriented to the wholeness of a total reality but picks and chooses and thus is a hindrance to true salvation. Nevertheless, in humans—if indeed they are to reach their perfection and their goal—the striving for reality and the striving for happiness do belong together, that is, the search for the correct answer to the *question of reality* (What is this?) and to the *question of happiness* (What does it mean for me?). Scripture, therefore, describes faith as the response to the word of divine revelation and promise, in the following terms: "Faith is the assurance of things hoped for and the proof of things unseen," which is to say that faith guarantees the reality of hoped-for things (eschatological salvation already present) and is the proof of (transcendental) realities that cannot be experienced with the senses. But this is actually not the achievement of faith as such; rather, it is the "amen" ("hypostasis" or substance) that faith gives to God's promises and revelations that alone is capable of "perceiving" these "realities" (Heb 11,1). If the mystery of the Holy Eucharist is to be correctly approached, it is nec-

essary to be aware of both these movements that constitute the act of faith and that must be kept in synchrony.

In the concrete life of our contemporary world, these
two simultaneous movements of the spirit, which are so
necessary for the interior maturation and perfection of
human beings, largely appear to be separated and one of
the movements thus becomes an obstacle for the other.
The natural sciences are busy developing their knowledge
of reality quite independently of the question of human
wholeness and salvation, without the human's being further formed as an ethical being to attain to the moral
stature required for him or her to use this new knowledge
only for his or her own welfare. The atom bomb, the very
first application of the new discoveries of atomic physics,
served only for annihilation.

We also have to reckon with the scientific development
of the question of earthly welfare or "salvation," for instance in Marxism and in the different forms of communism, which so severely subject people to the material
order that spiritual and moral freedom—and therefore the
proper being of the individual as person—are either endangered or destroyed.

The history of the doctrine of the Eucharist will show
how in this domain, too, the question concerning reality or
the question concerning salvation were at different times
approached one-sidedly, so that the answer given by the
eucharistic piety of Christians to these questions did not
always do full justice to the whole reality of eucharistic
faith.

2. These two fundamental human impulses (for truth
and for wholeness) are also a structural part of faith, and
this for three reasons: (1) because humans are living beings
that must mature by growing and must develop toward
their perfection; (2) because they are beings endowed with
spirit who, on the basis of a reflective understanding of
themselves, are capable of holding before their own eyes
the image of their proper goal and can strive toward it with

freedom; and (3) because they are personal beings whose mystery lies precisely in the fact that they must realize and perfect themselves not only through autonomous effort and self-asserting deeds but also through giving themselves in service to others. Finally, as persons humans are also (4) communitarian beings who, in these acts of giving, being themselves given and allowing themselves to be given to, can become perfected only to the extent that the fellow-human beings with whom and for whom they live are involved in their process of self-perfectioning. Thus, the two-sidedness of the act of faith, being an act of human existence, is seen to exhibit four aspects, all four of which are of great significance for a correct understanding of the Eucharist.

a) The reality of salvation given us in the mystery of the Eucharist becomes for us an event that involves both a believing acceptance of the *pledge of salvation* and a self-fulfilling *deed of salvation:* by celebrating the Eucharist we receive salvation, and, because we receive salvation, we are put in the position of being able to celebrate the Eucharist time and again: "Whoever eats my flesh and drinks my blood has life everlasting" (John 6,54).

b) Our celebration of the Eucharist, however, is not only a response to the pledge of salvation given us in this mystery: a believing understanding of the mystery enables and impels us as well to utter a human word ourselves; the accomplishment of the Eucharist is not only a reaction to God's promise, but also a spiritually free and loving action that is our shared participation of this divine mystery in Christ. The deepest meaning of the eucharistic mystery is its revelation of God's creative love. Our response to it, consequently, ought to be not a merely passive acquiescence in this creative love; it must be a creative and loving collaboration on our part if it is to be and remain truly a response of love.

c) The mystery of love is rooted in the essence of personhood. The mystery of personhood is manifested, how-

ever, precisely in the fact that in its existential self-realization personhood necessarily reaches the critical border-
line where it can preserve and perfect itself only by being
ready to give itself away lovingly and freely. But this in no
way implies self-rejection or loss of self; on the contrary, if
at this crucial point of its existence the person were to
clutch at itself egotistically so as to preserve itself whole,
it would by the very fact be hindering its own growth and
maturity: the person would then in truth be losing itself
exactly as if it were casting itself away downward into the
sphere of the sub-human and the sub-personal.

   d) In this mystery of personal being as a being in tension
between "preservation of self" and "bestowal of self" is
rooted the fact that, as persons and as individuals, humans
are necessarily oriented toward their fellow-human beings
and toward a community of reciprocal human relationships; both for the personal order of things and all other orders serving the personal dimension, humans need community, although this "need" means not only the need to
receive but much more so the need to give, culminating in
the need to give oneself.[2]

   3. It is only when we become aware of, understand, and
realize these structural elements of "faith" as the deepest
fulfillment of our human nature before God, our Creator
and supreme model, that we begin to have an inkling of
the wonder that is the manifold mystery of God and, therefore, of the Eucharist. This should become clear in Chapter
I, where we will deal especially with the particular nature
of this sacrament's sacramental sign, the sign that is not
only a sign for some indeterminate aid to salvation for
human beings but, rather, the sign of the actual aid to salvation that the living God has localized in Jesus Christ
himself. The recognition of the real presence of this aid to
salvation given us by God in the presence of Christ and his
deeds in this sacrament provides the condition and basis
for a correct understanding of the fact that here we have
been given the one and only sacrifice of redemption for all

time in the form of a memorial celebration. The Eucharist as sacramental sacrifice (Chapter II) thus provides the basis for correctly understanding the Eucharist as a meal—as a meal of participation in the sacrifice of Christ and as a meal of the celebrating community of Christ (Chapter III). In the correct understanding of the celebrating community of Christ, furthermore, lies the basis for seeing that the Eucharist itself can in some way be the object of cultic worship (Chapter IV). In these possibilities for the one Eucharist to become realized as sacrifice, meal, and cult, finally, lies the reason why the Eucharist in a particular way is ordered to the Church, the whole People of God, which, through sacrifice, cult, and meal, itself lives as Mystical Body of Christ in union with this sacramental Body of Christ, and which allows itself to be perfected by him who is the goal and the perfectioning of all created things and of all things needy for salvation in this world (Chapter V).

Before we proceed to examine these five structural elements in the mystery of the Eucharist, we will, by way of an introduction, prepare our access to the correct understanding of this mystery, first, by a technical consideration of method (1), and then by a short historical survey of the evolution of the doctrine of the Eucharist in our theology (2).

1. Toward an Understanding of the Eucharistic Mystery

1. As was already shown in the course of our General Doctrine of the Sacraments (see IV.3), the mystery of the Eucharist occupies an "exceptional place" in the context of the other sacraments. The reason for this is to be seen above all in the fact that the Eucharist alone not only is an effect of grace by virtue of Christ's redemptive deed (like the other sacraments), but actually makes present and communicates the Redeemer and his work of redemption itself in a sacramental and symbolic manner (*Summa*

theol. III, q. 65, a.3). This is why the Eucharist in some way is the last of the three great saving mysteries of revelation and of Christian faith: The eternal life of God—which unfolds in a timeless and essential way in the first Mystery of the Most Holy Trinity, and which in the second Mystery of the God-Man Christ is partaken of by humanity in the person and work, life, word, and redemptive deed of Christ— is present in all its fullness (Col 2,9f.; Eph 1,23) in the Mystery of the Eucharist in order to become communicated to the individual Christian with all the certitude of sacramental reality and efficacy.[3] As such, the mystery of the Eucharist is at once sacrifice and sacrament, sacrifice and sacrificial meal, center and zenith of the Church's cult, since the Church lives by virtue of this cult and incessantly renews and rejuvenates itself in it and from it to the end of time. All other sacraments, including baptism (Rom 6,2–12), which is the entry gate into the Kingdom of Christ, live from this saving mystery of Christ's sacrificial death that becomes present for us sacramentally in the Eucharist. Here we should remember that in the exodus from Egypt, which is the great type of the mystery of redemption proposed to us by salvation-history, we see at the very center of things what the Jews called פסח *pesach* (*pascha*), the sacrifice and sacrificial meal that protects Israel from the exterminating angel and leads to the liberation of Israel from Egypt (Ex 6,1–8; 12,1–13); the trek through the Red Sea under the cloud takes its place in the history of Israel's liberation from Egyptian slavery only later, that "crossing" that in 1 Cor 10,2, is called a "baptism into Moses' fellowship," since he is seen as the earthly founder of the Old Covenant.

2. Since the Eucharist, as a sacramental reality, wholly lives from its character as sign, the question arises as to the way in which the meaning of this sacramental sign best opens up to us or, more generally, the question of what methods might be most useful for a theological reflection on this sacramental mystery. As we shall see, dif-

ferent methods have been used in the course of theological history.

a) Above all, and from the outset, we have the method of *salvation-history* that was normative in Scripture itself and in the first Fathers. This method derives from the temple theology of the time and leads us most directly to the original understanding of the Eucharist as revealed reality.

b) Just as Jewish theology after the destruction of the temple, especially as it begins sinking roots within the Greek diaspora, developed the *allegorical-symbolic method*, so too did Christian theology use this method, particularly after the end of the second century. This method, too, was the favorite of the Germanic Middle Ages, which no longer understood the sense of biblical salvation-history; it was here above all applied to the explanation of the Sacrifice of the Mass, whose liturgy had by now become enhanced by many new prayers that reflect the fact that the Mass was no longer understood in its connection with the *pascha* within the context of salvation-history.

c) In view of the widespread use of this allegorical-symbolic method, the "reality" of the eucharistic mystery as perceived by faith had to be secured by applying the new *philosophic-metaphysical method*, just as had been done during the christological debates of the fourth century to secure the import of the figure of Christ. This approach produced in the twelfth century the concept of "transubstantiation," just as in the fourth century the concepts of "homoousios" and "hypostatic union" had been developed to shed some light on the problems of the christological controversy.

d) From the beginning the Reformation denied the sacrificial character of the Eucharist and understood the Eucharist only as a meal of the Christian community. In this context, and especially after the Enlightenment, what was used was more of a *phenomenological-idealistic method* in order to describe the Eucharist more precisely as Christian community meal. After the First World War this method stressing the "meal" also was used by Catholics (R. Guardini).

e) It is only in our own days that the mystery theology of Odo Casel and the liturgical movement have again oriented contemporary theology to the biblical method of salvation-history, which alone makes accessible the fundamental content of this mystery. The phenomenological attempts of Dutch theology (Schillebeeckx) to gain an understanding of the Holy Eucharist useful for contemporary natural science must be seen, in relation to the method of salvation-history, as but a supplement that assumes its rightful place on the basis of the pastoral task of all theology.

3. From this question of method we can understand where the correct theological point of entry must be located if the mystery of the Eucharist is to open up to us in all its uniqueness and essence. Whenever we attempt to understand a living reality correctly, the question of "point of entry" becomes of decisive importance for finding the point of contact from which we can contemplate the whole reality in both its order and its distinctions, and come to grasp the origin of the thing and the lines of its development, the archetype from which it emerges, and the fulfillment toward which it strives.

a) The first point of departure for an understanding of the eucharistic mystery is the *historical Last Supper of Jesus Christ*, as the scriptural tradition has preserved it for us in the post-paschal *kerygma*. This post-paschal kerygma, however, intends to portray only "the primitive community's new understanding of the historical event."

b) According to the portrayal we find in the Synoptics, the Last Supper is to be understood unequivocally as a *paschal meal* and a *sacrificial meal*, so that the meaning of this event for salvation-history must be deduced from the meaning for salvation-history of Israel's own paschal meal. In this connection we must remember that the real paschal meal was held only in Jerusalem, where the temple and its sacrificial ritual were found (Deut 16,6), and that

Jesus celebrated his Last Supper with his disciples in Jerusalem and not in his hometown of Nazareth or at the house of one of his disciples in Capharnaum, where there was only a synagogue but no temple and, therefore, no sacrifice: here only a house meal could have taken place.

c) The phrase concerning the "blood" possesses already in Mark (14,24) and even more so in Luke (22,20) a clear reference both to the sealing of the covenant (Exod 24,8) and to the fact that this covenantal act is occurring in the sacrifice of Christ himself, since Christ always speaks of "my blood of the covenant." Consequently, to understand the event of the Last Supper, we also need to understand Christ's death on the cross: that is, we need to understand that the death of Jesus was not merely the unfortunate ending of a life and a catastrophe, but rather that it was a voluntary sacrifice, as has already been shown in detail in volume 4, *The Mystery of Christ,* and as we will shortly see again.

d) Once we have seen these three historical bases for interpretation in their true light, we shall be in a position to bring the symbol of the "meal" as such to bear on our understanding of the eucharistic meal, particularly as we find it in John (13,2.26.28). For, as we just said, outside Jerusalem, in the provincial towns that possessed only a synagogue—a place for assembly and prayer but no place of sacrifice—what was celebrated was only a meal.

e) It is in this context, finally, that we are to understand Christ's numerous references to the *eschatological meal in the kingdom (house) of his Father* as being the completion of the work of redemption and the fulfillment of the life of the redeemed: reference to this is already made by the accompanying phrase (Mark 14,25; Luke 22,16–18; not the interpretive phrase) concerning the chalice in the description of the Last Supper. Theologically we can perhaps say the following: *Not only with reference to time but also with reference to content, the Eucharist has its locus between Jesus Christ's sacrifice on the cross and the eschatological meal in the house of the Father.*

4. From the perspective of these possible points of entry into our subject we can also interpret the names that are given to this mystery of the Eucharist by the Scripture and the Fathers. In the oldest passage referring to the "Lord's Supper" (κυριακὸν δεῖπνον: 1 Cor 11,20), Paul speaks of the "chalice of the Lord" (ποτήριον κυρίου: 1 Cor 11,27; 10,21) and of the "table of the Lord" (τραπέζη κυρίου: 1 Cor 10,21), here with clear reference to Malachi 1,7.12; but already here we must not overlook the fact that Paul is expressly bringing the meal into relation with the sacrifice when he writes, "Do not those who eat the sacrifices associate themselves with the altar of sacrifice?" (1 Cor 10,18; cf. 16f.). Likewise, in this connection, Mal 1,11f. speaks expressly and prophetically about the "sacrifice" that is offered to the name of God in all places.

In this same context Paul also speaks of "spiritual food" (πνευματικὸν βρῶμα) and "spiritual drink" (πνευματικὸν πόμα: 1 Cor 10,3f.), by which he means Christ himself. We again encounter this understanding of the Eucharist as "food" in John 6,57, in an idiom that is realistic and perhaps conditioned by anti-Gnostic concerns, where the Evangelist has Christ say: "As the living Father sent me, and I live because of the Father, so he who eats me will live because of me" (ὁ τρώγων με κἀκεῖνος ζήσει δι' ἐμέ). In John, Christ expressly contrasts the life-giving bread he calls "bread from heaven" (ὁ ἄρτος ὁ ἐκ τοῦ οὐρανοῦ) to the manna that cannot bestow eternal life (John 6,48ff.). For this reason a later time would apply the expression "bread of angels"[4] to the Eucharist.

In the same strain as Paul, but even more emphatically, the writer of the Letter to the Hebrews (surely after the destruction of the Jewish temple) speaks in this connection of an "altar of sacrifice" (θυσιαστήριον: Heb 13,10) from which the servers of the (Old Testament) Tent were not allowed to eat, and he describes the death of Christ repeatedly as a "sacrifice" (θυσία: Heb 10,5.10.14) through which Christ has forever led to perfection those who allow themselves to be sanctified by him. And yet in this passage the writer is not speaking specifically of the eucharistic sacrifice, as he is in 13,10, but rather of the one-time, unrepeatable, historical sacrificial death of Christ (cf. 10,18).

Echoing the text of the words of institution (Luke 22,17 = 1 Cor 11,24), this mystery is called *Eucharist* already by Ignatius of Antioch (d. 115) (Ad Phil. 4, *Ad Smyrn.* 7:PG 5, 700, 713), by Justin (d. 165) (*Apol* 1, 65: PG 6, 428), by Tertullian (d. 220) (*De Cor.* 3,3: "Eucharistiæ Sacramentum"; *De Cor.* 19, 2; *De Præscript.* 3, 6, 5: CC II 1043; I 267, 217), and by Irenæus (d. 202) (*Adv. hær.* IV 18,5: PG 7, 1029). The word *eulogia* (taken from Matt 26,26 and Mark 14,22 and meaning "blessed" or "consecrated bread") is only used now for the blessed bread of the Eastern Church. The term used by the Acts of the Apostles for this mystery (2,42), the "breaking of the bread" (κλάσις τοῦ ἄρτου), appears again in the *Didache.* But this title was most frequently used for the agapê and not for the Eucharist. The expression *sacrament of the altar* is first found in Augustine (*Sermo* 59,3: "Sacramentum altaris": PL 38, 401; cf. 562). Because of its internal connection with the worship of the Church, the title "Eucharist" imposed itself at least since the fourth century with the formation of the most important liturgies.

2. Short History of the Eucharistic Doctrine

A. BIBLICAL EVIDENCE

The mystery of the Eucharist has its historical origin in the "Last Supper," the farewell supper of Jesus with his Apostles concerning which we have received a so-called *Pauline account* (most likely the earlier one: 1 Cor 11,23–25; Luke 22,19–20) and another more liturgically oriented narrative, the so-called *Petrine account* (Mark 14,22–25; Matt 26,26–29). In connection with the multiplication of the bread (Mark 6,32–44 par.), John reports a great Bread of Life Discourse by Jesus (John 6,51–59) that in this version already clearly exhibits the anti-Gnostic characteristics of Johannine theology. The Letter to the Hebrews, very likely written after the destruction of the Jewish temple, deals in detail with the priesthood and sacrifice of Jesus Christ (chaps. 8–10), and here the statements of Paul concerning the Eucharist as sacrifice (1 Cor 10,16–18) undergo a decisive in-depth expansion. Seven very different ideas of salvation-history may be seen to converge in these eucharistic accounts:

(1) The point of departure is the Jewish *pascha* as it was celebrated in Jerusalem as both sacrifice and meal; redemption, liberation from slavery, is the determining idea of this highest of Israel's feasts.

(2) Intimately bound up with this *pascha* is the memorial, the *anamnesis* (in Hebrew *zakar*), which confers on the one-time historical happening a presence within salvation-history for all time and which makes the work and the person of Christ present.

(3) Through all the accounts there runs the unifying assertion that here Jesus is giving "his flesh" and "his blood" as food and drink, and to this Paul adds that what is involved is a sacrificial body ("given away": διδόμενον) and sacrificial blood ("poured out": ἐκχυννόμενον). Now these strong assertions relate the event of the Last Supper to the *sacrificial death on Good Friday* or incorporate this sacrificial death into the Last Supper event. According to Paul every eucharistic celebration proclaims "the death of the Lord, until he comes again" (1 Cor 11,26).

(4) Especially in the Pauline portrayal, the *figure of God's suffering servant* from Is 53, 4f. becomes incorporated into the event of the Supper through the specification "for you."

(5) In the phrase concerning the chalice, furthermore, which in a special way is the bearer of the theme of sacrifice, there enters into the eucharistic account the *theme of the covenant* so closely related to the Suffering Servant, as

can be seen in Isa 42,6 and 49,8. Basing himself on Jer 31,31, Luke calls this the New Covenant. The source for all of this is Exod 24,8, which speaks of the "blood of the covenant."

(6) Already the Synoptic accounts, even if in different places, connect the event of the Last Supper with Christ's reference to the *eschatological meal*, in the Kingdom of the Father, and this confers on the words of institution their whole breadth as a fundamental statement of salvation-history: the present event of the Supper points to the death on the cross and to the fulfillment of redemption in the Kingdom of God. (The first reference is in Luke 22,15–18, and this is then repeated in the Petrine account of Mark 14,25 and Matt 26,29.)

(7) Especially in Paul—and developed in a new way in what are known as "farewell addresses" John gives us— we see expressed the theme of *communion with Christ* in the Supper Room as a communion with the crucified and risen Lord. The farewell addresses anchor this relation of communion in that communion that takes place in the eucharistic meal through the eating of the Flesh and the drinking of the Blood, and this has its historical analogy in the story of the manna (John 6,49–59).

These seven ideas come together into one unified understanding of the Eucharist. The question of whether these ideas derive from Christ or were formulated only by the post-paschal kerygma is to be answered by saying that the Church's "supper" and Jesus' historical Last Supper are viewed by the biblical accounts in such an intimate relationship that the ecclesial meal has its meaning only in the light of Jesus' historical Supper and, likewise, the historical meal is portrayed in the light of the Church's supper.

B. PATRISTIC THEOLOGY

The first post-biblical writing that deals with the Eucharist is the *Didache* (chaps. 9 and 10): Here the Eucharist is called an "offering" or "sacrifice" with reference to Mal 1,11; and the prayers that are here provided are clearly agapê-type prayers. Ignatius of Antioch (d. 115) describes the Eucharist as the "flesh of Christ's passion" (*Smyrn.* 7, 1: PG 5, 713) and as "food of immortality" (*Eph* 20, 2: PG 5, 661), and he emphasizes the Eucharist's power to establish unity in the community (*Philad.* 4: PG 5, 700).

(1) The Eastern Church: To understand the further development of what is given us in revelation, we must note that the Eucharist is not only a doctrine and a practice, an object of scriptural commentary and of preaching—above all in the context of paschal sermons on the texts of the Last Supper (John Chrysostom, d. 407, and Cyril of Alexandria, d. 444)—but that it also is the fundamental idea and the interpretation of the Church's liturgy in its most central cultic event (cf. the sermons on the Eucharist of Pseudo-Cyril [John] of Jerusalem, d. 387, and of Theodore of Mopsuestia, d. 428). In all these writings the theology of the Eucharist is decisively shaped by contemporary christology and soteriology. A certain synthesis of eucharistic doctrines is attempted already by Gregory of Nyssa (d. 394) (*Or. cat.* 37: PG 45, 93–97), and later by John Damascene (d. 749) (*De fide orth.* IV 13: PG 94, 1137–1153). The presentation of the eucharistic celebration as liturgy first emerges in the *First Apology* of Justin Martyr (d. 165) (Chap. 66: PG 6, 428) and in the *Apostolic Constitutions* of the fifth century (VIII, chaps. 6–15: *Klementinische Liturgie*, ed. F. X. Funk, 46off.), and is developed by the explanation of this Liturgy by Pseudo-Dionysius around 520 (*De eccl. hier.* III, 1: PG 3, 424ff.), whose work is continued by Theodore of Andida (PG 140, 424ff.) in the seventh century and in the Middle Ages by Nicholas Cabasilas (d. 1390) (PG 150, 368–492) and Simeon of Thessalonica (d. 1429) (PG 155, 176–237). In all this literature the Eucharist is seen as the cultic actualization and representation (i.e., the making present)—effected by the action of the Church and the risen Lord himself—of the person of the Lord, of his re-

demptive sacrifice, and of the salvation given with it. The basis and guarantee for this actualization is the *anamnesis*,[5] that is, the fulfillment of Christ's action at the Last Supper by obedience to his command (Luke 22, 19; 1 Cor 11, 24ff.; Heb. 10, 3). The action of the Church and the objects of this action appear within this "memorial celebration" as "symbols," that is, as real modes and means for the manifestation and representation of the historical event and its objects. The anamnesis is also the basis for the "sacrificial character" of the eucharistic celebration, firmly invoked starting with *Didache* 15.1 with its reference to Mal 1,11, even if the Eucharist can be only the "sacramental" actualization of the absolutely unique, "historical" redemptive sacrifice of Christ (Heb 10,10.14; 9,12). The interpretive model for the manner in which the anamnesis has its effect is the image of the "incarnation"[6]; that is, the change of the elements is a real mystery like the Incarnation of the Logos.

Necessary to the completion of the anamnesis is the so-called *epiclesis*, that is, the invocation of the Spirit that he, who brought about the incarnation in Mary, may here too bring about the presence of Christ and of his redemptive sacrifice in the action of bread and wine. The event and the effect of this anamnesis are interpreted differently by the different theological schools. For the Platonizing *Alexandrian theologians*, the Eucharist too is determined by the "Logos' becoming flesh." The goal of the Eucharist is spiritual communion with the Logos, which is also made possible by reading the Scripture and by prayer. The sacramental means to this is the eating of the flesh, which becomes present by the "transformation" of the bread.[7] A grand summary of these doctrines is offered later on by John Damascene (d. 749) (*De fide orth.* IV, 13: PG 94, 1135ff.). In this more ontological and idealistic approach of the Alexandrians, the memorial of Christ's death retreats markedly into the background.

The other main school, that of the *Antiochians*, deeply

influenced by Aristotle, thinks more historically and real-
istically and is therefore more interested in the identity of
the eucharistic with the historical Body of Christ, especially John Chrysostom (d. 407), whose viewpoint merited
him in the Latin Middle Ages the name of *Doctor eu-
charisticus.* Extreme representatives of this Antiochian
school, such as Nestorius (d. 451) and Theodoret of Cyrr-
hus (d. 466), among others, apply Chalcedonian christology so rigorously to the Eucharist that the formula *un-
changeable* (ἀτρέπτως), understood and taught with full
earnestness, is taken to mean that no transformation takes
place in the bread, but that rather the bread, remaining
bread, is filled with the spirit or the grace of the redemption. The so-called Liturgies of St. Basil and St. John
Chrysostom, which reached their full development in the
ninth century, are quite explicit, each in its own way, in ex-
pressing in their anaphora and epiclesis prayers the faith in
the change that takes place in the bread and the wine.

(2) The Western Church: In the West, by contrast to
Alexandria, an interest in the question of Christ's *real
presence* occupies the foreground of discussion from the
outset.[8] Bread and wine, already as such, symbolize the
Passion of Christ since already in the Old Testament (according to Jer 11,19: *mittamus lignum in panem eius*) they
appear as salvation-historical signs of the relationship between the eucharistic bread and the Passion.[9] Particular realism is exhibited by the eucharistic *theology of transformation* of Ambrose (d. 397).[10] It was Augustine (d. 431)
who brought the problems of Platonic-Alexandrian theology into the Western doctrine of the Eucharist. Alongside
the realistic doctrine of Ambrose on the sacramental presence of Christ in the Eucharist,[11] Augustine sees the *Mystical Christ in the Mystical Body of the Church,* and therefore the Church itself, as symbolized in the Eucharist.[12]
Isidore of Seville (d. 636) does indeed speak often in the
language of Augustinian symbolism, but what he is actually teaching is the real metabolism of Ambrose.[13]

C. THE CAROLINGIAN PERIOD

Until the innovations of the Carolingian period, the deep eucharistic doctrine of the early Church was conveyed practically above all in the textbooks for the eucharistic cult known as *sacramentaries,* as well as in the different *commentaries* on these books, especially in the theologically sober commentary of Florus of Lyons (d. 860) (PL 119, 15–72). It is Amalarius of Metz (d. 850) (PL 105, 985–1242; cf. PL 119, 71–96) who inaugurated the purely allegorical interpretation of the texts, and this had dire consequences for the understanding of the Mass of the entire Middle Ages.

During this period the doctrine of the Eucharist undergoes a further and decisive development in the Western Church on the occasion of a *first eucharistic controversy.* The stimulus for this came from the first monograph on the subject by Abbot Paschasius Radbertus of Corbie (d. 850).[14] In contrast to the then-dominant Augustianian language, this writer affirmed the identity between the historical and the sacramental Body of Christ, in order thus to determine more closely the reality of his presence in the Eucharist. Rabanus Maurus (d. 856) and John Scotus Erigena (d. 877) react against such an affirmation in the name of the symbolic explanation given by the Augustinian tradition. To the question of Emperor Charles the Bald as to whether the Body and Blood of Christ are received in communion *in mysterio an in veritate,* Ratramnus (d. after 868) answers that the change does not occur *corporaliter* but rather *spiritualiter,* and that consequently the presence of Christ must be understood *figurate.*[15] Thus, the ametabolic character of the Augustinian interpretation is developed into an antimetabolic character. Radbertus takes a position against this by arguing that *figura* may be united with *veritas* (*Ep. ad Chrudegardum:* PL 120, 1351–1366).

These arguments had opened the way for a new explanation, but the problem that had emerged remained to be discussed in a *second eucharistic controversy*. A new theological answer was achieved at the end of this debate when the eucharistic change came to be described with the apparently philosophical term *transsubstantiatio*, which in fact was meant with reference to salvation-history. Berengar, the erudite leader of the cathedral school of Tours (d. 1088), basing himself on his dialectical theology, proposed a doctrine that culminated in a kind of dynamic symbolism. In order to safeguard the uniqueness of Christ's sacrifice, he declared that the Mass is to be understood as a symbolic memorial celebration. His first opponents, Hugh of Langres (d. 1051) (PL 142, 1325–1334) and Durandus of Troarn (d. 1088) (PL 149, 1375–1424), revitalized the realism of Radbertus by teaching that the real Body of Christ is touched and broken by the hands of the priest and crushed by the teeth of the faithful, which shows the terribly primitive character of the metabolic theology of that time. Then came Lanfranc of Canterbury (d. 1089) (PL 150, 407–442) and Guitmund of Aversa (d. 1095) (PL 149, 1427–1494), and especially Anselm of Laon (d. 1117) (PL 149, 435–436), Alger of Liège (d. 1132) (PL 180, 739–860), and Gregory of Bergamo (d. 1146), all of whom, among others, by their distinguishing *substance* from *accident*, prepared the way for the effective use of the term *transsubstantiatio*, a word that had been in use since about 1150 and now became the key word for the interpretation of the event of the change in the Eucharist. Special attention must be called to the Fourteen Chapters in which Hugh of St. Victor (d. 1141) (PL 176, 461–472) exposes his doctrine of the Eucharist and shows with particular clarity the identification in salvation-history of the historical Christ with the eucharistic Lord. The development of the doctrine of transubstantiation at this time, and the influence of Hugh of St. Victor, are shown by the numerous "sentence" works of the period (*summa sententiarum, sententiæ divinitatis,* and so on), by the work of the school of Gilbert of Poitiers (d. 1154), to which the book of *Sentences* of Peter Lombard (d. 1160)[16] is much indebted, as well as by the great summas of the time (Praepositinus of Cremona (d. 1210); William of Auxerre, (d. 1237), by the opuscula *De mysterio missæ* and *De corpore domini* of Albert the Great (d. 1280), and by the treatise *De sacramento eucharistiæ* of William of Auvergne (d. 1249). Particularly significant in this context was the influence of Pope Innocent III (1198–1216), who composed a great commentary on the Mass entitled *De sacro altaris mysterio libri sex.* The Fourth Book of this work ("On the Eucharist": PL 217, 763–916) already contains the fully explicit doctrine of transubstantiation, and it was under the governance of this pope during the Fourth Lateran Council of 1215 that the term first appears in an official decree of the Church (D 430; cf. 414ff.–DS 802; 782ff.).

E. THE HIGH SCHOLASTIC PERIOD

The great developments of High Scholasticism have to do above all with the further clarification of the doctrine of transubstantiation, which was intended to elucidate the particular form of the sacramental presence of the risen Lord and of his historically unrepeatable sacrifice. They also have to do with the new form acquired by the *eucharistic cult,* which now spread because of the introduction by Pope Urban IV in 1264 of the Feast of Corpus Christi, a move impelled by the private revelations of the Augustinian nun Juliana of Liège (d. 1258). This cult of the Eucharist itself was based on the doctrine of transubstantiation, which was more and more becoming the absolute point of reference. The broad and deep eucharistic theology of this time found its highest expression above all in the office composed by Thomas Aquinas (d. 1274) for the

Feast of Corpus Christi, with the sequence *Lauda Sion* and the hymns *Pange lingua, Sacris solemniis*, and *Verbum supernum*. It was only since the middle of the twelfth century that it became customary to light candles and to bend the knee before the Blessed Sacrament, reserved in ever more ornamental little houses since the early Gothic period, as well as to elevate the transformed species at the consecration of Holy Mass for the faithful to view them. The eucharistic cult spread throughout the whole West within only one generation, which is a sign for the fact that the Church's liturgy corresponded to a general tendency among the people. The doctrine of transubstantiation, however, more and more was becoming an almost wholly philosophical speculation concerning the relationship of substance and accident and the question of space and time in the event of transformation within the Mass. In J. Duns Scotus (d. 1308) we already see the theory of "adduction" replacing Thomas Aquinas' theory of transubstantiation, and with the nominalistic understanding of substance of William of Ockham (d. 1349: substance is determined by quantity) the doctrine of the Eucharist more and more came to lose its relationship to the historical event of redemption and to the question of salvation through the sacrament. In consequence, the allegorical explanation of the Mass introduced by Amalarius of Metz became so dominant that in the fourteenth and fifteenth centuries the Mass was no longer understood, not only by the simple people but even by theology itself. We therefore see the first erroneous doctrines developing already in the fourteenth century.

F. ERRONEOUS DOCTRINES ON THE EUCHARIST AND THE MASS UP TO THE TIME OF THE REFORMATION

The first signs of decline were seen especially in the case of John Wycliffe (d. 1384), who fought vigorously against the *doctrine of transubstantiation* (calling it a heretical and devilish invention) and whose doctrines were condemned in 1382 in Oxford, Canterbury, and London. In 1415 the Council of Constance condemned Wycliffe's four erroneous propositions: (1) The bread and wine are not changed, (2) because accidents that remain the same cannot exist without their natural substance; (3) therefore, Christ is not present *identice et realiter* (*in*) *propria præsentia corporali*; (4) the mass is an invention of the Church (D 581–DS 1151–1158). John Hus (d. 1415), or at least his followers, demanded the *laity's partaking of the chalice* in order for the sacrament to be valid. The Council of Constance rejected this demand on the basis of the fullness of the Eucharist in the form of bread alone (D 626–DS 1198–1200). What had been only a matter of church discipline thus became a dogmatic decision, and the weakening of the doctrine of transubstantiation resulted in the liturgical symbolism of the sacrament becoming obscured. In 1518 and 1519 Martin Luther (d. 1546) still had written treatises on the Eucharist along fully Catholic lines. Only in 1520 did he begin speaking of the "three captivities of the Church" in *De captivitate babylonica* (WA 6, 497–573): (1) the denial of the chalice to the laity; (2) the insistence on transubstantiation, while he himself adhered now to Wycliffe's doctrine of "impanation"; (3) the doctrine of the Mass as being a good work and a sacrifice. Still more violently did he fight against the Mass in 1522 in *De abroganda missa privata*, "that private Masses ought to be done away with" (WA 8, 413–481; 482–503). Even though Luther did teach at times that Christ is present only at the moment of reception, or explain Christ's presence with the erroneous idea of the ubiquity of the resurrected Body, nevertheless, in the name of the word of Scripture itself, he always held firmly to the real presence of the Lord in the sacrament; this can best be seen in his confession "On Christ's Supper" of 1528 against the doctrine of Oecolampadius (WA 26, 261–509; Cat. Major p. V. of 1529). For

Huldrich Zwingli (d. 1531) the Eucharist was only a sign of belonging to the Church, and John Calvin (d. 1564) interpreted the presence of Christ in a purely symbolic manner (*Institutio* IV, 17: Eucharist; 18: the Mass). He rejected the Mass in the most strenuous terms. The first and best known rebuttals of these new doctrines of the Reformation, those of Thomas Murner (d. 1537) and John Eck (d. 1543), were not able to demonstrate the identity between the Sacrifice of the Mass and the Sacrifice of the Cross adequately. The learned refutations of Kaspar Schatzgeyer, O.F.M. (d. 1527) and Cardinal Cajetan (d. 1534) were of a much higher theological quality but also much less known.

G. THE COUNCIL OF TRENT

From the moment it opened, the Council of Trent enunciated these important Catholic doctrines, but it needed a longer period of preparation before it could deal with them adequately. In 1551 (Session 13) it examined the doctrine of the Eucharist, especially the real presence of Christ in the sacrament, and in 1562 (Session 21) it discussed communion under one species and especially the Sacrifice of the Mass as a relative sacrifice in relation to the one absolute sacrifice of Jesus Christ on the cross (D 873a–893, 929a–956–DS 1635–1661, 1725–1754). Even though the Council elaborated the individual doctrines clearly and unambiguously, nonetheless its separating the matter of communion from the matter of the Sacrifice of the Mass had ominous consequences in the following centuries for the total understanding of the Eucharist. This imbalance manifested itself especially when one began to explain the sacrifice of the Mass after the Council, which had declared the Mass to be a real but relative sacrifice that had always to be interpreted in relation to Christ's sacrifice on the Cross. Vásquez (d. 1604) and the Thomists who followed him attempted to explain this "relative, representative, symbolic sacrifice" more precisely (*theories on the sacri-*

fice of the Mass). The separation of bread and wine, body and blood, was seen as the sacramental sign for the death of Christ. Still more pointed was the attempt by Suarez (d. 1619) and his Jesuit followers to explain the sacrifice of the Mass by an aspect of *destruction* of the species. Subsequently, his doctrine was resurrected above all by Cardinal J. B. Franzelin (d. 1887). Contrasting this whole tendency, the French School (Cardinal de Bérulle [d. 1629], J. J. Olier [d. 1657]) concentrated more on Christ's personal sacrifice on the Cross and approached the Mass more through the aspect of *oblation.* V. Thalhofer (d. 1925) attempted to explain the sacrifice of the Mass in terms of Jesus Christ's heavenly sacrifice.

The Eucharist is, indeed, a sacrifice of its own particular kind, a memorial, representative, sacramental sacrifice that cannot be interpreted with a concept of sacrifice derived from the science of comparative religion but that must primarily come from the sacrificial act in salvation-history performed by God himself in Jesus Christ.

H. THE MODERN PERIOD

In more recent times a real deepening of the doctrine of the Eucharist has taken place through the application of the doctrine of sacrifice. The two great theologians who must here be mentioned are L. Billot (d. 1931) and M. de La Taille (d. 1933), who more than anyone in the last two centuries approached the Eucharist by working with the symbolic character of the sacramental sacrifice. Of special significance, too, was the *Liturgical Movement,* which began by studying the external form of the sacrament. In his work *Preparation for Holy Mass* (1922), R. Guardini saw the essential characteristic of the Eucharist as residing in its "character as a meal," and he was followed in this later by J. Pascher and others. The unhappy separation of meal and sacrifice that had dominated Catholic theology since the Council of Trent began to be overcome gradually only under the influence of the new ideas on salvation-history proposed above all by A. Vonier (d. 1938) and Odo Casel (d. 1948). Regardless of how questionable the sense of the "presence of the mysteries" may remain both liturgically and theologically, the lasting contribution of this theology is that it has given us new and badly needed insight into the interior cohesiveness of sacrifice and sacrament, of actual presence and real presence (J. Betz), in the one sacrificial meal.

The *Evangelical Churches in Germany* appointed a theological commission in the decade 1947–1957 to work through the newer exegesis of the eucharistic passages in Sacred Scripture. The result was the eight so-called "Arnoldshain Theses," which represent a common statement on the Eucharist. Here the Catholic doctrine of transubstantiation and the doctrine of the Sacrifice of Mass are emphatically rejected. The Fourth Thesis attempts a synthesis of Lutheran and Calvinist theology, when it says: "In his body, given over to death for all, and in his blood, poured out for all, the crucified and risen Lord, according to his word of promise, allows himself to be taken by us with bread and wine, and thus, by the power of the Holy Spirit, he takes us into the victory of his majesty, so that we, through faith in his promise, may come to have forgiveness of sin, life and bliss."

The Second Vatican Council in almost all its decrees stressed the great significance of the Eucharist both for the Church as People of God and for the individual. Also, the central concerns of the mystery theology of O. Casel, which seemed to have been somehow rejected by the encyclical *Mediator Dei* (1947), were now incorporated rather globally by both the language and the intention of the Council. In view of new and necessary attempts to gain fresh insight into the fundamental term *transubstantiation* as it can be understood (physically, not metaphysically) by the natural sciences today,[17] as well as in reaction to rash experimentation in the area of liturgical renewal,

Pope Paul VI again expounded the traditional doctrines in the encyclical *Mysterium fidei.*[18]

Under the influence of the mystery theology of Maria Laach, V. Warnach[19] and J. P. de Jong[20] have attempted to make the doctrine of transubstantiation useful for our time by developing a renewed concept of symbol, the so-called "symbol-reality."

I. ICONOGRAPHIC REFERENCES

The oldest illustrations are references to the particularity of the mystery, which combines elements of the event of the Last Supper with elements of relevant miracles of Jesus. Since these portrayals can be understood only when they have been interpreted, it is difficult to decide which illustrations are truly images of the Eucharist. Surely many drawings in the Roman catacombs belong in this class: first of all, the frequent portrayal of a basket of bread over a fish (the "chapel of the Eucharist" in Licina's crypt at the catacomb of Callistus), which unites the motif of the eucharistic bread with the miracle of the multiplication of the bread and illustrates the mystery of Christ and Christians with the symbol of the fish. This theme is often accompanied by pictures of vines and banquet scenes. Besides these symbols of "things" we also find—at least since the fourth century—symbols of "events" for the Eucharist, portrayals of the multiplication of the bread in which Christ blesses the bread and breaks it (catacomb of Domitilla), and of the miracle at Cana, where Christ changes the water into wine (catacomb of Priscilla). Generic portrayals of meals can be references both to the eucharistic banquet and to the Christian community meal, the agapê. Since the fourth century we find, alongside these types of drawings, either in isolation or in conjunction, portrayals of the sacrifice of Abel, the sacrifice of Isaac by Abraham, and the sacrifice of Melchizedek, which point to the eucharistic sacrifice insofar as this is seen as uniting

the themes of sacrifice pleasing to God (Abel), sacrifice of
one's own son (Isaac), and sacrifice of bread and wine
(Melchizedek). In the Eucharistic Prayer of the Roman
Mass these three themes are specifically united.[21] Since
the seventh century we encounter various historical portrayals of the eucharistic events themselves, above all the
Last Supper (around a table that is either square or in the
shape of a sigma) with washing of the feet[22] and, often in
the East, the Apostles receiving communion (paten of
Richa).

To all of this the Renaissance adds the picture of the disciples of Emmaus and, since the fourteenth century, we
begin to see various portrayals of the mystical theme of
John on the Lord's breast. As early as the twelfth century
there exist numerous illustrations on objects destined for
the eucharistic cult, such as tabernacles, chalices, monstrances, reredoses. We also have "poor people's bibles"
that take the form of illustrated bibles, and, finally, paint-
ings of the eucharistic cult itself (of which the best known
is Raphael's *Disputation*). Since the Late Middle Ages we
also have numerous representations of legends, such as
miracles involving hosts, miracles of the Precious Blood,
the Mass of St. Gregory, as well as symbolic portrayals of
the mystical wine-press (Isa 63,2; Rev 14, 19f.; 19,15) or the
threshing-floor (2 Sam 24,18–25), host-mills, and eucharistic symbols as attributes of saints (Clare, Barbara). A rich
cyclical portrayal with many allegories is offered by the designs for tapestries of P. P. Rubens' *Triumph of the Eucharist* (painted in 1627).

Modern Christian craftsmanship has created new symbolic forms and new figural ornamentation, especially for
cultic objects (chalices, monstrances, tabernacles), for instance the tabernacle in Himmelstadt that has a one red
crystal surrounded by twelve white crystals.[23]

I

The Meaning of the Sacramental Sign in the Eucharistic Mystery

Sacramental signs are not like road signs whose forms are independent of the size, distance, and direction of the place they indicate. Sacramental signs must rather be always understood and interpreted anew on the basis of the visible form, the historical and objective locus, and the reality of the thing signified, just as the thing indicated can and must always be understood anew in the light of this new understanding of the sign. Consequently, we must now attempt to understand the sacramental *signs* of the Eucharist, first, from the standpoint of their *historical and objective locus,* given us in Jesus' "promises" address and in the words of institution (1); second, we must examine their *specific visible form* (2), and, finally, their *unique meaning as sign.* This "meaning" is here specifically understood as the particular manner of the presence of Christ and his redemptive work in this eucharistic mystery for the salvation of humankind (3).

1. Toward an Understanding of the Words of Promise and Institution

The sign for the Eucharist is not primarily to be derived from what we see and experience today when we celebrate the Eucharist. We are to look for it rather in the accounts

of the Eucharist given to us in Scripture, which themselves
are to be elucidated from their respective contexts in salvation-history. An understanding of the sacramental sign
of the Eucharist gained in this manner then ought to become the standard by which to judge the sign as we experience it in our present worship, and the concrete eucharistic cult ought always to be continually reformed and
rectified on the basis of the scriptural sign.

A. JOHN 6: BREAD OF LIFE DISCOURSE

We will seek access to a preliminary understanding of
the sacramental sign of the Eucharist in what is perhaps
the latest text of the New Testament—the promises of the
Bread of Life Discourse—and we do this because John 6
reached its present form on the basis of theological concerns and difficulties stemming from the contemporary
world: here certain tendencies become manifest that are
also relevant for us today.

Expanding on John 4 (John 5 is rather a development of
John 6), John 6, 1–12 deals with the (first) *multiplication
of the bread*, of which the Synoptics too give accounts
(Mark 6,32–44; Matt 14,13–21; Luke 9,10–17). This event
took place shortly before the feast of Easter (John 6,4) on
the eastern shore of the Lake of Tiberias, near Bethsaida
(Luke 9,10). On the next day Jesus spoke in the synagogue
of Capharnaum on the western shore of the lake (John
6,59). The three fundamental thoughts of the discourse are
(1) *Jesus is himself the bread of life* that human beings
seek and the Father gives and that must be received with
faith in Jesus (John 6,12–51); (2) *Jesus gives himself* as the
bread of life to men and women, and indeed in such a way
that he gives his flesh (σάρξ) to eat (τρώγειν) and his blood
(αἷμα) to drink (πίνειν); (3) in this meal Christ proves himself to be *bread for the life of the world* (6,51), a bread in
which each person receives the divine life just as Christ
too has received life from the Father (6,57).

In the face of the doubt and the turning away of people
as a result of this incomprehensible discourse, Christ again
stresses the need of simple faith in his word (6,60–66), and
he places the Twelve before the decision that Peter answers with a vigorous confession of faith ("You have the
words of life": 6,66–71).

If it is licit to detect theological clues behind the juxtaposition of this address with the event of the multiplication of the bread, then we could see in the multiplication
of the bread an indication of Jesus' power over material
bread, in his walking on the lake an indication of Jesus'
power over his earthly body, and in the healing of sick persons by touching the "seam of Christ's garment" (mentioned in Mark 6,53–56 and Matt 14,34–36) an indication
of the power that goes out from the corporeal Christ.

"The Word became flesh" (John 1,14), and consequently
"faith in Christ" too must receive its "incarnation" in the
eucharistic meal.

B. ACCOUNTS OF THE INSTITUTION[24]

We possess four accounts concerning the institution of
the Eucharist in the course of the Last Supper. Of these,
two pairs are largely in accord with one another, the so-
called *Petrine account* (Mark 14,22–25 and Matt 26, 26–28)
and the so-called *Pauline account* (1 Cor 11, 23–25 and
Luke 22, 19–20).

The special content of the Petrine account appears to be
(a) that the indication that the words concerning the bread
were spoken "during the meal"; (b) that for the bread and
the cup the command was spoken: Take and eat (or drink);
(c) that the words concerning the blood are uttered in a
liturgical manner to parallel the words concerning the
bread (my body–my blood); (d) the reference to the eschatological meal in the Kingdom of the Father is connected
to the word concerning the cup, while in Luke it is found
before the meal, at the time of the first cup.

Matt 26, 26–28	Mark 14, 22–25	Luke 22, 19–20	1 Cor 11,23–25
			23 For I have received from the Lord what I have also passed on to you, that the Lord Jesus, on the night on which
26 But as they were eating, Jesus took bread, spoke the blessing (over it), broke it and gave it to the disciples with the words: Take, eat, this is my body.	22 And as they were eating, he took bread, spoke the blessing (over it), broke it and gave it to them with the words: Take, this is my body.	19 And he took bread, spoke the thanksgiving, broke it and gave it to them with the words: This is my body, which is given for you. Do this in remembrance of me!	he was betrayed, took 24 bread, spoke the thanksgiving, broke it and said: This is my body, (which is given) for you. Do this in remembrance of me!
27 And he took a cup, spoke the thanksgiving and gave it to them	23 And he took a cup, spoke the thanksgiving and gave it to them and they all drank from it.	20 And in the same manner (he took) after the meal the cup	25 In the same manner (he took) also the cup after the meal
with the words: Drink from it all of you; 28 for this is my "blood of the covenant" (Exod 24, 8; Jer 31, 31; Zach 9, 11),	24 And he said to them: This is my "blood of the covenant" (Exod 24, 8; Jer 31, 31; Zach 9, 11),	with the words: This cup is the New Covenant (which is sealed) through my	with the words: This cup is the New Covenant (which is sealed) through my

.

Accounts of the Institution of the Eucharist

Matt 26, 26–28	Mark 14, 22–25	Luke 22, 19–20	1 Cor 11,23–25
which is poured out for many for the forgiveness of sins.	which is poured out for many.	blood, which is poured out for you.	blood.
			Do this, as often as you drink (it), in remembrance of me!

By contrast, the characteristics of the Pauline account are (a) the clear indication of the sacrificial character of the meal, leading to salvation, and this already in the words concerning the bread (in the Petrine account they are found only in the words concerning the cup); (b) the indication that the words concerning the cup are spoken "after the meal" (at the time of the third cup, the "cup of blessing"); (c) the words concerning the cup have the form "This cup is the New Covenant" (the Petrine account speaks only of "blood of the covenant," Exod 24,8) in my blood (Luke adds "poured out for you"); (d) the command to continue celebrating this meal "in remembrance of him" (something that is lacking in Mark and Matthew, who apparently are taking such a practice for granted).

The question concerning the *historical phrasing* of the words of institution cannot be answered unequivocally. The answer cannot be attained only through chronological ordering (Paul–Mark–Matthew–Luke), or only with philological methods (where are the Aramaisms mostly to be found?), or only form-critical methods (which account is most closely dependent on the Jewish paschal meal?), or only with the methods of liturgical archæology (where can we identify clear liturgical prescriptions?). All these methods must be used conjointly. If the reference to Exod 24,8 in the words concerning the blood in the Petrine account appear to be genuine, the parallel formulation "my flesh–

my blood" appears conditioned by the liturgical practice of the primitive community, and the words concerning the cup in the Pauline account would have been more easily understood by the Apostles and not shocking. The theme of the sacrificial character of the meal, especially in the words concerning the cup, is suggested by the context of the paschal meal (cf. Exod 12,21 [*pascha*] = 1 Cor 5,7; Exod 29,18 [sacrifice as a pleasing odor] = Eph 5,2; cf. Gal 2,20) and is bound up with the theme of atonement ("for the many") according to Isa 53. The assertion that these "references" cannot be attributed to the "historical Jesus" (but only to the Apostles and the primitive community) is very unconvincing and appears unfounded: it would make the historical Jesus into a very weak figure and would claim a much stronger "spirit" for the Apostles and the primitive community than it is willing to concede the historical Jesus himself. To describe the Last Supper accounts of Mark 14,22 and 1 Cor 11,24 as mere "cultic legends or cultic ætiologies"[25] would be wholly to overlook the unequivocal historical intention of the Jesus-kerygma of the Apostles (Acts 1,21f.). Even the cultic "anamnesis," despite all its cultic development of form and even more of intended content, is at bottom seeking to make present a historical fact and its original salvific meaning.

C. THE LAST SUPPER, A PASCHAL MEAL

The account of the institution of the Eucharist becomes comprehensible when it is seen within the framework of the then-customary paschal meal as portrayed by the Synoptics and by Paul.[26]

A. Preparation: (a) The community gathered for the meal consists of 10 to 20 persons, the number that can consume a sacrificial animal: Jesus and his twelve Apostles; (b) A room is found in Jerusalem (Mark 14,12ff. and par.): a furnished dining-room acquired free of charge (Mark 14,15); (c) acquisition of the sacrificial animal by the father of the house or someone appointed by him during the four days before the feast. (This is not mentioned in the Gospels: Could it be that Jesus celebrated the Passover without a paschal lamb but instead used other roasted flesh, according to Law 123 concerning heretics, which forbade a paschal sacrifice to a heretic?[27]); (d) the lamb is slaughtered in the afternoon in the inner courtyard of the temple by those entrusted with the task; the blood is gathered up by the priests into bowls and is taken to the altar of holocausts while the Hallel psalms are sung (Pss 113–155); the whole sacrificial animal is then skinned and drawn, and is carried home in its own skin; (e) the animal is roasted over an open fire on a spit of pomegranate wood or in fire-clay pots. (Other flesh is also roasted!) Nowhere in the accounts of the Last Supper is there any explicit talk of this paschal lamb!

A Passover meal of Jesus with his Apostles in Jerusalem without a paschal lamb previously slaughtered in the temple would indeed have made Christ's reference to "my sacrificial flesh" and "my sacrificial blood" into even more of a reference to the new "Passover" or "Pasch" (1 Cor 5,7).

B. Unfolding of the paschal meal: (a) A sober attitude sets in, beginning at three in the afternoon. The meal is eaten between sunset and midnight, and four cups of wine are drunk during the meal.

(b) The first cup is mixed and handed about (cf. Luke 22,17: reference to the eschatological meal), perhaps in keeping with the word of blessing over the wine and the feast-day that usually follows.

(c) First course: bitter lettuce, dipped into sweet fruit compote (cf. Matt 26,23: the dish Judas "dipped into"?; John 13,26).

(d) The second cup is handed about while the leader of the meal recites the story of the Passover based on Deut 26,5–11. The story must at least touch upon the *pesach* (Exod 12,27), the *mazzoth* (Exod 12,39), and the *merorim* (Exod 1,14: the bitterness of captivity, from which God liberates).

(e) The leader of the meal breaks the bread and distributes it with the flesh of the paschal lamb, and he gives the sign to eat by himself beginning to eat. Christ distributes only the broken bread (without flesh), which he declares to be his own sacrificial flesh, and he *commands* his Apostles to eat since he himself apparently is not eating. Only afterward is the flesh eaten, by all together.

(f) Then the first Hallel psalm is prayed (Ps 115) and the third cup (the "cup of blessing") is distributed: either all drink from one larger chalice or the wine is poured into individual cups. They are then commanded to drink: either Christ himself does not drink or this command is a later liturgical addition.

(g) Other Hallel psalms are prayed (Pss 117, 118) while Christ and his Apostles leave the room of the Last Supper, so that the fourth cup is omitted.

C. What was the day of the Last Supper? Christ surely did not adhere to the so-called Essene (solar) calendar, but to the official (lunar) calendar of the temple, so that the fourteenth Nisan was a Friday. The four scenes of judgment (before Annas and Caiaphas, the Sanhedrin, Herod, and Pilate) took place from Thursday evening to Friday noon, if what was involved was a trial for high treason with summary court of justice. At the time of Christ, because of the great number of pilgrims, sacrifices were already offered in the temple beginning on Thursday (and not only on Friday, according to E. Stauffer), so that Christ could have celebrated with a sacrificial lamb on the Thursday evening. In the Essene calendar the fourteenth Nisan would have been a Tuesday, so that the judicial procedures could have been prolonged from Tuesday to Friday.[28]

D. Ideas and realities that Passover and Eucharist have in common: (a) point of departure in a real historical happening; (b) the event signifies redemption and salvation; (c) unity between the sacrifice in the one temple and the many sacrifices in the communities celebrating the sacrificial meal, just as the one sacrifice of Christ is present in the many "sacrifices" of the Church; (e) the memorial celebration is an actualization of the events remembered, both in the Old Testament and in the mystery of the New Covenant; (f) the Passover meal of the Old Covenant is a sacramental, while the eucharistic meal of the New Covenant is a sacrament.

D. OTHER NEW TESTAMENT TEXTS

a) In 1 Cor 8, 1–11.1 Paul deals with the question whether a Christian can partake of flesh that has been offered to idols; in chapter 10 he attempts to give a proof from Scripture. He first of all says that the downfall of many Israelites at the time of the exodus from Egypt, despite the manna, ought to be a warning (reference to Exod 14–17). The Christian may eat flesh offered to idols since idols are not real; but he can do this only if his action does not offend the love he owes his brother who may be weaker in faith. It is love that lays the norm, and not knowledge alone (1 Cor 8,1–3).

Indeed, the knowledge that the Christian celebration of the Eucharist unites one really to the flesh and blood of Christ even makes Paul develop a second argument against the eating of flesh offered to idols: Pagan sacrifices, too, are offered to realities, not to idols that are not real but to the corporeal demons. Thus he writes: "Therefore, my beloved, shun the worship of idols! . . . The cup of blessing which we bless, is it not a participation in the blood of Christ? The bread that we break, is it not a participation in the body of Christ? Because there is one bread, we who are many are one body, for we all partake of the one bread. Consider the people of Israel are not those who eat the sacrifices partners of the altar? What do I imply then? That food offered to idols is anything, or that an idol is anything? No, I imply that what pagans sacrifice they offer to demons and not to God. I do not want you to be partners with demons. You cannot drink the cup of the Lord and the cup of demons. You cannot partake of the table of the Lord and the table of demons" (1 Cor 10,14.16–21) This is why Christians, even if they are invited by a pagan, cannot eat of sacrificial flesh if their host has expressly told them it is sacrificial flesh. Eating is here forbidden the Christian "for the sake of the host's conscience." The Eucharist is here clearly characterized as a *sacrificial meal.* 1 Cor 11 cannot be understood without 1 Cor 10!

b) In this context we must also mention Heb 13,10: "We have an altar from which those who serve the tent have no right to eat." On this much debated text O. Kuss says: "We have the perfect sacrifice that imparts definitive reconciliation on the altar of the Cross on Golgotha. No one partakes of its fruit of salvation who still clings directly or indirectly to the old order of salvation, fraught with shadows, which is henceforth wholly useless."[29] O. Michel brings this text into direct relationship with the eucharistic meal, with reference to 1 Cor 10,18 and 11,26, and he writes, "We are dealing here with a fundamental cultic principle that originally excluded Jewish priests from the meal of the Lord."[30]

c) Acts 2,42 also belongs with this group of texts: "They [the first Christians] met constantly to hear the apostles teach, and to share the common life, to break bread, and to pray." "Breaking of bread" and "prayer" must here refer to the cultic life of the primitive Church, in which the Eucharist occupied the central place. As in 1 Cor 10,16, "breaking of bread" should here be understood to mean the Eucharist.

2. The Particular Shape of the External Sign in the Eucharistic Sacrament

1. In keeping with our viewpoint of today, we will first approach the Eucharist in its widest sense as the center of the Church's worship. We must then say that what belongs primarily to the specific shape taken by the external

sign of this cultic act are the ordained priest, the priestly People of God, the service of prayers and readings, and the sacrificial celebration itself. For this sacrificial celebration, moreover, the constitutive elements are the sacrifice and the sacrificial meal. These "external signs" are the efficacious cause and the guarantee for the fact that, in this celebration, the historical Last Supper and, through it, the sacrifice of the Cross on Golgotha, become events for us in such a way that we come to partake of the sacrificial meal of Christ's sacrifice. The very heart of the sacramental effect and reality is the presence of the eucharistic Lord as sacrificing priest and as sacrificial offering, as Redeemer and mediator to the Father, and as head of the "Body of Christ," of Christ's community as Church, which is always renewing itself in this celebration.

2. If we understand the Eucharist in the more narrow sense as the "sacrament" of communion, then our question about the form taken by the external sign has to do exclusively with the species of communion: bread and wine. On this point the Church teaches as follows:

A. The matter necessary for the validity of the sacrificial sacrament of the Eucharist is bread (wheat bread) and wine (grape wine).

The reason for this unequivocal doctrine of the ancient Church in both East and West is to be found in the accounts of the Last Supper (see III.1.), according to which Christ himself celebrated the meal with this matter and commanded his Apostles to continue doing the same thing in remembrance of him (1 Cor 11,24; Luke 22,19: concerning the bread; 1 Cor 11,25: concerning the cup). From the very outset the Church acted in keeping with this principle, and already in the second and third centuries[31] opposed those who wanted to depart from this practice. In the course of the Church's history, a specific difference such as the use of leavened or unleavened bread became an object of dogmatic controversy between East and West on the occasion of the Schism.

The Roman Church has affirmed these doctrines expressly since the Middle Ages. Thus, in 1202 Innocent III responds as follows to a question concerning the words *mysterium fidei:* "Dicitur tamen 'mysterium fidei', quoniam et aliud ibi creditur, quam cernatur, et aliud cernitur, quam credatur. Cernitur enim species panis et vini, et creditur veritas carnis et sanguinis Christi ac virtus unitatis et caritas. . . . Forma est panis et vini, veritas carnis et sanguinis, virtus unitatis et caritatis. Primum est 'sacramentum et non res'. Secundum est 'sacramentum et res'. Tertium est 'res et non sacramentum'": "It is called a 'mystery of faith' because one thing is believed and another seen, one thing is seen and another believed. What we see is the form of bread and wine, and what we believe is the truth of Christ's flesh and blood as well as the effect of unity and love. . . . The species are those of bread and wine; the truth (or reality) is that of flesh and blood; the effect is that of unity and love. The first is 'sacramentum et non res'; the second is 'sacramentum et res'; the third is 'res et non sacramentum'" (D 414ff.–DS 782f.).

The Fourth Lateran Council of 1215 says concerning the Church: "In qua idem ipse sacerdos est sacrificium Jesus Christus, cuius corpus et sanguis in sacramento altaris sub speciebus panis et vini veraciter continentur, transsubstantiatis pane in corpus et vino in sanguinem potestate divina: ut ad perficiendum mysterium unitatis accipiamus ipsi de suo, quod accepit ipse de nostro": "In it [the Church] the priest himself is the sacrifice, Jesus Christ, whose body and blood are truly present in the sacrament of the altar under the species of bread and wine, since the bread has been changed ['transubstantiated'] into the body and the wine into the blood by the power of God; this has been done so that, in order to realize the mystery of unity, we may receive from him [the substance] that he has first received from us" (D 430–DS 802).

At the Council of Florence (1439) the controversy between East and West is put aside with this formulation "In

azymo sive fermentato pane triticeo corpus Christi veraciter confici; sacerdotesque in altero ipsorum domini
corpus conficere debere, unumquemque scilicet iuxta suæ
ecclesiæ sive occidentalis sive orientalis consuetudinem":
"The body of Christ is truly made present in either unleavened or leavened wheat bread, and the priests should
make present the body of Christ, each in his own bread, according to the custom [rite] of his own church, whether
Western or Eastern (D 692–DS 1303).

At this same time the Decree for the Armenians states:
"Tertium est eucharistiæ sacramentum, cuius materia est
panis triticeus, et vinum de vite, cui ante consecrationem
aqua modicissima admisceri debet": "The third [sacra-
ment] is the sacrament of the Eucharist, whose matter is
wheat bread and grape wine with which a very little water
should be mixed before the consecration" (D 698–DS
1320).

The following specific things are to be said concerning
these requirements for the matter of the Eucharist:

a) *The [1917] Code of Canon Law* (can. 814–816) requires
"wheat bread." Bread from other grains (barley, rye, oats,
buckwheat, etc.) is not allowed (D 692, 698–DS 1303,
1320–1322). In the *Roman Missal* of 1670 we read concerning this matter in the paragraph entitled "De defectibus
Missæ" (§ 3): "Si panis non sit triticeus . . . non conficitur
sacramentum." The *Roman Missal* of 1969 says in Number
282 of the "General Institution": "Panis . . . debet esse triticeus, iuxta traditionem totius Ecclesiæ, et azymus iuxta
traditionem Ecclesiæ latinæ."

b) For the *Western Church* the use of "unleavened bread"
(*azyma*) is prescribed, and "leavened bread" (*enzyma*) is
forbidden, although it is expressly stated that the validity of
the sacrament in no way depends on this. Since 1054,
(Michael Caerularius) the use of unleavened bread by the
Western Church has been criticized by the Greek Church
to the point of being condemned, and the Eucharist con-
fected with unleavened bread has mostly been declared to

be invalid; and yet this declaration seems to intend not so much the "validity" as the "licitness" of such a eucharistic celebration. The Eastern Church defends its leavened bread by referring to the fact that (1) Melchizedek surely used leavened bread, and that (2) only leavened bread, being "living" bread, can be a sign for the living Christ in the Eucharist. The Western Church, on the other hand, defends its use of unleavened bread (1) by pointing to the fact that Christ used unleavened bread at the Last Supper (Mark 14,12; Matt 26,17; Luke 22,7: "on the first day of the unleavened bread"). In the Old Testament *mazzoth,* that is, unleavened bread, was prescribed for all sacrifices (Exod 23,18; 34,25; Lev 2.4,11; 7.12; 8.2). (2) Fermentation was seen as decay, and thus *enzyma* or leavened bread was regarded allegorically as a sign of sin and evil (Matt 16,6,12; 1 Cor 5,7f.). Nonetheless, because of the ancient traditions that use both kinds of bread, the Western Church has always recognized them both as valid matter.

c) More in general we can say that the matter for the Eucharist must in any case be bread and not some other matter such as cheese or bread baked with other ingredients such as was the usage of Gnostic sects in the second and third centuries. As early as the Middle Ages (*Summa theol.* III, q.74, a.3) the question emerged whether "wheat bread" was absolutely required on dogmatic grounds, under danger of incurring invalidity, or whether bread made from "leguminous fruits common in a district" would suffice for validity. Thomas says that the bread must consist "primarily" of wheat flour, but that other kinds of flour could be mixed with it. This answer contradicts the tradition. The question remains, however, whether the reasons given by the Western Church for the strict use of "wheat bread" are so weighty as to be final, or whether the Church could not in exceptional cases allow the use of bread made from different kinds of grain according to geographic region. In light of the openness of travel and commerce in today's world, it would seem that the question of "expediency" can by rights be asked of the tradition alongside the questions of "objective validity" and of "ecclesiastical law and custom" (*Summa theol.* III, q. 74, a.1, ad 2).

d) Likewise, natural and pure grape wine is required as valid matter (Matt 26,29; Mark 14,25; Luke 22,18). In keeping with the Eastern custom, some water is mixed with the wine. Wine is the valid matter; the addition of water is required for the licitness, but not the validity, of the sacrament. (a) Ever since the time of Cyprian, the Church has always opposed those who prescribed the use of "water" or other non-alcoholic drinks instead of wine as valid matter (such persons are called "aquarians" or "hydroparastates") (D 876, 945 –DS 1639, 1748). (b) When in an emergency no water is mixed with the wine, the sacrament is not thereby rendered invalid. (c) As with the bread, the question whether wine is necessarily required must be answered in the affirmative. The other question whether it must be grape wine is to be left to the free determination of the Church, even if, as with the bread, the question of expediency is not easy to answer, since the use of any other kind of wine would be a departure from an ancient and closed tradition. (d) The question of the color of the wine (red as a sign of Christ's blood), which has variously emerged during controversies between the churches, is, objectively speaking, insignificant.

B. Form: "The form of the sacrificial sacrament is constituted by the words with which Christ gave his Apostles his body and blood at the Last Supper and which have been handed down in the Canon of the Mass."

This doctrine is expounded with clarity by Innocent III in 1202 in a letter to Archbishop John of Lyons, and the pope compares the words of the Canon in detail with the words of the Gospel. He expressly stresses the fact that, even though the words concerning the chalice in the Canon of the Mass cannot be shown to derive from any one Gospel account, and even though they contain elaborations, nonetheless the phrase *mysterium fidei* within the consecration ought not to be interpreted as meaning that what becomes present is only the *imago, species,* and *figura* of Christ's sacrifice; rather, it is the *veritas* of the sacrifice that is made present and actualized (PL 214, 1119–1121). When in the fifteenth century the controversy broke out between the Eastern and the Western Church concerning the form of the sacrament, the Decretum pro Armeniis (1439) declared expressly: "Forma huius sacramenti sunt verba salvatoris, quibus hoc confecit sacramentum; sacerdos enim in persona Christi loquens hoc conficit sacramentum. Nam ipsorum verborum virtute substantia panis in corpus Christi et substantia vini in sanguinem convertuntur": "The form of this sacrament is the words of the Savior, whereby he accomplished [instituted] this sacrament. For the priest accomplishes this sacrament by speaking in the place of Christ [*in persona Christi*]. For it is by the power of the words themselves that the substance of bread is changed into the body of Christ and the substance of wine is changed into his blood" (D 698–DS 1321). The same teaching is found in the Decretum pro Jacobitis (D 715–DS 1352ff.).

In the Roman Liturgy the words concerning the bread are "Hoc est enim corpus meum," to which the new Canons add "quod pro vobis tradetur." And the words concerning the wine: "Hic est enim calix sanguinis mei, novi et æterni testamenti, (mysterium fidei) qui pro vobis et pro multis effundetur in remissionem peccatorum. (Hæc quotiescumque feceritis, in mei memoriam facietis)."

a) The words with which Christ gave the bread and the cup to his Apostles were also the words of consecration.

Before his elevation to the papacy, Innocent III had held the following opinion, derived in part from Stephen of Autun (d. 1139) and Praepositinus of Cremona (d. 1200), among others: Christ effected the transformation in silence when he blessed the bread (εὐλογήσας), and when he handed the changed species to the Apostles he declared that this was his flesh and blood. This opinion is in no way based on Scripture; it does not fit the Aramaic phrasing; and it stands in contradiction to the tradition of the Church and to the express formulations of the ecclesiastical decrees enumerated previously. The liturgical character of the Last Supper, too, requires that these words be not merely words of explanation but "words of accomplishment."

b) At least since the fourth century different conceptions of the *form* of the eucharistic sacrament predominate in the Eastern and Western Churches. Until this time there was general agreement that what was necessary and efficacious for the eucharistic celebration was the actualization of the event of the Last Supper—that is, of the account of the institution of the Eucharist as a whole—performed and uttered following the Lord's command. Beginning in the fourth century, however, it became more and more customary to add to this account of eucharist institution a sacrificial prayer of entreaty either to the Logos or to the Spirit. John Damascene expressly says that the efficacious formula of consecration is to be seen in the words of institution as spoken by the priest following Christ's command, but that the agent who effects the change is the Holy Spirit, who also effected the incarnation of the Logos in Mary (PG 94, 1140ff.). The subsequent prayer to the Holy Spirit—the so-called *consecration epiclesis*—asking him to "sanctify" the species over which the words of consecration have already been spoken, is first found in Cyril of Jerusalem (d. 387) (*Cat. myst.* V, 7; PG 33, 1113–1116) and then especially in the Syrian liturgies. In the *liturgies of Egypt and of Rome (Const. Apost.* VIII). this prayer is found before the words of consecration and it here has the character of a *communion epiclesis:* that is, it is a prayer that the Eucharist may bring salvation to its recipient through the action of the Holy Spirit. The "consecration epiclesis" became an object of controversy especially after the fourteenth century, when it was no longer regarded liturgically but only as a question of sacramental theology and when the East began attributing to it more and more the specific power of consecration. In the background of this development in the East we have the understanding of the Eucharist current there, as represented by a Theodore of Mopsuestia (d. 428) (*Hom. cat.* 15 and 16: *Studi e Testi,* 145: 465ff., 533ff.). He identified two parts of the Canon. The first part actualizes the Lord's death in a sacramental manner, through the recitation of the account of institution and through the separation of the species. The second part symbolizes the Lord's resurrection and exaltation. This second phase culminates in the epiclesis and in the mixing of the eucharistic species, an action that symbolically represents Christ's *transfiguratio.* Thus, here too the so-called "consecration epiclesis" practically becomes a "communion epiclesis" that guarantees that we receive Christ's spiritual nourishment in the Spirit.

In this sense, the Nestorians tended to understand what we receive in communion more as the *Kyrios exaltatus* (and communion, therefore, as the food of immortality), whereas the Greek Fathers saw it more as the *Logos incarnatus* (and communion as a communion in the Logos). In any case, in the *Eastern Church* the epiclesis subsequently came more and more to be seen as the element that actually effects the sacrifice. In the *West,* especially since the twelfth century, the sacrificial death was primarily attributed *vi verborum* to the effect of the words of institution, while the transfigured Lord is present in the transformed species *vi concomitantiæ,* and in the communion he makes the receiver a partaker in his own glorification. In this way, the two phases that Theodore of Mopsuestia had distinguished in his eucharistic theology were put together in the account of institution, and the eucharistic celebration became purely and exclusively a "sacrificial celebration." This development in the Western Church derived especially from Paschasius Radbertus (d. 860) (*De corpore et sanguine Domini,* c. 15, n. 1: PL 120, 1322) and Peter Lombard (*Sent.* IV, d 8 c 4).

On this point we should say that the *epiclesis* as prayer

of entreaty has no basis in the scriptural accounts and shows no trace in the Last Supper. Consequently, at the Councils of Union the Western Church always sought from the Eastern Church the recognition of the fact that the sacrifice of the Mass occurred by virtue of the words of institution (D 698, 715–DS 1320, 1352ff.). Nonetheless, if Theodore of Mopsuestia's teaching on the two phases of the Eucharist is an adequate analysis of the eucharistic sacrifice (and the distinction between sacrifice and sacrificial meal is certainly drawing great attention in today's understanding of the liturgy), the Western Church must still respond to the question of a solid communion epiclesis. The new Eucharistic Prayers offer a clear consecration epiclesis and communion epiclesis.[32] (See Appendix to the text, page 371.)

c) Of absolute necessity for the consecration are the following words: "Hoc est corpus meum—Hic est sanguis meus." Thomas is of the opinion that the whole addendum to the words of consecration for the chalice are necessary for the sacrificial character of the Mass (*Summa theol.* III, q. 78, a.3), but this cannot be correct since the Eastern Churches do not have most of this addendum and their eucharistic liturgy has always been held to be valid by the Western Church.

As example of an *epiclesis* from the Eastern Churches we here quote that of the *Liturgy of St. John Chrysostom:* "We ask and pray and entreat Thee: send down Thy Holy Spirit upon us and upon these gifts here offered on the altar. Bless the holy bread, Lord, and make this bread the precious body of Thy Christ! Amen!—Bless, Lord, the holy chalice and make what is in this chalice the precious blood of Thy Christ! Amen!—Bless both things, Lord, and change them by Thy Holy Spirit! Amen! Amen! Amen!"

d) In the history of theology a problem had already been discussed in the Middle Ages that acquired new relevance with the liturgical reforms of the Second Vatican Council: the question of the correct dogmatic understanding of *con-*

celebration. From the outset the Eucharist was understood to be the Church's central act of worship, accomplished by the presider of the community and celebrated with him by the whole community. In keeping with the development of the understanding of the Church, the president was often not an individual person but the whole presbytery and, since Ignatius of Antioch in the second century, the *bishop* with his presbytery. Even into the twelfth century the celebration of the Eucharist occurred in such a manner that this presiding group acted together, but the words of consecration were spoken by only one person, as a rule the bishop or his representative. The word *con-celebratio* for the concerted action of several priests in one and the same Eucharist, under the leadership of a chief celebrant, appears for the first time in the twelfth century, and with it emerges the problem. The immediate source of the problem is that, since the twelfth century at an episcopal consecration, since the thirteenth at a priestly ordination, and since the sixteenth century in general, the words of consecration at a concelebration are spoken together by all concelebrating priests. The specific question here is whether the uttering of the words of consecration by the noncelebrating priests adds anything to the act of consecration performed by the chief celebrant. This view of the Eucharistic celebration, deriving from our new understanding of sacrament, poses the question in our new liturgical science whether concelebration as practiced up to the twelfth century should not be termed *liturgical,* as opposed to our concelebration today, which we should perhaps call *sacramental,* since it results from everyone's speaking the words of consecration together.[33] Or perhaps we should say that the Church has always had a sacramental concelebration, only that before the Middle Ages it occurred silently, residing in the common *intention to consecrate* of the concelebrating priests; afterward, it became an explicit and spoken concelebration. This is the opinion of B. Botte and most modern liturgists.

Several factors contributed to the eucharistic celebration's becoming ever more decidedly the affair of an individual priest and his congregation. Among these causes we can identify the organization of the Church into parish churches as subdivisions of the episcopal diocese since the sixth century, also the increasingly objectified conception of the Eucharist since the High Middle Ages, and especially the more nearly juristic conception of the priestly office above all since the Council of Trent. This led to the situation that, when several different congregations would come together for a special communal eucharistic celebration (services for the dead, for instance), it became customary for the individual presiders from each community to celebrate each his own "private Mass" within the same church space ("corner Masses," as Luther called them) and the result was that "concelebration" wholly fell into oblivion. It was only the act of concelebration by cardinals and bishops at the Eucharistic Congress in Rome in 1922 (in the context of the liturgical movement of the time) that again brought this problem into the limelight: concelebration by priests began to be juxtaposed to what since the time of Pius X had been called *actuosa participatio fidelium*—active participation in the Mass by the faithful. At the International Congress of Pastoral Liturgy in Assisi, Pius XII declared on September 22, 1956, that concelebration necessarily required the uttering of the words of consecration by all concelebrating priests. This was again affirmed by the Holy Office in answer to a query on May 23, 1957, and by the directive of September 3, 1958. According to these documents, concelebration is a collegial act of the priests celebrating together, an act that actualizes the one sacrifice of the Mass (not a plurality of sacrifices); and yet each of the concelebrating priests can regard the act as "his sacrifice," and therefore each of the concelebrating priests may bring to it his own Mass intention in fulfillment of his Mass stipend. Indeed, the sacrifice of the Mass not only constitutes one whole in its form (it is not a sum of parts), but is also of infinite value, a value that likewise cannot be divided and in which all can participate. Article 57 of the Constitution on the Liturgy of 1963 gives a whole range of possibilities for the use of concelebration that go beyond what had been allowed up until then (consecration of bishops, ordination of priests, and so on), and the Rite of Concelebration promulgated on March 7, 1965, extends the possibility for concelebration, with permission of the ordinary, to every eucharistic celebration where there are more than one priest present who wish to concelebrate. This development does not exactly exclude the notion of a *Levitical high priesthood* that would have even priests (and not just bishops) pontificate as Levites; but it does make the concept problematic. A number of Masses being celebrated at the same time within the same church space is now regarded as an erroneous development that ought to be done away with. Concelebration gives particularly clear expression to the reality of the ecclesial community, and in this vein the Constitution on the Liturgy says (art. 41): "Everyone . . . should be convinced that the Church is visible in a preeminent manner when the whole of God's holy People participates fully and actively in the same liturgical celebration, particularly in the same eucharistic celebration: in the unity of prayer, at the same altar, presided over by the bishop surrounded by his presbytery and the servers of the altar."[34]

3. The Unique Symbolic Meaning of the External Sign in the Eucharistic Sacrament

The unique "symbolic meaning" of the external sign in the eucharistic sacrament consists in the fact that, because of the words spoken over it, the material object in its appearance and species becomes in a unique manner the valid and efficacious sign for the "real presence of Christ" and thus for the "actual presence of his work of salvation" in the liturgical celebration. We will attempt to understand this most important aspect of the doctrine of the Eucharist by asking in their proper order questions concerning: (a) the fact of this presence, (b) the particular manner of this presence, (c) the formal cause of this becoming present, (d) the duration of this state of presence, and (e) the special intellectual difficulties that this doctrine occasions.

A. FACTUALNESS OF CHRIST'S REAL PRESENCE AND OF THE ACTUAL PRESENCE OF HIS WORK OF REDEMPTION

In order to establish the factualness of this unique mode of presence of the person of Christ and his redemptive work, we will first examine the accounts of the eucharistic institution; second, we will review differing conceptions of this question; and, third, we will survey the Church's teaching and the tradition of this teaching.

1. The point of departure for this exploration are the *accounts of institution* (see above, p. 179ff.).

a) To understand the words of institution today, we must start from the fact that during the Last Supper Christ was speaking his mother-tongue, Aramaic. The words of Jesus cannot be reconstructed with total certainty, especially the phrase concerning the blood. But from our knowledge of Aramaic idiom we can say that the only possible "retrospective" translation of the Greek words handed down to us would have us affirm that Christ gave the bread and the cup to his Apostles, accompanying this action with a "word of indication" and a "word of interpretation," since the Aramaic language, unlike the Greek, does not have a copula. The words of Jesus, therefore, must have been *Den bisry*, literally "There, my flesh" (in keeping with the Pauline account: "My sacrificial flesh for you"). The word concerning the cup must have been *Den damj di qejamj*, literally "There, my blood of the covenant" (as in the Pauline account: of the "new covenant, poured out for the many"). In keeping with their place within the Passover liturgy, these words could be understood only in the sense that in place of the real sacrificial flesh of the Passover that would be lying there on the table, Jesus offers himself as the new paschal victim (flesh and blood) under the form of bread and wine; in this action, the flesh points more directly to the "sacrificial meal" itself, to the eating of the sacrificial meal, and the liturgical meaning of the cup and the wine in the context of salvation-history points rather to the sealing of the "covenant through the pouring out of the blood." It is precisely in the union of the two phrases that the real presence of Christ and the actual presence of his sacrifice, which inaugurates the New Covenant, become clear in a particular way, and the totality of the Eucharist is shown to be the "paschal sacrifice and sacrificial meal of the New Testament." This understanding of the words of institution, derived from the historical (Aramaic) formulation, shows that the question concerning the interpretation of the "is" comes up only with the Greek text. Therefore, there can be no question here that Jesus might have been speaking in an allegorical or metaphorical manner, such as Matt 16,11f. relates concerning the "leaven of the Pharisees" and John 2,19–22 concerning the "temple of his body."

b) We also encounter this original realistic understanding in the first account, that of Paul, when he says: "I speak to people who understand: judge for yourselves what I say! The cup of blessing which we bless, is it not a participation [communion] (κοινωνία) in [with] the blood of Christ? The bread which we break, is it not a participation [communion] (κοινωνία) in [with] the body of the Christ? Because it is only one bread, we who are many are one body, for we all partake (μετέχωμεν) of the one bread" (1 Cor 10,15–17). The realism of the eucharistic body and blood of Christ is even more corroborated and made clear with this reference to the interior community of Christians in the Church as "body of Christ."

c) Developing the meaning of his account of the institution itself, Paul enhances this realistic understanding of the words of institution even more when he writes: "Whoever, therefore, eats the bread or drinks the cup of the Lord in an unworthy manner will be guilty of profaning the body and blood of the Lord. Let a man examine himself, and so eat of the bread and drink of the cup. For any one who *eats and drinks* without discerning the body of the Lord [from other food], *eats and drinks judgment upon himself* (κρίμα ἑαυτῷ ἐσθίει καὶ πίνει: 1 Cor 11,27–29).

d) Looking back on the event of the Last Supper from the perspective of these affirmations of Paul's, we could perhaps interpret the Pauline phrase "body which is given for you" (τὸ ὑπὲρ ὑμῶν διδόμενον: Luke 22,19) with reference to both Christ's giving of himself in the meal and his giving of himself to death, in the same way that the phrase "the blood which is poured out for many for the forgiveness of sins" in the three Synoptics refers to the blood shed for the sacrifice of the New Covenant. These *appositions*, finally, emphasize the particular form taken by the real presence of Christ and his sacrifice.

To all these linguistic formulas we may also juxtapose the text of the Bread of Life Discourse (John 6,32): "My Father gives you the true bread from heaven (τὸν ἄρτον . . . τὸν ἀληθινόν)." The past historical event—Moses gave the fathers the manna in the desert—is contrasted with the fact that God is the supratemporal, ever-present giver of the true bread from heaven. "The bread that I will give is my flesh for the life of the world" (John 6,51). This sentence is to be understood only in a literal way:

a) because of the indication of the future event: "the bread that I will give (δώσω) [in the room of the Last Supper];

b) because of the word for 'eating' (τρώγειν = 'to crush with the teeth') that John uses continually after v. 54;

c) because of the effect of this bread, which communicates eternal life to the whole world, while those who ate the manna died (6,58);

d) because, as a metaphor, the phrase "to eat someone's flesh" in contemporary speech would have meant "to hate someone to death."

Therefore, John 6,55 ("Whoever eats my flesh and drinks my blood") and 6,57 ("Just as the living Father has sent me and I have life from the Father, so too the person who eats me has life from me") are to be understood only in a literal sense. The latter verse expresses with particular clarity the fact that here "flesh" means nothing other than the living body of the Lord, the person to the Lord himself (ὁ τρώγων με κακεῖνος ζήσει δι᾽ ἐμέ).

All the following verses speak against a symbolic or allegorical interpretation, especially v. 53–56, where, in response to the doubt "How can this man give us his flesh to eat?" Christ answers only: "My flesh is truly food and my blood is truly drink. . . . If you do not eat the flesh of the Son of man and drink his blood, you do not have the life in you." When in John 6,62–68 Jesus says that his words are "spirit and life" and that "it is the spirit that gives life," what is intended is a contrast between the "spiritual," that is, the believing reception, and a merely naturalistic reception in the manner of the people of Capharnaum. Peter's confession, too ("You have the words of everlasting life" and "We have believed and come to know that you are the holy one of God": 69f.), is but an answer to the Lord's demand that this food be received in a believing and spiritual manner. The literal understanding of this address in John is also the basis for the first great christological decision, taken at the Council of Ephesus (D 123), when what was at stake was "the life-giving flesh of Christ."

2. Starting from the Greek text and departing from the literal interpretation, it was possible to arrive at a confusing array of opinions, as we can see in the book of C. Rasperger, *Ducentae verborum: Hoc est corpus meum, etc., interpretationes* [Two-Hundred Interpretations of the Words: "This Is My Body, etc.", 1577]. R. Bellarmine (d. 1621) groups the different opinions into ten categories,[35] in

which four teachers of error call into question the word
hoc, two the word *est,* three the word *corpus,* and one the
word *meum.* The errors may basically be reduced to three
types:

a) The *copula* "est" is interpreted in a figurative symbolic sense: "this means." As basis for this interpretation
reference is made to numerous metaphorical expressions
in Scripture, such as Matt 13,38 ("the field is the world"),
Rev 1,20 ("the seven candlesticks are the seven churches,"
1 Cor 10,4 ("but the rock was Christ"). A figurative expression or *tropos,* however, is only to be accepted as such
(1) when the nature of the thing (images, parables, allegories) or linguistic usage (metonymy, synecdoche) requires it (which is not the case in the account of institution); (2) when one complete substance is attributed to another complete substance (for instance, "I am the vine"),
which is not the case here, for the demonstrative word in
Aramaic *den* ('there', 'here') is not an object, and even the
Greek text could at most be interpreted as "that which I
here have in my hands"; (3) when mutual agreement is
present concerning a figurative manner of speaking (for example, in John 3,14 where the brazen serpent is an image
of the Crucified), which is not the case either with the account of institution. It was above all Zwingli who worked
with this figurative interpretation.

b) The word "body" ($\sigma\tilde{\omega}\mu\alpha$) was used in a figurative sense
to mean an "image for my body" especially by J. Oecolam-
padius and by Calvin. In his interpretation Calvin based
himself on the parallel phrases in Gen 17,10, "Hoc [cir-
cumcision] est pactum meum" ("This is [a sign of] my
covenant"), and Exod 12,11. But these appeals, too, are not
valid even in the text, since the first member of the statement is each time a rite.

c) The demonstrative word *hoc* or *hic* was referred by
Bonaventure to the "terminus a quo" (the bread to be
transformed), by J. Duns Scotus to the "terminus ad quem"
(the body of the Lord: this interpretation is most faithful to

the Aramaic manner of expression, which lacks a copula),
and by Thomas, Bellarmine, and others to the substance in
general, without specific determination. This latter view
is closest to the doctrine of transubstantiation.

In summary we should again repeat that, in light of the
Aramaic text, these questions of linguistic interpretation
are no longer of great significance.

3. The Church's doctrine found its definitive expression
at the Council of Trent (Session 13 on October 11, 1551),
when it was stated: "Si quis negaverit in sanctissimæ eucharistiæ sacramento contineri vere, realiter, substantialiter corpus et sanguinem una cum anima et divinitate
Domini nostri Jesu Christi ac proinde totum Christum;
sed dixerit, tantummodo esse in eo ut in signo vel figura,
aut virtute, *anathema sit.*": "If anyone denies that in the
sacrament of the most Holy Eucharist there is contained
truly, really, substantially, the body and blood together
with the soul and the divinity of Our Lord Jesus Christ,
and therefore the whole Christ, but says that He is present
in it only in the manner of a sign or figure or only as an effect, *anathema sit.*" (D 883–DS 1651).

The word *substantialiter* had first appeared in the confession of faith that Berengar of Tours was asked to pro-
fess at the Sixth Roman Council in 1079: "I, Berengar, believe with my heart and confess with my mouth that the
bread and wine that are placed upon the altar are changed
in their substance [*substantialiter*] through the mystery
of holy prayer and through the words of our Redeemer
into the true and real and life-giving Flesh and Blood of
Jesus Christ, Our Lord, and that after the consecration
they are the true Body of Christ, born from the Virgin,
which hung on the cross offered there for the salvation of
the world and which sits at the right hand of the Father,
and the true Blood of Christ, which flowed out of the
wound on his side: not only as a sign or by the effect of
the sacrament, but in the reality of their nature and in the
truth of their substance, as is stated here in this short

confession, as I have read it out and as you have heard it"
(D 355–DS 700).

The Fourth Lateran Council of 1215 affirmed the same
doctrine (D 430–DS 802). The *vere* has its basis in John
6,32, and hearkens back above all to Thomas Aquinas, who
taught that only such realism in our understanding of
Jesus' words does full justice (1) to the perfection of the
sacrifice of the New Testament (cf. Heb 10,1); (2) to the
love of Christ, which led to the incarnation of the Logos
and urged him to abide among us forever corporeally that
we might abide in him (John 6,57); and (3) to the perfection
of Christian faith, which gratefully believes in the God
who performs wonders (Ps 107.8,15,21,31: *Summa Theol.*
III, q. 75, a.1). The *realiter* refers especially to the real identity between the sacramental Christ and the historical
Christ, a doctrine that was stressed repeatedly, especially
in the Western Church, since the time of Paschasius Radbertus.

The first nine centuries of Christian history showed no
controversy in this doctrine, and apparently symbolic interpretations are to be understood on the basis of the historical circumstances and the language of the various theologians.[36] The most important liturgical texts, which at
the same time manifest the realism of the Church's understanding of the Eucharist, have been collected by Johannes
Quasten in the *Monumenta eucharistica et liturgica ve-
tustissima.*[37]

In general, although not always with sufficient clarity,
three modes of Christ's existence came to be distinguished: (1) the *status connaturalis mortalis* in Palestine
and on earth (the "historical Jesus"); (2) the *status connaturalis gloriosus* (the risen Christ); and (3) the *status sacramentalis* (Christ in the Eucharist and the sacrifice of the
Mass), which was often called typical, antitypical, or symbolic, but this in no way intending to deny the real presence. Accordingly, Augustine spoke of a *threefold manner
of partaking* in the Eucharist: (1) a "Capharnaitic" com-

munion without faith, (2) a merely sacramental reception in the state of mortal sin and without the effect of grace, and (3) the worthy sacrament and spiritual (*spiritualiter et sacramentaliter*) partaking of the sacrament, with the effect of grace.

B. MANNER OF CHRIST'S REAL PRESENCE IN THE SACRAMENT

The second eucharistic controversy with Berengar of Tours had introduced the sensualistic and historical element in Germanic thinking into theological reflections concerning the Eucharist; by the same token, this controversy had elicited, not only the "doctrine of transubstantiation" that remains to be discussed here, but also the questions concerning the relationship between the external form of bread and wine and the external form of Christ. Parallel to this philosophical question, the controversy had also developed the doctrine of so-called "concomitance." In his *Summa theologiæ* (III, q. 76) Thomas dealt with these questions in their interrelationship for the first time, and the Council of Trent took a position with regard to these problems basing itself on Thomas and late-medieval speculation. These questions resulted in a strong "materialization" [*Verdinglichung*] of the doctrine of the Eucharist; but we will here discuss them briefly because they still are of great significance today for "eucharistic piety."

1. The decisive doctrine is, *In the Eucharist is present the living Christ with his flesh and blood, his body and his soul, his divinity and his humanity* (D 874, 883–DS 1636ff., 1651). The basis for this doctrine is the fact that the expression used by Christ ("my flesh") in the original language refers to the whole, living person, that is, the living God-Man in Christ. In John 6,57 this is expressed when Christ says: "As the living Father has sent me and I have life from the Father, so too the person who eats me [not only "my flesh"] will have life from me." On the basis of

a literal understanding of the account of institution, the
Middle Ages made the following distinctions possible: (a)
After the consecration, the "flesh of Christ" is present in
the bread and the "blood of Christ" is present in the wine
vi verborum; (b) *per concomitantiam*, that is, by a fuller
understanding of these words, the living corporeality of
Christ is present under each of the species: the "flesh and
blood" of Christ together and his "body and soul" together; (c) because of the *hypostatic union,* the whole
Christ is always present, the God-Man with his "divinity
and humanity"; (d) a later theology that had wandered
even further away from the fundamental mystery of the
Eucharist in the paschal context extended this "syllogis-
tic" habit of thought ever more and, by introducing the
doctrine of *perichoresis in God,* affirmed that in the Eucharist also the "whole, living and triune God," Father,
Son, and Holy Spirit, is present. From this we can understand how there came to be attributed to the effects of the
Eucharist, not only redemption and sanctification through
Christ, but also creative renewal by the Father and the beginnings of glorification through the action of the Holy
Spirit.[38]

2. The Council of Trent took what the High Middle Ages
had still seen in all its unity and proceeded to view it and
explain it more in the distinction and isolation of its parts,
in the manner of the Late Middle Ages: (a) The whole
Christ is contained in *each of the two species* (D 885,
698–DS 1653, 1321) (while 1 Cor 11,27 speaks of the sac-
rilege against flesh and blood through the unworthy eating
of the bread or drinking of the wine); (b) the whole Christ
is wholly present in *each material part* of the host or the
wine, at least after the separation (D 885–DS 1653). Since
the time of Odo of Ourscamp (d. 1150), this doctrine has
been affirmed with reference to the liturgical breaking of
the host on this basis of Christ's breaking of the bread at
the Last Supper. From this derives the reverence to be
shown to the tiniest little fragment, and the "doctrine of

transubstantiation" again made the problem of "material-ization" relevant. (c) The Eucharist is viewed in a purely philosophical way when the question, as in Late Scholas-ticism, is extended to ask whether Christ is already wholly present in every part of the whole even before the breaking of the bread or the distribution of the wine. The reason for this question was not a false physical train of thought but rather the affirmation that the presence of the whole Christ in the materially limited species could only be un-derstood analogously to the presence of the whole soul of the human being in the one, materially limited body. For the Middle Ages taught that the soul is wholly present in the whole body and in each part of the body,[39] since by "soul" it correctly understood the personal being of the human being. And this statement applies when human be-ings, in a healthy manner, understand all of their members in a genuine personal sense as being "members of their body."

The presence of Christ in the sacrament is not to be un-derstood in the sense of matter and physical makeup, but in the sense of mystery and personal presence.

C. ON THE FORMAL CAUSE OF THE REAL PRESENCE: THE DOCTRINE OF TRANSUBSTANTIATION

1. Historical Background

Already very early on, the Church's theologians strove to make the real presence of Christ comprehensible by seeking to understand the "happening" that led to this real presence. The bread itself cannot be Christ: the mystery of faith concerning the real presence becomes a reality only when Christ's words are spoken over the bread and over the wine. What happens when these words are spoken? Nor can the bread be the matter in which Christ abides

and is present. Such an externalistic manner of thought
was expressly rejected with Nestorius' Christology in 431
and was no longer of any use for the doctrine of the Eucharist. The bread in itself cannot be a natural sign for
Christ either; on the contrary, this material reality would
have to be an obstacle to thinking of the glorified Lord.

A. Here are different concepts and analogies from the
Greek theologians:

a) To become = γίγνεσθαι: It is in Irenæus that we first
encounter a theological reflection on the "happening" that
leads to the real presence of Christ in the bread. His debate
with Gnosticism gave him occasion to emphasize the reality of the Logos' becoming human being in the same way
as the reality of the bread and wine's becoming the Eucharist once they have received the Word of God. In each
case, Irenæus is stressing Christ's "corporeality" in this
world; for, on the basis of a spiritualistic conception such
as the Gnostics adhered to because of their Manichæan
understanding of the body, human beings would not have
been redeemed precisely in their corporeality and human
frailty. But, for Irenæus, we are redeemed because the
Logos in Christ became a man corporeally, "with flesh and
bones and nerves," and because he nourishes our body
with this his body. In this connection Irenæus says that
"the mixed chalice and the prepared bread" perceive or
admit (ἐπιδέχεται)[40] the Word (λόγος) of God and become
(γίνεται) the Eucharist of the Blood and Body of Christ,
nourished on which the very substance (ὑπόστασις) of our
flesh grows. "How can [the Gnostics] deny that the flesh
is capable of receiving the gift of God, which is eternal life,
when this flesh is nourished from the blood and flesh of
Christ and is a member of him? (Eph 5,30)" (*Adv. Hær.* V, 2,
2–3: PG 7, 1124ff.). This becoming (γίγνεσθαι) has its salvation-historical analogy in the *Logos' becoming man*
(John 1,14). Commenting on 1 Cor 10,16, Irenæus again
says in this context: "Blood derives only from flesh and
veins and the rest of the human substance, which is what

the Word of God in truth has become" (John 1,14) (*Adv. Hær.*, V, 2, 2–3: PG 7, 1125). "Wine and bread admit the Word of God and become Eucharist, that is, the body and blood of Christ (εὐχαριστία γίνεται, ὅπερ ἐστὶ σῶμα καὶ αἷμα τοῦ χριστοῦ) (*Adv. Hær.* V, 2, 2–3: PG 7, 1127).

The way to this doctrine had been prepared by Justin Martyr, who in his *First Apology* says: "Jesus Christ, our redeemer, took on flesh and blood for the sake of our salvation when he became incarnate through God's Logos. In the same way, we have been taught that the food that is consecrated with thanksgiving through a prayer for the Logos who proceeds from God is the flesh and blood of our Jesus who became flesh, and that this is the food with which our flesh and blood are nourished through transformation (μεταβολή)" (I, 66; PG 6, 428ff.). In reverential manner, Justin here uses not a philosophical but a biblical expression to describe the event of eucharistic transformation; and yet this very expression, because of its analogy to the mystery of the Incarnation, is particularly suited to probe the *mystery of the Eucharist*. Just as in Christ we can only see the man and yet it is the God-Man and the Redeemer who stands before us, so too in the Eucharist we can only see bread and wine and yet the reality before us is Christ and his redemptive sacrifice. As earnest and real as the event of "God's becoming man" are the earnestness and reality of the event whereby bread and wine are made to become the Eucharist. A more significant expression than this will never again be found, even though other, more philosophical expressions may be of further aid to our natural way of thinking.

b) To sanctify = ἁγιάζειν: We must now refer to another biblical expression that has its origin in the cultic order of the Eucharist. Already the *Didache* (9,5) calls the Eucharist "the Holy Thing" (ἅγιον), and on the basis of Matt 7,6 the oldest liturgies, especially among the Syrians, have this exclamation by the deacon before the communion: "The Holy Thing for the holy!" *Holy*, in the biblical sense, means *what has been separated from the profane to be turned over to the Divine and has become filled with the Divine.* Above all in John (6,69; 1 John 2,20; Rev 3,7) Christ is called "the Holy One of God" because he is believed to have divine being. At the same time, "the holy" is in the Old Testament a term closely connected with sacrifice, and "to sanctify" (ἁγιάζειν) has the sense of *making something into a sacrificial offering before God,* which also has an echo in Christ's farewell address, when he says: "I sanctify myself [= make myself into a sacrificial offering] for them, that they too may be sanctified [= become sacrificial offerings]" (John 17,19). Thus, Clement of Alexandria calls the Eucharist "the food which is the Lord Jesus, which is the Logos of God, Spirit become flesh, sanctified, heavenly flesh" (πνεῦμα σαρκούμενον, ἁγιαζομένη σὰρξ οὐράνιος) (*Paid.* I, 6, 43, 2ff.: PG 8, 301). Likewise, alluding to 1 Tim 4,5 (ἁγιάζεται γὰρ διὰ λόγου θεοῦ καὶ ἐντεύξεως), Origen speaks time and again of the Eucharist as the "bread" that is "sanctified through the Word of God and prayer" (*In Mt* 11.14: PG 13, 948 d; 949b), and he calls it "the typical and symbolic body of Christ." He continues: "A great deal could still be said concerning the Logos himself, who became flesh and true food. Whoever eats it will live eternally, for a bad person cannot [really] eat it" (*Paid.* I, 6, 43, 2f.: PG 8, 952a).

Later theologians interpret this "to sanctify" with the new *concept of transformation,* as when John Chrysostom says, "Our sacrifice today . . . is not less than that other one [of the Last Supper], since it is not men who sanctify it, but he himself who sanctified that other one" (*In 1 Tim* 2.2: PG 33, 1113–1116).

c) To transform = μεταβάλλειν: A philosophical term begins to be used to elucidate the event whereby the bread becomes Eucharist; but this term is first used with reference to the narrative of the *miracle of Cana* (John 2,1–10), where water became wine. John (Cyril) of Jerusalem says this of the Eucharist: "After we have sanctified ourselves through these spiritual songs of praise [the preface], we implore the good God that He send the Holy Spirit down upon the offered gifts in order that He might make the bread into the body and the wine into the blood of Christ. For whatever the Holy Spirit touches is sanctified and transformed" (τοῦτο ἡγίασται καὶ μεταβέβληται) (*Cat. myst.* V, 7: PG 33, 1113–1116). He bases this transformation on the words "Once, in Cana of Galilee, he transformed (μεταβέβληκεν) water into wine, which is related to blood. And should it not be believable that he transforms (μεταβαλλών) wine into blood?" (*Cat. myst.* IV, 2: PG 33, 1097–1100). The term appears to be transferred from the change or "transformation" that the food we eat undergoes in us. Justin already referred to this in his *Apology* (I, 66: PG 6, 428ff.), saying that the Eucharist is a nourishment (τροφή) that nourishes our blood and our flesh by transformation (μεταβολή). The term "transformation" should not indeed here be understood in that spectacular sense that the Gnostics wanted to give it already in the second century. Irenæus reports concerning the Gnostic Markos that, when celebrating the Eucharist, by a trick he made his chalice, filled with white wine, bubble up *red* and run over so as to prove that his sect possessed the true Eucharist! (*Adv. Hær.* I, 13, 1f: PG 7, 577–581).

d) To change = μεταποιεῖν, μεθιστάναι: This term, which carries a different emphasis, seems to appear first in Gregory of Nyssa and is then frequently used for μεταβάλλειν ("to transform"). According to Gregory, the soul comes to partake of the divine through spiritual faith, and the body must by means of food receive the divine in a corporeal manner. This became possible through Christ's incarnation and by the fact that Christ has made himself to be the nourishment of the body through the bread and wine of the Eucharist. But, just as the Logos not only assumed human nature but also elevated it to his own divine being, so too not only does the Eucharist effect participation in Christ but this elevation of human beings results in union with the Logos. Union in the Incarnation with the Logos, reception of food into the body, elevation of human nature through the eucharistic food to the immortality of the Logos: all these processes have their mysterious depths in the union of the lower with the higher. These processes of "interior appropriation" are summed up with the term "change" = μεταποιεῖν, which suggests both the "interior occupation [by God]" and the event of "creative transformation" (in Gen 1.1 the verb ποιεῖν is the term for God's creative act). Gregory of Nyssa writes in this vein: "Through union with God's Logos, the body was raised (μεταποιήθη) to the divine dignity. With reason, then, do we believe that now, too, the bread that has been sanctified (ἁγιαζόμενον ἄρτον) becomes changed (μεταποιεῖσθαι) into the body of God's Logos. For that body too [of the historical Jesus] was possibly bread [since it had to live on bread]. It became sanctified through the indwelling (ἐπισκήνωσις) of the Logos who dwelt in the flesh (John 1,14). Now, just as the bread that was changed (μετεποιηθεὶς ἄρτος) into that body was raised (μεθίσθη) to possess efficacious divine power, so now too the same thing happens in the same way. For there [in the event of the Incarnation] the grace of the Logos created (ἐποιεῖτο) a holy body for itself, a body that derived its substance from bread and therefore was itself bread in some way; and here [in the event of the consecration], as the Apostle says, in the same manner the bread is sanctified through the Word of God and prayer (1 Tim 4,5)—not that, as food and drink, it becomes the body of the Logos [by nourishing it historically], but rather because it is directly changed (μεταποιούμενος) into the body of the Logos, as was proclaimed by the Logos himself: 'This is my body!' . . . For this reason the Logos, at his epiphany, becomes intermingled with fallen human nature, that the human might become divinized (συναποθεωτήθη) by its communion with the divine. This is why he implants himself through his flesh into all who believe in his order of grace—into all whose existence depends on bread and wine. And so he intermingles with the bodies of believers in the manner of a union with what is immortal, in order that the human being too may become a participant in imperishability. This he conferred by the efficacious power of his blessing (εὐλογία), through which he radically transformed (μεταστοιχειώσας = "trans-elemented") the nature of visible things from the ground up to that immortal reality" (Or. cat., c. 37: PG 45, 96ff.).

Similarly, Cyril of Alexandria teaches: "We should not think that the visible elements are only a type; rather, they have been truly changed (μεταποιεῖσθαι) by a mystery of the omnipotent God into the sacrificial body and blood of Christ. When we partake of them, we take to ourselves the life-giving and sanctifying power of Christ (τὴν ζωοποιὸν καὶ ἁγιαστικὴν δύναμιν τοῦ Χριστοῦ)." (In Mt. 26, 27: PG 72, 452).

John Damascene summarizes the reality of this event of transformation and the mystery of faith underlying it when he says: "The body [of Christ in the Eucharist] is truly united with the divinity—I speak of that body that derives from the Holy Virgin—not because the ascended body somehow comes down again from heaven, but because the bread and the wine are changed (μεταποιοῦνται) into God's body and blood. But if you ask me about the way in which this happens, you must be satisfied with hearing the following: [This occurs] through the Holy Spirit, just as the Lord also received his carnal existence from the Holy Virgin through the Holy Spirit, for himself and in himself. More we do not know, except that the Logos of God is true and efficacious and omnipotent, but the manner of it is unfathomable (ὅτι ὁ λόγος τοῦ θεοῦ ἀληθής ἐστι καὶ ἐνεργὴς καὶ παντοδύναμος, ὁ δὲ τρόπος ἀνεξερεύνετος)" (De fide orthodoxa, IV, 13: PG 94, 1144ff.). By way of explanation John Damascene, like Gregory of Nyssa, also points to the transformation of good and drink into our body.

e) Essential change = μεταστοιχείωσις: The depths of the

mystery are even more apparent in the word that we have already encountered just now in Gregory of Nyssa, the word μεταστοιχείωσις, in Latin *transelementatio*, meaning "essential change or transformation." In another passage Gregory again explains it in terms of the mystery of the Incarnation: "The power of the All-High God, which is an essence without matter or form, assumed a servant's form as hypostasis from the Virgin and raised it up to his own heights by radically transforming (μεταστοιχειώσασα) it into the divine and simple [unmixed] nature" (*Adv. Apol.* 25: PG 45, 1177C). Of all the patristic vocabulary, this word is perhaps what comes closest to the medieval term "transubstantiation."

f) Change of meaning = μεταρρυθμίζειν, μετασκευάζειν: John Chrysostom contributes two new terms for this mysterious event whereby Christ's body and blood become present in bread and wine. Concerning Christ's words of consecration he says, "These words transform (μεταρρυθμίζειν) the gifts presented" (*De pro. Jud.* I: PG 49, 380.389). The usual sense of this word connotes that the gifts that have been presented, namely bread and wine as means of nourishment for the physical body, receive a new and essentially different "meaning" through the event of consecration. Chrysostom goes on to speak of human beings' new attitude toward the bread, and he warns against receiving it unworthily, giving the example of Judas. In the same connection the great preacher uses the word μετασκευάζειν, again for "to transform": "We [priests] have the rank of servants [at the sacrifice of the Mass]; but he himself [Christ] is the one who sanctifies and transforms (ὁ δὲ ἁγιάζων καὶ μετασκευάζων αὐτός)" (*In Mt.* 82, 5: PG 58, 744). One could compare these terms of Chrysostom's with the recent attempts at definition by E. H. Schillebeeckx, who calls the mystery of the consecration an "objective transfinalization," an essential change in the ontological meaning of the thing.[41]

All of these affirmations show how earnestly and realis-

tically the "event of transformation" of the consecration
was taken, but at the same time how, from the outset, its
character as mystery was emphasized. What is presented
to faith in the salvation-historical mystery of the "Logos'
becoming flesh" is elucidated for human thought by the
natural mysteries of the change of water into wine at Cana
or of the change of food and drink into our bodily nature.
To this the terms used by John Chrysostom add a reflection on meaning drawn from the Stoics. The decisive factor in all of this for the whole subsequent development of
the doctrine is the fact that, in all these considerations, *the
eucharistic mystery is placed on the same immediate ontological level as the mystery of the Incarnation.* Here is
where it must always remain if it is to be correctly understood by faith in the sense of the primitive Church.

The *Latin Fathers* add nothing essentially new to the
doctrine of the Greek Fathers, unless we consider new Ambrose's particular emphasis on the realism of the eucharistic change by his reference to the historical Christ: "Vera
utique caro Christi, quæ crucifixa est, quæ sepulta est,
veræ ergo carnis illius sacramentum est": "[The Eucharist]
is the sacrament of that true flesh, the true flesh of Christ
which was crucified and buried" (*De myst.* IX, 51–54: PL
16, 406ff.). Augustine, on the other hand, against the background of his Platonism, tends more to think about the
meaning and realistic symbolic character of the Eucharist:
"Nisi manducaveritis carnem. . . . (John 6,53). . . . Figura
ergo est præcipiens passioni dominicæ esse communican-
dum et suaviter atque utiliter recondendum in memoria,
quod pro nobis caro eius crucifixa et vulnerata sit": "[The
Eucharist] is thus an image that instructs [us] to participate in the Passion of the Lord, and to store in our memory
the delectable and beneficial thought that his flesh was
crucified and wounded for our sake" (*De doctr. chr.* III, 16,
24: PL 34, 74f.).

B. In the *first eucharistic controversy*, against Paschasius
Radbertus, all the distinctions introduced by Augustine,

Ambrose, and Jerome are further systematized. Ratramnus of Corbie responds thus to the first question of Charles the Bald: ". . . quod corpus et sanguis Christi, quæ fidelium ore in ecclesia percipiuntur, figuræ sint secundum speciem visibilem at vero secundum invisibilem substantiam, id est divini potentiam verbi, corpus et sanguis vere Christi existunt": ". . . the body and blood of Christ, which are received by the faithful in the Church with their mouth, are images [figuræ] with regard to their visible appearance, but with regard to their invisible substance (that is, the power of the divine Word) they exist truly as the body and blood of Christ" (De corpore et sanguine Domini, c. 49: ed. Bakhuizen [Amsterdam, 1954], p. 46; PL 121, 147). To the second question concerning the identity of the historical, the glorified, and the sacramental Christ, Ratramnus responds by clearly distinguishing these three manners of existence (c. 89). He especially emphasizes the fact that Christ's sacramental manner of existence rests on *significatio* (c. 69), which for the recipient means *spiritus et vita* and which in cultic worship exists *in memoria* (c. 101f).

It was only during the *second eucharistic controversy*, against Berengar of Tours in 1044, that a new term for the event of the consecration was developed and, with it, a new theological understanding of the Eucharist. In the process, the question concerning the presence of Christ in the sacrament became detached from its traditional connection with the question of salvation (bread for the life of the world) and with the question of the Trinity (the Spirit as consecrator). As a result, a kind of abstract juxtaposition began to be practiced whereby the only realities considered—and as autonomous entities—were bread and wine over against the body and blood of Christ, in keeping with Ambrose's linkage of the idea of consecration with the idea of creation.[42]

In contrast to the Capernaitic view of Paschasius Radbertus, which still largely determined the formula of recantation (PL 148, 1455) presented to Berengar of Tours by Cardinal Humbertus of Silva Candida in 1049, Lanfranc of Canterbury stated in his response to Berengar in 1050: "Credimus terrenas substantias . . . converti in essentiam dominici corporis reservatis ipsarum rerum speciebus" (c. 18: PL 150, 430). Around 1070 Guitmund of Aversa was teaching as follows: "Panem et vinum altaris Domini in corpus et sanguinem Christi substantialiter commutari" (PL 149, 1488B). Similarly Gregory VII affirmed in his formula of confession to Berengar in 1079 that the bread and wine "substantialiter converti in veram et propriam ac vivificatricem carnem et sanguinem J. C. D. N" (D 335–DS 700). The reflections of Alger of Liège (about 1120) led considerably further. He continued Ambrose's train of thought using the analogy of the miracle of creation *ex nihilo* and of the transformation of Aaron's rod into a snake. On this basis he discussed in detail the questions concerning the relationship between the reality of the Lord's body and the reality of the forms (species) of bread and wine after the consecration, between spiritual and real presence, between the spatial presence of Christ's body in heaven and on the altar, between the unity of Christ's sacrifice and the many sacrifices on the altar. Concerning the event of transformation in the consecration he writes: "Nec de nihilo credatur corpus Christi creari in sacramento secundum primariæ naturæ originem nec panis formam mutari secundum naturæ communicatam consuetudinem, sed novo et inaudito modo ita mutari substantiam panis in substantiam corporis Christi, ut panis non sit, sed appareat esse quod fuerat, et corpus Christi non desistat esse quod erat": "Let us not believe that the body of Christ is created *de nihilo* in the sacrament, with regard to the origin of its first nature, or that the form of the bread is changed in keeping with the usual manner of its nature. Rather, the substance of the bread is changed into the substance of the body of Christ in a new and unheard-of manner, so that it is no longer bread but only appears to be what it had been, and the body of Christ does not stop being what it was" (*De sacr.* I, 9: PL 180, 768).

We may perhaps attribute the development of the concept of *transubstantiation* to the School of Gilbert of Poitiers (d. 1154), since here is where the distinction between *substantia* and *accidentia* was introduced (and not only *species*).[43] In his book of *Sentences*, Peter of Poitiers (d. 1205) distinguishes three kinds of transformation: a change of matter and form at once (from an egg comes a chicken), a change that involves only form (soft bread becomes hard bread), and the change involved in the Holy Eucharist: "Substantia panis in substantiam corporis Christi transit, manentibus tamen omnibus proprietatibus, quæ erant in pane." After responding to different objections, he further describes this change: "Iste panis vertetur in corpus Christi; transibit, et quoties sumuntur ibi verba ad mutationem pertinentia, concedi potest, præcipue tamen cum dicitur 'panis iste transsubstantiatur in corpus Christi', quia nullum verbum adeo proprie hic ponitur sicut 'transsubstantiari', quia substantia in substantiam transit, manentibus eisdem proprietatibus": "This bread will be transformed into the body of Christ; it shall go over [into that new reality: *transibit*]; as often as the words pertaining to the change are perceived there, this can be affirmed, but especially when the words are said 'this bread is transubstantiated into the body of Christ', because no word can so aptly be used here as *transsubstantiari* ['to be transubstantiated'], since [one] substance goes over into [another] substance, even though the properties remain the same" (*Sent.* V, c. 12: PL 211, 1247B; cf. 1246 C and D). After rejecting the expression *transformari*, he repeatedly stresses the following: "Facta transsubstantiatione panis in corpus, non remanet ibi panis" (*Sent.* V, c. 12: PL 211, 1248a). Who it is that bears the accidents here can only be known, Peter says, by him who has effected the change: God (*Sent.* V, c. 12: PL 211, 1248C).

Innocent III already uses this word as a current term in his work "On the Sacrament of the Altar (IV, cap. 7, cap. 19 and 20: PL 217, 859; cf. 869–871): "Porro cum panis transsubstantiatur in corpus, itaque rationale animatum, videtur quod panis transsubstantiatur in hominem, et pari ratione in Christum transsubstantiatur et ita in creatorem. . . ." (IV, PL 217, 869). And he inserts this term also into the Decree of the Fourth Lateran Council (1215): "Jesus Christus, cuius corpus et sanguis in sacramento altaris sub speciebus panis et vini veraciter continentur, transsubstantiatis pane in corpus et vino in sanguinem potestate divina: ut ad perficiendum mysterium unitatis accipiamus ipsi de suo, quod accepit ipse de nostro."[44] It is significant that at this same time and similarly to the Western Church, the Synod of Constantinople in the Eastern Church under Emperor Manuel I Komnenos and Patriarch Lukas on January 26, 1156, expressly used the term *metastoicheiosis* for the Eucharist.

High Scholasticism then took up this precisely defined term (*transubstantiation*) and proceeded to specify it further in an unshackled theological manner according to the different understandings of *substantia.* It is Thomas Aquinas who thought through the doctrine of transubstantiation with greatest consistency.[45] The controversy surrounding the concept became most evident in the dispute of Giles of Rome with Thomas in his work *Centum theoremata*, in the critique of Richard of Middleton and of William of Ware, but especially in Duns Scotus, who, alongside the usual understanding of transubstantiation (= *transitio totalis substantiæ in substantiam*[46]), also distinguishes a *transsubstantiatio productiva* (for the transition from non-being to being)[47] and a *transsubstantiatio adductiva* (= transitus substantiæ in substantiam quantum ad hic esse[48]). The critique of dissolution was performed on the concept by William of Ockham, since for him the concept of substance was essentially determined by the concept of quantity.[49] From the Armenians, who adhered to a more spiritualistic viewpoint, Pope Benedict XII in 1341 exacted the confession of the doctrine of transubstantiation (D 544–DS 1018). The Council of Trent, in its Session

13 in 1551, prescribed the doctrine of transubstantiation in the understanding of St. Thomas (D 884–DS 1652).

C. The Doctrine of Impanation: It is significant that, after the beginning of the second eucharistic controversy in the Early Middle Ages and up to St. Thomas' presentation of the doctrine of transubstantiation, the doctrine that Christ's body is present in bread that remains bread ("impanation") was consistently rejected. Only with John of Paris was it again introduced as a possibility in 1280, and Durandus of Saint Pourçain (d. 1334) gave it a whole new cast: he stated that in transubstantiation what ceases to exist is only the substantial form of bread and wine, but that the matter, which is bearer of the accidents, remains. After Luther and Osiander, and despite the formulations of the Council of Trent, this doctrine again made a certain comeback in the explanation of the Eucharist of A. Rosmini-Serbati (d. 1855), who believed that the transformation of bread and wine is sufficiently described once it is said that they become animated by the soul of Christ (D 1919–DS 3229ff.). The error of this doctrine lies in the fact that, for the sake of answering the question concerning the meaning of the Holy Eucharist, it makes affirmations that are so spiritualistic that they no longer do justice to the reality of Christ's presence.

The Eastern Church is essentially in agreement with the Roman Church's doctrine of transubstantiation, even if it has no interest in the categories of Aristotelian philosophy being used and instead stresses the unfathomableness of the mystery contained in this sacrament. In the Anglican Church we find the whole gamut of doctrine, from the Lutheran and Calvinistic understanding of the Eucharist to, among the Anglo-Catholics, and Catholic doctrine.

D. Transfinalization: The more recent attempts to secure an authentic Catholic understanding of the sacrament are based above all in a new emphasis on the question of meaning. In this line, B. Welte was already in 1959 attempting to explain the meaning of the eucharistic change by means of a new "system of relations" in which some specific thing, for instance, becomes food, or an ordinary piece of cloth becomes a flag.[50] The same concern was addressed in 1959 by H. R. Schlette's portrayal of eucharistic communion as "communion of persons,[51] and in the same year K. Rahner was thinking along the same lines.[52] One who especially moved in this same direction was P. Schoonenberg, S.J. (1964). This Jesuit understood the doctrine of transubstantiation in its traditional formulation more as a spatial presence, and as such he criticized it; he called for greater awareness of the personal presence and personal communication in the liturgical presence and thus he qualified transubstantiation as being "transfinalization" or "transignification." In 1965 the Capuchin L. Smits, in his *Questions on the Eucharist,* declared himself against the static understanding of the doctrine of transubstantiation and wanted to replace it with an understanding based on the analogy of the hypostatic union. "The consecrated bread is not itself the body of Christ; it is the bread taken up by Christ and as such it is his body." Smits here speaks of what he calls "transessentiation." The response to Smits came from the Jesuit S. Trooster, who in turn spoke of "transfinalization": "From earthly bread heavenly food comes into being." This concern is also shared by E. H. Schillebeeckx, when he distinguishes three steps of theological reflection: first, the level of faith; then the ontological level (in medieval language, metaphysical reflection); these two steps are permanent and irreplaceable. The third level, that of physical reflection on the philosophy of nature, is rejected by Schillebeeckx. The phenomenological method with which he seeks to grasp the mystery leads him to the *doctrine of transfinalization,* even if he understands it in a wholly objective manner as John Chrysostom did before him. On May 9, 1965, the Pastoral Letter of the Dutch Bishops expressly opened up for discussion the question concerning the manner of Christ's presence in the Eucharist. The encyclical *Mysterium Fidei* of September 3, 1965, on the other hand, again expounded the old doctrine of transubstantiation, which it also calls *doctrine of transelementation* (as translation of the Greek term μεταστοιχείωσις).[53]

Subsequently, V. Warnach[54] and J. P. de Jong[55] have made new attempts to reexpress the meaning of the traditional doctrine of transubstantiation through a new conception of the Greek idea of symbol. They declare "symbol" to be a "symbolic reality," and in so doing Warnach leans more decisively on the Greek Fathers, while de Jong seeks to explain and establish this new interpretation of symbol on the basis of an immanent phenomenological consideration of bread as food and wine as drink. "Symbol," in this view, is not to have the sense of "spiritual sign," which is how it has been understood in the West since the time of Berengar of Tours; rather, it is understood to refer to the designated reality itself. This interpretation overlooks the manner in which the cultural-historical context of the Germanic Middle Ages changed the meaning of the Greek conception of symbol, and de Jong's discussions do not offer a sufficient footing for the necessary historical connections without which the Eucharist cannot be presented satisfactorily as the making present of Christ's sacrifice. A. Gerken attempts a similar solution.[56]

2. *Speculative Considerations*

The Council of Trent gives the following definition: "Si quis negaverit mirabilem illam et singularem conversionem totius substantiæ panis in corpus et totius substantiæ vini in sanguinem, manentibus dumtaxat speciebus panis et vini, quam quidem conversionem catholica ecclesia aptissime transsubstantiationem appellat, *anathema sit": "Whoever denies that wonderful and unique conversion of the whole substance of the bread into the Body and of the whole substance of the wine into the Blood, with only the species of bread and wine abiding, which conversion the Catholic Church most aptly calls 'transubstantiation' *anathema sit*" (Session 13, canon 2 *de Eucharistia*) (D 884–DS 1652). Although no direct proof from Scripture can be adduced for this doctrine, nonetheless we may say that the texts of the eucharistic institution and promise are not sufficiently accounted for by the doctrine of "impanation." Neither does a merely "symbolic interpretation" do justice to the liturgical sense of the institution. As the history of the Church's understanding of eucharistic consecration has shown, from the outset the faith of the Church attributed a "realistic meaning" to the words of institution, a meaning that, in the metaphysical language of the Middle Ages, was adequately expressed with the term "transubstantiation."

To be sure, the *concept of substance* underlying this definition is difficult to define, since it always emerges as a functional concept within a broader conceptual system. The "understanding of substance" adequate for the doctrine of transubstantiation was developed above all by Aristotle and, following his lead, by Thomas Aquinas. "Substance" is a category that interrelates the following four attributes: By substance we mean (a) the exclusive *being of a subject* over against multiplicity and change of predicates; and (b) the essential *identity* and unity of this subject with itself (essentia = οὐσία); (c) the *permanence* of this subject over against the changes in the subject's modes of appearance; and (d) the *function of this subject as bearer* with regard to both essential and accidental appearances ("accidents" over against "substance," understood as ὑποκείμενον).[57] Later on, Thomas clearly distinguishes the *essentia* (*esse quid*), which is determined by content; the *substantia* (*esse in se*), which is determined by form; the *prima substantia*, which he calls *hypostasis*; and, finally, the *subsistentia*, which means the *esse per se*. This *esse per se*, when found in rational substances, is the foundation for "personal being" (*Summa theol.* I, q. 29, a.2, c).

The decisive aspect of the concept of substance is that it

implies a categorical and transcendental reality. This substance cannot belong to the realm of what can be physically experienced. Precisely this gives particular significance to this concept when applied to the event of consecration of the Holy Eucharist.[58]

We here distinguish transubstantiation in its intransitive sense, as the wonderful *event* ("conversio mirabilis et singularis") through which Christ becomes present on the altar under the species, and in the transitive sense, as the mysterious *deed of God* through which the transformation occurs.

To explain the event of *transubstantiation in the intransitive sense* we must distinguish as follows: In the *object* (bread and wine) there is the *substance* (= the being residing as bearer behind the properties that emerge and are experienced in the appearances) and there are the *accidents* (= the properties that make their appearance and can be experienced and expressed). In the *event of transformation* there is the *terminus a quo* (the substance of bread and wine that are transformed), the *terminus ad quem* (the body and blood of Christ, into which the bread and the wine are transformed), and the *terminus manens* or the *tertium commune* (which remains the same for both realities and states: these are the accidents, namely, smell, taste, shape, color, species, etc.). If nothing remained the same, this would imply that the first substance is simply destroyed and that the body and blood of Christ are created from nothing. Insofar as matter and form may be distinguished in the substance, both are transformed together, and not only the form of the substance (this is what Durandus of Saint Pourçain and A. Rosmini called *transformatio*), but the matter is also transformed as a subject of the form. A mere transformation (such as that of wine into vinegar) would be a natural transformation, not a genuinely supernatural change such as occurs in this sacrament. The *terminus ad quem*, therefore, does not experience any change in this sacramental transformation such as must be experienced in every natural change (for instance, the vinegar resulting is always different according to the kind of wine used to produce it). The body and blood of the Lord are preexistent, and they are as unalterable as the one and unique sacrificial death of Christ.

Transubstantiation in the transitive sense, the deed of transformation by the divine omnipotence, is therefore not to be thought of simply as a creative act of God. What is involved here is a wholly new act of the divine omnipotence whereby God's power so influences the substance of the species that it is directly transformed into its *terminus ad quem,* the bread into the body and the wine into the blood of Christ, while the accidents of bread and wine remain perfectly unchanged. It is this process that the theology of the Middle Ages intended to express with the concept "transubstantiation."

The differences among the metaphysical systems resulted in the portrayal of this one truth in different ways in each different school of thought. Thomas[59] spoke of a "beginning of being" (*incipit fieri*), which is explained on the basis of Ambrose's analogy to the process of the virgin birth or of the transformation of Aaron's rod into a snake. Later Thomists speak of a *productio* (from the standpoint of the *terminus ad quem*) or of a *reproductio* (from the standpoint of the heavenly Christ). This last consideration led J. Duns Scotus[60] to speak of an *adductio* in connection with the consecration, the bringing of the glorified Lord into the transformed species. The difficulty with this view lies in the fact that here what is involved is not the making present of the glorified Lord but rather the making present of his sacrifice on the Cross.

The "doctrine of transubstantiation" adds *two new teachings* to the dogma of Christ's "real presence" in the sacrament: the teaching that the *accidents* of bread and wine remain preserved even though the natural substances are no longer present, and the teaching that the substances of bread and wine are not destroyed and replaced by

Christ's body and blood but, rather, that they undergo a genuine and astonishing *transformation*. The doctrine of transubstantiation, correctly understood, elucidates and supports the doctrine of the real presence of Christ. It is for this reason that Pius VI, in his bull *Auctorem fidei* (1794), condemned the statement of the would-be Synod of Pistoia of 1786 (under Bishop Scipio de Ricci) that the presence of Christ in the Blessed Sacrament ought to be zealously preached about, but omitting reference to the doctrine of transubstantiation (D 1529–DS 2629). An analogy for this "transformation" is the "transition" of Jesus' corpse of Good Friday to the glorified and risen Lord of Easter morning.

D. THE DURATION OF THE REAL PRESENCE

Under the influence of M. Butzer and P. Melanchthon, M. Luther taught beginning in 1536 that the real presence of Christ was to be found only at the moment of reception (*in usu*). The *Formula of Concord* (1577) cast the doctrine in this way: "Extra usum, dum reponitur aut asservatur in pyxide aut ostenditur in processionibus, ut fit apud papistas, sentiunt corpus Christi non adesse." In opposition to this, the Council of Trent defined: "Si quis dixerit peracta consecratione in admirabili eucharistiæ sacramento non esse corpus et sanguinem D. N. J. C., sed tantum in usu, dum sumitur, non autem ante vel post, et in hostiis seu particulis consecratis, quæ post communionem reservantur vel supersunt, non remanere verum corpus Domini, *anathema sit*": "Whoever says that after the consecration the body and blood of Our Lord Jesus Christ are not present in the wonderful sacrament of Eucharist, but only *in usu*, that is, while it is being received, but not before or after, or that the true body of the Lord does not abide in the hosts and consecrated particles which are reserved after communion or are left over, *anathema sit*" (D 886–DS 1654). The words of institution and of promise clearly testify to the fact that the flesh and the blood of Christ are here *salvation-historical objective* and *transcendental realities* that are not *dependent on the act of reception* (cf. John 6,55: "My flesh is truly food . ." and 1 Cor 11,29: ". . . because he does not distinguish the body of the Lord [from other food]"). The Fathers enunciate this doctrine most clearly. Cyril of Alexandria says it would be foolish to deny salvific effect to the reserved species, "for neither Christ is altered nor is his holy body changed; the power of blessing as well as the life-giving grace remain constantly in him" (*Ep. ad Calosyrium*: PG 76, 1076). Similarly, John Chrysostom compares the altar with Christ's abode in the crib (*De beato Philogonio*: PG 48, 753). Jerome declares those fortunate who "are allowed to bear the body and blood of Christ in woven baskets and in a glass" (*Ep* 125, 20 *ad Rusticum*: PL 22, 1085). The use of "pastophoria" since the time of the *Apostolic Constitutions* (VIII, 13), and especially the "Mass of the Presanctified," known since the fourth century, as well as the reservation of the sacred species for house communion, for the communion of the sick, and for trips—all of which is documented since the time of Tertullian—are unequivocal witnesses for the ancient faith of the Church. By comparison to all the other sacraments, the Eucharist is an exception. All the other sacraments become a reality only in their accomplishment, while the Eucharist has to be granted as a preexistent reality that makes its human reception possible (D 876, 879–DS 1639, 1645). While the *beginning of Christ's presence* may be determined exactly with the uttering of the words of consecration, the *cessation of the presence* is difficult to ascertain. We may say that it sets in when the accidents are so changed that we must presume the presence of a substance other than the substance of bread and wine natural to the accidents. It is even more difficult to explain the "how" of this cessation of Christ's presence, since with the cessation of this presence the new natural substance proper to the changed and "spoiled" accidents must enter in. We must interpret the presence of Christ as a permanently astonishing event, and the entering in of the new natural substance for the spoiled accidents simply as a dissolution of this wonderful event.

E. REFLECTIONS ON THE DIFFICULTIES FOR THOUGHT RESULTING FROM THE DOCTRINE OF TRANSUBSTANTIATION

For a modern person, who thinks with the categories of the natural sciences, the metaphysical concept of substance we have been discussing exhibits an "occult quality." The modern Catholic who thinks along the lines of the natural sciences will most likely attempt to make comprehensible what is expressed in the doctrine of "transubstantiation" as being an "objective change of meaning" ("transfinalization" in salvation-historical and liturgical thought), and he or she will do this in the name of his or her natural manner of thinking and of his or her scientific image of the world. Although it may be that this train of thought will satisfy the demand of our age for rational interpretations, we must affirm that the mystery of the Eucharist cannot find its full and adequate expression in such an approach. As long as a better term is not found, we will have to keep on going back to the concept of "transubstantiation" from different angles, in spite of its paradoxical character, because precisely this paradox will most aptly safeguard the mystery of faith for our thought.

The unsolvable problematic stemming from the concept of "transubstantiation" was evident from the very beginning of its history. The concept was nevertheless further developed and endorsed by the magisterial definitions of the Church because of its capacity for dogmatic expression. The problematic of the concept is evident especially in two places: when considering the relationship between substance and species (*accidens, accidentia*[61]) and when considering the questions of the spatial and temporal manner of Christ's presence in the sacrament.

i. The Relationship between Substance and Accident

Once the metaphysical concept of substance was introduced into theological reflection on the mystery of faith that is the Holy Eucharist, and once the affirmation had been made that the substance of bread becomes converted into the substance of the Body of Christ, then the questions had to be answered concerning the new subject of the accidents that remain the same. It very soon became clear that the species could not subsist without a "bearer" or *subject,* and that the bearer of the natural accidents of bread and wine could not be the sacramental Christ, his body and his blood. Two main attempts were made to resolve this problem. The first was the statement of Peter Abelard that after transubstantiation the accidents of bread and wine are borne by the air surrounding them, much as the human form of an angelic apparition.[62] The other attempted solution was the teaching of St. Thomas that God in a wonderful way maintains the "quantity" of bread and wine after the consecration, and this "quantity" can then in turn become the subject of the other accidents, such as taste, smell, color (*Summa theol.* III, q. 7, a.1–2). These two attempts clearly show the limitations of the application of the thought-patterns deriving from the concept of transubstantiation. The surrounding air can never be the unifying subject for a multiplicity of accidents, and the quantity cannot be the natural subject of color, smell, and taste. Even if in our natural experience color is not perceived without extension, still the metaphysical relationship between subject and accidents cannot be applied to the metaphysical relationship between extension and color. All accidents, including extension, can have only one substance as subject in the metaphysical sense.

With regard to the Church's dogma, which is binding to faith, in relation to this theological dilemma, the following thoughts suggest themselves:

a) Despite the great efforts by medieval thought to elucidate the mystery of the Eucharist from the perspective of the general objective relationship between substance and accident, we must be clear that the *doctrine of transubstantiation* as an attempt to explicate the mystery of faith *in no way intends to make a pronouncement concerning the physical matter of bread and wine;* and just such an idea is what enters the field of discussion today as soon as the word "substance" is spoken. Today, before we can apply metaphysical thought-patterns to realities such as the matter of bread and wine, we must first have stated and responded to the physical and chemical questions concerning this matter. In terms of physical chemistry bread and wine are "conglomerates," and therefore it makes no sense to speak in this case of a unified "substance" that makes the bread to be what it is as bread or that makes the wine to be what it is as wine. This has made all metaphysical talk concerning a "substance" of the bread or the wine to be extremely problematic.

b) A glance at the event of the sacrament's institution clearly shows us that Christ here wanted to say nothing about the physical and chemical nature of bread and wine; the one thing he intended to do was to give himself to us in the rite of the paschal meal as sacrifice and sacrificial victim under the form of the sacrificial food and drink—give himself to us truly, really, and essentially, that is, with all the realism attained by salvation-history in the midst of the world's history, which means in the midst of the real, human, and material world.

c) The deep insights gained in our time by the modern natural sciences (above all physics and chemistry) into the makeup of matter, therefore, can contribute nothing positive to the elucidation of the eucharistic mystery. But those insights can and should warn the theologians to be critical of so-called "metaphysical schemata" developed by human thought concerning the things of the world before natural science was in a position of saying anything to us about these things "from the inside"; the result of this desirable critical attitude would be to dismantle those schemata to the extent necessary in order for our vision of the mystery itself to become ever freer and more expansive. As an attempt by intellectual knowledge to comprehend being, even material being, metaphysics must in this age of atomic physics think through again many of its traditional statements and concepts, formulating them anew and reconsidering their basis. Physics cannot replace metaphysics; rather, in its deeper ramifications, it presupposes metaphysics. Nonetheless, in the age of atomic physics, metaphysics can no longer have the form and attitudes that were legitimate in an age when the exact natural sciences were still not known.

d) What theological thinking in the Church and the thinking of the modern natural sciences have in common is the task of holding on firmly to the historical verity and reality, over against all thinking that tends in a sensualistic, idealistic, or purely positivistic direction. With regard to the problem of the Eucharist, this means three fundamental affirmations: (a) The so-called "accidents" are realities, and not merely sensory illusions, regardless of whether we should understand them to be more objectively or more subjectively conditioned. There have been some theologians who held this theory of "sensory illusion" in connection with the Eucharist on the basis of the philosophy of Descartes, teaching that after the consecration God produces the necessary sensory illusions in the person.[63] (b) Bread and wine belong to inanimate nature, and consequently all forms of metaphysical hylozoism, panpsychism, or pantheism are eliminated from a discussion on the doctrine of the Eucharist and transubstantiation. (c) Genuine thinking is always "related to an object" [*gegenstandsbezogen*], and therefore physicochemical thought (proper to the natural sciences), anthropological and philosophical thought (that builds itself up on the basis of reflection and understanding), and theological thought (bound up with revelation and the act of faith), each has its own "objective locus" and its own methods, and one cannot be substituted for by the other or be explained in terms of the other.

ii. The Question of Space and Time in the Eucharistic Presence

After stating these restrictions, we may still pose the serious question of what the Church's doctrine of transubstantiation still has to offer positively. The meaning and the value of the concept of transubstantiation become evident when we remember the point in time and the circumstances when it was introduced into the theological meditation on the eucharistic mystery. What was involved at that moment was the debate with the extreme *Capernaitic historical realism* of Paschasius Radbertus, who said that when the species were broken and bitten, it was the historical Christ himself who was broken and bitten. At the same time, the other side of the debate was with the *spiritualistic symbolism* of Berengar of Tours, who wholly excluded historical realism. The burning concern in the controversy, therefore, was to grasp more exactly the particular *quality of reality belonging by rights to the historicity of the sacramental Christ.* This historicity had to be upheld from two different sides if justice were to be done to the *sacramental historicity of the mystery:* from the side of the spatiality of the species and from the side of the temporality of the species. The realism deriving from the sacramental signs was determined precisely by this yoking of space and time. Spatiotemporality that can be experienced is indeed the constitutive element for real earthly historicity; and *sacramental historicity had to be anchored in this earthly historicity* if the *historicity of the mystery* was not to be emptied out spiritualistically. The problem then was how to avoid a *Capernaitic* realism. As a solution to this problem, the Aristotelian idea of substance and the substance/accident schema were ready at hand.

We have already said something on the idea of substance (3.c.2). The extent to which here "substance" was not understood in a physical but in a purely metaphysical way may already be gauged from the objection we find in Hugh of St. Victor: "Conversio ipsa non secundum unionem, sed secundum transitionem credenda est; quoniam nequaquam essentiæ in augmentum accidit . . . nec sic in pane corpus Christi consecrari dicimus, ut de pane corpus Christi esse accipiat nec quasi novum corpus subito factum de mutata essentia, sed in ipsum corpus verum [historicum] mutatam essentiam": "We believe in the conversion [transformation] not in the sense of a unification but in the sense of a transition. For it adds nothing to the essence [in the sense of an increase]. . . . Nor do we say that the body of Christ is so consecrated in the bread that the body of Christ is thought to receive its being from the bread, or that a new body suddenly is made from the transformed essence [of the bread]. Rather do we teach that the essence [of the bread] is transformed into the true [historical] body [of Christ]" (*De sacr.* II, 8, c. 9: PL 176, 468B). The change of the substance of bread, therefore, does not imply an augment of the body of Christ, as if with each consecration the body of Christ became greater according to the increase in the spatial substance of the bread. The consecration, rather, always makes present the one, true, historical, and now glorified body of the Lord. It is just as false to say that the substance of the bread is annihilated as to say that the glorified Lord is somehow "resubstantialized" in the physical sense in place of the bread's substance. For this reason J. Duns Scotus later on introduced the concept of *adductio.* Even though this expression can be misleading when understood in the sense of natural space, still it is apt in the authentic metaphysical sense. Transubstantiation simply makes possible the *repræsentatio,* the salvation-historical *making present* of the one and always iden-

tical Lord for all spaces and all times in which the transformed bread and wine exist. This is why the spatial presence of Christ under the species of bread and wine is not a
natural, spatial presence (*circumscriptive*) but rather a
presence corresponding to Christ's personal and essential
nature (*definitive*). The physical accidents, thus, guarantee
the spatiotemporal presence of the one, historical, and salvation-historical Christ, and they do this on the basis of
their necessary relationship to a substance as being their
subject. By virtue of the consecration, the accidents come
to exist without a natural subject, and yet, through the
compelling power of the fact that they can really be experienced, the accidents point to a real subject, a subject that
our faith in Christ's words of consecration makes us identify as being the true, historical, and salvation-historical
Christ.

What is here answered is *not a question concerning
matter, but rather a question concerning spatiotemporal
existence* such as is proper to a historical human being
and, therefore, also to the God-Man Christ as person.
Thomas expresses this truth with words such as "Sacrificium novæ legis a Christo institutum, ut scilicet, con-
tineret ipsum Christum passum . . . in rei veritate . . . sui
præsentiam corporalem nobis promittit in præmium"
(*Summa theol.* III q. 75, a.1, c). Thomas expressly rejects a
spatial presence of Christ in the physical sense (*Summa
theol.* III q. 75, a.2 and 4.c; q. 76, a.4), and likewise that the
transformation occurs within physical time; rather, he
says, it occurs *in instanti,* which is to say in a timeless moment (*Summa theol.* III, q. 76, a.7). St. Thomas is continually distinguishing this supernatural change from every
other natural change and from God's original act of creation (*Summa theol.* III, q. 76, a.8). The insistence that the
accidents can be experienced and that the reality of Christ
cannot be experienced, but is accessible only to faith,
brings Thomas to assert that the accidents continue in existence without a subject through a miraculous act of

God's power (*Summa theol.* III, q. 77, a.1, c). This makes it possible to affirm the following truths concerning the mystery of Christ's presence brought about through Christ's words of institution:

a) Whenever the words of institution are spoken over bread and wine by someone empowered by Christ, commissioned by Christ, and in the sense of this commission, the sensory tokens of this matter are to us the guarantee that here and now the historical Christ and his historical work of redemption are present. The spatiality and temporality of the accidents, which we can experience, are for us in this case the guarantee for the reality of the presence of the supraspatial and supratemporal Christ and of his work of redemption, *hic et nunc.* The metaphysical term *transubstantiation* gives unique and apt expression to the fact that *the sacramental presence of Christ* and of his work of redemption in the Holy Eucharist are not merely a subjective matter of faith, not merely an objective sensory reality, but rather a historical truth that possesses a real and immediate relation to our physical conditions of space and time, even if this truth may be grasped only by faith.

b) With this the command to eat and to drink acquires a whole new meaning: what is at stake is not so much coming to participate in the unique historical event of the Last Supper as represented in the eucharistic meal; the crucial point, rather, is that we, through the act of the sacrificial meal with real eating and drinking, come to participate again here and now in the sacrifice itself. "Take and eat, there, my sacrificial body," does not mean only one reality, but quite clearly expresses two very different realities: The words exhort us to eat and to drink, and they also affirm in a unique way that what here is offered for eating and drinking is the true, living, and sacrificial body of the historical Christ himself. Just as for believers the sacrificial meal is in a particular way the sacramental and spatiotemporal realization of the Eucharist, so too, for the ministry of the empowered and commissioned priest, the uttering of the words of consecration, the *actio* of the Mass, is in a particular way the realization of this sacrifice.

The reality of the accidents of bread and wine, the reality of the priestly words of consecration, the reality of the meal received with faith: each of these things is, in its own way, the guarantee for the reality of the historicity of Christ and his sacrifice *hic et nunc* in the worship of the Church.

c) The interpretation of the event of consecration with the term *transubstantiation* guarantees for us today, as it did in the Middle Ages in response to Paschasius Radbertus, that the presence of Christ and the encounter with the Christ and his sacrifice must be understood not in a physical sense but in an authentically "pneumatic" manner, in the sense of the presence of the Mysteries. Physicomaterial thinking is here expressly directed at the accidental signs in order to free up the metaphysical and personal relation for encounter with the Lord, who cannot be affected by the breaking and biting of the species but who is present here *per modum substantiæ* (that is, really) *et spiritus* (that is, pneumatically). Thus, Ambrose already said: "Corpus Christi corpus est divini Spiritus" (*De myst.* IX, 58: PL 16, 409) (the Lord is the Spirit [2 Cor 3, 17; cf. 1 Cor 10, 3; *Lam* 4.20]), and Peter Comestor ascribes to the Christ in the sacrament *spiritualem quandam existendi modum* (PL 171, 1151).

d) Because of the fact that the relationship of substance and accident after the consecration here represents the relationship between an incommensurable substance and the species of bread and wine, which can be experienced, it becomes understandable and possible that Christ should always be present simultaneously in many places without this implying any kind of multilocation or multipresence. The plurality is supplied only by the accidents that are experienced, while by contrast Christ, as their subject and substance, is always the same and one historical and salvation-historical Christ. The *metaphysical* relationship between substance and accident, when it is simultaneously attributed to the *physical* reality of the species of bread and wine and to the *salvation-historical* event of Christ and his redemptive deed (mediated by the paschal rite of the Last Supper), proves to be an extremely valuable dialectical instrument in the service of the uncompromising mysteriological affirmations on the sacramental presence of Christ in the Holy Eucharist. When M. Luther teaches in his *Great Catechism* (part V): "Est verum corpus et sanguis D. N. J. C. *in et sub pane et vino* per verbum Christi nobis christianis ad manducandum et bibendum institutum et mandatum," he is thinking in a very Catholic manner indeed, even if he, as a non-philosophical religious man, vigorously rejects the metaphysical explanation attached to "transubstantiation."

e) Through this correct understanding of transubstantiation we guarantee the correct conception of the "eating and drinking" involved in this sacrament: a crude physical Capernaitic understanding is thus avoided every bit as much as a non-realistic, merely spiritualistic, and personalistic encounter with Christ. In this manner the right conception of the sacramental actualization of the sacrifice of the Cross in the sense of mystery theology also is made possible, as we will see further on.

f) This understanding of the doctrine of transubstantiation also begins to lay down the correct foundations for the eucharistic cult, which we will deal with later on.

The Eucharist as Sacramental Sacrifice (The Meal-Sacrifice)

We must first consider the Eucharist's basis in salvation-history. This becomes evident only if we approach the Eucharist as a sacrifice in which we participate through the sacramental meal. After a brief reflection on the relationship of sacrifice and sacrament (1), we will study the reality of the Sacrifice of the Mass (2), the theological understanding of the nature of the Sacrifice of the Mass (3), and the effects of the Sacrifice of the Mass (4).

1. Sacrifice and Sacrament

A. HISTORICAL CONTEXT

While the Bread of Life Discourse in John 6 portrays the Eucharist in a special manner as being a "sacramental meal," in the Synoptics' accounts of the institution it clearly appears as a "sacrificial meal" in the context of the paschal meal with a necessary connection to the paschal sacrifice, without which this meal would be neither possible nor comprehensible. Christ's reference to the once and for all sacrifice of his life for the redemption of humankind makes the "sacrifice on the cross" of Jesus Christ to be the event from which this sacrament receives its meaning and in which it has the basis for its existence. In the place of the paschal lamb Christ gave his own sacrifical flesh, and in the chalice he gives his own blood to drink as the blood of the New Covenant, "which is poured out for you and for all, for the forgiveness of sins." This fulfillment, which the Old Testament's *paschal meal receives from the sacrifice of the cross in the room of the Last Supper,* became evident to Christians first of all in the living faith of the Church and in their living out of an ecclesial life.

Even though in 1 Cor 11, 26ff. the paschal meal's character as *meal* is strongly emphasized, still at the same time Paul is stressing the following: "As often as you eat this bread and drink the cup, you proclaim (καταγγέλετε) the death of the Lord, until he comes again." In 1 Cor 10,14–18 Paul expressly compares eucharistic participation in the body and blood of Christ with Israel's participation in *its* sacrifices: "Do not those who eat of the sacrifices (θυσίαι) participate in the altar of sacrifice (θυσιαστήριον)?" The author of the Letter to the Hebrews makes a parallel between the priesthood and the sacrifices of the Old Covenant and Christ and his sacrifice, and he teaches concerning the Eucharist: "We have an altar from which those who serve the tent have no right to eat" (Heb 13,10).[64] Thus, the celebration of the breaking of the bread on the first day of the week[65] is the New Testament's celebration of the death of the Lord with a community sacrifical meal. It appears that, particularly in Africa, and in connection with the fourth petition of the Our Father, "daily Mass with communion" became current practice rather early on.[66]

This daily celebration of Holy Mass must be seen in the context of other contemporary phenomena: difficulties during times of persecution, the influx of lukewarm Christians after 312 when the Church won its freedom, the lack of priests, the development of communities of lay monks, especially in Egypt. All of this led to the practice and, in some places, the custom of self-administered communion by laypersons outside the sacrifical celebration.[67] But wherever the Sacrifice of the Mass was preserved along with priestly presence and daily service by a priest, the practice of daily self-administered communion by laypeople outside Mass underwent steady decline. The battle against Arianism so exalted the divinity of Christ that the overemphasis given to awe and reverence tended to obstruct a trusting approach to the table of the Lord. A process of religious externalization on the part of the Church's membership—enormously increasing after the times of persecution—may also have contributed something to the decline of daily communion.

The most serious blow to daily communion came at the time of the mission to the Germans, since on the basis of their religious history and their own religious feeling the Germans did not see the necessary connection between sacrifice and communion; moreover, the reference to the Jewish paschal meal had no place in Christian preaching, particularly during periods of persecution of the Jews in the Middle Ages. In the Middle Ages communion was as a rule received only three times a year, on the great feasts of the Lord, and it was a special privilege when in the Rule of his order Francis allowed his brothers communion on a fourth occasion. The Fourth Lateran Council of 1215 prescribed communion once a year, this in spite of the existing "Sunday obligation."

In the thirteenth century, eucharistic piety received a wholly new theme with the cult of the Eucharist and the Feast of Corpus Christi, at the expense of a piety centered about sacrifice and the sacrificial meal. In the Late Middle Ages the economic difficulties of a very numerous clergy resulted in the practice of daily celebrating several Masses. Another resulting practice was the so-called *missa sicca* or "dry Mass," which referred to a Mass-like devotion that included only the preparatory prayers, the Liturgy of Word, the Our Father, and the final blessing and thus excluded the actual sacrificial liturgy. With this, the internal connection between sacrifice and sacrificial meal and the wholeness of the event of the Last Supper as prefigured in the Jewish paschal meal may be said to have quite definitively disappeared from the general consciousness of the Christian people. Thus, the Reformation (Luther) could retain the sacrament and in some sense renew it, while wholly rejecting the Sacrifice of the Mass. In so doing the Reformers did not realize that in this way they were also robbing the sacrament of its most authentic meaning.

For the decrees of the Council of Trent what became normative was not the draft of August 1562, which on the basis of the words of institution stressed the character of the Mass as meal, but the draft of September of the same year. This later draft, on the basis of the Letter to the Hebrews, again correctly proclaimed the Eucharist to be both sacrifice and sacrificial meal: the Sacrifice of the Mass, in which Christ's sacrifice on the cross is manifestly represented.[68] Reception of Holy Communion increased in frequency as a result of the Council's decrees and of the Counter-Reformation. But Jansenistic rigorism, as portrayed for instance in Antoine Arnauld's *De la fréquente communion* (1643), did its share in having a contrary effect. A negative influence was also the Enlightenment, which made it a rule that Catholics were bound only to fulfill the church law of 1215, requiring that the faithful communicate only once a year. In a contrary direction, the daily celebration of Mass as *the* daily duty of a priest became a rule after the Council of Trent. It was only the *Decree Concerning Holy Communion* of Pope Pius X (20 December 1905) and his encouragement of communion by children (1910) that ushered in a new springtime in eucharistic practice, which in turn was given a deepened theological foundation especially by the *Liturgical Movement* beginning after World War I and by *mystery theology*. Thus, for the first time since the early Christian era, the intrinsic relation existing between sacrifice and sacrament, between the *sacrifice* that is a meal and the *meal* that is a sacrifice, has again been seen and proclaimed in all its balance and richness. We can consider it a fruit of this development when the *Constitution on the Liturgy* of Vatican II introduces the Eucharist in the following terms: "At the Last Supper on the night on which he was betrayed, our Savior instituted the eucharistic sacrifice of his Body and Blood in order thus to perpetuate throughout all time the sacrifice of the cross until he comes again. In this way he entrusted to the Church, his beloved Bride, a memorial celebration of his death and resurrection: the sacrament of gracious mercy, the sign of unity, the bond of love, the paschal meal in which Christ is eaten, the heart is filled with grace and we are given the pledge of future glory" (Article 47).

B. POINTS FOR REFLECTION

Concerning the Eucharist as "sacrifice" and as "sacrificial meal" we must say the following: The primary *meaning of sacrifice* is giving honor to God, the attempt by the sinner to achieve reconciliation by participating contritely and somehow actively in Christ's atoning sacrifice. This enables human beings to bring the creature's thanksgiving and praise before the Creator in a new way. In the depths of their personal being humans can understand themselves only as creatures and as sinners before God, the absolute Creator and the one who alone is holy. But through the eucharistic sacrifice they can open out in a new manner and move along the path toward this absolute and holy God— and here it makes no difference whether we consider this movement primarily as an effort by humans or primarily as an act of God's grace. As a religious reality it could only be considered both things at once. An essential part of sacrifice is the gesture of giving away, surrendering, offering up, and therefore sacrifice, in its basic phenomenal form, is an *"act" by a human being reaching out over himself or herself,* even though such an act may indeed be said to have its roots in the human interior disposition. The eucharistic sacrifice, for all its uniqueness, cannot dispense with these fundamental elements of human sacrifice.

By contrast to the sacrifice, the *sacrament* has the primary meaning of "sanctifying human beings through a gift of God." Because of the human being's spiritual nature as person this sanctification cannot take place without interior cooperation in faith, hope, and love, and such sanctification must also serve objectively to glorify God. Furthermore, humans can subjectively direct the sacramental act secondarily to God's glorification. All of this notwithstanding, we may say that in its phenomenal form the accomplishment of the sacrament is a *receptive action*, a *taking and accepting*. Now, because of the greatness of the gift involved, we may say that this action in the end necessarily includes an act of self-surrender; but such self-surrender of human beings can nevertheless become the primary and specific theme of the sacrament.

We would misunderstand and even tend to do away with the richness of the religious possibilities in the act of human existence before God were we to reduce these two essentially different dimensions—sacrifice and sacrament, offering up and receiving—to one single thing or attempt to derive one from the other. Along with this loving *offering up* and this believing and trusting *reception* we must also include in the Christian understanding of sacrifice and sacrament a hope-filled *existence into the future*. As we have seen, it is not only sacrament that has an eschatological character that both points to the future and is shaped by the future; sacrifice itself, in the Christian sense, cannot lack this relationship with the future. The sacrificial surrender somehow contains the idea that everything can reach its fulfillment and perfection only in the future, and that therefore the sacrifice is also a surrender that will find its actual fulfillment and perfection only in God. Here, a *sacrifice* by human beings is no longer a surrender in the sense of "renunciation or abandonment" but rather sheer *participation in the act of being accepted by God*, of being taken up by him "who fulfills all in all" (Eph 1,23). For this is the goal of all creation, and most especially of human beings: to be filled even to the very fullness of God (Eph 3,19), who alone is "all in all" (1 Cor 15,28).

Liturgical studies deal with the concrete historical form and evolution of the Christian sacrifice. Dogmatics limits itself to clarifying the basic questions concerning the reality of the Sacrifice of the Mass (2), its nature (3), and its effects (4).

2. The Reality of the Sacrifice of the Mass

Before we go on to discuss the historical reality of sacrifice in the New Testament (B), we must first be clear on the concept and nature of sacrifice as such (A).

A. WHAT IS A SACRIFICE?

i. The Theological Concept of "Sacrifice" as Defined by the History of Religions

Christian theology cannot really understand the affirmations and events of revelation without first applying to these mysteries of faith the categories of natural, non-revealed thought as these categories have become manifest in natural language and natural thought. Although we must indeed stress from the outset that these natural concepts are to be understood in an "analogical sense," still we cannot ignore the fact that the pressures of our everyday manner of thinking and speaking often lead us—through sheer "understandable presentation"—to miss the Christian mystery quite wholly, since this is a reality that always becomes manifest somewhere in the realm of paradox.

To come to a theological understanding of the sacrifice of Christ, theology has generally used the concept of sacrifice developed by research in the history of religions, which investigates the phenomenon of sacrifice in the different non-Christian religions.

The essential aspects of this understanding of sacrifice are as follows:

a) A sacrifice is usually a public cultic act of a religious community, even when it is accomplished by individuals and for personal reasons. The structural elements of sacrifice are an *offerer of sacrifice* who is somehow qualified (in the higher religions this is mostly an official religious minister such as a priest, otherwise a natural authority such as the father of the family or the eldest member of a tribe), a qualified *sacrificial gift,* and a *sacrificial action,* which mostly involves symbolic rites. To this may be added a *purpose for sacrifice* which determines the different kinds of sacrifices, as well as the requirement that the appropriate subjective *sacrificial disposition* be present, since this is what imparts to the symbolic gifts and actions their right meaning.

b) The loftiness of a *religion* and its sacrificial cult is not determined by the loftiness of its contextual *culture.* In the cultures of the ancient world it appears that "low" motivations, such as appeasing the wrath of the gods or manipulating the gods by means of magical powers, were of greater significance than was the case in primitive nature religions, as has been shown by the school of W. Schmidt in connection with the Bush People of Australia and the original inhabitants of the islands of Tierra del Fuego.

c) The *natural origin* of sacrifice appears to lie in the human desire to show *thanksgiving* to the deity (sacrifices of first-fruits and young animals) and in the human being's need, in his or her guilt-consciousness, to achieve *atonement* with the deity. This latter motivation has easily led to lower and religiously aberrant forms of the sacrificial cult, such as human sacrifices.[69]

ii. Stages of the Development of Sacrifice in the History of Judæo-Christian Revelation

Throughout the variety of its historical layers, revelation itself exhibits a variegated picture of "sacrifice," and at the same time it shows us a line of development within salvation-history that can enlighten us by imparting a deeper understanding of Christian sacrifice.

Here we can distinguish five different periods in the history of sacrifice:

a) Within Scripture's manner of understanding the world through faith, the first sacrifices are those of Cain and Abel. This same scriptural understanding of the world and of humankind, however, places at the very origin of history a primordial state of innocence that corresponds to eschatological fulfillment, a state that Scripture has clothed in the "narrative of paradise." The Christian understanding of the world is deeply nourished by the prophets' eschatological image of the world and it must, consequently, consider the question concerning the so-called "paradisal state" with full theological seriousness, quite apart from the question concerning the historicity of paradise. (This does not mean, however, that the Christian must naïvely accept the mythical portrayal of the paradisal state in Scripture.) It is thus that the theological question arises (one that has been increasingly asked since the nineteenth century) *whether sacrifice was already a part of this so-called paradisal state of human beings* or whether sacrifice has any meaning only beginning with the human sinful state. The answer to this question presupposes a certain understanding of sacrifice and is significant for any further discussion of the concept of sacrifice. Augustine rejected the notion of sacrifice in the paradisal state by referring to the biblical account, and Dominic Soto likewise rejected it on the grounds that sacrifice makes sense only in the context of sinfulness. By contrast, in our twentieth century, M. ten Hompel and V. Thalhofer have supported the existence of sacrifice even in the paradisal state by arguing that the original meaning of sacrifice should be sought in human beings' total surrender of their person to God in obedience and love, and not in the cultic destruction of a sacrificial gift.

b) *After the Fall,* in the time of the patriarchs, which is already colored by human sinfulness, we encounter in Scripture numerous portrayals of sacrifice beginning with Cain and Abel, Noah and Abraham. After humans had fallen away from God by their sin and had fallen prey to the world, which was cursed on their account, sacrifice came to consist of the attempt by humans again to attain to communion with God through the acknowledgment of God's supremacy, the active confession of their own guilt, and the surrender by humans to God of a world which humans had usurped, even to the point of destroying specific things within the world. Now humans began to sacrifice anything that was of value: the food and drink, for instance, on which they lived, as if to say, "All of my existence I owe to God." They slaughtered their domestic animals, as if to say, "My life has been forfeited through sin, like the life of this animal that belongs to me and which I am giving to God." Fire, with its purifying and destructive power, was widely used in sacrifice since it also is a symbol for God himself (cf. 1 Kgs 18,38). Such an understanding of sacrifice gave rise to both the liturgical cult and the priesthood, and the sacrificial gift became a substitute for humans' own self-surrender. In the Abraham narrative (Gen 22) for the first time we see a sacrifice as something demanded by God.

c) With the coming into possession of the land and with Israel's becoming a people under Moses the sacrifical cult, which had until now been a matter of human necessity and the call of God's grace to the individual, became a public affair of the People of God. Revelation clarifies and justifies this process in its account of the exodus from Egypt and of the *Covenant on Sinai.* God's saving activity on behalf of Israel was reciprocated by a *differentiated sacrificial cult* that profoundly left its mark in the history of the people and every individual within it. The place of sacrifice (the tent of the Covenant and afterward the temple) and the sacrificial rite, the sacrificial gifts and the sacrifi-

cial priesthood, the times of sacrifice and the forms of sacrifice, all found their specific expressions that continued to
evolve through Jewish history (Exod 25–32; and for the
temple priesthood see Leviticus). Of special significance,
beginning with the paschal sacrifice at the exodus from
Egypt, appears to be the connection between sacrifice and
sacrificial meal, whereby the "sacrificial meal" gives access to fruitful participation in the sacrifice itself.

As far as the *matter for sacrifice* is concerned, the Law
ordains food offerings (flour, oil, wine), slaughtered victims
(the flesh of domestic and herd animals, with the exception of unclean animals), drink offerings, and the offering
of incense. In what concerns the *manner of sacrifice*, we
can distinguish the burned offering (unknown in ancient
times in the Near East outside Israel), the roast offering,
the raised offering, the woven offering, and the libation.
According to the *intention* for sacrificing, we have the sacrifice for atonement, the sacrifice for sin, and the sacrifice
of praise and thanksgiving. With regard to the *times* when
sacrifice took place, we have the daily sacrifice, the evening and morning sacrifice, and the great sacrifices on the
solemn feasts.

The Aaronic priesthood and the sacrificial prescriptions
of Leviticus clearly show us an institutionalized cult that
does not always escape the dangers of every kind of institutionalization, which we can sum up with the one word
"externalization."

Against this decadence of the religious element in the
cult it was above all the penitential prophets of the Old
Testament who took a stance. Hosea and Amos fought
against this *externalized cult* in the Northern Kingdom,
where it was often associated with immoral aberrations
(Hos 4,8–14.18; Amos 2,7f; cf. Ezek 16,16–19). Hosea has
Yahweh himself speak: "I desire steadfast love and not sacrifice, the knowledge of God, rather than burnt offerings"
(Hos 6,6). Isaiah (1,10–16;29,13), Micah (6,6–8) and Jeremiah (7,21–23) also denounced a sacrificial cult that no

longer served to further ethical justice and authentic piety
before Yahweh. But this critique of externalization did not
imply a rejection of sacrifice as such: for the prophets had
a high regard for the temple as the house of God (Jer
7,7–11;26,2) and for Israel's solemnities as well (Isa 30,29;
Jer 3,11), and it is with melancholy that Hosea remarks
that during the exile Israel had to do without the cult (Hos
9,4f.). The writers of the Psalms (Ps 40,7–11;69,31f.) and
the authors of the Wisdom Books (Prov 16,6;21,3) make
their own the prophets' criticism, and they emphasized
the fact that Yahweh does not need the blood and flesh of
sacrificial animals, since the whole world belongs to him
(Ps 50,8–15). Psalm 51 (18f.) stresses the point that it is the
sacrifice's *intention* that is decisive: "The sacrifice acceptable to God is a broken spirit, a broken and contrite heart."

Such *internalization of the notion of sacrifice by the
prophets* was to be sure followed in the post-exilic period
by a *new institutionalization in the temple cult,* which
made sacrifice to be essentially a work of obedience toward the temple and the law of the temple. Consequently,
works of charity (Prov 16,6; Tob 4,11), of reverence toward
one's parents (Sir 3,3), and of justice (Sir 3,30) were henceforth also to be regarded as sacrifices.

By contrast to the idea of the scapegoat (Lev 16), Second
Isaiah (53f.) introduced the wholly new conception of the
"Servant of God" who offers himself as sacrifice for the
sins of others. But this idea of a *vicarious sacrifice of aton-
ment* and of a *sacrifice of self for others* appears not to have
been fully understood before the New Testament's proclamation of redemption.

d) In the light of the teaching, life, and work of Christ
the decisive question arises: *What does Christ say to the
notion of sacrifice* as it had developed up to his time
within the faith-community of the Old Testament and
that had reached its high point in the temple cult? Christ
did not expressly reject the sacrifices; he showed reverence
before the temple and the priesthood of the Old Testament

(Mark 11,17 and parallels, with reference to Isa 56,7: "My house is a house of prayer"). Nevertheless, he made his own the prophetic criticism of the externalization of sacrifice and the prophets' demand for interiority (Matt 9,13-Hos 6,6: "I want mercy and not sacrifice"), and he saw the Law and the Prophets as summarized in the great "commandment of love" (Mark 12,28–32 par.). Indeed, he prophesied the destruction of the temple and, along with it, the end of its sacrificial cult (Mark 13,2 par.), and he proclaimed a New Covenant to be sealed "in his own blood" (Mark 14,24 par.), a blood that was to be a ransom "for many" (cf. Mark 10,45; Matt 20,28; Eph 1,7; Tit 2,14).

In such a fashion Christ portrayed himself as *the Servant of God* of Second Isaiah (52,13–53,12), and the whole narrative of the Passion, which most likely is the oldest part of the tradition in the Synoptic Gospels, presents itself as the real and sole fulfillment of the idea contained in the prophecies of the Servant of God.[70]

Paul expressly characterized the death of Christ as an "atoning sacrifice" (1 Cor 15,3; Rom 5,8-10; Col 1,19-22), and the author of the Letter to the Hebrews incessantly stresses the fact that the sacrifice of Christ surpasses by far all the sacrifices of the Old Testament, and how Christ, through his one and unique immaculate sacrifice, fulfilled all other sacrifices. In the Letter to the Hebrews we read: "Through the eternal Spirit Christ offered himself as spotless sacrifice to God" (9,14; cf. Eph 5,2), and such a statement may well be seen as providing the basis for Christ's new understanding of sacrifice.

Being both God and man, *Christ* offered himself to God once and for all as wholly valid sacrifice of reconciliation and redemption on behalf of humankind. In him sacrifice became something totally new. All previous sacrifices had been attempts by ephemeral and sinful human beings to attain again to communion with God, the eternal and holy one, by means of human gifts. These attempts, moreover, had received their confirmation and ordering from God himself in the revelation of the Old Testament. In this context, sacrifice acquires a wholly new fundamental structure by virtue of *Christ's sacrifice of himself.*

1) Christ offers *himself* as sacrifice: In the person of Christ the sacrificial gift and the sacrificing priest are one and the same. From this perspective the question concerning the sacrifices of humans in paradise gains a new relevance.

2) Since theological thought must distinguish in Christ between the divine and the human reality, the doctrine of the hypostatic union is the guarantee for the fact that it is the one concrete historical Jesus Christ who as God-Man offers the sacrifice, which means that his sacrifice in a mysterious way is anchored in God himself: God [the Father] so loved the world that he gave [ἔδωκεν = offered as sacrificial gift] his only-begotten Son, that whoever believes in him should not perish but have eternal life" (John 3,16).

3) Because Christ's sacrifice is an atoning sacrifice for sin and the wages of sin is death, this atoning sacrifice had to be a "sacrifice of self through death:" it could no longer be a merely spiritual sacrifice of self as would have been appropriate to the paradisal state.

4) Because Christ, the God-Man, is an absolutely unique historical reality, this sacrifice of his could enter history only as an absolutely unique and unrepeatable sacrifice.

5) With this we must finally ask the question concerning *sacrifice in Christ's Church*, which is to say in the people of God's New Covenant. Since "sacrifice" is an essential part of revealed "religion," the latter resting on the relation of creature and Creator and of sin and grace between God and human beings, Christianity cannot be a "religion without sacrifice" such as we encounter in Buddhism and Jainism, in which we would also have difficulty speaking of a "personal God." On the other hand, the sacrifice of Christ remains of an absolutely unique nature. Through the "sacramental celebration of his sacrificial death" accomplished in the paschal rite of the Last Supper and through his com-

mand to celebrate a "memorial sacrifice," Christ himself created the possibility of wholly new sacrificial event in his Church, a sacrificial event we have still to discuss later on when we develop our theological analysis of what we call "Sacrifice of the Mass." We shall see the essential element in this "sacramental rite" to be the fact that it is not primarily an institutionalized rite, even more fundamentally than this, the Mass is a co-enactment by the members of Christ's Body through their participation in the sacrifice of Christ their Head. This line of thought already appears quite expresssly formulated in St. Paul's theology of sacrifice: "I appeal to you, brethren, by the mercies of God, to present your bodies [yourselves] as a living sacrifice, holy and acceptable to God, which is your rational [spiritual] worship" (Rom 12,1). 1 Peter 2,5 expresses a similar thought: "Like living stones be yourselves built into a spiritual temple, to be a holy priesthood, to offer spiritual sacrifices acceptable to God through Jesus Christ!"

Finally, the description of the "slaughtered Lamb," around whom the redeemed and the elect throng in the Kingdom of Heaven and whose wedding with the Church represents the ultimate fulfillment of revelation (Rev 5,6; 7,9.7; 14,1ff; 19,7ff.), may be seen as prophetically announcing the eschatological meaning of this sacrifice of the Church.

iii. The Objective Structural Elements of Sacrifice

In its cultic sense, the word "offering" is a close equivalent of "sacrifice." Deriving from the Latin *offerre*, it denotes a gift that is brought before the face of God. The Greek ἀναφέρειν translates the Hebrew *quarab*, and προσφέρειν renders *olah*, which is the technical term for the verb "to sacrifice" especially in the priestly code (Lev 17,5; cf. Isaiah 57,6; Heb 7,27; 11,17; 1 Pet 2,24: "to lay a gift on the altar of sacrifice"). In a transferred sense it is also applied to "spiritual sacrifices" (1 Peter 2,5).

In spite of all its unique interior development, reaching down to the very foundations of religious realities, a living salvation-history cannot exclude any authentic elements essential to the human experience as these have emerged in previous stages of development. For this reason it would be very valuable for us to review in brief the objective structural elements of sacrifice as these have developed in the course of the history of sacrifice with its different stages. Such a study will then enable us to understand whether (and how) these elements still appear in all their meaning and justification at the stage of the fulfillment of sacrifice, namely, in the Sacrifice of the Mass.

a) The first element is the person who brings the sacrifice, "*the sacrificer.*" In a purely anthropological sense every individual has both the right and the duty to engage in such sacrificial service. But from the standpoint of a correct understanding of God and of religion we must affirm that this "sacrificer" must be a socially and ethicoreligiously qualified person, or must become such by virtue of the sacrifice. God is not simply there for each individual as "his or her God"; he is necessarily the "one and sole God of all humankind," and wherever this God is invoked "against other people" (even if these should be personal enemies) the true image of God is compromised and endangered. Likewise religion, in the sense of Christ's requirements and in a fashion corresponding to his unique image of God, must always lead the individual person to think not only of his or her own salvation but of the salvation of all, and particularly of those who most appear to live in the way of perdition or whose life most threatens to develop into eternal perdition. Finally, beyond any thought of human salvation, the goal and perfection of all fundamental religious attitudes in human beings is the stance of thanksgiving, praise, and adoration before the almighty, all-good, and all-holy God himself. Thus we see how the "sacrificer" necessarily stands in the place of the greater human community, and that his role must be seen as determined not only by this human community itself but also by the deity whose reality is grasped by faith. Our understanding of the religious relationship of human beings to their God also has much bearing on our understanding of the "sacrificer." The figures, therefore, of the sacrificing head of a household or eldest member of a tribe, of the person called to minister (*sacerdos*) in the holy tent or in the temple of Yahweh by virtue of his belonging to the tribe of Aaron, of the minister of the cult of the People of Israel—all these figures are an expression of the way the religion of the Old Testament understood itself at different stages of its development. Christ's sacrificial office has its basis solely in his own person and in his one–time atoning sacrifice for the redemption of humankind and for the establishment of a New Covenant with God (Mark 14,24; Exodus 24,8). The command to celebrate the memorial of the Last Supper (Luke 22,19; 1 Cor 11,26), the handing over of the power to bind and to loose (Mt 18.8) as well as the comprehensive entrusing of his own divine mission to his Apostles (John 20,21; 17,18f.) are the foundation for the fact that, in Christ's Church, the *Apostles* may and must exercise in their own manner Christ's unique office. The example of St. Paul shows that this apostolic office is passed on, "in succession and tradition" and through the Jewish rite of the laying on of hands, to those whom the Apostles themselves select as successors.[71] It is not the ministry itrself that is decisive; rather, it is the "mission" that entitles one to be a minister.[72]

b) Another part of sacrifice is the *sacrifical gift* (*mincha:* Gen 4,3), which is always a necessary or very valuable reality that people remove from their own area of use and give away, either symbolically or by destroying it. Since it is to the deity that people give it away, it becomes a "consecrated gift" (*kodashim*), and insofar as this handing over occurs through a particular rite, the sacrificial gift is called *korban* ("offering") in Ezekiel and in the priestly code. Along with the unbloody sacrifice of food and drink (which

also takes the form of burnt offering), particular significance is taken on by the bloody slain sacrifice, since the
destruction of life and the pouring out of the blood, which
is the bearer of life, make crystal clear humans' total in-
debtedness to God. Along with the "whole offering" (*holo-
caustum*), the "sacrificial meal" has special significance in
Israel, since through a sacrificial meal there is symbolized
and effected the communion of the believers among themselves and with the deity (e.g., the paschal meal) and the
meal is a sign that the deity has accepted the sacrifice.
Paul interprets the "memorial celebration" that followed
Christ's Last Supper as the "meal of the Lord" (1 Cor 11,20),
and he terms it a "sacrificial meal" (1 Cor 10,16–22) that
conferes participation in Christ and his sacrifice. Just as
Christ offers "himself" as sacrificial gift to the Father, so
too the Christian cannot but partake of this sacrificial gift,
which is Christ himself. This imposes on Christians, as
members of Christ, the duty of offering themselves with
Christ to the Father as a holy gift (Rom 12,1) and a precious
and fragrant sacrifice to God (Eph 5,2; Lev 1,9).

c) The *sacrificial action* in which the gift is offered to
God is quite varied according to the kind of gift involved
and the human attitude toward sacrifice. In the course of
the development of the cult it has assumed a rich variety
of forms, in which a significant role is played by the sense
of giving away the human possession (the "destruction")
and surrendering it to God (the "immolation"), as well as
by the search for a sign that the deity has accepted the sacrifice (cf. 1 Kgs 18,36–39: the sacrifice of Elijah; and in the
sacrificial meals in the temple, the meal itself). In the case
of Christ's sacrifice of himself, the sign of its acceptance is
his Resurrection by the Father (Phil 2,5–11). Like the Last
Supper, the Sacrifice of the Mass represents the unique and
sole sacrifice of Christ on the cross, and the rite of the
commingling of the Body and the Blood just before communion is intended to symbolize the fact that the meal is

a participation not only in Christ's sacrifice but also in the risen and living Lord.[73]

d) Insofar as the "sacrificial action" as such has any meaning only on the basis of a transcendental reality, every sacrifice also involves a human "intentionality." Without such intentionality the event of sacrifice remains a mere ceremonial. The fundamental *goals of sacrifice* are atonement for one's own guilt, reconciliation with God, human beings' deliverance from sin, rendering of praise to God, self–surrender to God, communion, and community with God. Especially the temple cult of Israel greatly developed these sacrificial ends in sacrifices of thanksgiving and imploration, sacrifices of praise and atonement, sacrifices of conciliation, and as fulfillment of vows.

e) The sacrifice of the New Testament is not an action of humans themselves, but rather the obedient enactment and participation in Christ's one–time atoning sacrifice to the point where the Christians, as members of Christ, must offer themselves as sacrifice as well. For this very reason in the New Testament, along with the intention of the sacrifice, the *attitude of sacrifice* gains particular significance. Here this does not so much connote the subjecive attitude of the spirit and the heart, but rather the way to an objective understanding of self out of faith. The basic components of a Christian attitude of sacrifice are the sense of being a creature, the consciousness of being a sinner, the awareness of divine filiation, having one's life from being a member of Christ. "I have been crucified with Christ; it is no longer I who live, but Christ who lives in me; and the life I now live in the flesh I live by faith in the Son of God, who loved me and gave himself for me" (Gal 2,20). "One has died for all; therefore all have died. And [Christ] died for all, that those who live might live no longer for themselves but for him who for their sake died and was raised" (2 Cor 5,15).

B. EXISTENCE OF THE SACRIFICE OF THE MASS

Although the New Testament itself does not explicitly use the term "sacrifice" with reference to the Eucharist, "sacrifice" does become the fundamental definition for it that the Church's self-understanding in faith developed in the period immediately following the New Testament. Especially beginning with the struggle against Gnosticism, the different liturgies[74] further qualify this "sacrifice" as being an "anamnesis"[75] of the whole work of redemption: "We proclaim your death, O Lord, and we praise your resurrection, until you come in glory!" This *memorial celebration* is, in keeping with the ancient Jewish understanding of *zakar*, not merely a subjective remembering but rather the liturgical (sacramental) "representation" (i.e., "making present again") of something that is past in a historical sense, for the purpose of our being able to participate in it fruitfully for all time, for all epochs, every one of which is in need of this "historical deed."

In response to the denial of the sacrificial nature of the Mass by the Reformers, the Council of Trent expressly declared: "Si quis dixerit, in Missa non offerri Deo verum et proprium sacrificium, aut quod offerri non sit aliud quam nobis Christum ad manducandum dari, *anathema sit*": "If anyone should say that in the Mass a true and real sacrifice is not offered to God, or that this offering is nothing other than Christ's being given to us as food, *anathema sit*" (D 948; cf. 938 – DS 1751; 1739ff.). This is not only a statement against the Reformation; it is also an expression and a confession of what the Church has believed from the beginning: That, in the Church's understanding, the *Mass is a true and real sacrifice* in the sacramental sense and that, with reference to the one-time sacrifice of the Cross, the *Mass is a relative sacrifice,* which means that it is real in an ontic sense but not autonomous.

i. Proof from Scripture

In an effort to understand the eucharistic event of the New Testament as a fulfillment of the promises of the Old Testament, thus to come to grasp it better in all its newness, theology since the second century has repeatedly used two favorite texts from the Old Testament:

Malachi 1,10f.: "I have no pleasure in you, says the Lord of hosts, and I will not accept a sacrifice from your hand. For from the rising of the sun to its setting my name shall be great among the nations, and in every place incense shall be offered to my name and a pure food-offering (*mincha*) shall be brought." In view of the grievances found in the community returning to Palestine from the Babylonian captivity, the prophet here prophesies concerning a new sacrifice to come. It is to be an unbloody, universal, perfect, liturgical sacrifice that already the primitive Church saw realized in the Eucharist, as can be seen from the way this passage is quoted in the *Didache* around 110 A.D. From this point on the passage is quoted with great frequency, for instance, by Justin, Irenæus, Tertullian, Clement of Alexandria, Cyprian, and so on. (The texts will be given in a moment.)

Isaiah 66,20: "They shall bring all our brethren from all the nations as an offering to the Lord to my holy mountain Jersulalem, says the Lord, just as the Israelites bring their cereal sacrifice in a clean vessel to the house of the Lord." It was the spiritual interpretation of the Malachi passage, especially by Tertullian[76] that led to the use of this passage of Isaiah. As members of Christ, Christians are incorporated into Christ's sacrifice by the priests who offer the sacrifice and, ultimately, by Christ himself, who alone is the High Priest.

Even though, as we have said, the eucharist is never called a "sacrifice" expressly in the New Testament, the whole context of the institution and the New Testament's own interpretation of the meaning of the Eucharist point beyond doubt to the Eucharist's "sacrificial character." We here enumerate the most important evidence:

a) In the context of the paschal meal (Luke 22,15; 1 Cor 5,7), which itself is a "sacrificial meal" and a "memorial meal," Christ gives himself out in place of the sacrificial flesh when he declares the bread to be "his [sacrificial] flesh" and distributes it to the Apostles.

b) In the oldest eucharistic account, in Paul (1 Cor 11,24; cf. Luke 22,19), Christ himself refers indirectly to Isaiah 53,4–6 when he hands his sacrificial body (διδόμενον = given) and his sacrificial blood (ἐκχυνόμενον = poured out) to the Apostles and says that these are surrendered "for you."

c) The words concerning the cup in Mark (14,24) and Matthew (26,28), in a manner analogous to Exodus 24,8, present the blood contained in the cup as the "blood of the covenant" separated from the flesh, which means it is "sacrificial blood." It has been acquired by the act of slaying and, as such, is the sign for the surrender of life and an expression of the sacrifice of life.

d) In a deep symbolic sense, the manner in which Christ "gives himself—his sacrificial body and blood—away" (ἔδωκεν) to the Apostles may be regarded not only as a sign but as the actual opening up or representation of the "surrender" with which Christ handed himself over to the Father on Good Friday as a sacrifice for many. (Cf. John 3,16; Gal 1,4; Tit 2,14; 1 Tim 2,6: "he gave himself as a ransom for all".)

e) Paul therefore expressly compares the "Lord's Supper" with pagan sacrificial meals, which are nothing more than a ritual participation in the sacrifice involved (1 Cor 10, 18–22),

f) According to 1 Cor 11, 24–26, the breaking of the bread with thanksgiving and the offering of the wine in the cup are mandated as a "memorial celebration," which can mean nothing other than the (in a cultic sense) real "proclamation (καταγγέλλετε, in the indicative) of the death of the Lord, until he comes again."

g) Just as Paul presents the death of Christ as a "sacrificial death for us sinners," so too the Letter to the Hebrews in particular develops the doctrine of Christ as the sole and new high priest according to the order of Melchizedek (4,14–16; 5,6 = Ps 110,4). In this manner his sacrifice of himself is portrayed as the sole and definitive sacrifice (7,26–28), which he, moreover, is always offering for us in heaven to the Father (8,1–3; 7,25; 9,24; 10,12). This makes Christ to be the mediator of the New Covenant, and "by a single sacrifice he has perfected for all time those who are sanctified (i.e., sacrificed)" (10,14).

h) The Gospel of John too views the Eucharist as "sacrificial flesh for the life of the world" (6,51), and Jesus dies as the true paschal lamb (19.34ff. = Exodus 12,46). The statement "whoever has the Son of God, has the life" (1 John 5,12) refers to the crucified Christ (1 John 5,6), through whose sacrificial death the life has been given to us.

ii. Proof from Tradition

The *disciplina arcani* notwithstanding, from the earliest periods of Christian history we already have evidence of an uninterrupted testimony concerning the Sacrifice of the Mass. We briefly cite the following as being most important:

Didache 14, 1–3[77]: "On the Day of the Lord, come together, break the bread and give thanks after first having confessed your sins: in this way your sacrifice will be pure. Anyone who has a quarrel with his friend shall not take his place among you until they have been reconciled, so that your sacrifice not be desecrated (cf. Matt 5,23f.). For such is the Lord's command: 'In evey place and at every time a pure sacrifice shall be offered to me, because I am a great king, says the Lord, and my name is wonderful among the nations' (Mal 1,11.14)."

Clement of Rome (*First Letter to the Corinthians*, 40, 1–5; written 95/97 A.D.) (PG 1,288ff.): "We must accomplish in right order everything that the Lord appointed we should carry out at specified times. He wished sacrifices and divine services (θυσίαι καὶ λειτουργίαι) should take place, but this was not to happen haphazardly and without order but at definite times and hours. He himself determined according to his all-exalted will where and by whom these things should be established, so that all should occur in holy fashion and be acceptable and pleasing to his will. Those who now offer their sacrifices at the prescribed time are pleasing and praiseworthy. For to the chief priest his own ordinances have been appointed, and the other priests have also been shown their own place, and appropriate services are assigned to the Levites. And the layman is bound to the prescriptions for laymen."

Thus, according to these two documents from before the turn to the second century, it is already taken for granted as a tradition coming from the apostolic period that the "sacrifice" is precisely regulated as a public and communal cult to be offered at specific times and places by specific persons.

Ignatius of Antioch (*Ad Phil.* 4): "Strive to celebrate only one eucharist. For there is only one flesh of our Lord Jesus Christ and only one cup for union with his blood, only one altar (θυσιαστήριον), just as there is only one bishop in union with the presbytery and the deacons, my fellow servants. The end is that, whatever you do, you should do it according to God's will" (PG 5, 700). In his *Letter to the Smyrnæans* (7) Ignatius calls the "eucharist the flesh of our redeemer, Jesus Christ, the flesh that suffered for our sins and which God the Father awakened in his goodness (PG 5, 713).

In his *Dialogue with the Jew Tryphon,* Justin Martyr three times makes reference to Malachi 1,10f.,[78] and he says that the prophet is speaking in advance about the sacrifices that we, the heathen nations, would bring to God in all places, which is to say the bread of the Eucharist.

Clement of Alexandria too quotes Malachi (*Stromata* V, 261 [PG 9, 200 B]).

Irenaeus of Lyons makes reference to Mal 1.10f. in connection with the account of the institution, and then he
says: "This clearly means that first of all the people [of Is-
rael] would cease making sacrifice to God, and that then a
sacrifice would be offered him in every place, a pure sacrifice, and that his name would become glorious among the
nations. And this name which is to be glorified among the
nations is no other than our Lord's, through whom the Father is glorified as well as man" (*Adv. Hær.* IV, 17,5: PG 7,
1023f.). The "pure sacrifice" in question is, for Irenæus, the
Eucharist as a "sacrificial liturgy"; and, in keeping with
Rev 5,8, he applies the term "sacrifice of incense (*mincha*)
to the "prayers of the saints," which is to say the "prayer
liturgy." In considerable detail he then explains why only
the sacrifice of the Church is pleasing to God; he does this
by taking as his basis the Prophets' own critique of sacrifice: "Thus, the notion of sacrifice has not been rejected,
for there are sacrifices in both places—sacrifices in the
synagogue and sacrifices in the Church. But it is the manner of offering sacrifice that has changed, since now it is no
longer offered by slaves but by free men" (*Adv. Hær.* IV,
18,2: PG 7, 1025). Irenæus sees evidence for this change especially in the totality of the sacrifice and in the childlike
attitude of the one offering the sacrifice: "It is not the sacrifices that make men holy, for God does not need any sacrifice; rather, it is the conscience of the offerer that sanctifies the sacrifice, provided this conscience is pure; it then
has the effect that God accepts the sacrifice as from a
friend" (*Adv. Hær.* IV, 18,5: PG 7, 1026). "We offer to [God]
from what is his own when in a fitting manner we proclaim the inseparable unity of flesh and spirit; for, just as
the bread that comes from the earth, receiving the invocation of God, is no longer ordinary bread but the Eucharist,
which consists of two elements—an earthly one and a
heavenly one—so too our bodies no longer belong to the
realm of the corruptible once they have received the Eur-
charist, but possess hope of resurrection" (*Adv. Hær.* IV,

18,5: PG 7, 1029). "It is not, therefore, on account of his needing anything that we make sacrifice to [God], but in order to give thanks to his majesty and to sanctify his gift; for, in the same way that God does not need our gifts, *we* do have the need to offer something to him (works of mercy). Although he does not need it, then, he nonetheless desires that we do it for our sake so that we will not remain bereft of fruit. This is why the very same word gave the people the commandment to offer sacrifices, not because he [God] needs them, but so that we should in that way learn to serve God. He therefore desires from us that we should always unceasingly bring the sacrifice to the altar. The real altar, however, is heaven, which is the goal of all our prayers and sacrifices" (*Adv. Hær.* IV, 18,8 : PG 7, 1029).

On the basis of the sacrifices of Cain and Abel, Tertullian (*Adversus Judæos,* 5 and 6) says that the sacrifices of the Jews are carnal and the sacrifices of the Christians spiritual, and commenting on Mal 1,10 he adds that in Christ has come "the giver of the new law, the heir of the new covenant, the priest of the new sacrifices who purifies the new circumcision and celebrates the eternal sabbath—he has come to establish the New Covenant, to offer the new sacrifices and to proclaim the new kingly rule [of God], which shall never know decline (*CChr* 2,1351–1353). In Tertullian's opinion, God gave Christians sacrifices in order to keep a people prone to idolatry (*populum pronum in idolatriam et transgressionem*) in his own religion, by means of appropriate *officia* (*Adv. Marc.* 18,3: *CChr* 1, 496). Tertullian expressly mentions that we Christians *oblationes pro defunctis, pro nataliciis annua die facimus* (*De Cor.* 3,3: *CChr* 1, 1043), and he encourages his readers not only to conclude stational fasting with reception of the Eucharist but also, in so doing, to participate in the sacrifice (*sacrificiorum orationibus*)(*De or.* 19,1: *CChr* 1,267).

Cyprian treats the Eucharist as a sacrifice (Ep. 63) when, on the basis of Hebrews 7, he presents the sacrifices of

Melchizedek as an example (Chapter 4) and Isaiah's treader of the winepress (63,2) as a model. He says expressly: "The Lord's Passion is the sacrifice that we offer" (Chapter 17: PL 4, 387). "Christ Jesus, our God and Lord, is himself the highest priest of God the Father and has presented and offered himself to the Father as a sacrifice so that this be done in memory of him. If this is so, then only that priest truly occupies the place of Christ who imitates what Christ has done, and he offers in the Church to God the Father a true and perfect sacrifice only when he does it in the manner he sees Christ himself to have offered it" (Chapter 14: PL 4, 385ff.; aimed against the Aquarians).

Cyril (John) of Jerusalem says: "We offer up the Chirst who has been slain for our sins; in this way we reconcile God with them [the dead] and with us" (*Cat. myst.* 5,10: PG 33, 1117).

In an instruction concerning thanksgiving, John Chrysostom says,[79] "This is why the priest also exhorts us in the presence of that sacrifice (Θυσία) to give thanks for the whole world, for the past and the present and for what is to happen to us only later."

In his first homily on Christ's Passover, Cyrillonas writes: "Our Lord first sacrificed his body himself, and only afterwards did men sacrifice it. He sacrificed and slew his own self; he gave and pressed out[80] his life-bestowing blood."

Especially in his work *The City of God*, Augustine developed not only a theological, but also an anthropological and ecclesiological theory of sacrifice. God does not need our sacrifices, but we need them in order to worship God: *"Sacrificium ergo visibile invisibilis sacrificii sacramentum, id est sacrum signum, est"*(X,5: PL 41, 282). On the basis of Ps 51,18f., 50,12–15 and Mic 6,6–8, he affirms that the decisive sacrifices are mercy, thanksgiving, and love. The aim of sacrifice is communion with God: *Verum sacrificium est omne opus, quod agitur, ut sancta societate inhæreamus Deo . . . quo veraciter beati esse possimus:* "A true sacrifice is every work which is done that we may

cling to God in holy fellowship . . . , and this makes us to
be truly blessed" (X,6: PL 41,283). Later on Augustine
speaks of the Church's sacrifice in the ecclesiological
sense: "This is the sacrifice of Christians: the many are
one body in Christ. It is this that the Church time and
again offers in the sacrament of the altar, so well-known to
believers. In [this sacrament] it is shown to her [the
Church] that in the object which she brings for the sacrifice she is to offer herself" (PL 41,284). His classical theology of sacrifice, however, runs as follows: "Because he has
taken on the form of a slave, that true mediator has become the mediator between God and men, the man Jesus
Christ (1 Tim 2,5). Insofar as he is in the form of God (Phil
2,5ff.), he accepts the sacrifice together with the Father,
with whom he is one God. Nevertheless, he preferred the
form of a slave so as to *be* a sacrifice rather than receive
one; therefore no one should believe, on account of this
sacrifice, that sacrifice should be offered to any creature
whatever. Thus he himself is the sacrificing priest, and, at
the same time, the sacrificial gift. The daily symbolic enactment of this reality (*sacramentum*) should, according to
his will, be the sacrifice of the Church, which, being the
body of precisely this Head, learns to offer itself as sacrifice
through him. The ancient sacrifices of the saints [of the
Old Testament] were the manifold and different signs for
this true sacrifice [of the Church], for this one reality is
represented by a variety of many [symbols], just as one single thing is expressed by means of many words. Therefore,
all false sacrifices had to yield to this one and true sacrifice
[of the Church] (X,20: PL 41,298).

In the short summary of John Damascene, the chief interest already goes to the mystery of the real presence of
Christ's body and blood through the transformation. Concerning the Sacrifice of the Mass he writes as follows with
reference to Melchizedek (Gen 14,18; Heb 7,1) and Mal
1,11: "This sacrifice [of the Mass] is the purely and indeed
also unbloody sacrifice of which the Lord says through the

prophet that it is offered from the rising of the sun to its setting (*De Fide orthodoxa* IV, 13: PG 94, 1149–1151).

The *Early Middle Ages* followed Augustine for the most part and was more interested in the anthropological and ecclesiological perspectives of the Mass; this may be seen above all in the symbolic interpretations of the Mass, starting with Amalarius of Metz. The more dialectical theology that emerges toward the beginning of the twelfth century concentrated more on the Mass as a memorial sacrifice.

High Scholasticism produced great allegorical commentaries on the liturgy of the Mass and profound investigations on the doctrine of transubstantiation; but the question concerning the sacrificial character of the Mass was dealt with only from three angles that St. Thomas repeatedly examines in his *Summa theologiæ:* the Mass is the *commemoratio* and the *repræsentatio* of the sacrifice of the Cross (*Summa theol.* II, q. 73, a. 4, c; a. 5, c; q. 79, a. 1, c.) and the *participatio fructus dominicæ passionis* (*Summa theol.* III, 7. 83, a. 1). Therefore, the Mass itself is called *sacrificium* or *immolatio Christi.* The *commemoratio* and the *repræsentatio* are basically understood in the spirit of St. Augustine's theology as a 'representation" (i.e., "making-present-again") effected by means of "image and likeness" (*figura et signis*) and a "commemoration" guaranteed by means of the reenactment of the event of the Lord's Supper. The *participatio fructus* is accomplished through the manner of the sacrament's effect (*ex opere operato*). Decisive for the further development of the Western understanding of the Eucharist is the fact that the fourth characteristic —namely, that the Mass is somehow an *oblatio* also as a "sacrifice of the Church," as is still stressed by Albert the Great (*Sent.* IV, d 13 a 23) and the *Summa Halensis* (IV, q 10 m 8 a 1)—is ever more strongly understood in an ethical sense and misinterpreted in terms of personal asceticism, this under the influence of the contemporary development of a Pauline-Augustinian Christ-mysticism. The result was the distortion of the true meaning of the Mass as "sacrifice of the Church." This, together with all the late medieval misinterpretations, was the basis for the Reformation's wholesale rejection of the Mass as such, or of its total ignorance concerning the essentially sacrifical character of the Mass as representation of Christ's sacrifice.

Even though Luther still accepted the Mass as a "service of praise and thanksgiving for Christ's redemption" (WA 6, 368ff.; 302, 692), nevertheless even he fundamentally denied the atoning character of the Mass (as re-presentation of Christ's atoning sacrifice), since he no longer possessed the theological resources to be aware of the possibility of such sacramental re-presentation. All the Reformers understand the definition of the Mass as "sacrifice of the Church" in the sense of human "justification through works," and therefore as a denial of Christ's one and only atoning sacrifice. Consequently, they can conceive of the Mass only as "communion" but not as "sacrifice."[81] Sometimes it is even regarded as "idolatry"[82], even when in the rituals the form of the old Roman Mass is mostly preserved.

In response, the Council of Trent decreed the above mentioned doctrines by affirming the teaching of the Tradition on the Mass as *true and real although relative sacrifice,* as a sacrifice that is to be offered for both the living and the dead and that, like every other sacrament, effects grace and salvation *ex opere operato,* that is, from its own sacramental nature and not through meritorious human works.

It was only the post-Tridentine period that sought to develop a specialized "theology of the Mass" and, with it, new theories concerning the Sacrifice of the Mass.

3. The Nature of the Sacrifice of the Mass

A. DOCTRINE OF THE CHURCH

Because of their nominalistic misunderstanding of "sacrament" the Reformers had had to reject the teaching of the Fathers and the Tradition on the Mass, since in the Catholic Mass they saw either a renewal or a repetition of the Sacrifice of the Cross, or a merely human work.

In his *De captivitate babylonica* (1520) Luther taught that Christ indeed instituted the Mass in the room of the Last Supper, but that here Christ was not sacrificing himself but only leaving behind a meal as sign of promise of the forgiveness of sins. Hence, according to Luther, the Mass is *memoriale eiusdem promissionis. . . . Quod cum frequentaris, mei memor sis, hanc meam in te caritatem et largitatem prædices et laudes et gratias agas* (WA 6, 512–526; 515). The Mass, therefore, is only a worship service, and the fruits of the Mass are given on the basis of our faith. Consequently, in his work *De abroganda missa privata* (1523), Luther rejects the private Mass in which only the priest communicates since here, according to him, the character of the meal has been lost (WA 8, 423–481).

In his *Loci communes* (1521) Melanchthon taught that all *impie errant* who accept the Catholic understanding of the Mass, for the Mass is only a communion that strengthens faith.[83]

Zwingli (1484–1531) rejected the Mass as identified with Christ's Sacrifice of the Cross, and he taught that Christ's one–time Sacrifice on the Cross was possible only through Christ's suffering, shedding of blood, and dying. But now Christ has been gloried, and thus there can be no more sacrifice by him.

In his *Institutiones* (1536) Calvin sought to synthesize the various ideas of the other Reformers. He carried on a polemics particularly against the Sacrifice of the Mass, saying that it was blasphemy against Christ since it tended to abolish Christ's sufferings, push Christ's death into oblivion, and rob the fruit of Christ's death. He expressly distinguishes between the "atoning sacrifice," which in the New Testament is only Christ's Sacrifice of the Cross, and sacrifices of praise and thanksgiving *for* Christ's Sacrifice, which are numerous in the New Testament (IV, c.18).

Also along these lines, in his *Loci præcipui theologici* (1559),[84] Melanchthon distinguishes clearly between *sacrificia propitiatoria* (in the New Testament only Christ's sacrifice of himself) and *sacrificia eucharistica,* that is, sacrifices of praise and thanksgiving for the redemption that has been accomplished (these are all actions that in the New Testament are still called "sacrifices" because they are external works of faith).

Over against these teachings, the Council of Trent[85] exposed the sacramental understanding of the Sacrifice of the Mass as it had evolved in the Tradition. Trent taught as follows: (1.) The Sacrifice of the Mass is a true, real sacrifice and not only a "meal" instituted by Christ (D 948–DS 1751) or a mere remembrance of the Sacrifice of the Cross (D 950–DS 1753). (2.) However, the Sacrifice of the Mass in no way does violence to Christ's unique and one-time Sacrifice of the Cross, nor does it belittle this sacrifice (D 951–DS 1754): although it is a true sacrifice, the Mass is but the sacramental representation of the Sacrifice of the Cross: "He, our God and Lord (Christ), indeed chose to offer himself in death to God the Father as a sacrifice on the altar of the Cross only once, in order to effect eternal redemption for mankind. However, his priesthood was not to be extinguished with his death (Heb 7,24); and so, at the Last Supper on the night of his betrayal, he wanted to leave his beloved Bride, the Church, a visible sacrifice as required by human nature. In this visible sacrifice, the bloody sacrifice that was to be offered only once on the Cross was again to be represented; in it, his memory was to be preserved until the end of time (1 Cor 11,24ff.); and, through it, his saving power for the forgiveness of the sins we daily commit was incessantly to be applied (D 938–DS 1739 ff.).

This makes for a very clear doctrine: the sole, real, self-sufficient sacrifice of the New Testament is Jesus Christ's Sacrifice on the Cross, which is made present in the Sacrifice of the Mass for our salvation. For this reason, the Mass is a relative sacrifice, the unbloody, sacramental representation of the once and for all, bloody Sacrifice of the Cross. "For it is one and the same sacrificial gift, the same sacrificing priest who now makes the offering through the ministry of the (earthly) priest and who once offered himself on the Cross. It is only the manner of the offering that is different (*sola offerendi ratione diversa*)" (D 940–DS 1743).

B. THE PHYSICAL NATURE OF THE SACRIFICE OF THE MASS

In order to understand the physical nature of the Sacrifice of the Mass, we must recall the following historical elements in the phenomena we are here examining:

1. The sole absolute sacrifice of the New Testament is the bloody sacrifice of Jesus Christ on the Cross. Heb 9,12: "Christ entered once for all into the Holy Place, taking his own blood, thus securing an eternal redemption." Heb 9,26: "He has appeared once for all at the end of the age to put away sin by the sacrifice of himself." Heb 9,28: "Christ sacrified himself once for all to bear away the sins of many." Heb 10,12: "When Christ had offered for all time a single sacrifice for sins, he sat down at the right hand of God forever."

2. In the room of the Last Supper, Christ instituted a sacramental rite that was based on the paschal meal. This rite (a) was to be performed by the Apostles and their successors ("Do this in memory of me") and (b) it had a direct relation with Christ's Sacrifice on the Cross ("my sacrificial body–my sacrificial blood"). (c) The sacrificial character of this rite becomes clear through the fact that it was

instituted during the sacrificial meal of the Passover: in place of the sacrificial flesh, it is Christ's own flesh that is offered and partaken.

3. What Christ did in the room of the Last Supper and commanded his apostles to do after him was called by the Council of Trent *memoria* (memorial rite), *repræsentatio* (making present of the Sacrifice of the Cross through the sacramental rite), and *applicatio* (applying the fruits of redemption through the action of the Church to her individual members). An erroneous conception would be to think of the Sacrifice of the Mass as a "repetition" of the one-time historial Sacrifice of the Cross (unfortunately the Roman Catechism does in fact call the Mass a *renovatio*), and just as erroneous would be the other conception of the Mass as only a human and psychological memorial celebration, something that is already excluded by the real presence of Christ's sacrificial body and blood under the changed forms.

4. The difference between the *Sacrifice of the Mass* and the *Sacrifice of the Cross* may be described as follows according to Trent: (a) The Sacrifice of the Cross is absolute, occurring only once, whereas the Sacrifice of the Mass is relative and repeatable (Mal 1,10f.). (b) The Sacrifice of the Cross is a bloody sacrifice of human life, whereas the Sacrifice of the Mass is an unbloody sacrifice of food (*mincha*). (c) The sacrifice of the Cross worked redemption; the Sacrifice of the Mass (together with other means of salvation) applies the redemption to us. (d) In the Sacrifice of the Cross Christ is the sole officiating priest; in celebrations of the Mass many human priests officiate as ministers, even though Christ remains the *sacerdos principalis*. (e) In the Sacrifice of the Cross Christ offered himself *specie propria* ("under his own form"); in the Sacrifice of the Mass he offers himself *specie aliena*, under the sacramental forms and through the action of the Church. (f) In the Sacrifice of the Cross suffering, spilling of blood, and death dominate the events; in the Sacrifice of the Mass there no longer is

any spilling of blood or death. We will later on deal with the question whether the suffering of Christ is present in the Church sacramentally, that is, in the manner of a sign, in the Sacrifice of the Mass.[86]

5. The Last Supper is different from the Sacrifice of the Mass in the following two manners: (a) In the former, as on the Cross, Christ was the visible priest, whereas in the latter he is only the invisible priest. (b) In the former we have both the institution of the sacrament and the command to offer the sacrifice, whereas in the latter we have but the execution and the fulfillment.

6. The element of the Sacrifice of the Mass that makes the Sacrifice of the Cross to be present is solely that which is an imitation of what Christ did in the room of the Last Supper when he instituted this sacrifice and commanded the Apostles that they too should accomplish: and this element is the narrative of the institution with the words of consecration (*actio*). This is why the double transformation of bread and wine is an essential part of the Sacrifice of the Mass, since only with it is Christ's command totally fulfilled. It remains a question of theological interpretation whether one sees Christ's death signified in the double transformation through the separate forms (as has been the opinion of many, chiefly Vásquez) or whether in the change of the bread one sees more the form of the meal and in the change of the cup one sees more the indication of a living sacrifice and the sealing of the covenant.

C. THE THEOLOGICAL (METAPHYSICAL?)
   NATURE OF THE SACRIFICE OF THE MASS:
   THEORIES ABOUT THE MASS

If we are to understand the Mass in a theologically correct manner (and so overcome the nominalistic misunderstanding of the Reformers), it is above all necessary for us to consider the Johannine conception of the "mystery of the Incarnation" and the Pauline conception of a "mystical life centered on Christ." The Johannine statement "The Word became flesh" (John 1,14) means that, in the Incarnation, the Creator God really entered his creation and that, in Jesus Christ, the creation has really been taken up into the Creator God. The Church has at times expressly attempted to give utterance to this ineffable mystery—the arch-mystery of Christian faith—especially in the doctrine of the hypostatic union of the Council of Ephesus (431) and later on other occasions.

In his Christ-centered mystical doctrine Paul has made this truth to bear fruit for the life of Christians: he understood all human action as "Christian action," as an "acting in Christ." This means not only in the power and at the command of Christ, but rather in personal communion with Christ, the Head of the body whose members Christians are. This Christ-centered mysticism is not only a religious interpretation of human action; in the sacrament of baptism (cf. Rom 6,1–12) it has become a reality. Consequently, the Apostle can say: "No longer do I live, but Christ lives in me" (Gal 2,20). Here the possibility of a genuine *commercium* is given that the liturgical texts of the Mass often speak of: Christ has us human beings participate in his work and takes our human efforts up into his holy activity.

From the perspective of this theological truth we can say the following concerning *theories of the Mass* that have sprung up especially since the Council of Trent. We must first of all remark that the theological attempts to interpret the Mass correctly as Sacrifice of Christ and of the Church suffer from their not seeking the locus the Sacrifice of the Mass occupies within salvation-history—the locus we discussed earlier. Rather those attempts proceed on the basis of a metaphysics of natural human sacrifices. A case in point is Thomas Aquinas, who made sacrifice as such, for instance as found among pagans, to be the heuristic basis for his conception of sacrifice.

The *first attempts* in this direction in the sixteenth century (Melchior Cano, O.P., d. 1560, and Dominic Soto, O.P., d. 1560), in the line of the Council of Trent, see in the Sacrifice of the Mass simply a sense-perceptible representation of Christ's historical sacrifice, since the priest consecrates (that is, sanctifies the offering and thus makes it a sacrifice) and since the blood of Christ is spilled (in communion from the chalice it is consumed by human beings). The Jesuits A. Salmerón (d. 1585) and J. Maldonatus (d. 1583) take the breaking of the host, the communion, and the prayer *Offerimus* after the consecration as signs of the offering of the sacrifice.

A *second theory* objectifies these ideas even more. This theory requires a real change (*destructio*) of the sacrificial matter as essential to the sacrifice; consequently, it sees the sacrificial character of the Mass as residing in the separation of flesh and blood under the forms of bread and wine after the consecration. This opinion was held by J. M. de Bay (d. 1589), and F. Suárez (d. 1617) developed this doctrine when he spoke of a *ratio sacrificii sub ratione mysticæ mactationis ac separationis corporis et sanguinis ex vi verborum*.[87]

A *third theory* would have this change (*immutatio*) in the sacrificial matter of bread and wine have an effect on the real Christ, who becomes present under the forms; in this way it strove to make the Sacrifice of the Mass a "sacrifice of Christ" in the real sense. Such a theory makes questionable in part the relationship between the Sacrifice of the Mass and Christ's one-time and unique Sacrifice on the Cross. According to J. Hessels (d. 1566) among others, the living Christ is affected by the separation of flesh and blood in the consecration. And R. Bellarmine (d. 1621) represents those who would see the Lord's suffering as present especially in the eating and drinking at communion time because of the change of form these actions involve. Similarly, de Lugo (d. 1660)[88] exacted a moral *immutatio,* which he located in the *reductio corporis et sanguinis Christi ad statum cibi et potus.* For his part, A. Cienfuegos (d. 1739)[89] located Christ's humiliation in the fact that, because of the separation of the species, Christ is deprived of all perceptible activity between the consecration and the mingling of the species. The humiliation of Christ as the food and drink of human beings also plays a significant role in the understanding of sacrifice of J. B. Franzelin, S.J., and, in more modern times, of A. Winklhofer.

A *fourth theory* affirmed the necessity of a real *immutatio* in the species of the sacrifice themselves, but it saw these changes in the bread and the wine, more correctly understood, to be merely sacramental signs or symbols for Christ's true sacrificial action. It was especially G. Vásquez, S. J. (d. 1604) who developed this doctrine in his commentary on Thomas. He made a precise distinction between the actual sacrifice of Christ and the sacramental representation of this sacrifice in the Mass. He again excluded the communion as sign of the sacrifice and saw this sacrifice present in a symbolic and sacramental manner only in the change in the species. L. Lessius, S.J. (d. 1623), further developed this theory by saying that the words of transformation are the mystical sword whereby this *mactatio mystica* occurs. J. B. Gonet, O. P. (d. 1681), C. R. Billuart, O. P. (d. 1757), A. Berlage, F. X. Dieringer, and above all L. Billot, S.J. (d. 1931), all spoke of such a *mactatio mystica*.

The *fifth theory*, which was developed especially by the "Ecole française" of the seventeenth century, provided a new and fundamental insight that was to lead in our time to an acceptable theory of the Sacrifice of the Mass. Alongside the idea of the *immutatio* of the sacrificial gifts there developed the recognition that the very heart of the sacrifice must be a personal *oblatio* or *immolatio*; the point of departure for this insight was the meditation on the life of Jesus as conducted by Cardinal P. de Bérulle (d. 1629) and his school. It was above all C. de Condren (d. 1641) who most deeply developed this thought. The meaning of the sacrifice was seen by him to reside not so much in Christ's atonement and a unique sacrificial death but rather in the adoration and honor he rendered to God's holiness and greatness throughout his whole life: *pour honorer son souverain domaine, non seulement sur la vie et la mort, mais sur l'être même.*[90]

Jesus' whole life was considered to be Christ's sacrifice, already before the death on the Cross, especially by L. Thomassin (d. 1695): *Non sacerdos tantum fuit iam a principio sui conceptus, sed et immolare et sacerdotio suo fungi iam tum cœpit Christus-homo; et ipsa incarnatio . . . summum sacrificium est.*[91]

J. B. Bossuet (d. 1704) provided a *sixth theory* when he expanded this doctrine even further. He saw Christ's sacrifice as occurring not only in his Incarnation and throughout his life, coming to a climax in his death, but on the basis of Heb 9,24 held that an essential part of this sacrifice of Christ's is his interceding for us continually in heaven before his Father. All of these aspects together constitute, according to Bossuet, "the one sacrifice through which he has brought to perfection all those who allow themselves to be sanctified" (Heb 10,14).[92]

The great theologians of the nineteenth century then combined the various elements of these theories concerning the Mass in different ways. Special significance goes to the opinion of J. A. Möhler (d. 1828)—and this is almost a *seventh theory*—who on the basis of the fifth theory brought the Church more into play as the bearer of the sacrifice. Also worthy of mention is V. Thalhofer (d.1891), who stressed Christ's continual sacrifice in heaven as the foundation for the reality of the Sacrifice of the Mass. "When the words of consecration are uttered, he [Christ] makes himself present on the altar in the form of separation, *in forma sacrificii.* Thus he is performing on the altar, which is to say within space and time, what in essence is the very same sacrificial act which he once accomplished on the Cross and which he does not cease to accomplish in the heavenly sacrifice.[93]

Starting with A. Vonier and O. Casel, the approach of

mystery theology has brought new possibilities to our understanding of the Mass, and this could be considered an *eighth theory.* This approach has deliberately used the Pauline "mystery of Christ" in a new and fruitful way by applying it to an understanding of the sacraments and especially the Eucharist. At the conclusion of what constitutes the most significant historical study to date on theories of the Mass, J. M. Lepin states concerning the Sacrifice of the Mass that it is *l'oblation que le Christ fait de lui-même et que l'église fait du Christ sous les signes représentatifs de son immolation passée.*[94]

But it was by reincorporating dogmatic mediation into a liturgical context that the nature of the Mass could best be illuminated in a new way: the liturgy confronts us with the rich *totality of Christ's image in all his saving events*—Christ incarnate, Christ crucified, Christ risen from the dead, Christ the transfigured intercessor with the Father, Christ the head of the Church and principal celebrant at the community's every Mass as well as Christ the head of every individual Christian who in baptism has been made a member of his body, Christ in us and we in Christ: these are the essential manifestations of the one reality of Christ, the reality that is the very ground of the Mass. Into this reality, through the Church in this world, *the whole world* is taken up—not only the officiating priest but likewise the community of those celebrating with him and the whole People of God, not only the saints but especially the sinners who most need the grace of Christ's redeeming sacrifice, the nonhuman world of creation along with its share in the curse brought on by human sin, the universe itself and the history of all humankind: all of this is taken up into the Sacrifice of the Mass so that it will come to participate in Christ's unrepeatable and irreplaceable sacrifice of redemption, which sovereignly applies to all times and all places of this world. It was especially the encyclical *Mediator Dei* (November 20, 1947) that best portrayed the Church's doctrine on the Mass according to the state of theology at that time.

Through all six editions of his *Catholic Dogmatics,* M. Schmaus attempted in ever more precise ways to describe the nature of the Sacrifice of the Mass with particular reference to mystery theology. Thus he writes: "The Sacrifice of the Mass is made present by the Church in the symbols instituted by Christ so that she, the Church, can enter into Christ's saving event. She accomplishes this by offering to the heavenly Father as sacrificial gift the body and the blood that have been made present by her own action as she participates in Christ's gift of self. The basis for the Church's being capable of participating in such an event lies in the fact that Christ is her head and she is his body, that Christ is her bridegroom and she is his bride. Her sacrifice carries with it the plea that the heavenly Father may be pleased to look upon the sacrifice of his Son not only as his personal, individual sacrifice but to accept it as the sacrifice of the Head, in which the whole Body partakes, as the sacrifice of the Bridegroom to which the Bride gives her consent. In every eucharistic celebration the Church declares ever anew that she looks upon Christ's sacrifice as a representative sacrifice. Just as the priest plays the role of Christ in the eucharistic sacrifice, so did Christ play the role of all mankind in the historical event of his death. The Church is fully conscious at every eucharistic celebration that this representation Christ accomplishes occurs solely by virtue of grace: his representation of mankind in the Passion bears the character of grace. And the Church express this awareness on her part by the numerous prayers of acceptance of the liturgy."[95]

D. ATTEMPT AT A SUMMARY

We must first of all affirm that both the Last Supper and the Sacrifice of the Mass have their very foundation and reason-for-being in Christ's Sacrifice on the Cross. The fact that Christ instituted the Eucharist in the form of the paschal meal may indeed show that the Mass is a sacrifice that takes the form of a meal (*Mahlopfer*), that is, that the Mass has the form of a sacrifice in which we participate through a meal. Nevertheless, this meal cannot be primarily understood as a community meal; rather, its most genuine and unique meaning lies in its being a *sacrificial meal* (*Opfermahl*).[96] *Mediator Dei* clearly declares: "One would be straying from the way of truth if one were shrewdly to assert that what is involved here is not only a sacrifice but a sacrifice and *at the same time* a meal on the part of a fraternal community, and that the climax, so to speak, of the whole sacrificial celebration is the communion received as a community."[97]

We must further affirm that one cannot do justice to an understanding of the sacramental and symbolic nature of the Mass as long as one refuses to leave the perspective of "historicism": from this perspective, the sacrifice of Christ can be considered only a one-time event in the continuum of world history and, therefore, the Sacrifice of the Mass can only be taken to be a subjective memorial celebration.

As error, too, would be to look at the Mass in a strict positivistic manner from the perspective of its rites. This would lead to seeing the essence of the Mass as residing only in the destruction or the immutation of the sacrificial species, or in the sacrificial attitude and function of the risen Lord in heaven. This perspective, too, blocks the way to understanding the sacramental nature of the Sacrifice of the Mass.

Finally, a purely "mystical" approach would also impede a correct understanding of the Mass, because this approach would not sufficiently differentiate the specific forms taken by the action of Christ, the action of the priest, and the action of the believing people.

In order to be able to make an accurate judgment of the specific ontological character of the supernatural mystery contained in the Mass, it would be good not to lose sight

of the threefold nature of the supernatural, which, for lack
of better expressions, we have termed the dimensions of
the objective-metaphysical, the psychic-moral, and the
personal-mystical.

If, from the perspective of these preconditions, we were
to look again at the abovementioned five aspects of the
physical understanding of sacrifice (sacrificial gifts and
sacrificing priest, sacrificial action, purpose of the sacrifice, and attitude in sacrificing), we could say the following
about each of these aspects:

i. Sacrificial Gift

In the Sacrifice of the Cross and of the Mass, the sacrifical gift is "the divine Redeemer in his human nature and
in the reality of his body and blood."[98] Today we would expand this assertion by saying that, in the Mass, this sacrifical gift includes also the Church as Body of Christ and,
through the Church, the whole world. The mystery remains, moreover, of how the divine nature of Christ itself
also belongs to the sacrificial gift by virtue of the hypostatic union. For the distinction of two natures in Christ
must not be understood as a trenchant reality, in Nestorian
fashion.

ii. The Sacrificing Priest

The sacrificing priest is the one Christ, who on the Cross
offered the sacrifice once and for all and who, in heaven,
sits at the Father's right hand as high priest constantly interceding for us (Heb 7,24; 10,12; Rom 8,34; 1 Pet 3,22). In
the Sacrifice of the Mass "his holy person" is represented
by "his chosen servant who, through priestly ordination,
has come to resemble the High Priest and possesses the authority to act with the power and in the person of Christ
himself."[99] It would be false to say that Christ himself acts
directly through and in the priest; and it would be equally
false to say that the priest acts alone and self-efficiently,

only carrying out Christ's command. Rather are we to say that, in a mysterious manner, three elements are here operating together: Christ uses the priest instrumentally; the priest surrenders himself to Christ in obedience and love; the priest performs a work (words and action) that belongs to the earthly, objective reality and that through Christ's command and co-active deed becomes an efficacious and most real sign (this is the meaning of *memoria*).

The encyclical *Mediator Dei* describes as follows the relationship of the ministerial priesthood to the general priesthood of believers: "The unbloody sacrifice in which, through the words of consecration, Christ becomes present on the altar in the condition of a victim, is the work of the priest alone in so far as he represents the person of Christ, but not in so far as he represents the person of the faithful. The priest acts in place of the believing people only because he represents the person of our Lord Jesus Christ, insofar as He is the Head of all the members and offers himself for them. The priest, consequently, goes to the altar as a servant of Christ, standing lower than Christ but higher than the people."[100]

Our more recent understanding of the liturgy since Vatican II would need to expand these assertions by saying that the believing people itself not only stands before Christ by mediation of the priest but, by virtue of its being Christ's Mystical Body, it too has an immediate relationship to Christ, even if this relationship is not based on direct apostolic mission, as is the ministerial priest's. Thus, the memorial acclamation by the people after the words of consecration ("O Lord, we proclaim your death and we praise your resurrection until you come in glory!", cf. 1 Cor 11,26) not only affirms that the ministerial priest has accomplished the sacrifice; these words indicate, rather, the active incorporation of the People of God, of the believing communilty, into the offering of the sacrifice, even if this sacrifice, in order to be sacramentally valid, must be carried out only by the ministerial priest.

iii. The Sacrificial Action

The Council of Trent taught that, through the Sacrifice of the Mass, redemption was not effected but rather applied to us (*applicari*) (D 938–DS 1740). This helps us to understand the correct meaning of the Sacrifice of the Mass as being a true but only relative sacrifice. The one Sacrifice of the Cross becomes sacramentally present, which for our earthy existence means a visible sacrificial action even though Christ is not killed, nor does he die once again. We can distinguish three elements in the historical Sacrifice of the Cross and likewise in the Mass: (a) the killing or dying (objective-metaphysical element), (b) the suffering that precedes and accompanies the dying (psychic-moral element), and (c) the sacrifical action as a deed of the human and divine person to whom revelation attributes the words "Not my will be done, but yours" (Luke 22,42); "My God, my God, why have you forsaken me?" (Mark 15,34); and "Father, into your hands I commend my spirit!" (Luke 23,46: personal-mystical element).

a) *Death, Killing, and Dying:* Killing was the work of the executioner; dying was the result of the killing and an essential part of the Sacrifice of the Cross because Christ freely allowed it to happen to him in obedience to the Father and out of love for humankind: he accomplished it insofar as dying is something that can be "accomplished." "The memorial of his death, which truly occurred on Calvary, is again realized in every sacrifice of the altar in so far as here Jesus Christ's presence is represented and shown in his condition as victim through clear symbols."[101] Theologically it remains an open question whether the separated forms as a sign for the separation of body and blood are the sign for Christ's death, or whether the sign for his death is the cup with the blood alone as a sign for the bloody sacrifice of the New Covenant. A still more difficult question is whether, with the making present of the death, the killing too must necessarily be made present, so that we would correctly have to speak of a *mactatio mystica* and the words of consecration could be considered the instrument of this killing.[102] As integrally as Christ's being killed by human beings belongs to his historical sacrificial death, we must, from the standpoint of that death's strict meaning, say that the work of redemption is essentially linked only to Christ's act of dying and not to his having been killed. We may indeed ask whether requiring a liturgical sign for his killing is not too historicist a demand.

b) *The Suffering:* Here the question arises whether we cannot find in the Sacrifice of the Mass a sacramental sign for the physical and psychic suffering (pain and mortal anguish) that characterizes the long road of Christ's suffering until he reached his death. If we look first of all to the consecrated species, we will see that here are contained Christ's sacrificial Body and sacrificial Blood, and thus his very sacrifice. An objective reality is symbolized through objective signs. But the question is whether a suffering that is ordered not to the objective but to the experimental world can have a corresponding sign. Maybe the following thought can be of help: Just as the sacrificial gift of the cross is present under the species of bread and wine, and just as Christ's priesthood is operative in the ministry of the human priest, so too the suffering of Christ, the now transfigured Lord, must enter into the Sacrifice of the Mass as sacrifice of Christ the Head *through the human suffering of the faithful who constitute the Mystical Body of Christ.* It is primarily in this manner that the Sacrifice of the Mass becomes "the sacrifice of the Church," too, which here means not only a sacrifice belonging *to* the Church but especially the Church *as sacrifice.* Precisely in this manner does the Sacrifice of the Cross continue to be efficacious in this world in the Sacrifice of the Mass. The event of the Church's being sacrificed along with Christ in the Mass is not only of a personal and spiritual nature; it incorporates humans as a whole in this present world and time, in the condition that makes them to be sinners in pilgrimage who need Christ's redemptive sacrifice: "Dear brothers, I appeal to you by God's mercies to offer up your bodies as a living and hold sacrifice, consecrated to God and worthy of his acceptance; this is the worship due from you as rational creatures" (Rom 12,1). "I am glad of my sufferings on your behalf, as, in this mortal frame of mine, I help to pay off the debt which the afflictions of Christ still leave to be paid, for the sake of his body, the Church" (Col 1,24).

c) *The Sacrificial Action:* The sacrificial gesture as innermost personal existential attitude and deed is the soul of sacrifice. In the Sacrifice of the Cross this deed was accomplished as the personal deed of the God-Man, in obedience and love. The question now is, Is there a sacramental sign for this in the Sacrifice of the Mass? Since in the Mystical Body of Christ we must clearly distinguish between the person of Christ and the persons of Christians as individuals, we must affirm that for this most interior personal element of the sacrifice there can be no real sacramental sign. This central element of the sacrifice, rather, is really present in the Christ who is present in the sacrifice itself *vere, realiter, et substantialiter.* This interior and personal sacrifical attitude remains the same in Christ both on the Cross and in heaven, where he is offering his sacrifice for us before the Father. In the Eucharist the attitude becomes really present with this same Christ, so that we can participate in Christ's sacrifice just as Mary and John and the pious women and the centurion participated in Christ's one-time historical sacrifice. Now Christ's sacrificial attitude on the Cross was the sacrificial attitude of his divine and human self and not merely that of the divine Logos. Consequently, Christians too can participate in such a sacrificial attitude in the Mass, since they are members of Christ's Body. Just as Christ created and acquired the Church in his sacrifice on the Cross, so too does he, as head of the Church, offer the same sacrifice sacramentally in every Mass. The result is that we, as members of the Church and members of Christ, in a sacramentally real manner come to partake in his sacrificial attitude through our human attitude of self-surrender to the Father in obedience and love, an attitude we attain to through Christ's grace, particularly when in the communion we unite ourselves with Christ, who is both sacrificing priest and sacrificial victim. In this way we participate in the redemption itself, which was merited for us by Christ's sacrifice on the Cross and which makes us to be the Church. Thus, the Sacrifice of the Mass involves not only Christ's "coming down upon our altars" but equally (if such a spatial image may be used at all) a going up of Christ's members to their Head in heaven: it involves, in a sacramentally real sense, not only human purification from sin but also human glorification, and all of this in Christ and in the power of the Holy Spirit, that the Father and the triune God may be honored and adored.

d) *The Sacrificial Purpose:* All of this makes possible an answer to the question concerning the purpose of the Sacrifice of the Mass. The purpose or finality of the Sacrifice of the Cross is above all to be sought, for our human manner of thought, in the "atonement" for the sins of humankind, as Scripture (alluding to Isaiah 53) says of Christ himself when he instituted the Holy Eucharist. But the portrayal of the heavenly liturgy in the Book of the Apocalypse clearly shows that the purpose of the Sacrifice of the Cross is at the same time to be sought in the "adoration and glorification of God." It is in the context of this heavenly liturgy that we encounter the "slain Lamb" (5,12) that not only intercedes for us before God but to which adoration and glorification are likewise given. And just as Christ himself continually offered "praise and thanksgiving" to the Father in his prayers during his earthly sojourn (Luke 10,21; John 11,41), so too must the Mass be regarded as a sacrifice of thanksgiving and praise, insofar as it was given to us by Christ himself as "sacrifice," and sacrifice, when accomplilshed by human beings in a natural sense, must always be an expression of "praise and thanksgiving" before God. Thus, the purpose of the Sacrifice of the Mass may be seen in its totality only when we look simultaneously at the purpose of the *Sacrifice of the Cross*, of the *heavenly sacrifice*, and of the *human sacrifice* and understand these together from the perspective of the mystery of the divine and human deed of redemption. The decisive point is that the purpose of the Sacrifice of the Mass is not a human institution, but rather a participation in the immanent purpose of the divine gift itself—and this is of the utmost importance for our understanding of the value of the Mass.

(e) *The Sacrificial Attitude:* From these discussions it is now evident that the sacrificial attitude that should fill us during the Mass cannot be any other than Christ's own sacrificial attitude, which essentially expressed consisted of "obedience to the Father and love for humankind." As we make it our own, this attitude must still be completed at a fundamental level by the attitude of "contrition and penance" proper to us as sinners: this penitential attitude is obviously the prerequisite for our being able at all to assume Christ's attitude of obedience and love. In the same way, our "praise and thanksgiving" for Christ and his work—and through him to God the Father in the Holy Spirit—are the prerequisite for our being able to participate in the attitude of "adoration and glorification" that according to the Apocalypse are to be rendered to Christ and, through him, to the Father. Here it becomes clear that the Sacrifice of the Mass cannot be only a "representation of Christ's historical sacrifice on the Cross transposed into a non-historical sphere." Rather, the Mass can become a representation within the historical space of our world and of our time and within our Church only in the measure that we allow ourselves to be grasped by the grace-filled mystery of this sacrifice: this means that we must be ready to cooperate with the grace of Christ that is always coming to our encounter and thus prepare ourselves to walk the *via purgativa,* which in this world can never fully become the *via illuminativa* that follows it and that will be fully surpassed by the *via unitiva* that belongs only to our fulfillment in God.

The Constitution on the Liturgy of the Second Vatican Council teachers as follows: "They [the believers] should offer the spotless sacrificial gift not only through the hands of the priest but also together with him; thus they learn to offer themselves. In this way, through Christ the Mediator, they will day to day attain to ever greater unity with God and one another, so that in the end God may be all in all" (art. 48).

4. The Effects of the Sacrifice of the Mass

The holy has its value in itself, and it is because of this intrinsic value that it is to be honored religiously. A reflection of the effects of the Mass, therefore, in no way deals with the intrinsic value of the Sacrifice of the Mass: such a reflection intends to be a stimulus so that people will not only reverence the Mass for its own sake but also allow it to become fruitful in their lives. For the Sacrifice of the Mass is the sacrifice that Christ has instituted "for us": "This is my body which is given for you. This cup is the new covenant in my blood, which is poured out for you (and for many: Mark 14,24)" (Luke 22,19f). Thus, the meditation of this section is nothing more than a modest attempt to consider and apply to ourselves the explicit theme of this "for you and for many."

A. THE EFFECTS IN GENERAL

The Reformers saw in the Eucharist only the sacrament that is beneficial to its recipient. By contrast the Council of Trent emphasized the general intercessory and atoning character of the Sacrifice of the Mass: a sacrifice for others, for the whole Church, to bring blessings on the whole of creation (Cf. D 940). "Whoever says that the Mass is only an act of praise and thanksgiving, or the mere remembrance of the Sacrifice of the Cross but not an atoning sacrifice; or that the Mass is beneficial only to the person who communicates and that one consequently ought not to offer it for the living and the dead, for sins and punishments, for reparation and other needs, *anathema sit"*(D 950–DS 1753).

1. The encyclical *Mediator Dei* (November 20, 1947)[103] affirms in its second part the equality between the Sacrifice of the Cross and the Sacrifice of the Mass, stressing the equality in both of the four ends of sacrifice, which it describes as follows:

a) *Finis primus gloria est cælesti Patri tribuenda:* "The first end of the Mass is to render the glory due to the heavenly Father." With and through Christ, and in union with all saints and all angels, we are to render praise and honor to the Lord God. This is why the preface usually ends with the words *Hymnum gloriæ tuæ canimus sine fine dicentes*, and the ending of the canon, which is the *actio* of Holy Mass, reads *Per ipsum [Christum], et cum ipso, et in ipso, est tibi Deo Patri omnipotenti, in unitate Spiritus Sancti, omnis honor et gloria per omnia sæcula sæculorum. Amen.*

b) *Alter . . . finis eo spectat, ut gratiæ adhibeantur Deo debitæ:* "The second intention is that the thanksgiving owed to God should be rendered." Thanksgiving is the very meaning of the Eucharist. This is why the Roman canon of the Mass begins: *Vere dignum et iustum est, æquum et salutare, nos tibi semper et ubique gratias agere, Domine, sancte Pater, omnipotens æterne Deus, per Christum Dominum nostrum.*

c) *Tertio autem loco, expiationis, placationis reconciliationisque proponitur finis.* Just as the Sacrifice of the Cross brought not only atonement, satisfaction, reconciliation for our sins, but also for those "of the whole world" (1 John 2,2), so too the Sacrifice of the Mass is offered as a *sacrifi-*

cium, tibi acceptabile et toti mundo salutare (Fourth Eucharistic Prayer).

d) *Quarto denique loco impetrationis habetur finis.* Just as Christ "during the days of his earthly life, offered prayer and entreaty to the God who could save him from death, not without a piercing cry, not without tears, yet with such piety as won him a hearing" (Heb 5,7) so too the Mass itself is offered as an intercessory sacrifice and in the Mass are offered entreaties for the living and the dead *per Christum Dominum nostrum.*[104]

2. The fact that the Mass is an atoning sacrifice for humankind and an intercessory sacrifice for the Church has since ancient times been expressed in two practices: in the prayers of intercession during the liturgy and in the fact that the Mass is celebrated for the dead.

a) *Intercessions:* Already in 1 Tim 2,1–4 we read the exhortation "This first of all, I ask: that petition, prayer, entreaty and thanksgiving should be offered for all mankind, especially for kings and others in high station, so that we [in the Church] can live a calm and tranquil life, as dutifully and decently as we may. Such prayer is our duty, it is what God, our Saviour, expects of us, since it is his will that all men should be saved, and be led to recognize the truth." Accordingly, from the very beginning of the Church and corresponding to the Jewish prayer *Shemone Esre,* "general prayers of intercession for the Church," for the worldly authorities, and for individual emergencies and concerns of all kinds have been offered. Already Justin[105] speaks of these "general intercessions" (κοινὰς εὐχάς); *precationes* are likewise mentioned by Tertullian[106] and Augustine,[107] and Cyprian calls them *publica et communis oratio.*[108] Both Hippolytus[109] and the *Apostolic Constitutions*[110] contain wonderful examples of such prayers, and the *Indiculus de gratia Dei* (D 139–DS 246) speaks of the apostolicity and catholicity of these intercessions, which were usually uttered at the conclusion of the Liturgy of the Word. Pope Gelasius I introduced these prayers into the be-

ginning of the Liturgy of the Word (a vestige of this is the
Kyrie at the beginning of Holy Mass (PL 101, 56of.). Later
on intercessions for the living and the dead take place, re-
spectively, before and after the consecration.[111] The ever
stronger emphasis given intercessory prayer in the Middle
Ages—something that obscured the genuine mystery
character of the Mass—contributed to the development of
the practice of applying the Mass to particular intentions
(Mass stipends). The Second Vatican Council's Constitution on the Liturgy (art. 53) expressly reintroduced these
intercessions after the Gospel and the homily, calling them
"general intercessions" or "prayer of the faithful."

   b) *Masses for the Dead:* The Council of Trent expressly
emphasizes the fact that the Mass *et pro defunctis in
Christo, nondum ad plenum purgatis, rite iuxta Apostolo-
rum traditionem offertur* (D 940–DS 1743). Around the
year 170 the eucharistic celebration at the grave of the
dead (or even in the presence of the corpse) had already displaced the pagan *refrigeria* or funeral meals.[112] These sacrifices for the dead are intercessory sacrifices and especially
yearly memorial sacrifices that stand alongside the sacrifices of praise and thanksgiving at the graves of the martyrs that are emerging around this same time. One witness
is Tertullian: *Oblationes pro defunctis pro nataliciis
annua die facimus* (*De Cor.* 3,3: *CChr* 2,1043). *Et pro
anima eius [mulieris] orat, et refrigerium interim adpos-
tulat ei . . . et offert annuis diebus dormitionis eius* (*De
monogam.* 10,4: *CChr* 2,1243). *Pro qua oblationes annuas
reddis . . . et offeres pro duabus* [for the two women] *et
commendabis illas duas per sacerdotem de monogamia
ordinatum aut etiam de virginitate sancitum, circumda-
tum viduis univiris? Et ascendet sacrificium tuum libera
fronte?* ["For her (the one woman) you offer the yearly
memorial sacrifice. . . . Will you also offer a sacrifice for
the two women (of one man who has married twice), and
you commend the two of them to God also through the
priest, who is monogamous or consecrated to virginity, and

surrounded by widows who were married only once? Will
your sacrifice arise from a pure conscience?" (*De exhort.
cast.* 11,1-2:*CChr* 2, 1031).

In 249 Cyprian forbids the offering of sacrifice on behalf
of a Christian who has made a priest the executor of his
will and has thus enticed him away from his real ministry:
*Non offerretur pro eo nec sacrificium pro dormitione eius
celebraretur* (Ep. 66: PL 4,399). In his Fifth Mystagogical
Catechesis, Cyril of Jerusalem writes as follows elaborating his explanation of intercessory or general prayer:
"Then we remember those who have already gone to sleep,
above all the patriarchs, prophets, apostles, martyrs, so
that God through their prayers and intercessions may give
heed to our supplication. Then we pray for the holy fathers
and bishops and all our dead in general who have already
gone to sleep. For we believe that great profit comes to
those souls for whom we pray during the most holy sacrifice" (V, 8-10: PG 33, 1116f.). To the question of what use it
is to a soul who has departed this world in sin to be remembered during the sacrifice, Cyril answers: "We offer
our prayers to God on behalf of the dead, even though they
were sinners. We weave no garland, but rather offer Christ
who was slain for our sins. In this manner we reconcile the
merciful God both with them and with us. (V, 8–10: PG
33, 1116f.).

Around 410 Balæus the Syrian says in a poem: "For
those who have understanding it is clear that the dead derive benefit from our vigils, from the [eucharistic] sacrifice
and from the thurible of reconciliation when the priest remembers their names before the altar. Then do both the
heaven-dwellers and the earth-dwellers rejoice, and also
the dead leap for joy, for they are today being convoked to
be consoled by the heavenly sacrifice. Honor be given to
the Living One [Christ], who has awakened the dead
through his death and granted them the hope of resurrection, who will also return and awaken them that they may
sing praise to him!"[113]

Our theme is developed in a particularly detailed way by
Jacob of Sarug (Batnan), at the beginning of the sixth century, in a homily concerning the remembrance of the dead
and the eucharistic sacrifice: the fact that the dead derive
benefit from the sacrificial gifts and alms that are given on
their behalf.[114] He tries to base his doctrine especially on 2
Macc. 12,43. Augustine too deals expressly with sacrifices
for the dead.[115] Especially clear on this point are passages
from liturgical prayers, the fourth-century canon of the
Roman Mass, and so on. Heb 5,1 says expressly that a
priest "is made a representative of human beings in their
dealings with God; he is to offer gifts and sacrifices in expiation for their sins."

3. The fact that the Sacrifice of the Mass is a sacrifice of
praise and thanksgiving before God is also expressed in the
sacrificial celebrations offered "in honor of the saints."
The origin of this theme in the Mass is the "cult of the
martyrs" emerging in the beginning of the third century:
praise and thanksgiving are offered God for the grace he
has given those who have withstood trials victoriously in
his grace; being perfected, they are now asked to intercede
for us with God (*Deo de illorum victoriis gratias agens,
eorum patrocinia implorat [sacerdos]*) (D 941–DS 1744).

Since Carolingian times, both in Trier and in the East,
the custom develops of offering several loaves of bread
symbolically in Holy Mass. In the East it is mostly five
loaves: one for Christ, the Lamb; one in memory of Mary;
one in memory of the saints; one as entreaty for the living,
and one (or more) for the dead (cf. the Rite of Preparation in
the Liturgy of St. John Chrysostom). A particularly hard
blow was struck against these Masses in honor of the
saints by the verdict of the Reformers, who did not recognize the cult of the saints. In response the Council of Trent
declared: "Whoever says it is improper to offer Masses in
honor of the saints, as the Church does, to obtain their intercession before God, *anathema sit*" (D 952–DS 1755).

A medieval prayer concluding the offertory expresses

these thoughts well: "Holy Trinity, accept these gifts which we offer Thee in memory of the suffering, resurrection and ascension of Our Lord Jesus Christ, in honor of the blessed and ever pure Virgin Mary, of St. John the Baptist, of the holy Apostles Peter and Paul, of these and all the saints. Let [these gifts] redound to their honor, but to our salvation, and let them be our intercessors in heaven whose memory we celebrate on earth."[116]

If we review as a whole the development of the liturgy in our Church as it has occurred from the beginnings of the liturgical movement around 1920 all the way to Vatican II's Constitution on the Liturgy of 1963, including the manner this Constitution was implemented in the three new Eucharistic Prayers, we can happily affirm that, while retaining the valid doctrines concerning the Masses for the dead and in honor of the saints, still the Church has clearly emphasized that the real and sole meaning of the Sacrifice of the Mass is the *sacramental celebration of our redemption in the sacrifice of Christ*: it is this that remains the central theme of each and every Mass.[117]

B. ON THE SPECIFIC EFFECTS OF THE MASS AND ON THE MODES OF THESE EFFECTS (FRUITS OF THE SACRIFICE OF THE MASS)

The question that, especially since the Middle Ages, was developed under the theme "fruits of the Mass" must in our day be considered from the perspective of the newer and more profound insight into the nature of the Mass as being "the sacramental celebration of the mystery of our salvation in the sacrifice of Christ."

A. To understand this theme let us introduce the following historical considerations: From the very beginning the Mass was the central mystery of the community and, as such, of the Church as a whole. From early on the priests lived exclusively from their service at the altar and as proclaimers of the Gospel, as Paul writes: "You know surely that those who do the temple's work live on the temple's revenues; that those who preside at the altar share the altar's offerings. And so it is that the Lord has bidden the heralds of the gospel to live by preaching the gospel" (1 Cor 9,13f.). The ministers of the altar, thus, received their sustenance through gifts that were formally given for and in connection with the sacrifice but that were not really needed for the sacrifice; rather, they were intended for the ministers of the sacrifice. During the first few centuries, therefore, which were the era of persecutions, it was taken for granted that only a believing Christian gave contributions for the sacrifice and for the priests; in other words, the economic gift was an expression of authentic faith. Only later, when the Church came to enjoy civic freedom, did it become possible to give the impression of belonging to the Church by making monetary contributions to a Church with which one had no bonds of faith and love. The situation became particularly difficult in the Middle Ages when big monasteries, often with hundreds of monks, had to live on gifts given for the liturgy, preaching, and sundry devotions. It is in this context that an abuse developed in connection with the institution of what are known as *mass stipends,* which was a hallmark of medieval piety and produced phenomena of Mass-like devotions such as the *missa sicca* or "dry mass": all of this provoked the violent criticism of the Reformation.

This was the spirit in which the questions concerning the "fruits" of the Sacrifice of the Mass were more and more developed. Three kinds of "fruits" came to be distinguished: (a) The *fructus generales* ("general fruits"), shared by those who are specifically named in the Mass, above all in the intercessions (all ecclesiastical orders, the believing people, the living and the dead); (b) the *fructus speciales* ("special fruits"), shared only by those to whom the Sacrifice of the Mass is applied, either as a free gift or by virtue of a mass stipend;[118] finally, (c) the *fructus specialissimi* ("very special fruits"), shared only by the officiating priest or priests as free instruments of Christ. Such a manner of looking at the fruits of the Mass, while valid in itself, is nevertheless too objectifying and even materializing; in our day it needs to be somewhat corrected and deepened on the basis of our understanding of the Mass as the "sacramental celebration of the mystery of Christ's redemptive deed."

The specifc questions concerning "mass stipends" fall in the realm of Canon Law. Here we will be dealing only with some fundamental dogmatic questions.[119]

B. The Sacrifice of the Mass belongs in the order of sacraments, and as a "sacramental mystery" it has to do both with Christ as Head of the Church and with believers as members of Christ's Body. In this connection, a fundamental question concerning the "manner of the efficacy of the Mass" is the question that the Middle Ages expressed in the terminology of "efficacy *ex opere operato*" and "efficacy *ex opere operantis.*" The Reformers' understanding of grace, determined as it was by nominalism and the humanism of the times, rejected this distinction; but from the Catholic perspective, such a distinction remains a valid attempt at addressing and enunciating the ever impenetrable "mystery of Christ" in the concrete Church in this world. The intention of this distinction is certainly not to provide a ready recipe for a rational solution: there is no such thing when it comes to the mystery of faith. Rather, this distinction only strives to make us continually aware of the "Christ-mystery" itself as a human mode of existence within the sphere of the truth "Christ in us and we in Christ"; it strives to liberate us for this mode of existence—free from all magical-material thinking in connection with the Mass as well as from any form of the purely ethical will-to-achieve, free for life out of the grace, in the grace, and with the grace that was revealed to us in Christ himself and has become the reality of faith.

The following brief points on this theme will have to suffice:

1. According to what has been said, we can affirm that

the Sacrifice of the Mass is the mystery-event and the action of the Church and in the Church, the event in this world that alone possesses "infinite value," until the consummation at the Lord's Second Coming. It is Christ's sacrificial event, which Christ himself bestows; but it is also the action of the Church, of the individual community, of the individual priest in the community and with the community, insofar as it is only the obedient accomplishment of this memorial celebration that makes possible the re-presentation—the making present—of Christ's sacrifice. The relationship between supernatural divine gift and human act in this event is similar, *mutatis mutandis*, to the collaboration between nature and human activity in human non-technical cultural works. The decisive difference remains that human natural cultural works must continually be furthered by human initiative (through an expansion of insights in experimentation and planning), while in the supernatural event God's free gift of grace itself remains the ever greater and more efficacious factor. In both cases what has been given in advance remains the element that is more "pregnant" with powerful reality and the bearer of more significant efficacy. This is why Paul himself could say of his missionary work: "It was for me to plant the seed, for Apollo to water it, but it was for God who gave the increase. And if so, the person who plants, the person who waters, count for nothing; God is everything, since it is he who gives the increase. This person plants, that person waters; it is all one. And yet either will receive his or her own wages, in proportion to his or her own work. You [the believers] are a field of God's tilling, a structure of God's design; and we [the apostles] are only God's fellow-workers (συνεργοὶ θεοῦ)" (1 Cor 3,6–9).

2. The question is, How does this infinite value of the Sacrifice of the Mass become applied to us humans as "fellow-workers"? To understand an answer to this question we must first keep in mind the following four truths:

a) Human beings are finite and, therefore, they can ever

receive infinite realities only according to the measure of their finitude. But here we must not forget what Thomistic theology rightly teaches, namely, that God himself in his graciousness expands our ability to receive divine grace, and that it remains God's affair to what degree he wills to carry this expansion as Creator. God's infinite generosity finds no barrier in our weakness and poverty.

b) As bodily-spiritual beings, humans either are always under way to development and growth, or they atrophy. Immobility is not possible over any considerable time-lapse. Even being grounded in God's grace cannot consist of merely retaining what one has received. Frequent reception of the sacraments and attendance at Mass, therefore, cannot mean a mere "addition of proofs of grace"; such acts, rather, must have their effect in an "existential intensity" that itself is both a gift and a task. It is from this fact that the question concerning the "many Masses and the one Sacrifice" (Karl Rahner) must receive its meaning and its answer.

c) Both the Sacrifice of the Mass and the sacraments are indeed bound to the character of sacramental signs. Nevertheless we may say that a sacrament must primarily be "received" and that it benefits only the person who receives it, whereas the Mass, unlike the sacraments, must be "co-enacted" in the sense of a personal and existential opening up and self-surrender to Christ, his sacrificial attitude, and his sacrificial gift; for this reason the Mass can be validly applied to others "in and with and through Christ." The aspect of *opus operantis* consequently has in the Sacrifice in the Mass, because of its "fundamentally social character," a different and higher significance than in the reception of the sacraments: there is no such thing as a "private Mass"; every Mass is a Mass of the whole Church.

d) The answer to the question of how the infinite value of the Mass can be received by us as "co-laborers" is also affected by the fundamental problem of all theology: how we can grasp God because of our spiritual nature created in God's image, and likewise how God encompasses us through his creative and infinite being (and this reciprocal "grasping" and "encompassing" cannot be further dissociated, since they have their reality only within this reciprocal and paramensural uniqueness). In the same manner, as a rule the action of divine favor and predestination, on the one hand, and, on the other, our action in and with and through the favor of divine grace are ordered to one another. Even though God's action, being always antecedent and greater, has from the outset already overtaken and surpassed all human action, still our personal freedom presents a limit for God. Indeed, it is a law of salvation-history that *the many are saved by the few*, which means that God wills it that individuals called by him are, through their free obedience and their action in God's grace, responsible for the salvation of the others, the many.

3. The four truths we have just named are at work in the Mass both with respect to the "sacrifice of praise and thanksgiving" and with respect to the "sacrifice of entreaty and atonement," although in differing measures.

a) In the *sacrifice of praise and thanksgiving* we can add nothing to the work of Christ. As sacrifice of praise and thinksgiving, the Mass is the greatest thing that God himself has placed in our hands, to the end that we should offer it to him. This is where the "Sunday obligation" has its deeper reason: one time, at the end of the week of creation or at the beginning of the week of redemption, we should have the opportunity of offering *this* thanksgiving to God, his Lord, through and with and in Christ, since this thanksgiving is owed by us and is the sole valid and wholly worthy one.

The extent to which this thanksgiving becomes our personal thanksgiving depends on the intensity with which we give ourselves to this sacrifice of Christ's, allow ourselves to be grasped by it: it will coincide with the extent to which we ourselves become, in union with Christ, a sacrifice of praise and thanksgiving to God the Father. A fundamental mystery remains in this connection: that here praise and thanksgiving do not consist merely in shouts of jubilation or in a raising up of the heart, but rather in the willingness to become a sacrifice unto death.

b) Even less can we add anything to the *Mass as a sacrifice of atonement.* Christ alone is atonement for all human sins. Now the Church and the individual Christian can celebrate and offer the Sacrifice of the Mass, as representation of Christ's Sacrifice of the Cross, not only for their own sins but vicariously and intercessorially also for the sins of others, for other sinners. But the application of this particular manner of sacrifice is in many ways subject to limitations. One limitation is surely the disposition of the recipient to whom this atoning sacrifice is to be applied through intercession. The other limitation lies in our intercession itself, which cannot dispose and "direct" the sacrifice but can "effect" the application of the sacrifice only through Christ himself, only through insistent prayer like that of the friend in the Gospel (Luke 11,6), through believing trust in Christ's limitless love of sinners (Matt 9,13; Luke 19,10), or through one's own grace-impelled entering into the "suffering of Christ for sinners" (cf. Col 1,24).

If the Church celebrates "several Masses" for the same intention or for the same deceased person, and has made provision for such "multiplication of Masses" in the custom of "applying particular intentions," the reason for this practice is not a belief in an "extensive limit" of application (that is, a quantitative measuring of the fruits of the Mass) but rather faith's insight into human historicity: in this repetition and in the resulting accumulation of the Church's sacrificial acts, both the living person who is making intercession and applying the sacrifice and the dead person for whom the applicaton is intended are seen as persons standing in a constant process of growth and maturation. Although, to be sure, we cannot apply to human existence after death our manner of thinking about space and time in this world, still the essential view of humans as beings who are always "growing and maturing" remains valid. Even when we find ourselves *in statu comprehensoris*, we cannot in our spiritual nature enter a state of immobility; rather, the constant growth of what is essentially finite toward what is always essentially infinite is the very meaning of all our fulfillment.

c) As *intercessory sacrifice*, characterized by the liturgy's many entreaties and intercessions, the Sacrifice of the Mass is surely also of infinite value in itself, and yet more bound to human limitations than as atoning sacrifice. Even though God's grace knows no absolute limit, nonetheless some limits to the application of God's gracious favor through the Sacrifice of the Mass would be not only the thing itself prayed for (decisive here is the thing's proximity to or distance from the meaning of God's Kingdom on earth), but likewise the mysterious saving will of God, which has standards quite different from even the most loving human attitude (Is 55,8f.), and the receptive capability and readiness of the person for whom something is being asked. And yet the image of knocking at God's so-called *absoluta potestas*, which we frequently encounter in a Late Scholasticism tinged with nominalism and in the Reformers, is not in keeping with the biblical image of God, which includes not only God's love but also his justice, not only God's mercy but also his wrath.

d) Theology has made the following assertions concerning the effects of the Mass as an atoning sacrifice for our sins. The Mass, as re-presentation of Christ's Sacrifice on the Cross, surely contains within itself the power and the intention to wipe out all sins. But because of its sacramental form, which is given for us and requires our free co-operation, it does not *delete grave sin* immediately and in a quasi-magical manner but does so only immediately through the conferral of graces of conversion: it is only through repentance and a penitential attitude that we become fit to receive the forgiveness of grave sin (as separation from God) in a moral manner.[120]

The Mass also deletes venial and *everyday sins* mediately through the grace of repentance, whereas unwilled quotidian weaknesses can be healed immediately through the power of the eucharistic sacrament in sacramental communion with Christ (D 938–DS 1740).

Temporal punishment for sin is deleted by the Mass immediately, because punishment may be waived without our cooperation whereas guilt requires our collaboration for it be deleted.

The conditions for the reception of these graces are the *ability* to receive them (*capacitas:* to be a Christian; but the graces of the Mass can also be applied to non-Christians through intercession), the *condition of pilgrim* (*status viæ;* but the fruits of the Mass can also be applied to the dead through intercession), *proper disposition* (*dispositio;* but the strengthening and ordering of the disposition are likewise a grace of the Mass), *need* (*indigentia;* such objective need should nonetheless be attuned to the personal structure of the celebration of the eucharistic mystery through an awareness of one's neediness).

e) For all active participants the fruit of the Sacrifice of the Mass is connected in a particular way to the *opus operantis.* (*Mediator Dei,* in Part II, 2, names the following as being particular means of participation in the Mass by the faithful: [a] uniting one's own attitude of praise and thanksgiving, atonement, and intercession, with that of the celebrating priest, and then all of this finds its sacramental expression in the rite of the sacrifice and its highest fulfillment in Christ himself, who is the sacrificing *sacerdos primarius;* [b] personal self–surrender as sacrificial gift through the purification of the soul in repentance, penance, renunciation and love, and formation in the image of Christ through the obedience of faith and in love for God; [c] sacramental communion, which means actual participation in the Mass and which communicates the fruits of the Mass in a sacramentally real manner.)

Francis of Assisi and the theology elaborated by his Order have especially recommended, as fundamental eucharistic attitude, the practice of including oneself spiritually in the intentions of all Masses everywhere on earth, since in this way an opportunity is given to participate in a spiritual manner in Christ's sacrifice at every moment of the day. Wherever this high Franciscan esteem and gratitude for the Mass have come to predominate, the Mass stipend may also become an expression and an actualization of such a mentality and as such an aid to a more personal participation in the Sacrifice of the Mass.

Thus does the believing Christian have a part in the blessings of the Mass, objectively as a member of Christ's Body, the Church, and subjectively through personal corealization ("Have the mind which was the mind of Christ," Phil 2,5), much as a person has a share in the goods of his or her family first of all objectively, simply by belonging to the family and possessing the objective spirit of the family, and then subjectively by his or her cultivation of the family spirit and care of the family's goods.

The dead cannot of themselves gain a share in the fruits of the Mass; these can be applied to them only through intercession by others. For such application to take place, too, a decisive significance goes, first of all, to God's unmerited love and predestination, and then to the community of believers with one another, to the community of believers with Christ the Head who is always interceding for us before the Father, to the adequate disposition of the earthly intercessor, and also to the disposition for and esteem of the Holy Mass that have remained present in the dead person from the time of his or her earthly sojourn.

f) Much profit can be derived for a deepened understanding of the Mass from the theological discipline known as *liturgiology*, which began developing a little over a century ago. The correct historical, theological, and religious understanding of the texts of the Mass can help in a particular way to foster in us the genuine theological understanding of this sacramental Christ-mystery. This is why Vatican II published the *Constitution on the Sacred Liturgy* as its first decree, thereby recognizing liturgiology as a primary theological discipline. "All the more surely, then, now that we have found justification through his blood, shall we be saved, through him, from God's displeasure. Enemies of God, we were reconciled to him through his Son's death; reconciled to him, we are surer than ever of finding salvation in his Son's life!" (Rom 5,9–10).

III

The Eucharist as Sacrificial Meal (The Meal as Sacrament)

The sacrament of the Holy Eucharist, being a meal, cannot be regarded as an autonomous sacrament but must always be understood as a participation in the Sacrifice of the Mass. Even when it is distributed as viaticum to the sick or, exceptionally, to anyone outside the celebration of Mass, still it retains its primary meaning as sacramental participation in the Sacrifice of the Mass.

We have already dealt with the aspects of the matter, form, and institution of the sacrament by Christ (see Introduction, No. 2, and Chap. I.1). Here we will limit ourselves to a brief discussion of the minister and recipient of the sacrament (1), intercommunion and "open communion" (2), the effects of the sacrament (3), and the necessity of the sacrament (4).

1. The Minister and the Recipient of the Holy Eucharist

As with every other sacrament, so too in this sacrament the minister and the recipient must be two different persons. This fact implies that the action of the minister must be phenomenally distinct from the action of the recipient.

A. THE MINISTER

The actual "ministration" of the Eucharist is the institution of this sacrament in the Mass, something that can be accomplished only by an ordained priest. The distribution of the consecrated species is a question of the liturgical order of the Church, not a question having to do with the dogmatic basis of this sacrament.

In the third and fourth centuries both Montanists and Priscillianists had conferred priestly ordination and the priestly office on women. Epiphanius took an emphatic stand against this.[121] Much later, Albigensians and Waldensians gave the laity the full power to consecrate, something that the Church explicitly opposed in 1208 (D 424–DS 794), and the Fourth Lateran Council of 1215 proclaimed that the eucharistic sacrifice can be offered only by a priest who has been duly ordained (D 430–DS 802).

The Reformation definitively abandoned the specific office of ordained priesthood and replaced it with the general priesthood of all the baptized (1 Pet 2,5.9). Thus, Luther taught that in the New Testament there is no special priesthood to offer sacrifice, and that the eucharistic sacrament is not brought about by the words of the priest.[122] Calvin rejected the sacrament of orders with sarcastic disdain.[123] Ordination now became the mission entrusted to the minister by the community, and its whole sense was an appointment to the preaching office. The Mass survived as a service of prayer and readings with a sermon and, if desired, with communion as well; but its character as sacrifice was expressly denied with the affirmation that only Christ's unique sacrifice on Calvary had validity. The Council of Trent repeatedly responded by making the authentic Catholic position clear.[124] "If anyone should say that with the words 'Do this in memory of me' (Luke 22,19; 1 Cor 11,24) Christ did not institute the apostles as priests and did not command that they and other priests offer up the body and blood of the Lord, *anathema sit*" (D 949–DS 1752).

The proof from Scripture should be based on Christ's command to the aspostles at the institution of the Holy Eucharist (see Introduction, No. 2), as well as on 1 Cor 4,1 (ὑπηρέτας χριστοῦ καὶ οἰκονόμους μυστηρίων Θεοῦ) and Heb 5, 1–3, and 8, 1–3, where both the calling and the ordination of the priest are portrayed as being constitutive of his office (see volume 8 on the sacrament of holy orders).

From the most ancient tradition we should note the following: Pope Clement I presents apostles and bishops pointedly as being successors in Christ's mission.[125] Ignatius of Antioch writes: "Only that eucharist is to be considered valid which is celebrated in the presence of the bishop or by those commissioned by him. Without the bishop no one may either baptize or celebrate the love-meal" (*Ad Smyrn.* 8,1: PG 5, 713).

Justin Martyr writes: "Then they bring to the presider of the brethren (προεστῶτι τῶν ἀδελφῶν) bread and a cup with water and wine. He takes these and offers praise and glorification to the Father of the universe in the name of the Son and the Holy Spirit, and he then accomplishes the eucharist (or thanksgiving) for the gifts received from Him. After he has finished the intercessions and the eucharistic celebration, the whole people answers: 'Amen'. Now the Hebrew word 'amen' means: 'So be it!' Then, after the presider has celebrated the eucharist and the whole people has agreed (through its acclamation), those whom we call deacons distribute to each person present the bread and the wine with water over which the thanksgiving has been spoken, and to the absent these things are sent" (*Apol.* I, cap. 65: PG 6, 428). It is questionable whether the "prophets" who, according to the *Didache*,[126] celebrated the Eucharist, were always consecrated bishops; the title of "prophets" is thereafter no longer used for the ordained priests.

The distribution of the consecrated species ordinarily is the proper task of the priest, and extraordinarily of the deacon, as the Code of Canon Law of 1917 orders (can. 845).

This was already the practice at the time of Ignatius of Antioch, Justin Martyr, and Cyprian. Nevertheless, already in
these earliest times, and especially in periods of persecution and in the case of the Desert Fathers, we do find evidence of the practice of the laity administering communion to themselves, as attested by both Tertullian[127] and
Basil.[128] In this passage Basil writes: "When persecution
makes it necessary, and in the absence of both priest and
deacon, it is not a sin to take the Eucharist with one's own
hand; and I must not prove this, since custom and the facts
have long since demonstrated it. For all hermits in the
desert, living without a priest, have communion [reserved]
in their dwellings and take it with their own hand. In
Alexandria and Egypt every layman normally has it at
home and communicates himself as often as he wants.
However, once the priest has offered and distributed the
sacrifice, the person who has received it and daily eats of it
must still believe that he is duly receiving it and eating it
from the minister. In the church, too, the priest only hands
the portion out and the recipient takes it to his mouth
with his own hand."

The newer regulations concerning eucharistic practices
after Vatican II make provision for the distribution of Holy
Communion by laypersons even during the liturgy.

Questions concerning the manner of distribution belong
to the field of liturgical history. As evidenced by the text of
Basil just quoted, and also by a text of Cyril of Jerusalem,[129]
in the fourth century the host was placed in the hand of
the recipient and he or she then took it to his or her
mouth. In the Middle Ages, because of the danger of profa-
nation, the host was placed directly into the recipient's
mouth.

The oldest formula accompanying the distribution of
the consecrated species was "Body of Christ unto life eternal." The communicant answered, "Amen." In the Middle
Ages this formula of entreaty was preferred: "May the
body of our Lord Jesus Christ preserve your soul unto life

eternal." Since Vatican II the formula of the Eastern Church is used: "The body of Christ!" And the communicant answers, "Amen!"

B. THE RECIPIENT

All believers in the state of grace may receive the sacrament of the Eucharist efficaciously. Even though, in and of itself, it is a sacrament for adults, it was often given to newly baptized children under the form of wine alone.[130] Beginning in the Middle Ages the practice became established of giving the Eucharist only to adults, and it was only Pius X's Decree concerning Holy Communion (August 8, 1910) that specified the age of seven as norm for the reception of First Communion (D 2137–DS 3530). The decisive factor is that the person (the child) be able to distinguish Holy Communion from ordinary food, and that he or she be capable of certain religious encounter with Christ. Consequently, the specific age will have to vary in specifc cases.

The Council of Trent stresses that *reverentia et sanctitas* are conditions for communicating (D 880–DS 1646 ff.), and it condemns the opinion that faith alone suffices as preparation (D 881–DS 1648). The Council distinguishes between merely spiritual and sacramental reception and affirms that only the latter is real communion and hence must be sought as normal goal (D 890–DS 1658). In the case of the presence of mortal sin the Council enjoins confession before communion, when this is possible. Mere perfect contrition would not suffice *habita copia confessorum*, that is, when an adequate number of confessors are available (D890–DS 1661). [See Appendix to the text, page 372.]

The condition of the state of grace is justified with reference to the washing of feet before the Last Supper as a symbol of purification (John 13,2–20; 1 Cor 11,27). The *Didache* says: "Break the bread after you have first confessed

your sins" (14.1). The Church's ancient call to communion
was "Holy things for the holy!" as attested by Cyprian,
Cyril of Jerusalem, and the Eastern liturgies.

Abstention before communion from even the legitimate
use of the sexual act in marriage is expected from the most
numerous sources, usually on the basis of 1 Sam 21,5f. (the
"Bread of the Presence," the Showbread, is given to David
and his men): Origen, Jerome, Gregory the Great, Isidore of
Seville, numerous Scholastics, and even the Roman Catechism. A correct understanding of the act of love in marriage, as well as the Church's exhortation to daily communion in our day, have rendered that older injunction
both pointless and invalid.

Since the second century we see the advisability of ob-
serving a certain period of *fasting* before the reception of
Holy Communion, especially since the separation of the
agapê-meal from the Eucharist, and this practice has undergone many changes in the course of time.[131] In our day
the rule is a fast of at least one hour, and water does not
break it.

It is from the medieval period that we have most evidence of the Eucharist in the form of communion for the
sick or *sacrament of the dying (viaticum).* In the ancient
Church communion for the dying took the form only of
the reconciliation of penitents. When he was dying, Augustine meditated on the penitential psalms,[132] and Ambrose had the Eucharist brought to him.[133] Nonetheless, if
there is a specific sacrament for the particular situation of
dying, then the Eucharist is that sacrament. It should help
us so to unite our dying with Christ's dying that, at this decisive hour of our life, we may participate in the special
grace of Christ's redemptive sacrifice *(viaticum–ἐφόδιον).*

At different times a particular role was taken in the
Church by what was known as the "communion of poor
sinners." The name of "poor sinner" was given to a condemned criminal. From the seventh to the eighteenth centuries these condemned criminals were routinely denied

communion. Starting in the nineteenth century adequate preparations for dying and communion for condemned criminals were enjoined in a particular manner.[134]

On the question of *frequency of communion,* we would point to the following facts: In the early Church, communion was normally received every time one participated in the eucharistic sacrifice. It was only with the development of penance as an institution that exceptions began to be made. Since daily Mass became a practice toward the end of the second century, at least in Egypt and Rome, this likewise meant daily communion. Basil[135] and Jerome[136] still speak in the late fourth century of daily communion by the laity. After the end of the fourth century the practice of daily communion declined significantly, and this for various reasons: greater reverence for the sacrament after the Council of Nicæa, penance developed as an institution, laxity among believers after the period of persecutions and in Late Antiquity, and so on. In the Middle Ages the rule was to receive communion on the three great feasts of the liturgical year: Christmas, Easter, and Pentecost. The reasons for this decisive regression in the Middle Ages were both financial and pastoral: financial, because a donation had to be given the priests for bringing Holy Communion to one's house; pastoral, because pastoral conditions in the Middle Ages were extraordinarily bad, partly because of the huge size of parishes, and partly because of the poor education of the clergy. But there were also ascetical and dogmatic reasons: in the Germanic thinking of the Middle Ages, more ascetical practices were demanded as preparation for Holy Communion than in the early Church or in our day.[137]

On the question of frequent communion Augustine writes: "Some receive communion daily, others only on certain days. In one place no day passes without the sacrifice being offered, in another place this occurs only on Saturday and Sunday. All these customs admit freedom, and for the serious and intelligent Christian no one of them is better than the others. Each one is to do what he sees the Church do in the place to which he comes. For, what is not against faith and good morals is to be treated as of equal value and to be observed according to the community in which one lives" (*Ep. 54 ad inq. Jan.*, c. 2: PL 33, 200). In similar manner Jerome says: "I am acquainted with the Roman manner always to receive the Body of the Lord. I want neither to praise it nor to censure it. In this each one can follow his own opinion" (*Ep.* 71, n. 6: PL 22, 672). Toward the end of the fifth century Gennadius writes similarly: *Quotidie Eucharistiæ communionem recipere nec laudo nec vitupero* (*De eccles. dogm.*, c. 5). This text was also incorporated into the *Decretum Gratiani* (Part 3, dist. 2, c.13). The Synod of Agde (506) decreed that laypersons who did not receive communion on Christmas, Easter, and Pentecost were no longer to be considered Catholic.[138] Gratian and Thomas Aquinas erroneously attribute this decree to Pope Fabian (258). The Fourth Lateran Council (1215) required, as a minimum, communion once a year during Eastertide, something that had already been done earlier by a synod under St. Patrick and was to be done later by the Council of Trent. This requirement became a part of the Code of Canon Law (can. 859). But Canon 863 exhorts as follows: *Excitentur fideles, ut frequenter, etiam quotidie communicent:* "The faithful are to be encouraged to communicate frequently, even daily."

An important issue, debated since the fifteenth century, is the question of *communion under both species.* In 1404, and for the first time in a public manner, Master Peter of Dresden proclaimed that Christ had instituted communion under two species and that it must be received in this way. In their struggle against the Church's hierarchy, the "Bohemian Brethren"—the Hussites—again championed this opinion. Jacob of Misa, the head of the Calixtines or "Utraquists" (from *utraque* = "both"), defended the doctrine passionately, and Ciska, the leader of the Taborites, introduced communion under both species very successfully into his communities. But the Council of Constance (1415) ruled that only the priest has to communicate under both species for the Mass to be valid, and that communion under one species suffices for the laity (D626–DS 1188ff.). Both Calvin[139] and Luther[140] again demanded communion under both species.

Opposing all this, the Council of Trent proclaimed that, for the laity and for those priests who are not themselves consecrating, communion is necessary under only one species, since in this one species the whole, living Christ is present and participation in the sacrifice is perfect.[141]

The doctrine of Trent is based on the Bread of Life Discourse in John 6, where we find the double expression referring to "eating and drinking" only as often as the single expression "whoever eats has eternal life." The unbroken tradition of the Church witnesses to the fact that it has never doubted that communion under one species alone is fully valid and sufficient. Examples of this belief are communion at home, especially for the sick, under the form of bread only, or the communion of children under the form of wine only, or the practice of what is known as "Mass of the Presanctified," reaching back to the fifth century and observed to this day by the Eastern Church during Lent and by the Western Church on Good Friday.

John of Ragusa preached on this matter at the Council of Basel, incorporating, among many others, the views of Innocent III, Alexander of Hales, Albert the Great, Thomas Aquinas, and Bonaventure.[142] For important and just reasons, the Council of Trent conceded communion from the chalice to the laity in Bavaria and Austria, but this had to be retracted after barely two years.

The view, represented by P. Merendino, that the chalice is important because it expresses the sacrifice of the Covenant, while the bread bears only the character of the meal, is wholly unfounded.

Vatican II, and the ecclesiastical regulations concerning the Eucharist deriving from the Council, have up to now

allowed communion from the chalice by the laity in fourteen circumstances: at the baptism of adults, to the newly
baptized and his or her close relatives attending the ceremony; to the newly married at their nuptial Mass, as well
as at anniversary celebrations of the marriage; to new
priests at their ordination, and to all priests during their retreats or during concelebrated Masses, even when they are
not concelebrating; to abbesses on the day of their blessing
and on the anniversaries thereof, and to religious sisters on
the day of their profession and the anniversaries thereof;
also to close relatives of newly ordained priests and pro-
fessed religious at their corresponding ordination and profession Masses; to lay auxiliaries at the Mass when they
are entrusted with their mission; during Mass in a sick-
room when the viaticum is given; to all servers at the altar
during an episcopal Mass; at the concluding Mass of a re-
treat, to all retreatants; to participants in special festive
Masses in a religious community.[143] On September 2, 1970,
the express ruling was made that the ordinary of a place
has the power to determine when communion may be
given under both species over and beyond the occasions
just listed.

In the line of Augustine and the Schoolmen, the Council
of Trent distinguishes three *manners of reception* for this
sacrament (D 881–DS 1648). The sacrament is received
sacramentally only *(sacramentaliter tantum)* by whoever
receives it unworthily, such as the person in grave sin.
Others receive it spiritually only *(spiritualiter tantum)*
when they long for it with a living faith that works
through real love. The Council expressly states that these
people too experience the fruit and the benefit of this
sacrament. A third group receives the sacrament *sacramentaliter et spiritualiter;* these are the people who receive it in their bodies and in the state of grace, with good
intention and good preparation.

The second manner of receiving the sacrament was
largely called "spiritual communion" from the Council of

Trent to Vatican II and involved fervent acts of love and yearning for the sacrament in Holy Mass, without sacramental reception of communion. To such a disposition, at least since Vatican II, must be added an "encounter with Christ" made possible not by the sacrament of his flesh and blood but rather by "the Word of God." On this point Vatican II expressly says the following in the Dogmatic Constitution of Divine Revelation (art. 21): "The Church has always revered the Holy Scriptures as well as the Lord's Body itself: especially in the Sacred Liturgy, it does not cease to take the Bread of Life from the table both of the Word of God and of the Body of Chirst, in order to distribute it to believers. So great is the efficacy that indwells the Word of God that for the Church it signifies support and life and, for the children of the Church, the strength of faith: it is food for the soul and a pure and unceasing stream for the spiritual life" (Heb 4,12; Acts 20,32). Consider also Article 26: "Just as from the constant celebration of the eucharistic mystery the life of the Church is multiplied, so too may we hope for a new impulse for the spiritual life from deepened reverence for the Word of God, which perdures for all eternity" (Isa 40,8). "You have all been born anew with an immortal, imperishable birth, through the Word of God that lives and abides forever" (1 Pet 1,23).

In this sense, therefore, a well-ordered Christian day could take shape around the Eucharist: in the morning, Mass with a fitting communion *(sacramentaliter et spiritualiter)*; during the day a visit to the church, including an encounter with Christ full of fervent thanksgiving and yearning for him; then, in the evening and before the closing of the day, a short reading from Scripture as spiritual and deeply felt encounter with Christ *(communio cum verbo Domini)* to round off what has been a "day of communion" and to prepare the next day to be the same.[144]

By *spiritualiter communicare* the Middle Ages understood the worthy and hence fruitful sacramental reception of communion in the grace of the Holy Spirit. Since the Council of Trent, and especially in the nineteenth century, *spiritualiter communicare* came to mean the non-sacramental reception of communion by desire.[145]

2. Intercommunion and "Open Communion"

The word *intercommunion* has come to have special significance for many years now. We first see it used in the Lambeth Conference Report of 1867, the work of F. G. Lee and his "Association for the Promotion of the Unity of Christendom (A.P.U.C.)," founded in 1857. Subsequently, the idea gained ever greater interest in the ecumenical dialogues of the reformed churches among themselves and with the ancient churches of East and West. Since the time of the World Conference of Faith and Order held in Lund in 1952, the concept of *intercommunion* has constantly been given a more precise interpretation by the use of newer terms such as "open and closed communion," "full sharing in the Lord's Supper," "intercelebration," and "general reciprocal admission" or "limited admission." Beginning with the question concerning the possibility of the reception of communion and even full participation in the eucharistic celebration by members of one confession in the other "churches," it has become increasingly clear that the problem this brings up does not primarily belong in the field of sacramental theology but rather that of ecclesiology, insofar as it is in the eucharistic celebration that the Church has the very center of its existence and that it both shows who it is and actualizes itself.

Within the Catholic Church it was the far-reaching vision of Pope Leo XIII (1878–1903)[146] that introduced the ecumenical ideal, which continued to be powerfully promoted by the ecumenical movement in both the Anglican and the Reformed Churches. The word "ecumenism" was used for the first time in 1919. One result of all this was the establishment by Pope John XXIII, through his Motu Proprio *Superno Dei nutu* of June 5, 1960, of the Secretariat for the Unity of Christians under Cardinal Bea. On November 21, 1964, the Second Vatican Council approved the decree On Ecumenism *(Unitatis Redintegratio* [UR]), which was signed and proclaimed on this same day by Pope Paul VI together with the decree On the Eastern Catholic Churches (*Orientalium Ecclesiarum* [OE]) and the Dogmatic Constitution on the Church *(Lumen Gentium*: [LG]).

In these documents, prayer for the unity of Christian is recommended as the very "soul of the whole ecumenical movement," but, as a "generally accepted and unqualified means for the restoration of the unity of Christians," the communal celebration of the liturgy *(communicatio in sacris)* is rejected. "In most circumstances, witnessing to unity forbids a common liturgy, but in some instances the need for grace would seem to impose it" (UR 8). This decree expressly distinguishes between the Eastern Churches and the ecclesial communities in the West that have derived from the Reformation. In what concerns its liturgical and spiritual tradition, the Roman Church knows itself to be one with the Eastern Churches, especially on the basis of the seven sacraments and the priesthood, which rests on real apostolic succession. The bond to the reformed churches, on the other hand, is based only on faith in Christ, the possession of the Scriptures, and the sacrament of baptism. The decree "On the Eastern Catholic Churches" therefore disposes that, whenever "there is a serious need or a real spiritual benefit" to be derived, Eastern Christians may receive the sacraments of penance, the Eucharist, and the anointing of the sick in the Roman Church, and Roman Christians in the Eastern Churches" (OE 27). Whereas the Russian Church has accepted this offer, the Greek Church has to date rejected it, on the grounds that sacramental unity is not possible without doctrinal unity. The Greeks say there is no doctrinal unity with a Rome whose pope has been declared to be infallible and to have the power of universal jurisdiction, and that once the power of jurisdiction has been separated from the power of ordination, the doctrine of the sacraments too becomes uncertain (see LG 15; 23). The Greeks further say that sharing in the sacraments is possible only as an expression of full unity in the one Church of Christ, in the *koinonia* that is given in the sacrificial sacrament of the Eucharist (cf. 1 Cor 10, 16–18). They argue that, intimately connected with the eucharistic sacrifice, there are three important aspects: in the liturgy, Eucharist is intimately connected with unity in the teachings of the Apostles and in prayer (cf. Acts 2,42); in the Church, Eucharist is bound up with unity in faith in Jesus, the Son of God, and in his Father (cf. 1 John 1,1–3); and in spirituality, Eucharist is connected with the disposition shaped by the Spirit of God (cf. Phil 2, 1–4; 1 Cor 2,16). This "oneness through community" (κοινωνία) is the expression of the "unity through unicity" (ἑνότης) that comes from God. This is why the Apostle writes: "Be eager to preserve that unity the Spirit gives you (σπουδάζοντες τηρεῖν τὴν ἑνότητα τοῦ Πνεύματος), through the bond of peace: you are one body, with a single Spirit; each of you, when he was called, called in the one and only hope; with the one Lord, the one faith, the one baptism; with the one God, the one Father of all of us, who is above all beings, pervades all things, and lives in all of us" (Eph 4,3–6).

The Roman Church believes that the conditions for this "unity of the Spirit through the bond of peace" with the Orthodox Churches already exist in spite of the developments that it has undergone since 1054. These are developments that the Roman Church since Vatican II has been striving to bring into harmony with the doctrines and practices of the first millennium of Christianity. A good example of these efforts is the liturgical reform.

With the Reformed Churches different accords have been reached on the question of "intercommunion," especially since in some of these churches the "one catholic Church" has taken the form rather of a "spirtual church" that would only require certain sociological agreements for it to be made visible at the earthly level. This holds particularly for the High Anglican Church, which itself unites many different forms, for the churches of the Nordic countries, and for the Old Catholic Church, which enjoys unity of communion with the Eastern Churches. Alongside these more formal accords, more spontaneous attempts at liturgical communion are frequently being made without explicit deliberation among the churches.

The principles of the Decree on Ecumenism were more precisely clarified by the Roman Church by means of the "Ecumenical Directory."[147] They were updated in the "Declaration of the Secretariat for Christian Unity"[148] and further specified through the Instruction of this same Secretariat dated June 1, 1972.[149] The little progress that may be concretely noted in the practice of the churches should not conceal from us the fact that dogmatically something has really begun to grow in this dialogue, characterized by the following statements. With reference to the Eastern Churches, the Ecumenical Directory says in article 40: "Through the celebration of the Lord's Eucharist in these individual churches the Church of God is built up and grows" *(per celebrationem Eucharistiæ Domini in his singulis ecclesiis Ecclesia Dei ædificatur et crescit.).* The Instruction of June 1, 1972, quotes a letter of Pope Paul VI to Patriarch Athenagoras (February 8, 1971) in which the pope writes that "between Our Church and the venerable Orthodox Churches there exists, not indeed a perfect communion, but already an almost full communion *(communio fere totalis)* which results from Our common participation in the mystery of Christ and his Church *(e communi nostra participatione in mysterio Christi eiusque Ecclesia . . .).*[150] Both these statements go beyond the formulations of the Constitution on the Church, which says that the one Church of Christ "is realized in the Catholic Church, which is led by the successor of Peter and by the bishops in communion with him" (LG 8). These later statements envision the Church of God and Christ even more clearly as that eschatological Church in this world that is constantly being built up by the celebration of the Eucharist within each individual (partial) church: and both the Eastern and the Western Churches are seen as participating in this eschatological Church. Thus, the one Church of God is seen as standing before these two Churches as a goal they must strive for anew. Since the Second Vatican Council the Roman Church has deliberately avoided identifying itself fully and exclusively with the one Church of Christ. This is a solid start on the road of authentic ecumenism, which does not use an overly hasty *communicatio in sacris* (to date official Church documents do not use the term "intercommunion") to precipitate or even to feign a situation of unity that, after the thousand-year separation between East and West, can be reached only slowly and patiently through much common work and prayer.[151]

The dialogue on intercommunion between Lutherans and Catholics gained a new impulse from the decision of the Council of the German Evangelical Church (EKD) in the summer of 1975 to allow Lutherans to receive the Holy Eucharist in the Catholic Church, and to admit Catholics to the celebration of the Lord's Supper in the Lutheran Church.[152] After negotiations of the Common Synod of the Bishops of the Federal Republic of Germany,[153] the "Statement on Ecumenical Collaboration," presented by Archbishop Degenhardt,[154] once again confirmed the following principles: (1) Communion is not a means toward but an expression of Church unity. (2) Between the Eastern Churches and the Roman Catholic Church intercommunion is possible in the event of serious need or of desire. (3) With regard to intercommunion between the Catholic Church and Lutherans or other Reformed Churches, the prescriptions of the Ecumenical Directory are still binding.

In 1979 *The Eucharist* published the latest results of the dialogues of the "Roman Catholic/Evangelical Lutheran Commission" (Paderborn-Frankfurt), and it also discussed comparable texts for bilateral dialogues with the Anglican Church,[155] with the Group of Les Dombes in France[156] and in America,[157] and the position papers of Accra, Malta, and Windsor.

All of these dialogues have made it ever more evident that, in order to reach final clarity on the nature of the Church as *Una Sancta*, what is most necessary are a unifying vision of the different questions (real presence, sacrifice, priestly office, liturgical practice) and the active cooperation of the official Church, the Church's theologians, and the Church's whole people, especially when engaged in concrete liturgical prayer.[158]

3. The Effects of the Holy Eucharist

The *Eucharist* is not an "object": along with the *Sacred Scriptures* of the New Testament as God's witness to Christ and the *Church* as Mystical Body of Christ, the *Eucharist* is the most concentrated form of the Christ-mystery in this world. For this reason, the question concerning the effects of the Holy Eucharist is a different and particularly significant question that is inseparable from the question concerning the very nature of the Holy Eucharist. The question concerning these effects makes the Christ-mystery itself come to new life in its unique relationship with the Christian mystery of human beings, of the Church, and of the world itself. Consequently, it is important to clarify as much as possible our methodological principles as we attempt to answer such a question.

A. THE EFFECTS IN GENERAL

To do this we will first enlist the support of some historical observations. The first thing that strikes us is that, until well into the twelfth century, the Eucharist was primarily approached in a more objective manner, while starting around this time it began to be seen more subjectively, especially by the Victorines, by Franciscan theologians, and by the mystics. The normative image first used to approach the Eucharist was that of *new manna.* Then Origen adds the insight that the Eucharist above all confers participation in the *Spirit of Christ.* Hilary of Poitiers, for his part, teaches that the Eucharist makes one a partaker in the *Logos of the Father.* For Augustine the Eucharist is above all the *sacrament of the Church,* and its effect is therefore to be sought particularly in the unity of love within the Church, in the intensive growth of the Church's interior reality. From his Alexandrian theology, Cyril of Alexandria derives the Origenistic conception of the bestowal of Christ's Spirit. But he develops this conception in the context of his anti-Nestorian polemic by speculating on the physical efficacy of the Eucharist especially as it tends to weaken the lusts of the flesh and communicates a participation in the illumination that at death will become manifest. The Middle Ages then synthesizes these different viewpoints and orders them variously under three primary effects, which according to St. Thomas are "abolition of sin and concupiscence, communication and increase of grace, providing the path to interior purification and eternal illumination" (*Summa theol.* III, q.79). Interpreting the twelve fruits of the Tree of Life of the Apocalypse (Rev 22,2), many medieval theologians (such as Peter of Tarantaise and Richard of Middleton) summarize the different doctrines on the effects of the Eucharist under the heading of these twelve fruits.

The new contribution that this period makes to the question is the subjective and personalistic manner of considering the eucharistic effects, above all in the personal encounter of the communicant with Christ and of all communicants with one another.[159] This is an idea that will be further developed by fourteenth-century mysticism (H. Suso, J. Tauler, Marquard of Lindau, Rudolf of Biberach) on the basis of St. Paul's Christ-mysticism.

The great theological effort of the post-Tridentine period will be intensely occupied with this question.[160] It is significant that only the Carmelite theologians (the Salmanticenses) deal with the personalistic dimension: *Devotio et dulcedo spiritualis, unio cum Christo et inter fideles.*

More recent research on this question, represented by M. de La Taille, J. Filograssi, and M. Schmaus, orders the fruits of this sacrament under these three headings: (1) personal union with Christ (christological dimension); (2) union of Christians with one another (ecclesiological dimension); and (3) pledge of eternal life and resurrection (eschatological dimension). The older discussions (such as those of J. Pohle, F. Diekamp, L. Ott, etc.) also emphasize another dimension: (4) the increase of grace and the blotting out of daily faults (soteriological dimension). Our newer understanding of the Eucharist as the "sacramental mystery that celebrates Christ's redemptive deed" can be seen as contributing (5) the dimension of salvation-history, with its several elements. The essential thing here is to see the Sacrifice of the Mass and the Sacrificial Meal as pointing to the one Christ-mystery. *In missa ergo sacrificium et sacramenti convivium ita ad idem mysterium pertinent, ut arctissimo vinculo alterum cum altero cohæreat.*[161] "In the Mass, the Sacrifice and the Sacramental Meal so refer to the one and only [Christ-] mystery that they are bound together by a most tight bond."

B. THE EFFECTS IN PARTICULAR

a) In attempting to answer our question we must first of all address two errors that continue to surface all along the history of our problem. It is an error to attribute to Holy Communion as sacramental meal the primary effect of "forgiving sin," especially the forgiveness of grave sin. This was done by most of the Reformers—Luther, Calvin, Martin of Chemnitz, among others. Such a teaching was contested vigorously by R. Bellarmine[162] and of course, before him, by the Council of Trent (D 887–DS 1655). The Sacrifice of the Mass does not, in and of itself, effect the forgiveness of grave sin; rather, if God will it, it gives the grace of conversion through remorse, penance, and confession. For the reception of communion as a sacrament, therefore, the state of grace is all the more required. Here the Apostle's warning against an unworthy reception of communion is especially relevant: "A man must examine himself first, and then eat of that bread and drink of that cup" (1 Cor. 11,27–32).

On the other hand, a Jansenistic error must be detected when communion is seen too much as a reward for a holy life and as a gift for the predestined. Such a thing would require an ascetical preparation that, moreover, would never by sufficient, and it also overlooks the fact that this sacrament is intended as a "fruit of the Cross for our salvation" and thus as an aid for the needs of our earthly life on our way home to God. "Come to me, all of you who are weary and burdened; I will give you rest" (Matt 11,28).

b) According to the doctrine of the ancient Church, the first fruit of this sacrament is the *strengthening and increasing of grace in us.* Here "grace" ought to be understood not only according to the interpretations of the various theological schools but also in its wide diversity according to the differences of the particular persons who receive it.[163] The point of the departure for this doctrine is the Bread of Life Discourse in John's Gospel (John 6), where the Eucharist is compared with the manna in the desert. Every effect normally attributed to physical food and drink for the life of the body—it is sustained and renewed, increased and strengthened, refreshed and gladdened—may be expected from this spiritual food also for our spiritual life: *Sustentando, augendo, reparando et delectando, sacramentum hoc quoad vitam operatur spiritualem* (*Decree for the Armenians* [D 698–DS 1322]). Such an effect may be understood at an even deeper level when we consider that the Eucharist unites us not only with Christ but, through him, with the life of the *holy and triune God* (John 14,10.23), and when we remember that the innermost mystery of all grace is *participation in the divine life*: this is why "eternal life" (John 6,58) is promised as a fruit of communion. In the context of his anti-Nestorian theology Cyril of Alexandria in this connection developed the concept of the "life-giving flesh of the Lord" (σὰρξ ζωοποιόν).[164]

c) On the basis of this notion of "Christ's life-giving flesh" we can well understand why one fruit of this sacrament is said to be the "tempering of lusts and passions" and, hence, a healing of the sicknesses and wounds that sins inflict on the whole human being and not just on our spirit. In this connection, too, we listen once again to Cyril of Alexandria. He says that "those who still suffer from interior weaknesses may indeed partake of Christ's *eulogia*, but not in the manner of the saints, who do so to make progress in their sanctification, to strengthen their minds and to persevere in their pursuit of excellence, but above all in a manner that befits sick persons—to rid themselves of ills, to put a stop to sin, to mortify the passions and to attain again to healthy pneumatic behavior. According to Scripture, Christ is 'a new creation', and we receive him into ourselves by means of his holy flesh and blood, that we, having been transformed into newness of life, may put off the old man through him and in him" (2 Cor 5,17f.) (*De ador.* 1, 12: PG 58, 793 BD). In considering this text we must remember that, in Cyril's day, there was still no private confession. The Council of Trent calls the Eucharist an *antidotum, quo liberemur a culpis quotidianis et a peccatis mortalibus præservemur* (D 875 –DS 1638), a "gift (of

God) whereby we are freed from our daily faults and preserved from mortal sins."

d) The Eucharist is, therefore, the special sacrament that
confers the necessary graces for the daily struggle, the daily
suffering, and the daily tasks of one's calling, which means
the particular work one does in the place God has assigned
us in the Mystical Body of Christ. In a particular way the
Eucharist is the "sacrament of one's state in life." Thus, the
encyclical *Mediator Dei* (Part II, 3) exhorts everyone, whatever one's age or profession, to receive sacramental communion or at least spiritual communion as often as possible—even daily—and it singles out children, married people, and workers especially. "Call all persons [of every
condition] and compel them to come in" (Luke 14,23). Especially the daily cross of authentic Christian living must
receive its saving meaning and value by being united with
Christ's Sacrifice on the Cross. "In my flesh I complete
what is lacking in Christ's afflictions (θλύψεις) for the sake
of his body, that is, the Church" (Col 1,24). The Eucharist,
consequently, is the very source of Christian mystical suffering, that is, suffering in union with Christ's Passion.

e) Furthermore, another fruit of the Eucharist is the personal encounter with Christ that has been progressively
defined beginning with the German mystics of the Middle
Ages, continuing with the piety of the seventeenth century, and culminating in popular pietism in the wake of the
Romantic movement. The basis for this may be seen in the
following passage from the discourse of promises: "He
who eats my flesh and drinks my blood abides in me, and
I in him (ἐν ἐμοὶ μένει καγὼ ἐν αὐτῷ). As the living Father
sent me, and I live because of the Father, so he who eats me
(ὁ τρώγων με) will live because of me" (John 6,56f.). What
first impresses us here is John's very Jewish manner of
viewing Christ as a bodily person. What is meant is not
merely a spiritual and interpersonal relationship, but a
genuine sacramental communion with the bodily Lord. It
is a communion that is as concrete and living as a com-

munion of spouses; it is a communion of covenant that fully corresponds to Jewish thought.

Already in Paul the influence of Greek thought, which tends to make of this encounter a more pneumatic reality, is noticeable. For instance, by contrast to Gen 2,24 and in connection with marriage, Paul writes: "He who clings to the Lord becomes one spirit (ἕν πνεῦμα) with him" (1 Cor 6,17). And he also teaches: "The Lord is the Spirit" (2 Cor 3,17). Christ, as second Adam, is the "life-giving spirit" (1 Cor 15,45). Origen made this "spirit-christology" his specialty, the Alexandrians cultivated it, and John Damascene termed the Lord's flesh "life-giving spirit" (*De Fide orth.* IV, 13: PG 94, 1152 B).

On the basis of the Song of Songs in particular, medieval mysticism developed a full-blown "eucharistic bridal mysticism" starting from this personal encounter with Christ in the Eucharist. William of Auxerre saw the effects of this sacrament in the special joy received by the five interior senses: *Delectat visum spiritualem per pulchritudinem* (Ps 44,3), *delectat auditum spiritualem per melodiam* (Ps 90,9), *delectat olfactum spiritualem per odorem* (Cant 1,3), *delectat gustum spiritualem per dulcedinem* (Cant 1,3), *delectat tactum spiritualem per suavitatem* (Ps 34,9). . . . *Delectat ut divitiæ, quia in eo omnes thesauri sapientiæ et scientiæ sunt absconditi* (Col 3,3) (*Summa aurea* [Paris, 1500], IV, tr.5 c. 1f. 16bc).

Commenting on Ps 34,9 ("Taste and see the sweetness of the Lord") Bonaventure often developed certain traits for such a eucharistic mysticism on the basis of Christ's personal presence in the sacrament.[165] The mystics of the fourteenth century frequently dealt with the theme at length.[166] As an example let us look at a text of Henry Suso (d. 1366).[167]

Congratulamini mihi omnes, qui diligitis Dominum, quia inveni dilectum meum non solum secundum divinitatem omnibus præsidentem, sed et secundum humanitatem sacramentaliter

*præsentem. . . . Dominum meum præsentem habeo non solum
spiritualiter, sed et corporaliter, non solum ut deum, sed ut
fratrem et amicum meum dilectum. . . . Tua præsentia meum ve-
hementer accendet amorem. . . . Amor cogit tam dilectum spon-
sum affectuose amplecti. Tu quidem es deus meus et dominus
meus, sed et frater meus, et, sic dicere audeo, dilectus sponsus
meus. . . . Quid enim magis est amoris, quid dilectionis, quam
coniunctio dilecti cum dilecto familiaris . . . ?*

Rejoice with me, all you who love the Lord, because I have found
my beloved not only in his divinity, as presiding over all things,
but also in his humanity, as present in the sacrament. . . . I have
my Lord present not only spiritually but also corporeally, not only
as God but as my beloved brother and friend. . . . Your presence
powerfully enkindles my love. . . . Love compels [me] to embrace
tenderly so dear a bridegroom. You are indeed my God and my
Lord, but you are also my brother, and thus I dare to call you "my
dear bride-groom." . . . What is more proper to love, what more
proper to fondness, than the intimate union of beloved and
beloved . . . ?

Suso then goes on to meditate at length on the love of
God that chose the mystery of this sacrament in order to
make possible a real union with him which would never
have been possible to human beings otherwise. Throughout his contemplations these questions continually are
asked: Who is coming to me? (The holy God!) To whom is
he coming? (To me who am a sinner! cf. 1 Sam 18, 18).
Why is he coming? (Out of sheer love!) The main concern
remains: How can I prepare myself? And the answer: *Ar-
dentissimis affectibus et sanctissimis meditationibus
tamquam rosis rubescentibus et liliis albescentibus hospi-
tiolum cordis tui ei adorna et thalamum tanto sponso per
veram cordis pacem repara. Et cum præsentem senseris,
inter cordis bracchia ipsum reclina per exclusionem omnis
terreni amoris et inclusionem sponsi cælestis:* "Adorn the
humble inn of your heart for him with the most ardent desires and the most holy thoughts as with red roses and
white lilies, and prepare the bridal chamber for such a

bridegroom by establishing true peace of heart. And when you feel his presence, embrace him in the arms of your heart. Leave aside all earthly loves and belong wholly to your heavenly bridegroom."[168] [See Appendix to the text, page 373.]

f) In a special way, the Eucharist is the "sacrament of the Church," the sacrament that creates church and sustains church. Thus, Paul could already write: "Is not the bread that we break a participation in Christ's body? The one bread makes us one body; the same bread is shared by all" (1 Cor 10,16f.). Paul is here proceeding on the assumption that the community of the Church is established through communion in Christ's meal. Soon after Paul, the *Didache* says (9,4): "Just as this bread was scattered over the hills and now, after being gathered, it has become one, so may your Church be brought together from the ends of the earth into your Kingdom." The prayer is based on the image of bread and wine becoming one from many parts. Subsequently this same image appears time and again in all eucharistic discourses (Tertullian, Cyprian, Augustine, Cyril of Alexandria, and even Thomas Aquinas). Paul likewise writes: "We are limbs of his body, flesh of his flesh and bone of his bone" (Eph 5,30). And Irenæus comments, "He does not say this of a spiritual and invisible body, since a spirit has neither flesh nor bones (Luke 24, 39), but of a truly human organism that consists of flesh and nerves and bones, which is nourished from the cup of his blood and receives growth from the bread of his body (*Adv. Hær.* V, 2, 3: PG 7, 1125ff.).

According to 1 Cor 10,18, however, the community realized by the Eucharist is not only a community based on the *meal* but also one based on the *sacrifice*. This means that eucharistic community and communion in the Church are not only a *gift* of God's but also an *obligation*, as Paul explains in detail also in 1 Cor 11,20–22.

As we have seen in the case of the eucharistic mysticism deriving from bridal mysticism, eucharistic community in

the Church is also a "communion of life with Christ." Paul
himself indicates in Eph 3,6 that the pagans are not only
"co–heirs" (συγκληρονόμα) and sharers of the inheritance
in Christ along with the Jews, but also that they "form one
body" (σύσσωμα) with Christ.

Cyril of Jerusalem later explains that, through the Eucharist, we are one flesh and one blood (σύσσωμος καὶ
σύναιμος) with Christ.[169] And it was above all Augustine
who, in his polemic against the Donatists, often stressed
this connection between the Eucharist and the Church.

Our newer understanding of the Church allows us to
grasp how, precisely in the celebration of the Eucharist,
the two realms—the individual, personal dimension and
the social dimension—must interpenetrate one another
through communion with Christ in the Church, and this
both as a mystery of grace and as a task to be accomplished. To be sure, this truth of the unity of the Church
in the eucharistic Christ will come to perfection only in
the eschatological fulfillment. Quite correctly, M. de La
Taille identifies the following three aspects of this unification with Christ: *Incorporatio nostra ad Christum, et
incorporatio nostra ad Christum caput corporis ecclesiæ,
et incorporatio nostra ad Christum caput corporis ecclesiastici in cælis congregandi.*[170] "Our incorporation into
Christ [as such], and our incorporation into Christ who is
the head of the body of the Church, and our incorporation
into Christ, head of the body of the Church which is still
to be gathered together in heaven." The Eucharist, then,
remains a *signum unitatis*, a *vinculum caritatis*, and a
symbolum concordiæ.[171]

g) On the basis of this significance of the Holy Eucharist,
at once personal and ecclesial, our current understanding
of the Church also makes it possible for us to consider the
"salvation-historical" perspective of the Eucharist, something that was already hinted at when we were examining
the Eucharist as a sacrament of one's state of life. Christ
gave us this sacrament not only for him to remain among

us, always the same until the end of time (Matt 26,29;
28,20), but also for him to be the Savior needed at each moment of time by each individual person. According to the
account of the Gospels, Jesus personally lived through all
aspects of being human, sin excepted, something frequently stressed by the anti-Gnostic theologians of the
second century (Tertullian, Irenæus, Origen). In the same
way, we too should seek to encounter *the* Christ we need
in keeping with our state within the history of salvation:
Christ the child or Christ the man; Christ as he is quietly
at work in the family's everyday life at Nazareth or Christ
as he fights for the Kingdom of God in the eyes of all;
Christ as he wrestles with his Father in prayer, Christ the
savior of sinners, Christ spending himself for the Kingdom
of God, Christ who has compassion on his people, Christ
praying in the night, Christ being tempted, Christ abandoned by all. Only this multifaceted image of Christ presented to us by the Bible permits us to grasp the living
Christ in all the width and depth of his being. Could not
we say that often we have only a skeletal image of Christ
in our consciousness, so that in communion what we encounter is more this schematic Christ than the living
Christ himself, the Lord and Brother who wants to come to
us, who wants to take us up as we are, and who wants to
help us precisely where we need him to? Every state in life
and every vocational situation and every human circum-
stance needs an appropriate image of Christ if the eucharistic encounter is to be concrete and alive. The sacrament of
the Eucharist will be able to unfold this, its "salvation-
historical," effect in the measure in which we are ready and
inclined to consider the magnitude of the total image of
Christ.

h) Both as sacrifice and as sacrament the Eucharist possesses a particular "eschatological" character. The Eucharist is the Church's sacrificial meal within the time between the Lord's Ascension and his Second Coming. It is
our heavenly food along this pilgrimage. It is a sacrifical

liturgy that unites us with the eternal heavenly liturgy. It is a sign, commencement, and pledge of the bliss that is ours with Christ before the Father—of that state of beatitude that Christ himself so often portrays to us in the image of the "wedding banquet."[172] As both gift and task, the Eucharist brings together the three basic elements of our eschatological Christian attitude in this world: our immediate presence before God in Christ, the readiness to die on Christ's cross to everything that irretrievably separates us from Christ, the continual readiness and the effort— grounded in Christ's grace—to allow oneself and one's world to become transformed into the transfigured Lord.

4. The Necessity of the Eucharist for Eternal Salvation

1. The Council of Trent expressly defines the following: "Whoever denies that every Christian of both sexes who has reached the age of reason must every year, at least at Easter time, go to communion in keeping with the prescription of Holy Mother Church, *anathema sit*."[173] The Council expounds a teaching concerning the moment in time of the obligation and the frequency of the reception. In so doing it expressly invokes a commandment of the Church and not a passage of Scripture.

In the Bread of Life Discourse in John's Gospel we read: "Truly, truly I say to you, unless you eat the flesh of the Son of man and drink his blood, you have no life in you. He who eats my flesh and drinks my blood has eternal life, and I will raise him up at the last day. For my flesh is food indeed, and my blood is drink indeed" (John 6,53–55). The theological question here is whether John 6,53 establishes the Eucharist's necessity for salvation in the same sense that John 3,5 establishes baptism's necessity: "Truly, truly I say to you, unless one is born of water and the Spirit, he cannot enter the kingdom of God." With reference to the

Eucharist, the Church's decrees do not speak of its absolute necessity for salvation *(necessitas medii)* as they
teach with regard to baptism (D 861–DS 1618) or confession in the case of grave sin (D 917–DS 1707). With regard
to the Eucharist the decrees speak of a *necessitas præcepti
divini (et ecclesiastici).*

During World War I there arose a controversy concerning
the Eucharist's necessity for salvation. The Eucharistines
J. D. Nicolussi and G. Klodnicki, as well as the Jesuits E.
Springer and M. de La Taille, strove to prove the absolute
necessity of the Eucharist for salvation on the basis of John
6,53, papal documents from the first centuries, and especially Augustine and Thomas. Against them, O. Lutz in
particular defended the doctrine of Trent by trying to dis-
solve the evidence from the tradition that the other group
had presented.

Between the fourth and the eleventh centuries, and according to a custom that was even older, the Eucharist was
given under the form of wine to infants immediately after
baptism or at least in the imminent danger of death.[174] The
Council of Trent expressly declared that what was involved here was a practical matter, one that had as little to
do with the imperative of the *necessitas medii* as the practice of attaching the sacrament of confirmation to that of
baptism. "Whoever teaches that communion is necessary
to salvation for children before they reach the age of reason, *anathema sit*" (D 933, 937–DS 1730, 1734).

In our time, when we attempt to consider the question
of the Eucharist's absolute necessity to salvation *(necessitas medii)* in the context of an understanding of Christ's
redemptive work and of the history of humankind that is
open to the world, the issue generally appears more problematic, already in the way we ask the question and even
before we search for an answer. The question concerning
the salvation of "children who die unbaptized" (which already posed such difficulties for Augustine), or of people
who have not yet heard of Christ ("pagans"), or of those

who have known Christianity only as the cultural power of a particular Western group: this question can today— with our understanding of human beings and their history, with our insight into the psychology and sociology of faith—no longer be answered as easily as in former times that had a more narrow scientific and historical horizon. The Decree on the Missions, the Decree on Ecumenism, the questions concerning atheism in our time, which were raised and discussed at the Second Vatican Council: all of these bear eloquent witness to this difficulty.

Nor, conversely, is the question concerning the Eucharist's necessity for the salvation of the individual Christian any longer so simple to answer. Even the individual Christian is no longer to be regarded so much as an individual as a member of the Church; and for the Church—as "Mystical Body of Christ" living from the redemptive graces of Christ's sacrifice—the Eucharist appears "necessary" in a manner different from its necessity for the individual as such. The brief discussions in Chapter V, 1 and 2, will consider other aspects of this question.

The Eucharist as an Object Worthy of Adoration

1. Adoration and Veneration of the Blessed Sacrament

1. In Christian antiquity, and generally still today in the Eastern Church, the Eucharist was celebrated as both a sacrifice and a sacrificial meal. The consecrated species were handled with reverence; and yet a special veneration of the species outside of Mass, a public exposition or adoration of the Lord in the Sacrament, were unknown.

But there were many elements that eventually led to specialized "cult of the Eucharist": some of these were, first, the medieval Germanic understanding of the liturgy, which always saw the Mass more as a spectacle in which the individual events of Christ's Passion were symbolically made present (see the medieval explanations of the Sacrifice of the Mass); second, the new outlook on the manner of Christ's presence deriving from the doctrine of transubstantiation after the debate with Berengar of Tours; finally, the personalistic understanding of Christ in the Eucharist. More specifically, the eucharistic cult was launched by the visions of the Augustinian nun Juliana of Liège (d. 1258). Beginning in 1209, her visions showed her the liturgical year in the form a moon marred by one black spot: this was interpreted to her as the lack of a special feast for the Eucharist. In 1246 Bishop Robert of Liège ordered such a special feast of the Eucharist to be celebrated in his diocese, with the intention of opposing heretics and atoning for negligence in giving God thanks for this Sacrament. In

1230 Juliana had reported her visions to Archdeacon Jacob Pantaleon of Liège, who subsequently became Pope Urban IV and instituted in 1264, for the whole Western Church, what later came to be known as the "Feast of Corpus Christi." Thomas Aquinas composed for the Office of this feast well-known hymns and the sequence *Lauda Sion.* In Rome the feast was introduced only in 1317 by John XXII. In the Germanic north it was immediately adopted, spreading far and wide and undergoing a rich development. In 1277 both the feast and the procession are already in evidence at Cologne, and in 1286 at Benediktbeuern. At this latter location the processions were enhanced by including the older custom of walking around the town and through the fields, which was a part of public life. At least since the fifteenth century this procession was combined with the rite of carrying the four gospels and imparting a fourfold blessing toward the four regions of the heavens, a practice that was formally recognized and approved by the Sacred Congregation of Rites in 1820.

Given their understanding of the Eucharist, the Reformers naturally had to reject the reservation of the Eucharist and especially any form of eucharistic cult. The Council of Trent, consequently, expressly had to ratify both these things (D 879–DS 1645, 1656), and the encyclical *Mediator Dei* (1947, Part II, 4) most emphatically recommended all forms of the eucharistic cult.

Adopting the principles of the liturgical movement and of mystery theology, the Second Vatican Council made the eucharistic celebration in the community to be once again the center of eucharistic life, and the newer legislation resulting from the Council expressly decreed as follows in 1967: "The first and proper finality of the reservation of the Blessed Sacrament outside of Mass is the *administratio viatici*—[the need to administer communion to the dying]. The secondary purposes are the distribution of communion outside of Mass and the adoration of the Lord under the consecrated species."[175]

2. It was in opposing the Reformers that the Church first dealt expressly and in detail with the eucharistic cult. Thus it taught as follows at Trent: "Whoever says that Christ, the only-begotten Son of God, ought not to be adored in the Blessed Sacrament with the external marks of reverence proper to God's majesty, and that therefore He ought not to be honored with the particular external solemnity, and that one ought not to carry [the Blessed Sacrament] about solemnly according to the praiseworthy and general practice and custom of Holy Church or show it publicly to the people for adoration, and that those who so adore [the Sacrament] are idolaters: *anathema sit*" (D 888–DS 1656). "Whoever says it is not permitted to reserve the Most Holy Eucharist in the tabernacle, but that immediately after consecration it must be distributed to those present, or that it is not permitted to bring it solemnly to the sick: *anathema sit*" (D 889–DS 1657).

As mentioned, these practices represent a development in the Western Church that the Eastern Church has never known, and at no council for reunion has the former demanded that the latter either approve or adopt such practices. The reason for this far-reaching distinction is that, on the basis of its Græco-Platonic thinking, the Eastern Church can have no interest in the exterior form (the species of the Sacrament) but only in the invisible reality. The external cult offered in the Western Church to the Blessed Sacrament is, in the Eastern Church, given perhaps only to *icons*, which are a sign for the epiphany of the divine, which is why the figures of saints come forth from their golden background. The desire to have a visible reality led, already at the time of the polemic with Berengar of Tours, to the *elevatio*, that is, the practice of raising the consecrated species. This same desire later on introduced many elements of a "spectacle" into the eucharistic cult, and especially into the eucharistic processions, a part of which was the carrying of the mysteries of salvation-history—from the world's creation to the Last Judgment—in the form of as many as fifty pictures.

3. During the celebration of the Mysteries, the Church has been rendering adoration to its eucharistic Lord at least since the Council of Nicæa. Cyril of Jerusalem says: "Bow down and utter an amen of adoration and worship!" (*Cat. myst.* 5, 22:PG 33, 1126). Augustine writes: "No one eats this flesh without first adoring it" (*In Ps.* 98, 9: PL 37, 1264).

The adoration of the Lord present in the Sacrament, closely connected in the Western Church with the eucharistic cult, has great significance for an understanding of the *church as house of God* and not just as a place where the community assembles for services. Such a view has greatly fostered both *silent adoration* and the special worship given to the "Sacred Heart of Jesus" and the "Passion of Christ."

Two special kinds of adoration have developed in this area. The *Forty Hours Devotion* emerged from combining the practice of fasting for forty hours in honor of the forty hours Christ spent in the grave (from Good Friday to Easter Sunday)—something already done in the second century[176]—with the adoration of the Lord present in the Eucharist, a practice that started in the thirteenth century. Under the influence of Ignatius of Loyola, Philip Neri, and others, the Forty Hours Devotion was detached from Holy Week to become an independent devotion. It was formally recognized by Clement VIII in his bull *Graves et diuturnæ* (1592), and hence served as the basis for the second special kind of adoration, the custom that became known as *perpetual adoration*, that is, the practice of adoring the Blessed Sacrament continually in the course of one year by having parishes take turns, either within one or more dioceses or throughout a whole country. For this purposes "Sodalities of Perpetual Adoration" began to be formed, particularly since the seventeenth century, and many branches of the older orders (especially Benedictine nuns) chose this theme of "eucharistic adoration" to revitalize their orders. For laypeople special "confraternities" were created for perpetual adoration.

To the extent that these practices foster the worship of Christ and intercessory prayer for the great needs of the times, they retain their lasting value and are necessary to the Church.

4. Limits of the eucharistic cult: In our age of televison and illustrated magazines it seems somewhat questionable to us to "expose the species for adoration" (*ostensio:* "ostensories" = "monstrances"), since in these species there is nothing extraordinary to be seen, nothing that points to something higher: it is "faith" and faith alone that sees the reality and is the basis for adoration. On the other hand, concerning this form of the eucharistic cult, which exposes the Blessed Sacrament in a monstrance to carry it in processions and impart blessings with it, we must say the following: Insofar as the visible sign is the warrant of the sacramental reality of Christ's presence, this visible form too is of great significance for the believer. However, modern people's senses have become dulled by the flood of optical stimuli that bombard them, and this results in their no longer being so open to perceive simple symbols as they should. And insofar as the public sector has been secularized more than in former times, precisely this form of the eucharistic cult may indeed be more harshly judged by the public.

Consequently, after the Second Vatican Council, the Church ruled that it was up to the ordinary to determine whether a eucharistic procession should take place, and, if so, where and in what form. And the celebration of Mass before the exposed Blessed Sacrament was expressly forbidden.[177]

This same document goes on to enumerate the *modes of Christ's presence*, not according to "rank" but rather according to the external data of experience: (1) presence in the community of believers that has assembled for worship in the name of Christ, (2) presence in his Word in the Scripture that is read and proclaimed, (3) presence in the person of the ordained priest who presides over the worship ser-

vice, (4) presence in the eucharistic species after the consecration (this is the reason for the ordinance that the tabernacle containing the consecrated species should not be
found on the altar where the sacrifice is being celebrated.[178]

This critical attitude toward our own "piety" has its
basis in the need for critical self-evaluation (1 Cor 3, 18ff.;
4,6f.) out of respect for the conscience of those of weaker
faith (1 Cor 10,28f.) and out of care not to give an occasion
to unbelievers to slander our Church (1 Cor 10,32f.). Nevertheless, our age's clamor for *desacralization* can be widely
misunderstood. Ever since the Incarnation, ever since God
became man in Christ, "spiritualism," both in its enlight-
ened and in its Neo-Platonic form, is an aberration from the
reality of salvation-history as God himself has instituted.

Already in 1950 the attempt was made to free the Corpus Christi procession from its agricultural origins by se-
lecting different Gospel readings for the four stations and
by composing different intercessory prayers, namely, for
the Church, the country, the fruits of the land, and human
work, and for the intentions of the individual parish communities. Since 1967, a new meaning has been sought for
the Corpus Christi procession: it is to be a yearly eucharistic stational celebration for bigger dioceses, with all
parishes of an episcopal city or of a deanery participating
and holding a procession from the cathedral back to their
parish churches or it is reinterpreted as a "representation
of the Church on pilgrimage with her Lord."

V

The Eucharist and the Church

Since the Eucharist is the central mystery of Christ's concrete saving will in his Church, we set it apart from the number of the seven sacraments, and when we dealt with the general doctrine of the sacraments we treated the Eucharist as a reality *sui generis*. We did this because, as the "sacrifice and sacrificial meal of the church," the Eucharist has a different relation to the Church than do the other six sacraments. We would not be doing justice to the Eucharist as we see it in revelation and as it has developed in the Church through its efficacy as a reality all its own if we did not go on now to explore the different interior and exterior connections that exist between the Eucharist and the Church. It will be the content of the present concluding chapter to clarify the relationship of the eucharistic Body to the Mystical Body of Christ (1), and then to consider the coming-into-being and growth of the historical Church from the eucharistic mystery, into our present time and to the end of the world (2).

1. The Eucharistic Body and the Mystical Body of Christ

Modern thought is accustomed to draw conclusions concerning a reality by beginning with its effects and the forms of its manifestation. When dealing with realities of faith that cannot be "experienced" but that are known and can be reflected upon only from revelation, it is advantageous to proceed in reverse fashion, starting from revelation and theological reflection and going through this revelation in order then to grasp the believed reality in all its mysterious character. Then, and only then, on the basis of this understanding by faith, can we adequately understand and judge the reality's effects wihtin the space of the visible and historical world. We will first of all consider the essential relationship between the Church and the Eucharist, and we will then be in a better position to understand and interpret the significance of the Eucharist for the origins and life of the Church.

A. PRELIMINARY HISTORICAL REMARKS

1. The problem of "Eucharist and Church" has a history all its own that we will touch on here only to the extent necessary for an understanding of the problem. Three elements in our understanding of the Church have especially been crucial for this problem.

a) The great Catholic Church grew from individual communities that first had formed around the Apostles and the early missionaries of the faith. Still, from the very outset the individual community understood itself to be not an autonomous church but rather a cell of the one Church: this is shown by the way the word ἐκκλησία is used already in Sacred Scripture. This self-understanding by the individual community has its deepest reason in the uniqueness, the unicity, of the Sacrifice of the Cross of the one Lord and in the uniqueness of the meaning of the eucharistic sacrifice for the building of the Christian community. Just as the one Church becomes concretized in *individual communities*, so too the individual communities know themselves to be members and cells of this one *total Church*: it is to this Church that the individual communities owe their being a church even as individual communities. Eucharistic communion always was the bond of the communities within the one Catholic Church, and whenever a division arose among the communities it was manifested by the cessation of reciprocal eucharistic community and communion.

b) Very early on eucharistic communion also came to express the *interior dimension* of the Church. Even though unbaptized catechumens and baptized penitents, for instance, had many opportunities of participating in the Church's life, nonetheless they were barred from the Eucharist as communal life-center of the Church. Nothing expressed more eloquently the reality of an exterior and an interior membership in the Church.

c) This Church *order from the interior to the exterior* was then reversed by the more juridical-minded Middle Ages. For a while the practice was developed of compelling former heretics to partake externally of the Eucharist—even against their will—through a juridical act of communion so as to show clearly that the communicant henceforth belonged to the Church's interior community of grace. The Church very soon renounced and prohibited this form of conversion of heretics. Still, even in this abuse it is evident that the sacrament as an external sign—that is, visible eucharistic communion—is of decisive importance for interior membership in the Church's community of grace. Although it is of course true that authentic human religious identity must originate in the interior and proceed outward from there, nevertheless, for humans as corporal beings the way from the external to the internal can also offer a possibility to fulfill the way from the internal to the external as the authentic religious path.

The significance of the Eucharist for our understanding of the Church's very foundations, however, such as we see it explored in Augustine, no longer was a theme of theology in the post-medieval period, neither at the Council of Trent nor at Vatican I. It was only Vatican II that again exposed the Church's fundamentally eucharistic character.[179] "God became man so that man might in turn become

God": this is a paramount theme of Athanasius, Gregory of
Nazianzen, and Augustine. From this perspective the Eucharist should be seen as a gift and work of Christ to accomplish his primary goal in redeeming all humankind, all
times, and all regions of the world: it is the decisive aid we
need to become participants in Christ's redemption and be
able to live as redeemed beings. Thus, the Church may be
called the *continuatio Christi*, that is, the continuation of
the Christ-event for the redemption of the world (Dieck-
mann). Now this continuation does not occur without the
coöperation of human beings in this world, and therefore it
requires the reality of the Word and the Work and the Person of Christ to be present in a form that makes possible
the human acceptance of Christ's gift, the human cooperation with Christ's work, the human inherence within
Christ's earthly manner of existence. The locus where all of
this becomes possible and actually occurs is the "Church,"
the "Body of Christ" as *Christus totus, caput et membra*
(Augustine). The event and reality in the Church where
this *commercium* or *exchange between Christ and Christians* takes place is the Eucharist: Here it is Christ who
acts; here is where Christ's work in his Church is done;
here is where Christ's redemption becomes reality for each
individual Christian.

B. DOGMATIC REFLECTIONS

1. After what we have said it should be obvious that to
speak of the Eucharist is nothing other than to speak of
Christ. Until modern times it was even a matter of course
that to speak of the Eucharist was a special way of speaking
about Christ, whereas to speak of the Church was more understood as speaking about Christians in this world. Ever
since "Church" became a special theme of systematic theology, particularly since the nineteenth century,[180] a central
issue has once again become evident that was taken for
granted by patristic theology of both East and West, and

above all by Augustine: namely, that speaking about Christ cannot be separated from speaking about Christians, about the Church. The goal of the Incarnation is the *redemption of humankind*: In Christ God became the Son of Man, to the end that in this same Christ human beings might in turn become the children of God (Origen).

2. This is why the Eucharist, above all in its saving function for the whole Church, cannot be seen merely as a means of salvation for the individual. Just as in the Old Testament the Law and the temple, with its feasts and sacrifices and liturgical institutions, bound together Israel as God's People with God and among themselves, so too the New Covenant rests upon and is rooted in Jesus Christ. He himself—his person, his word, and his work—is the *Kingdom of God* that he has brought. In him humans are bound with God and one another, and it is in this bond that "God's lordship in this world" becomes possible and real.

The Pauline doctrine of the *Body of Christ*, whose head is Christ himself and whose members are the Christians,[181] is but the fuller development of the synoptic kerygma concerning the Kingdom of God, under the influence of St. Paul's Christ-mysticism, which has its roots even before the Damascus experience. The Christians that Saul is persecuting are Christ himself: "Saul, why do you persecute me?" (Acts 9,4). Christ in us (Gal 2,19; Col 1,2f.; 2 Cor 13,5) and we as Christians in Christ (2 Cor 5,17 and passim): this is the secret of Christian existence.

St. John developed this insight into Christian existence even further through his doctrine of the "mission." The source of the unity of Christians with Christ is located higher up, in the mysterious unity of Christ with his Father in heaven. The parable of the vine and the priestly prayer express this in an incomparable manner: "I am the vine, you are the branches; if a man abides in me, and I in him, then he will yield abundant fruit. Separated from me, you have no power to do anything" (John 15,5). "I have revealed your name to men. . . . The words you have given to me, I have given to them. . . . I pray for those you have given to me, for they are yours. . . . As you have sent me into the world, so have I sent them in to the world. . . . That all may be one, as you, Father, are in me and I am in you. . . . That the love with which you have loved me may be in them, and I may be in them" (John 17,6, 8f.;18,21,26). Now the way to this unity with Christ is the Eucharist, to which he refers with the following words: "He who eats my flesh and drinks my blood lives continually in me and I in him! As I live through the Father, the living Father who has sent me, so he who eats me will live, in his turn, through me (John 6,56f.).

3. The eucharistic event in the Church, whereby Christ abides in us and we abide in Christ in the midst of this world, is the mystery of his redemptive work, of his sacrificial death, and of his resurrection. It was in his own quality as sacrifice that Christ proclaimed this event: "For them do I consecrate myself [ἀγιάζω ἐμαυτόν = make myself a sacrificial offering], that they too may be consecrated [ὦσιν ἡγιασμένοι = may become a sacrificial offering]" (John 17,19). *Being a sacrifice* is the essential modality in which Christ became a Redeemer God, and therefore *to be a sacrifice* is also the essential modality of being a Christian. Just as the Church was born from Christ's wounded side (D 480–DS901), which means that the Church came forth from Christ's sacrificial death, so too does it belong to the essence of this Church that it become a sacrifice as it accomplishes the eucharistic sacrifice: a sacrifice for its own sins and a sacrifice for the sins of the world. In this world there can be no redemption without sacrifice, and one cannot live a redeemed existence in this world without its at the same time being a sacrificial existence. In a unique and incomparable manner the Eucharist is the presence of Christ's sacrifice, to the end that the Church and Christians of all times and places, of all languages and nations, may come to partake in Christ's sacrifice and may come to live a sacrificial existence out of faith that alone is

the realization of a redeemed existence and that will lead to the glorious Easter morning of the final fulfilment. It may be that the reality of the Lord who already has been glorified may now and then pierce through the *sacrificial existence* proper to this world and overwhelm it with extraordinary gifts of God's grace, just as Christ himself appeared to his Apostles before his Passion as their transfigured Lord (Mark 9,3f.). Nonetheless, it is the Christian's everyday existence that remains Christ's sacrificial existence. Just as Christ "took upon himself our sins and our sufferings and infirmities" (Isa 53: the "Servant of God") for the glory of God and out of love for his heavenly Father, so too Christian existence is summarized as follows by Paul: "Now I rejoice in my sufferings for your sake, and in my flesh I complete what is lacking in Christ's afflictions for the sake of his body, that is, the Church" (Col 1,24). In the Holy Eucharist Christ is present in the state of a victim, in order to be a way to sacrificial Christian existence for all who celebrate this mystery (cf. Rom 12,1; 2 Cor 9,12f.).

4. The soul of this sacrificial Christian existence is the *mystery of love*, which is likewise the mystery of the Church and the mystery of the Eucharist. Already in the Synoptics we see that Christ's only commandment is the great commandment of love, and this love is worth more than all slain sacrifices and holocausts (Mark 12,28–34). In this love a sacrificial existence is not "renunciation" but "fulfilment," since every genuine form of love always considers itself to be receiving the more it sacrifices itself and gives of itself. Being "sacrificial love," this love reaches all the way into the mystery of "love for one's enemies" (Matt 5,43–48) and has its roots and its very basis of possibility solely in the love of Christ and of God himself (John 15,9–17). This love is the foundation of the Church as "community and unity," as "communion of saints," as a community that is one "in Christ" and made holy "through Christ." The "Holy Things," moreover, which in the older

liturgies the deacon held forth with the cry "Holy Things for the holy" (*Didache* 9,5), is the Eucharist. Thus, the Eucharist in a unique way becomes the *mysterium unitatis et vinculum caritatis et pacis* in the Church, as Augustine especially repeats time and again.[182] He develops those thoughts of the unity of the mystical and the sacramental Body of Christ above all in his commentaries on 1 Cor 10,16f.: "The bread which we break, is it not a participation in the body of Christ? Because it is only *one* bread, so too all of us are only *one* body, since we all partake of the one bread." Hence Augustine can even write in his dialectical manner: *Si ergo vos estis Corpus Christi et membra, mysterium vestrum in mensa dominica positum est: mysterium vestrum accipitis. . . . Estote, quod videtis et accipite, quod estis* ["Thus, if you are the Body of Christ and his members, it is your own mystery which is placed upon the Lord's table: it is your own mystery which you receive. . . . Be what you see and receive what you are."[183] The Eucharist is not an act of initiation or of incorporation, as is baptism, but an act of communication."[184]

5. This reciprocal relationship and interpenetration between the Church and the Eucharist become evident in a special way in the Church's most important role, her *priestly office*. Just as Christ built his Church on the foundation of the Apostles (Eph 2,20)—which is what the priests of the new People of God are—so too it is to these Apostles that the commission has been given to celebrate the Eucharist "in remembrance" of Christ.[185] In the same way that all members belong to Christ's body and thus live and work from the power of the Head of this body (like branches on the vine: John 15,5), so too do they all participate in Christ's offices, one of which is the priestly office. But not all the members of Christ's body participate in the priestly office in the same way as do the Apostles, since these participate not only through community of life but also through their having explicitly been sent and commissioned by Christ. Insofar as the Eucharist is the source

of life for the Church, from which all must drink who desire to live from Christ (John 6, 53f.), all who belong to the
Church share an identical participation; but insofar as the
Eucharist is a sacrifice of the Church, it is a sacrifice of
Christ to be celebrated by those who have been commissioned for that purpose by Christ, even though at the same
time the Eucharist can be nothing other than "a sacrifice
of the Church," of the whole body and all the members
who build up the Body of Christ. Both the interior unity
and the organic differentiation of this one Body of Christ,
the Church (1 Cor 12), become evident precisely in the
Holy Eucharist as a celebration of the Church. This holds
not only for the eucharistic sacrifice itself, but also for the
different partial functions of the eucharistic celebration
(including the magisterial office and the pastoral office as
these become expressed in the celebration) as being the
central liturgy of the Church; and it also holds for the totality of the Church's acts of worship, which have their
center and apex, their origin and goal, in the Eucharist.

   6. Church and Eucharist are connected with one another
and determine one another also in that fundamental aspect
of Christian existence that contemporary theology usually
refers to with the term *eschatological*. This means that
both Church and Eucharist are to be seen as the fulfillment of promises made to the People of Israel and, through
it, to all of humankind. In Christ as the promised "Messiah" the promises of the Old Testament have found their
fulfillment. Such is the faith of the Apostles in the primitive community; and even though for humankind in this
world the cosmic and universal fulfillment must await the
end of the present æon, still "in Christ" this "end" is already a reality in this present æon, an incessantly occurring reality for everyone who lives in Christ: as the "exalted Lord," this Christ has already reached the final perfection that he will bring to this world when he returns in
judgment. The same Christ is the head of the historical
Church and "the slain Lamb" (Rev 5,12); as content of the

Eucharist, he is the Lamb who, together with the One sitting on the heavenly throne, receives praise and glory from the entire creation. Both the mystery of the Church and of the Eucharist run together in this central reality: that the fulfillment is given in Christ both as the Head of the historical Church and as the slain Lamb in heaven. But within the world's present age, which persists in shutting itself off from the Redeemer's work, this "fulfillment" produces a new promise. This promise has for its content the cosmic lordship of God over a new heaven and a new earth, which will come through judgment and ruination. Thus, in the room of the Last Supper, Jesus himself proclaimed when he instituted the Eucharist: "I shall not drink again of the fruit of the vine until that day when I drink it new in the kingdom of God" (Mark 14,25 par.), and "I shall not eat [this Passover lamb] until it is fulfilled in the kingdom of God" (Luke 22,16 par.). As the sacrificing priest of his Church and as the sacrificial food in the Eucharist, the exalted Lord is efficaciously present both in the form of the ministerial priesthood, sacramentally determined by his explicit commission, and in the forms of bread and wine that have been transformed by the Word. For everyone who offers sacrifice with the Church and lives the life of the Church, this glorified Lord is the pledge of future glory.

For all those who, "weary and burdened" (Matt 11,28), seek for salvation in Christ, the Church prepares and distributes the Eucharist as "Bread of Life" (John 6,35,51); and, through this sacrifice and sacrificial meal, the Church itself grows in its believing members to "the full stature of Jesus Christ" (Eph 4,13). So it is that the Church effects for the Eucharist and the Eucharist for the Church that *process of growth* that is the condition imposed on this æon between Christ's Ascension (or "exaltation") and his return to this world.

7. With this characterization of Church and Eucharist as eschatological realities existing for one another what is, in

conclusion, being said is that their present manner of existence is preliminary, that *both institutions are intended for the period of pilgrimage*, and that they will continue to exist even in the consummation at the end of time, even if this will be in a new way and in a new reciprocal relationship. This is why the only prophetic book of the New Testament, the Apocalypse, expressly says of the victor at the time of the consummation that he will receive "fruit from the Tree of Life that grows in the paradise of my God" (Rev 2,7; 22,14), and that he will "partake of the hidden manna (Rev 2,17); and of those who have come from the great tribulation and have washed their garments in the blood of the Lamb it is said that they will no longer hunger or thirst and that the Lamb will lead them to the springs whose water is life (Rev 7,14–17; 21,6). The point is no longer now being fortified for the journey; the whole event consists of delight in the enjoyment of the eternal banquet, the eternal wedding banquet (Matt 25,1). The new Jerusalem, the Church in its fulfillment, is the Bride of the Lamb (Rev 21,9). In the new heaven and in the new earth it is "the tent of God pitched among men: he will dwell with them and they will be his own people, and he will be among them, their own God (Rev 21,2–3). No longer now does the Church minister the Eucharist, nor does the Eucharist help in building up the Church: rather, now both are a gift of God in this time of fulfillment, a gift in which God gives himself: "See, I am coming, and with me comes my reward" (Rev 22,12).

It is thus that the reciprocal relationship of Church and Eucharist develops: they are both distinct from one another and yet for one another. And this development consists of seven stages, beginning from the foundation of the Church and the Eucharist in Christ's redemptive act all the way to the consummation of a redeemed world in the risen Lord. Therefore our question now is what significance the Eucharist has within this eschatological age for the development of the Church.

8. The relationship of "Church and Eucharist" in the last analysis points to a mystery that is difficult to grasp through sheer theological speculation, but that since ancient times has found a precise expression in liturgical piety: we mean the mystery that, according to God's eternal plan of salvation and according to the salvation-history of the New Testament, determines the *position of the Mother of Jesus, Mary, Mother of God, and her relationship to the Church and to the Holy Eucharist* within the Church. Vatican II's Constitution on the Church says the following in its concluding chapter "on the blessed and virginal Mother of God, Mary, within the mystery of Christ and of the Church": "This is why the Church, even in its apostolic activity, rightly looks up to her who gave birth to Christ, since Christ was conceived by the Holy Spirit and born of the Virgin in order to be born and grow through the Church also in the hearts of the faithful (LG 65). [Mary] conceived, gave birth to and nourished Christ, presented him in the temple to the Father and suffered with her Son as he was dying on the cross. As such she participated in the work of the Redeemer in a wholly unique manner through her obedience, faith, hope, and burning love, so as to restore the supernatural life to souls. Consequently, she is our Mother in the order of grace (LG 61).

Cardinal Augustine Bea found that the result of juxtaposing Acts 1,14 ("All these, with one mind, gave themselves up to prayer, together with Mary the mother of Jesus") and 2,42 ("These occupied themselves continually with the apostles' teaching, their fellowship in the breaking of bread, and the fixed times of prayer") was the precise biblical expression of the position of the Mother of God within the eucharistic community of prayer and sacrifice of the earliest Church. In the Eastern eucharistic liturgies, at least since the fifth century, she is invoked at the heart of the eucharistic action in the anamnesis (*Unde et memores . . .*). When arranging the sacrificial bread on the paten in preparation for the celebration, after the portion of bread representing Christ himself the priest places a portion in her honor. During the sacred action the Holy Spirit is invoked on this special portion for it to be transformed into the sacrificial flesh of the Lord, since it was from Mary through the Holy Spirit that the Body of Christ was born, the same body that on the cross became a sacrificial body. To be sure, Mary wholly belongs on the side of the saints, for whom likewise a portion of bread is arranged on the paten, and not on the side of the Son of God. Nevertheless, within God's saving action in this world she occupies an absolutely unique position as free instrumental cause, as is shown in volume 4, *The Mystery of Christ*. To stand with Mary, the Mother of Christ, at the foot of the cross is the ideal challenge to our Christian participation in the Sacrifice of the Mass. And to pray with Mary, the Mother of the Church, in the Upper Room for the "coming of the Spirit" that signals the birth of the Church in this world: this is of decisive importance for our relationship to the Church as Mystical Body of Christ.

2. Birth and Growth of the Church from the Eucharistic Mystery to the End of the World

According to Vatican II, which based itself particularly on the New Testament proclamation and on the theology of the first four centuries, the Church understands itself to be, not primarily and essentially an organization, but rather an "event within this world" that, as an undertaking of God's that relies on the cooperation of those persons whom God calls and sends forth, is to serve for the salvation of the whole world and all times and has as content and goal the growth of the "Kingdom of God." The *office* or *agency* that is to promote this event within the world, that is to administer, regulate, and lead the Church in this world to its goals, is threefold, as our meditation on the Church shows[186]: (1) the *pastoral office,* which has its center in the Petrine office (John 21,15ff.); (2) the *magisterial office*, which, other than in Peter (Acts 1–12), found a special exponent in the subsequent calling of Saul (Acts 9,15), who becomes Paul (Acts 13–28); finally (3) the *priestly office*, which is common to all the Apostles and has no special exponent. The priestly aspect is the innermost component of the ecclesial office, that aspect that is least determined by humans and most determined by God and that was entrusted to all the Apostles by Christ in the hour of farewell. This priestly office, moreoever, has its highest task in the celebration of the Eucharist (1 Cor 11,26) and in the forgiveness of sins (John 20,21–23; 2 Cor 5,18–21), that is, in the application of Christ's redemptive grace to all who would be sanctified. The most interior mystery of the life of the Church is the Eucharist, especially because it is the central mystery of the *liturgy*, which, as such, is the full blossoming of the Church's threefold office as well as of the life of Christians, built on the foundation of faith, love, and hope. We must, therefore, now briefly consider the coming-into-being and growth of the Church from the perspective of the *Eucharist as central mystery of the liturgy*.

1. Already in the oldest portrayals of the life of the Church we see to what extent *the Church derives its life from the act of divine worship.* Thus we read in Acts 2,42: "These [the first Christians] devoted themselves to the apostles' teaching and to the fellowship, to the breaking of the bread and the [fixed times of] prayers." The fellowship or community that grew out of this divine service extended also to the economic realm: "They sold their possessions and goods and distributed them to all, as any had need. And day by day they attended the temple together and broke bread in their homes..." (Acts 2,45f.). The so-called *Letter to Diognetus*, from the first half of the second century, could thus characterize the life of Christians in this world with the words "They are in this world what the soul is in the body" (ch. 6). In this world and for this

world and yet not of this world; and what Paul writes concerning his own apostolic life (2 Cor 6,4–10) appears to be the very essence of the life of all Christians. The reason for this peculiar life is to be sought in the fact that such a life receives its shape from the Eucharist, from the liturgy of the Church, in which the relationship of the individual Christian to Christ and the relationship of Christians to one another is formed and determined by the Word of proclamation as Word of instruction and by union with the eucharistic Lord. Vatican II (LG 7) says the following on this subject: "In the breaking of the eucharistic bread we receive real participation in the Body of the Lord and are raised to communion with him and one another . . . . (1 Cor 10,17; 12,27; Rom 12,5). . . . All members must be formed in conformity with him [Christ], until Christ becomes formed in them (cf. Gal 4,19). It is for this that we are taken up into the mysteries of his earthly life, for this that we are shaped in conformity with him, for this that we die and rise up with him, until we come to reign with him: (cf. Phil 3,21; 2 Tim 2,11; Eph 2,6; Col 2,12).

To be sure, what is said concerning Christians in the Acts of the Apostles and in the Letter to Diognetus is an ideal picture with apologetical intentions, as other documents of the same period show. What the Council says is an earthly statement about supernatural realities that can be understood as applying to human beings in the indicative mode only as a fulfillment of a command in the imperative mode. What does this mean? That the liturgy, with the Eucharist as its central mystery, is the actual and most interior source for the shaping of a Christian existence; and yet this same liturgy with its central eucharistic mystery is just as much a mandate as it is a gift, both for individual Christians and for the whole Church. The history of this eucharistic and liturgical mystery, as we have already described it from many different angles, has shown how Christians in the Church time and again have failed to grasp the meaning of this mystery and have therefore not been able to harvest the fruit the mystery contains. This is why we must take it seriously when the Apocalypse, in its own characteristic language, portrays the end of the world not as the end of a process of growth and development in which the Church and Christians have, through Christ, developed in the Eucharist and the liturgy and have reached some kind of ideal height where the Lord on his return already finds them. Rather, Christ comes in power and glory as the judge who passes judgment and separates the accursed from the blessed in order to give to the latter his Father's Kingdom, intended for them from the foundation of the world, and to consign the former into the eternal fire, prepared for the Devil and his followers (Mat 25,34,41; Rev 19,20–20,10). The final fulfillment, the new Heaven and the new Earth, the eternal Kingdom of God, is to be an intervention by God's and an undeserved gift, no less than the first coming of the Messiah was an unmerited gift at the end of the Old Covenant. The New Covenant, too, will in the earthly realm have no other conclusion than the Old Covenant had had. The only sense in which the New Covenant in its innermost substance remains the fulfillment of the Old Covenant and, thus, the definitive covenant is that its founder and lord is Christ, who even as man is already transfigured and glorified. In him the New Heaven and the New Earth are already existent, even if they will be revealed only at the end of time.

2. The Church's coming-into-being and growth from the eucharistic mystery therefore mean for the Church in this world that it must bear the Lord's earthly life and suffering throughout the ages. In this way, at the Lord's Second Coming, she will be able to receive his transfigured glory, to bestow it on this world. Vatican II's Constitution on the Church continues the text we have just quoted as follows (art. 7): "As long as we are on earth on pilgrimage and are following Him along His path in affliction and persecution, we shall be drawn into His own suffering because the

Body belongs to the Head and there exists a unity between Head and Body. We suffer with Him in order thus to be glorified with him (cf. Rom 8,17)."

What was said previously (III.3) concerning the effects of the eucharistic meal for the individual applies equally to the Church as a whole. *The Eucharist is for the Church not a reward for its holiness but a help for its time of pilgrimage.* All liturgy, especially the eucharistic liturgy, possesses a festive character and a particular joy that derive from this festive cult and should fill human beings when they appear before God to praise Him and thank Him. Nevertheless, it is not incompatible with this that all liturgy, in its capacity of atoning sacrifice for sin, likewise has the function of awakening in us the spirit of repentance and penance and the readiness to suffer and atone. If we forget this aspect of the Eucharist the danger could arise that worldly pomp and earthly joy might destroy the spiritual character of the liturgy, as is shown by the history of the liturgy especially in the Middle Ages, when the mysterial character of the Eucharist was ill understood. This, however, should not make us overlook the fact that the glad and loud alleluia belongs to the eucharistic cult of the New Testament insofar as this cult is a memorial celebration not only of the Lord's death but also of his resurrection.

3. When we speak of the Church's coming-into-being and growth, what first comes to mind is the sacrament of "baptism." And yet, even though "no one may eat or drink of the Eucharist without first having been baptized in the name of the Lord" (*Didache*, 9,5), nevertheless baptism is not properly speaking the Church's sacrament of life: indeed, rightly understood, the meaning of baptism itself may be grasped only on the basis of Christ's death and resurrection (Rom 6,2–11), which become sacramentally present in the Holy Eucharist. This is why the completion of baptism is not the Eucharist but confirmation, which, by the gift of the Spirit, brings to maturity the supernatural life conferred by baptism. Even if baptism, like the other

sacraments and perhaps in an even more particular manner, has a direct bearing on the totality of the Church, still it is not to be compared with the Eucharist. All other sacraments (originally penance too, which nowadays has become a repeatable sacrament) have the peculiarity that they are normally received only one time, either by the very nature of the sacrament (baptism, confirmation, priestly ordination) or because of their meaning (marriage, anointing of the sick). Peculiar to the Eucharist's meaning alone is the fact that it ought to be received as often as the eucharistic liturgy is celebrated. *Thus the Eucharist, both as sacrificial meal and as sacrifice, is an essential function of the life of the Church*, and the Church itself derives its essential life from this sacrificial sacrament. No life ever comes to a standstill: life always implies either growth or atrophy. Thus, insofar as the Church is always in the state of becoming, insofar as it must always become what it is intended to be, and can preserve its being only in this constant process of life, the Eucharist is the proper "sacrament of the Church's life."

4. The Church, then, is an event whereby God, with the aid of human beings called by him and who place themselves at his disposal, ever anew implants God's Kingdom into the ever-growing world, thus drawing the world to himself and bestowing himself upon the world. This being so, an essential element of such a Church is its *missionary work*, through which it fulfills Chirst's missionary mandate as his final inheritance: "Go forth, making disciples of all nations, and baptizing them in the name of the Father, and of the Son, and of the Holy Spirit, teaching them to observe all the commandments which I have given you. And behold I am with you all through the days that are coming, until the consummation of the world" (Matt 28,19f.). In this missionary work we are somehow to see the continuation of the Incarnation and of Christ's whole work of redemption, insofar as these two mysteries may be regarded as the sending of the Son by the Father and as self-surren-

der of the Son to the Father. Consequently, the Church not only has a missionary task imposed on it by Christ; it is *essentially* missionary. The missionary aspect is a structural element of its very nature: "The Church on pilgrimage is 'missionary' by nature since of itself it has its origin in the mission of the Son and in the mission of the Holy Spirit according to the plan of God the Father" (AG 2).

Precisely in order for it to realize this missionary aspect of its nature, for the Church the *Eucharist is the point of departure, the center and the aid for all its tasks.* This already holds for the Church's missionary activity in the smallest local communities: the care of souls at the parish level, understood as a missionary work of the church, must have its center in the eucharistic cult. In the local communities (or churches), "the faithful are gathered by the proclamation of Chrit's Good News. In these [local churches] the mystery of the Lord's Supper is celebrated, 'to the end that through the food *[esca]* and blood of the Lord's Body the whole community of brethren may be united. . . .[187] For the partaking in the Body and Blood of Christ has no result other than our passing over into what we receive.' "[188]

This missionary nature of the Church, however, must also have an effect outwardly, outside the Christian community, in obedience to the mandate given by the Church's Founder that the Gospel should be brought to all humankind. To be sure, in the context of the Church's outward missionary activity on behalf of humankind all kinds of undertakings are required, especially through language (dialogue, catechesis, preaching) and in the social order. Nevertheless, the interior coming-into-being and growth of the Church into the still non-Christian world have their very source in the Holy Eucharist, and Vatican II's Decree on the Church's missionary activity calls on the whole Church to carry out and foster this life-work with all the means available, especially through exemplary living and intercessory prayer in the eucharistic cult. "Priests . . .

should also be profoundly aware of the fact that their life is also consecrated to service in the missions. On the basis of their own ministry, which preeminently consists in the celebration of the Eucharist that perfects the Church, priests stand in intimate communion with Christ as Head, and they lead others to this communion. Therefore, priests cannot possibly overlook how much is still lacking to the full form of the Body, and thus how much still remains to be done that it [this Body] may ever continue to grow. They are consequently so to exercise their care of souls that it serves to spread the Gospel among non-Christians" (AG 39).

5. The missionary activity of the Church in this world has its center in the pastoral realm: its primary task is so to lead human beings to God that they will surrender themselves unreservedly to him.[189] But it would be an unhealthy narrowness and a misunderstanding among Christians—one that the Church has not always been able to escape during certain periods—if the Church were not to see and be fully aware of its mandate on behalf of the world, all of it created by God and redeemed by him and belonging to him in its totality. It was in its fight against Gnosticism that the early Church first saw this responsibility for the world. Above all Irenæus of Lyons gave expression to this in his central idea of the *recapitulation of the world in Christ* (Eph 1,10), and the great bishops and theologians of the Church have served this task through their incorporation of Greek philosophy and the Roman concept of empire and law. But the actual development of the Church often led even great apostolic figures in two undesirable directions. In their striving to win the world for Christ, they themselves sometimes succumbed to the danger of secularization (especially in what concerns possessions and power); and their spiritual striving often led to a world-rejecting spiritualism, this under the influence of Neo-Platonism, particularly as transmitted through the writings of Denis the Areopagite, which were the subject of much commentary beginning in the sixth century.

The secularization decrees of 1803 and the loss of the papal states in 1870 left the Church small in power and possessions in this world. And when Vatican II proclaimed its Pastoral Constitution on the Church in the Modern World as its final decree, the Church wanted to make clear in a new, biblical manner its understanding of its responsibility to the world. This *aggiornamento* thus undertaken by the Church ought to become an affirmation of the world, but "the world" correctly understood: the world that, until the end of time and even while being the creation and revelation of God's power, wisdom, and love, still labors under sin and stands under the Cross of Christ. The person who intends to accomplish this service for the world must find his or her foothold and center in the Eucharist, in which both the crucified and the risen Lord abides with us, in which the bread of life and the sacrifice of life are given to us for our salvation. The true *nobilitates creaturarum*, which the Franciscan theologian Marquard of Lindau (d. 1392) described in his Neo-Platonic manner, can be possessed and looked after in this world, even by the Church, only by means of that genuine "indifference" that Paul developed from the heart of his Christ-centered mysticism (cf. 1 Cor 7,29–31).[190] In the Greek Fathers this original Christian attitude underwent a transformation under the influence of Stoic and Neo-Platonic concepts, to become in some respects a spiritualistic attitude and sometimes even an outright rejection of the world and the body.

Ignatius Loyola reinterpreted this Pauline "indifference" anew on the basis of a Christian existentialism, derived from his understanding of the ever-greater God and of his membership in the *militia Christi*. And such "indifference" must respond to the challenge of a secularized world and be reconciled today with a genuine affirmation of the world. Even in our time, however, this Christian "indifference" cannot be correctly found and maintained without a fundamental attitude of the Church and the individual

Christian that is both bound to God and open to the world, that stands at the foot of the cross and is oriented to the risen Lord, and such a stance may only be acquired—and indeed on a continual basis—from living in the mystery of the Eucharist. The great tasks that this last decree of Vatican II more hints at than expounds either must be realized by a Church living on the Eucharist or will not be realized at all.

May the eucharistic Lord himself pilot his Church through the storms of this world's era, the same Lord who brought the Apostles' little boat to the shore on the Lake of Tiberias. May he pilot his Church to that shore that no longer belongs to this world but to that other æon in which Christ reigns since his Ascension, the same Christ who is present in the Eucharist in the hiddenness of his redemptive sacrifice.

Epilogue

Denis the Areopagite, who perhaps was a Syrian bishop of the early sixth century, through the mouth of his teacher Hierotheus, calls the Eucharist "the sacrament of sacraments," the mystery of mysteries, and in this manner introduces a commentary on the eucharistic celebration.[1] In his meditations concerning the growth of the life in Christ through the three great sacraments of initiation—baptism, chrismation, and the Holy Eucharist—Nicholas Cabasilas of Thessalonica, a Byzantine theologian of the fourteenth century, writes extensively in Book IV[2] on the singular meaning that communion at the altar has for the life in Christ. The great meditations on the Eucharist always occur within treatises on the Holy Liturgy, since the fullness of this mystery cannot be made accessible only through sober reflections but always in the context of the living, believing, and loving celebration of the Eucharist as center of all the Church's liturgy and of all the worship of the People of God.

A. Kirchgässner has said: "Christianity loves images, finds joy in miracles. It is a religion of holy signs, and these signs—above all the sacraments—are not only interpretations and indications, dry codes for the intellect. Rather, they are concretions, translations of the heavenly into the earthly, representations of the divine in the human: yes, *in the human*, since God has become man and the mystery of the Incarnation is forever ongoing." But these holy signs are alive only in their enactment; they are signs of the divine only when human beings accomplish them, since human beings were created in the image of God that they might rule over the things of creation and thus give glory to the Creator. This will be understood and experienced by whoever becomes a member of the community that forms itself and comes into being through the holy action taking place around the altar, by whoever engages soul and body to pray and sing the holy liturgy, accomplishing it through eloquent silence and human action, by whoever surrenders himself or herself wholly to God in the liturgy and receives from him forgiveness for sin, renewed favor, and finally himself, the infinite God, under the figure of holy signs. It would be good for us to experience this great mystery of the liturgy not only in the old accustomed form of our own Church, that is, in the austere Western liturgy, but also in all the diversity of the rich and variegated liturgies of the Eastern Churches.[3]

Only in the context of this liturgical action within the living eucharistic community can we gain the insight and the attitude necessary to understand the other six sacraments, which will be the subject of volume 7, *The Sacraments of the Church.*

Appendices to the Text

APPENDIX TO P. 25

To what has already been said we would add the following explanations and clarifications from R. Hotz' work *Sakramente im Wechselspiel zwischen Ost und West* (Cologne-Gütersloh, 1979):

1. The difference between the Eastern and Western doctrines of the sacraments has its basis not only in the difference between Neo-Platonic and Aristotelian philosophy but also in the opposition between lay and monastic theology. This East-West difference, moreover, was often widened by political controversies or, even at times, bridged over, as was the case when Reformation theology appeared in the East.

a. Beginning in the tenth century the disadvantages of Platonism for Christian theology became evident even in the East (cf. Michael Psellos, and the condemnation of his disciple John Italos), and in the thirteenth and fourteenth centuries Aristotle became in the East, as in the West, the supreme teacher in the secular sciences; in theology Platonism continued to remain largely normative. The Platonist Demetrios Kydonos even translated the *Summa* of Thomas Aquinas into Greek. The debate between Platonism and Aristotelianism took place largely in the secular centers of learning, which were under the direction of laymen, while the further development of theology became more the domain of charismatically oriented monks who subscribed to hesychasm, a current of mystical prayer practiced within the sphere of the sacramental and liturgical life. The founders and proponents of hesychasm were Simeon the New Theologian (917–1022)[1] and Gregory Palamas (1296–1359)[2]; and, following in their spirit, we may also include the writings of Nicholas Cabasilas (1290–1371) and Simeon of Thessalonica (d. 1429). In this theology, Platonism remained dominant, while in the West Aristotle was taking the forefront even in theology. As in the Reformed churches the Word came to take precedence over the Mystery, Eastern theology took an anti-Western (anti-Roman) direction.

b. When Byzantium began to look to the West because of the danger posed by the Turks, the "number seven" for the sacraments and the doctrine of "transubstantiation" for the Eucharist were agreed upon almost automatically by theologians participating in the Union Council of Lyons (1274) and even more that of Ferrara-Florence (1438–39). It must be added, however, that this agreement was not universal, especially not in monastic circles (Hotz, p. 111).

c. After the fall of Constantinople in 1453, the opponents of Union understandably gained the upper hand in the East, which led to Western Reformation theology's finding a willing audience there. Melanchthon had already sent to the East a Greek translation of the *Augsburg Confession* in 1559, and in the years 1574–1581 a lively correspondence developed between the theologians at Wittenberg and the patriarch of Constantinople. This exchange eventually showed that the Eastern Church had still not penetrated its great biblical and patristic understanding of the *mysterion* philosophically, with the result that Patriarch Cyril I Soukaris (1620–1635) could openly embrace Calvinist theses in his sacramental doctrine, beginning in 1627.

d. At this point it was Russian Orthodoxy that took over the leadership in defending Orthodox faith, and the metropolitan of Kiev, Peter Mogila, wrote in 1640 a *Confessio Fidei Orthodoxa* that exhibited a strong influence from the side of Western Scholasticism. This work was soon translated into Greek and contained a certain adaptation of the older Greek doctrine of the mysteries. In 1642 it received the recognition of the new patriarch of Constantinople at the Synod of Jassi, and in 1642 the approval of all four Greek patriarchs. On the occasion of the Council of Jerusalem (1672), Patriarch Dositheus II of Jerusalem published his own *Confessio Dosithei*.

e. These confessions, Western in their orientation, remained normative for Orthodoxy until a return to more native Eastern traditions began around the middle of the nineteenth century, especially in Russia. Of great import for this new theology, particularly in its understanding of the sacraments, was a universalistic way of thinking about the whole cosmos, rooted in the Incarnation of God in Christ (cf. Nikolai Berdyaev, 1874–1948), and about the Church (cf. Alexei Khomiakov, 1804–1866), which does not appear as a hierarchical instution or even merely as the People of God but rather as a eucharistic community sanctifying the entire cosmos (cf. A. Maltsev, 1854–1915, and P. Evdokimov, 1901–1970.[3]

2. The following may be noted concerning Luther's understanding of the sacraments: In his sacramental doctrine we may distinguish at least three stages: (a) The Catholic stage (1518–19), during which Luther still holds to the seven sacraments and understands the concept of sacrament as rooted in the three ele-

ments of sign, meaning of the sign for what is signified, and faith in the efficacy and reality of the sacraments. (b) Beginning in 1520 ("Sermon on the New Testament, that is on the Holy Mass") Luther brings the sacraments into closer relationship with the Word of God, that is a promise and a pledge for the interior person, like the Gospel itself, and as such is already efficacious in itself. For him, however, the sacramental sign is still given in addition for the sake of the exterior person. But it is the Word that remains the decisive element. (c) In the third period, that begins in 1525 with the pamphlet "Against the Heavenly Prophets: On Images and Sacraments," Luther teaches the existence of only two sacraments—baptism and the Eucharist—and these sacraments are determined not only through word and sign but also through Christ's explicit command and order. Here, in opposition to spiritual enthusiasts, he emphasizes more fully the real efficacy of signs on the basis of the Word, which is present in the sacraments for the individual and in the Gospel for all (Hotz, pp. 87–94).

3. Hotz also indicates that Vatican II and the subsequent liturgical reforms brought the sacramental theology and praxis of the Western Church much closer to those of the Eastern Church, even if there remain deep differences in the picture of the world underlying each theology (pp. 212–222). The task of the future shall be, not so much an approximation of Eastern and Western theology, but rather a deepened synoptic contemplation of the anthropological vision of the West together with the cosmic and biblical vision of salvation-history of the East. In so doing East and West should be able to retain the uniqueness of the picture of the world each has developed, since wiping away these deep differences would result in some kind of religious "romanticism" instead of the realism necessary for all religious understanding and action (cf. Hotz, pp. 297–300).

APPENDIX TO P. 67

As we have shown in the text, the doctrine of the *sphragis* (or *character indelebilis*) was clearly seen in the Eastern Church in the fourth century for the sacraments of baptism and priestly ordination; but it then lapsed into oblivion as a result of the practice of repeating these sacraments when apostates were reconciled. Under the influence of Western Scholastic doctrines, the doctrine of the indelible character reappears in the *Confessio Dosithei* (1672) and in some of Dositheus' disciples, and it then disappears again. More recent theologians clearly tend to deny this doctrine. In 1756 the patriarchs of Constantinople (Cyril V), Alexandria, and Jerusalem ruled that Catholics had to be baptized and confirmed again when received into Orthodoxy. Since 1757 the Russian Church demands only the repetition of chrismation. In 1903 the Greek Church made optional the repetition of baptism and confirmation in the case of Catholics. Since 1932 chrismation is once again repeated in this case. The juridical basis for these ordinances is found in the Third Synod of Constantinople of 692 (the "Trullanum," not recognized by Rome), which accepted Cyprian's view of the nullity of heretical baptism and thus circumvented the Western Church's decision that came out of the controversy over heretical baptism. The deeper reason for this split (efficacy of the sacraments through the Holy Spirit; and yet invalidity of heretical baptism) between East and West lies in the fact that the Eastern Church views the sacraments more from the totality of the Church, to which precisely heretics do not belong, whereas the West views the sacraments more as realities instituted by Christ and thus as signs that are efficacious in themselves. At the Second Vatican Council this difficulty again became evident even in the Western Roman Church with regard to the question of validity of episcopal consecration, for the conferral of which the assent (participation) of neighboring bishops again becomes desirable in keeping with the earliest Christian practice; but there is no implication that a consecration not preceded by such consultation and assent must be declared invalid (LG 21: "Nonnisi in hierarchica communione cum collegii capite et membris . . .") (Hotz, pp. 165–170).

APPENDIX TO P. 88

On the number seven for the sacraments in the Eastern Church we may note the following:

a) Enumeration depends on the clear specification of the counted objects. In the West, beginning in the twelfth century with Hugh of St. Victor, the concept of sacrament was expounded in such a way that the number of the sacraments both could and had to be fixed at seven. In the East the concept remained more open: Alongside the sacraments of *mysteria* there are other rites (*teletai*) and blessings (*hagiasmata*) of equal standing; that is, there does not obtain the rigorous distinction between sacraments and sacramentals that the Western Church has made since the Middle Ages.

b) On this basis may be explained why the more monastic understanding of world, Church, and Christian life in the East induces Denis the Areopagite[4] and Theodore the Studite to give the name of *mysteria* to monastic consecration and the consecration of churches, as well as to the blessing of oil and water and to the service of the dead.

c) In the thirteenth century, in the context of efforts toward Union, the number of seven *mysteria*, recently fixed in the West, was adopted also in the East, at first somewhat covertly. In order to adhere to this number many Orthodox theologians paired anointing of the sick and penance as one *mysterion* and excluded marriage from the number, thus making it possible to include monastic consecration and the service of the dead among the seven sacraments. Not only under Calvinistic influence, but also from the Eastern understanding of things, the three biblical sacraments of initiation—baptism, chrismation, and the Eucharist—received particular emphasis (for instance, in Gregory Palamas and Nicholas Cabasilas). The number seven was again strongly insisted upon when in the sixteenth century the Eastern Churches had to enter the debate with Reformation theology. Thus, the *Confessio Dosithei* (1672) branded any other enumeration of the sacraments an "outgrowth of heretical folly," and the *Grammata* of the Greek patriarchs (1723) declared in their Article 15 as follows: "In the Church we know nothing of either a smaller or a greater number of mysteries [than seven]."

d) But all of this ought not to obscure the fact that in the East the number seven is not conceived primarily numerically, as in the West, but rather symbolically as the number of perfection, which is quite in keeping with the mind of the ancient world and not least of all with Holy Scripture itself.[5] In more recent times this has led, particularly in the Russian Church, to the addition of the following kind of statement to the affirmation of the seven sacraments: "Beyond this, both in the ancient Fathers as in divine liturgy, there are blessings and important rites that receive the name of 'mystery': such are the great *hagiasma,* the great prayer on the day of Pentecost which is uttered on bent knees, the consecration of a church and the tonsure of a monk" (Synod of Karlvtsi, 1924). S. Bulgakov, N. Afanassieff, and other modern Russians wholly give up the Western distinction between sacraments and sacramentals and decline to say anything specific about the effect and instition of these rites; rather, they prefer to let it all be taken up into the efficacy of the Spirit within the holy Church, understood as a pan-cosmic reality. The Greek Church, however, is closer to the views of the Roman Church in this respect.[6]

APPENDIX TO P. 98

In his article "Why Are There Seven Sacraments?" (*Concilium* 31:67–86), J. Dournes orders the sacraments around the Eucharist as center into two chiastic groups of three each. He writes: "On the one hand we have the three sacraments (baptism, confirmation and holy orders) that irrevocably and perennially assign a person to serve in the Mystical Body; on the other hand we have the three sacraments intended for specific situations or states of human existence (the state of marriage, that of penance and that of sickness). The two groups of three, so constructed, emit 'waves', so to speak, that blend with one another and point to a unity which they also create. In an essential and overarching manner these 'waves' come into harmony in the Eucharist." By way of summary he concludes: " 'There are seven sacraments' means that there is one sacrament and that in it everything that is sacrament can be contained: one sacrament through which God's favor becomes manifold so that it can be realized in every moment of human existence. This one sacrament is Christ, the graspable sign of the mystery of God's love, who accepts humans as equals of his Child." Hotz (pp. 282–286) similarly takes a questioning stance with regard to the number seven for sacraments.

If we follow historically the internal unfolding of the concept of sacrament in the theology of the Western Church we will not be able to ignore the "logos" and the logic of this spiritual accomplishment. Indeed, in the "one house of wisdom with seven pillars" (Wis 9,1) we shall be able to admire the wisdom and the love of God better than in theological constructs that seek to abandon the quite meaningful sevenfold doctrine for the sake of an undifferentiated unity. Even a rightly understood ecumenical spirit cannot overlook the fact that unity can be served only by the person who is first ready to honor revealed truth (cf. volume 7, *The Sacraments of the Church*).

APPENDIX TO P. 121

Blessings and consecrations—which is to say, the sacramentals—presented particular difficulties at the time of the implementation of the reforms required by the Constitution on the Liturgy. Two particular aspects are to be noted in this liturgical renewal that are of import for the doctrine of the faith: (1) Following the spirit of the Constitution on the Liturgy, these new blessings strive to do justice not only to the theological truth involved but also to the concrete form of popular piety in a given situation, not least of all by careful scrutiny of the language used. In so doing, however, the richness of theological truth that has developed in the different cultures on the basis of Scripture and Tradition ought in no way to be compromised or given short shrift merely for the sake of popular piety, especially when this piety proves to be decidedly poorer in a theological sense. All peoples should become enriched by delving into the full spiritual depths of God's revelation ("Come, you who have no money, buy and eat wine and milk, without money, without a price," Isa 55,1). (2) According to the principle *sacramenta propter homines* ("the sacraments are for the sake of human beings"), together with what Paul says in Rom 8,20–23 (that creation "is to be freed from slavery to corruption and receive the freedom of the children of God"), we can understand why "when objects are being blessed the prayers should not be spoken over he object itself; rather, the prayer should have reference to the persons who make use of the object." We ourselves must qualify this remark by noting that the anthropocentric manner of looking at things especially corresponds to Western thought and the modern mentality. And yet for the sake of continuity with the Christian picture of the world proper to the Eastern Churches, and above all for the sake of continuity with the *biblical* picture of the world (cf. 1 Tim 4,4f.: "All is good that God has made, nothing is to be rejected; only we must give thanks to him when we partake of it, then it is hallloved for our use by God's blessing and the prayer which brings it"), we cannot deny that the non-human world, too, may be the subject of blessings and consecrations: after all, through the Incarnation it too has already been taken up into Christ's redemptive grace and, through their bodies, human beings themselves are a part of the cosmos. The modern anthropocentric tendency leads to an un-Christian idealism.

APPENDIX TO P. 195

R. Hotz (pp. 222–265) makes the following historical and dogmatic contributions to a deeper understanding of the *epiclesis:* According to the view of the Eastern Church, the ultimate goal of God's Incarnation in Christ is the sending of the Holy Spirit: "God has made himself a bearer of the flesh so that the human being might become a bearer of the Spirit."[7] If in the "Body of Christ" humans become one, so too does the Spirit call individuals again within this Body in order to perfect them.[8] Just as there is no access to the Father except through the Son, so too there is no access to the Son except through the Spirit (John 16,7; 1 Cor 12,3). But the way of the Church as such and of every Christian to the Spirit is the *epiclesis,* the essential component of every eucharistic action: it is the prayer that never goes unheard (John 16,23) and that in the last analysis is the action of the Spirit in us (Rom 8,26f.). (This is a subsequent development, for in the Scripture the verb ἐπικαλεῖσθαι ("to invoke") refers only to God or to the name of God and, in the New Testament in particular, to Jesus Christ himself.[9] Thus, the *epiclesis* is nothing other than the avowal in prayer of the dogma concerning the Holy Spirit; it is the fulfillment of the Church as a whole—both the hierarchy and the People of God—something that is given rich expression in the liturgy's forms of prayer. Although during the periods of controversy between East and West, especially in connection with the Slavic liturgy of the sixteenth and seventeenth centuries, the *epiclesis* came to be separated in various ways from the historical account of the institution of the Eucharist, in the original understanding of the Eastern Churches both the historical account and the *epiclesis* are most intimately united, like Christ and the Spirit in the Holy Trinity.

From this understanding of how the mystery is accomplished through the *epiclesis* we can also see why in the Eastern Church the formula for conferring the sacraments is basically "deprecative" (that is, always imploring God's presence), whereas in the Western Church it become "indicative" (that is, descriptive of a present reality) for all the sacraments, especially in keeping with the juridical mentality of the Middle Ages. This is the reason, too, why in the East the whole sub-human cosmos, the world of nature, itself belongs to the realm that "becomes sanctified" through blessings and consecrations, especially of water and different oils, so that they themselves become "bearers of the Spirit." The internal coherence of hierarchy and people in the celebration of the liturgy becomes evident to this date in the Eastern Church on the occasion of ordinations and consecrations to the ecclesial offices. This is true not only of priestly ordination—for which the giving of assent by the whole Christian people present has been retained also in the Western Church—but even of the consecration of a bishop, at the beginning of which rite the people are asked to give their approval to the candidate for consecration in question. It is above all in the rite of the consecration of a church in the Eastern Church that the cosmic meaning of the ceremony becomes evident. In the Western Church the liturgical reform itself has made this meaning all but disappear.

APPENDIX TO P. 309

Qualms in the Evangelical Church concerning the question of children's communion have also been the occasion for Catholics to rethink the proper age for First Communion. As in the early Church, so too here infants were already admitted to communion. In this custom a large part was played by the family's attitude and the adults' understanding of communion. Thus, at a time when there was still no obligatory school attendance, the age of receiving communion varied greatly in practice. This great variety continued even after the introduction of obligatory elementary education, and Pope Pius X finally saw himself constrained to intervene. His decree on children's communion *Quam singulari* (August 8, 1910) fixed the age for First Communion at seven. This decree was a continuation of the earlier decree *Sacra Tridentina Synodus* (December 16, 1905), which exhorted the faithful to frequent communion. (Cf. L. Braeckmans, *Confession et communion au Moyen Age et au Concile de Trente* [Gembloux, Editions Duculot, 1971].)

In the Evangelical Churches the age for First Communion was fixed at fifteen, which had already been introduced as the age for confirmation. The problem of alienation within the Church has led many evangelical churches, especially since 1975, to admit even primary school children to First Communion, and confirmation has been left as something celebrated in conjunction with graduation from high school, signifying a declaration of mature status within the Church.[10]

APPENDIX TO P. 329

The "breaking of bread" by the father of a household for the members of the family, a practice of ancient Judaism, becomes a religious rite during the paschal meal (Mark 4,22 par.; 1 Cor 11,24). It also becomes the technical term for the early Christian community meal, in which the agapê and the eucharistic celebration were still conjoined.[11] In keeping with ancient Jewish practice, "the joy of the feast and the care for individuals' needs" were thus intimately combined.[12] Abuses (cf. 1 Cor 11,20–22), as well as a deeper understanding of the religious import of the eucharistic celebration, led as early as the second century to the separation of agapê and Eucharist. (Cf. B. Kleinheyer, "Brotbrechen: Zeichen der Einheit und des Friedens," in: *Mysterium der Gnade* [Regensburg, 1975], pp. 175–182. WNT III [1950], 726–743: Behm.)

Notes

AN INTRODUCTION TO THE WORK OF JOHANN AUER

1. H. Rossmann and J. Ratzinger, eds., *Mysterium der Gnade. Festschrift für Johann Auer zum 65. Geburtstag* (Regensburg, 1975), p. 7.

2. For a brief biographical outline, see ibid., pp. 7–8.

3. *Die menschliche Willensfreiheit im Lehrsystem des Thomas von Aquin und Johannes Duns Scotus* (Munich, 1938).

4. Ibid., pp. 300–303.

5. *Die Entwicklung der Gnadenlehre in der Hochscholastik mit besonderer Berücksichtigung des Kardinals Matteo d'Acquasparta* (Freiburg im Breisgau, 1942; 1951).

6. Ibid., pp. 24–29.

7. Ibid., pp. 250–55.

8. Ibid., pp. 1–2.

9. H. Rossmann, "Das Schriftum von Professor DDr. Johann Auer," in *Mysterium der Gnade*, pp. 442–50.

A GENERAL DOCTRINE OF THE SACRAMENTS

1. Cf. *Mart.* 3.1:*CChr* I 5;*Spect.* 24.4: ibid. I 284;*Coro.* 11.1: ibid. II 1056; *Scorp* 4.5:ibid. II 1076;*Idol.* 19.2:ibid.II 1120.

2. Cf. KKD V, No. 16.

3. Cf. the *Glossa ordinaria* for John 13,8 on the washing of the feet: "Qui non lavatur per baptismum et confessionem pœnitentiæ, non habet partem cum Jesu" (PL 114,405).

4. Cf. the 1321 passional of Cunegunda: Prague, National Library, MS 14, A 17, and the Dominican breviary of Jean Pucelle.

5. This translation follows the Rösch rendering of the passage.

6. Cf. G. Anrich, *Das antike Mysterienwesen in seinem Einfluß auf das Christentum* (Göttingen, 1894), pp. 235 ff.

7. *Die Liturgie als Mysterienfeier* (Frieburg im Breisgau, 1922).

8. O. Casel, *Glaube, Gnosis, Mysterium* JLW 15 (1941).

9. Cf. R. Bultmann, *Theologie des NT.* (Tübingen, 1968), 6th ed, no. 13, ET: *Theology of the New Testament* (New York, 1955); O. Kuss, *Der Römerbrief* (Regensburg, 1959), pp. 307–381.

376 Notes

10. Cf. M. J. Vermaseren, *Mithras* (Stuttgart, 1965) Urban Books, no. 83; L. A. Campbell, *Mithraic Iconography and Ideology* (Leiden, 1968).

11. Cf. *De Bapt.* V 21,29: PL 43,191; *Ep.* 89,5: PL 33,311.

12. Cf. *In Ps.* 40.90, 56.11, 126.7, 138.2: PL 36,461, 668; 37, 1672, 1785.

13. Cf. PL 82,255/285, 347/428, 206/208.

14. Cf. *Institutio christianæ religionis*, IV 14, 1–26.

15. E. Kinder, LThK 9 (1964), 231.

16. *Symbol und Wirklichkeit im Kultmysterium* (Bonn, 1937); *Der Wesensaufbau des Mysteriums* (Bonn, 1938).

17. Cf. O. Casel, *Das Christliche Opfermysterium* (Cologne, 1968), xxviif.

18. LThK 9 (1964), 228.

19. Cf. J. Duns Scotus, *Ox.* IV, d 3 q 3 n 2.

20. *De sacramentis in genere* I, c. 1.9 J. Fèvre (ed.), *Opera omnia* (Paris, 1870), III, 379.

21. *Symbol und Wirklichkeit im Kultmysterium* (Bonn, 1937), pp. 89–92.

22. As a result of "perfect contrition," which can bestow the forgiveness of sins, since God has not made his grace dependent on the sacraments (*Summa theol.* III, q. 64, a.3 c; a.2, ad 1.

23. Regensburg, 1932; 4th ed. 1960.

24. Bonn, 1937.

25. Bonn, 1938.

26. *Liturgisches Leben* 5 (1938), pp. 9–39.

27. *Salzburger Klerusblatt*, December 25, 1948.

28. R. Bultmann, *Theologie des Neuen Testaments* (Tübingen, 1953), pp. 544–559; ET: *Theology of the New Testament* (New York, 1955); TWNT VI (1959), pp. 222–224.

29. Cf. R. Schnackenburg, *Das Heilsgeschehen bei der Taufe nach dem Apostel Paulus* (Munich, 1950); ET: *Baptism in the Thought of St. Paul* (New York, 1964); and in contrast to this see V. Warnach, ALW 3,2 (1954), pp. 284–366; 5,2 (1958), pp. 274–332. See also H. Frankemölle, *Das Taufverständnis des Paulus* (SBS 47) (Stuttgart, 1970).

30. Cf. S. Stricker, "Der Mysteriengedanke des hl. Paulus nach Römerbrief 6,2–11," in: *Liturgisches Leben* 1 (1934), pp. 285–296.

31. Cf. JLW 6 (1926), pp. 113–204; 8 (1928), pp. 145–224; 13 (1933), pp. 99–171; 15 (1941), pp. 155–305.

32. *Myst. Cat.* 2.6:BKV 371.

33. Ibid. 3.1: BKV 373.

34. Cf. JLW 13 (1933), p. 112.

35. ZAM 1 (1926), pp. 351–366; ZKTh 52 (1928), pp. 357–400;

cf. O. Casel, *Das christliche Kultmysterium*, 4th ed. (Regensburg, 1960), p. 58.

36. *Das christliche Kultmysterium*, 2nd ed. (Regensburg, 1935), p. 102.

37. "Glaube, Gnosis und Mysterium," JLW 15 (1941), p. 268.

38. 4th ed., Regensburg (1960), pp. 60f.

39. *Symbol und Wirklichkeit im Kultmysterium* (Bonn, 1937), p. 79.

40. Ibid., p. 93.

41. Bonn (1938), pp. 44–63.

42. III-1, 2nd ed., (Munich, 1948), p. 36.

43. "Zum Problem der Mysteriengegenwart," in: *Liturgisches Leben* 5 (1938), pp. 9–39.

44. *Das Mitsterben und Mitauferstehen bei Paulus* (1937).

45. 6th ed., IV-1 (Munich, 1964), p. 2.

46. Paris, 1950; ET: *The Resurrection: A Biblical Study* (London, 1960).

47. *Epp.* 69–75: CSEL 3/2, 749–827.

48. Canon 13:Mansi 2, 472.

49. *De virg. Maria* IV 9: CSCO 224, 26.

50. Hymn. epiph. 3, 16: CSCO 187, 137; 4,1: ibid. 142; 3.31: ibid. 140.

51. *Cat. 17 de Spir. S* 2, 36: PG 33, 1011.

52. *In 2 Cor Hom.* 3, 7: PG 61, 418.

53. *Ep. 98 ad Bonif.* n. 5: PL 33, 362.

54. *De bapt.* 6,1,1: PL 43, 197.

55. Cf. Thomas, *Summa theol.* III, q.63.

56. For the official decrees, see D 695 and D 852–DS 1310, 1609.

57. Bonaventure, *Sent.* IV d 6 p 1 a and q 3; Thomas, *Summa theol.* III, q.63, a.2.

58. Cf. Cyril of Jerusalem, *Cat. Myst.* 2, 4; Cyril of Alexandria, Augustine, etc.; see under specific sacraments.

59. LThK 9 (1964), p. 228.

60. Tr. V, ed. B. Geyer, p. 108f.

61. Bibl. Franc. Scholast. 15, Quaracchi, 1957, 40.

62. See, for instance, Simeon of Thessalonica, *De sacr.* c. 33: PG 155, 178.

63. *Dogm.* III-1, 1892, p. 436.

64. *De myst.* c 6, 31,f; PL 16 398; *De sacr.* III c 1, 48; PL 16, 432 f.; and the Ceremonial of Milan.

65. Cf. Georg Richter, *Die Fußwaschung im Johannesevangelium* (Regensburg, 1967).

66. Cf. *Kleine Kath. Dogmatik*, IV.1, no. 2.

67. Cf. Isa 6,2: Seraphim; 37,16: Cherubim; Deut 3,55.58; Matt

378   Notes

26,53; Heb 1,6; Rev 5,11; 7,11f. Cf. E. Peterson, *Das Buch von den Engeln* (Leipzig, 1935).

68. Cf. J. Brinktrine, *Die Lehre der Schöpfung* (Paderborn, 1956), pp. 170–173.

69. From the *Winkelmesse und Pfaffenweihe* of 1533: WA 38, 195–256.

70. Cf. on this Thomas of Strasbourg, *Sent.* IV, d 6 q 1 a 1.

71. Cf. E. Schlink, *Theologie der lutherischen Bekenntnisschriften* (Munich, 1940), pp. 325–333.

72. For the distinction between the common priesthood conferred by baptism and the priestly office as such, and between priest and layperson, cf. the discussions on the sacraments of baptism and priestly orders and on the Church

73. For marriage, for instance; cf. CIC, can. 1070.

74. See under the individual sacraments in volume 7, *The Sacraments of the Church.*

75. Cf. *Theol. Revue* 36 (1937), pp. 229ff.

76. Cf. the criticism Pope Cornelius (251–253) makes against the ordinations conferred by bishops of the antipope Novatian, after they had first been made drunk: Eusebius, *Hist. eccl.* VI, 43, 243: PG 20, 620f.

77. *De bapt.* VII, 53, 102: PL 43, 243; Rufinus, *Hist. eccl.* I, 14: PL 21, 487.

78. Cf. Thomas, *Summa theol.* III, q.64, a.8, ad 1.

79. P. Sarpi, *Istoria del Concilio di Trento*, II (Naples, 1935), chap. 8.

80. Cf. Juenin (d. 1713), *De sacr.* d 1 q 5 a 3 § 2.

81. D 1963f.–DS 3315ff.; cf. LThK 1 (1957) 554f.: "Anglikanische Artikel" (Kœnen).

82. Cf. J. J. Hughes, "The Papal Condemnation of the Anglican Orders in 1896," in: *Journal of Ecumenical Studies*, IV-2 (1967), pp. 235–267; ibid., pp. 290–297: editorials by E. A. Smith; cf. also appendices.

83. Cf. "Ego te baptizo"; "Absolvo"; "Hoc est enim . . ."; cf. especially the *error circa personam* in the sacrament of marriage (CIC, can. 1083).

84. Cf. D 957–DS 1764; condemnation of Simoniac ordinations on these grounds: D 354–DS 691–694.

85. Landgraf III/2 (1955), pp. 207–222.

86. E. B. Allo, *Erster Korintherbrief.* (Paris, 1934), pp. 411–414.

87. Cap. 3, can. 3:Mansi III, 865, 881.

88. Cf. the obstacles to ordination and marriage as given in Canon Law.

89. Cf. Landgraf III/1, 210–253: *sacramentum ex voto.*

90. *De bapt. contr. Dona*t. IV, c 22; 29: PL 43, 173; cf. Thomas, *Summa theol.* III, q. 66, a. 9, c.

91. Alger of Liège: PL 180, 797.

92. Cf. J. Pinsk and R. Guardini and their work on "holy signs," and L. Bopp and N. Dudli and their work on the liturgical books.

93. Freiburg im Breisgau, 1936.

94. Freiburg im Breisgau, 1938.

95. Cf. CIC, can. 1147–1150.

96. Cf. Christ's temptations: Matt 4; expulsion of demons: Mark 3,22, Luke 11,20; the Johannine proclamation, in which "Satan" appears as Christ's most real adversary. 1 John 3,8; theme of the ruler of this world: John 12,31; 14,30; 16,11; Paul calls him the "god of this world": 2 Cor 4,4.

97. Cf. Acts 13,10; 1 Pet 5, 8f.: Rev 12, 13-17.

98. Cf. N. Kehl, D*er Christushymnus im Kolosserbrief* (Stuttgart, 1967: Stuttgarter Biblische Monographien, 1).

99. Cf. V. Rüfner "Homo secundus Deus," in: PhJ 71 (1962), pp. 248–291.

100. If we have here termed the Incarnation and the Redemption "events of salvation-history" and not of "world-history," it is because God did not become man in such a way that he had to relinquish his divinity. Rather, it is as Son of God that he assumed human nature, so that the man Jesus could in all truth call himself the Son of God without this meaning that he himself had become God. The title of "God-man," too, which theology ascribes to Christ, is to be understood in the context of salvation-history, since an understanding of such a title in a world-historical sense would necessarily distort it in either a Monophysitic or an Arian direction. The point is that, for our human manner of thinking and formulating concepts, God and the human being essentially are different, and even the highest or deepest theological statement cannot renounce this natural human manner of thought, if it is to remain a human statement, that is.

101. Cf. Teilhard de Chardin, *The Divine Milieu*.

102. Cf. Tauler, *Sermons:* Vetter, 145.

103. Cf. *Phædrus*, 89d.

104. *Nichomachean Ethics*, I, 6, 1098a, 7.

105. Cf. Isa 40,26; Ez 37,4; Gen 1,3–12.

106. Cf. BL 486ff. ("Fluch" ["curse"]: P. van Imschoot); 1897ff. ("Wort Gottes" ["Word of God"]: P. van Imschoot).

107. Cf. Matt 3,15, 5,22, 5,34, 5,39, 7,28f.; Mark 1,22; Luke 4,32.

108. Cf. Eph. 1,9.

109. Cf. Eph 2,18; 2 Pet 1,4.

110. Cf. Col 1,15; 1 Tim 1,17.

111. Cf. Exod 33,11; John 15,14f.

112. Cf. Bar 3,38.

113. Rom 16,26; cf. Rom 1,5; 2 Cor 10,5–6.

114. Cf. Luke 2,19,51.

115. Cf. LThK 10 (1965), pp. 712f. (V. Schurr); RGG VI (3rd ed., 1962), pp. 1358ff. (K. E. Legstrup).

116. Cf. *Confessiones*, VIII, 12; PL 32, 762.

117. Cf. Mark 10,17–22: Athanasius, *Vita S. Antonii*, c. 2: PG 26,841.

THE MYSTERY OF THE EUCHARIST

1. Throughout this passage the German word *Heil* is used to mean both "wholeness" and "welfare" in a more general sense and "salvation" in the more technical theological sense. This felicitous ambiguity cannot be reproduced in English. Even though the German context here intends all these meanings at once, the translator must choose one of them somewhat arbitrarily. [Translator's note]

2. Cf. on this point J. Lotz, *Ich, Du, Wir* (Frankfurt, 1968).

3. Cf. M. J. Scheeben, *The Mystery of the Church and the Sacraments* (St. Meinrad, Indiana, 1953); Council of Trent, sess 13 c 3: D 876–DS 1639f.

4. Ἀρτος (τροφή) ἀγγέλων: Wis 16,20: which contains every delight and satisfies every taste; cf. Ps 78,24f. = manna = food from heaven; on the other hand, see Tob 12,19.

5. Cf. John Chrysostom, *In Heb*. 17,3: PG 63, 130f.

6. Justin, *Apol*. 1,66: PG 6, 429; Irenaeus, *Adv. hær*. V, 2 and 3: PG 7, 1123–1132; Clement of Alexandria, *Paid*. II, 2:PG 8, 429f.

7. Cf. Origen (d. 254), *In Ex*. 13, 3: PG 12, 391; *In Mt* 11.14: PG 13, 949f.; Gregory of Nyssa (d. 394), *Or. cat. myst*. 37: PG 45, 93–97; Cyril of Alexandria, 444, *In Mt* 26.26: PG 72, 452f.; *In Jo*. 4: PG 73, 579f.

8. Cf. Tertullian (d. 220), *Adv. Marc*. 3, 19; *Resur*. 8, 3:CChr I, 533, II, 931.

9. Thus Cyprian (d. 258), *Ep*. 63: PL 4, 372–389; Tertullian (d. 220), *Adv. Marc*. 4, 40:CChr I, 655–657.

10. *De myst*. 8 and 9: PL 16, 403–410; cf. *De sacramentis* IV, 4–6; V; 1–3; PL 16, 439–450; cf. also Irenaeus (d. 202), *Adv. hær*. IV, 17f.: PG 7, 1019–1029.

11. Cf. *Sermo* 227, 1: PL 38, 1099f.; *In Ps* 33, 1, 10: PL 36, 306; *Ep*. 98, 9: PL 33, 363f.

12. *In Jo*. tr. 26, 15–18: PL 5, 1613f.; *De civ. Dei* 21, 25: PL 41, 741f.; *Sermo* 229: PL 38, 1103.

13. *De eccl. off*. 18, *De sacrif*.: PL 83, 755–757.

14. *Liber de corpore et sanguine Domini*, written in 831 and published in 844: PL 120, 1267–1346.

15. *De corpore et sanguine Domini*, ed. J. N. Bakhuizen van den Brink (Amsterdam, 1954).

16. *Sent.* IV d 8–10; ed. Quaracchi (1916), 787–801.

17. Dutch theologians especially speak of transfinalization or transignification; cf. E. H. Schillebeeckx, *The Eucharist* (New York: Sheed and Ward, 1968).

18. AAS 57 (1965), pp. 753–774.

19. Victor Warnach, "Symbol and Reality in the Eucharist," in: *The Breaking of the Bread*, ed. Pierre Benoit, et al. (New York, 1968) = *Concilium* 40:82–105.

20. *Die Eucharistie als Symbolwirklichkeit* (Regensburg, 1969).

21. Cf. the beginning of the canon in the ninth-century *Sacramentary of Drogo* (Paris, Bibl. nat. ms. lat 9428).

22. Ravenna: San Vitale, San Apollinare Nuovo; Rome: St. Mary Major; numerous portrayals on sarcophagi; book miniatures: Codex Ronanensis.

23. Cf. W. Beinert, "Die neuen Deutungsversuche der Eucharistielehre und das Konzil von Trient," in: ZThPh 46 (1971), pp. 342–363. Also, S. Harkianakis, "Die heilige Eucharistie in orthodoxer Sicht," ibid., pp. 172–188.

24. Cf J. Schmid, *Synopse*, 3rd ed. (Regensburg, 1960).

25. L. Schenke, *Stuttgarter Bibelstudien* 33 (1968), p. 90, note 91.

26. Cf. on this H. Strack and P. Billerbeck, *Kommentar zum Neuen Testament aus Talmud und Midrasch.* IV, 1, Fourth Excursus (Munich, 1928), pp. 41–76.

27. Cf. E. Stauffer, *Jerusalem und Rom* (Zurich, 1957 [Dalp]), pp. 113–122.

28. Thus A. Jaubert, *La date de la cène, calendrier biblique et liturgie chrétienne* (Paris, 1957); B. Schwank, in: BM 33 (1957), 268–278.

29. RNT 8,1 (1966), p. 219.

30. Meyer KNT, 11th ed. (Göttingen, 1960), p. 343.

31. Cyprian, *Ep.* 63: PL 4, 372–389.

32. Cf. B. Kleinheyer, *Erneuerung des Hochgebetes* (Regensburg, 1969), pp. 83–87.

33. Thomas, *Summa theol.* III, q. 82 ad 2 and 3; cf. on this J. M. Hanssens, *Institutiones liturgicæ de ritibus orientalibus* (Rome, 1930/32).

34. Cf. DACL 3 (1914) 2470–2488; Hendrik Manders, "Concelebration," in: *The Church and the Liturgy* (New York, 1965) = *Concilium* 2:135–151; O. Nussbaum, *Liturgiereform und Konzelebration* (Cologne, 1966); A. Fries, "Die eucharistische Konzelebration in der theologischen Kontroverse des 13. Jahrhunderts,"

in: *Die Kirche im Wandel: Festschrift für Kardinal Höffner* (Cologne, 1971), pp. 341–352; A. Fries, "Die eucharistische Konzelebration als theologisches Problem vom 13. bis 15. Jahrhundert," in: *Studia Moralia* 10 (Rome, 1972), pp. 347–435.

35. *De Eucharistia*, I, 8: *Op. omn.*, ed. J. Fèvre (Paris, 1873), IV, 24f.

36. Cf. A. Arnauld, *La perpetuité de la foi de l'Eglise touchante l'eucharistie*, 3 vols. (Paris, 1669–1674).

37. *Flor. patrist. fasc.* 7 (Münster, 1935–37).

38. Cf. Bernadotte-Lippert, *Eucharistie* (Munich, 1927). A. Grillmeier, "Missio eucharistica," in: GuL 31 (1958), pp. 166-172.

39. *Summa theol.* I, q. 76, a.8; cf. Augustine, *De Trin.* VI, 6: PL 42, 929.

40. Cf. Plato, Timæus, 51A; 58D.

41. On this term, cf. Clement of Alexandria, *Strom.* IV, 23: PG 8, 1357 C.

42. *De myst.* IX, 51–54: PL 16, 406f; cf. *De sacram.* IV, 4 f.: ibid., 443–446.

43. Cf. Peter Lombard (d. 1160), *Sent.* IV, d 11 c 2 n 106 (ed. Quaracchi, 1916) II, 803.

44. D 430–DS 802; cf. Mansi XXII, 982; Hefele V, 78f.

45. *Summa theol.* III, qq. 75–77.

46. *Ox.* IV, d 11 q 1 and 2 (XVII, 319).

47. Ibid., q 4 n. 16 (458).

48. Ibid., 458.

49. Cf. E. Iserloh, *Gnade und Eucharistie in der philosophischen Theologie des Wilhelm von Ockham* (Wiesbaden, 1956), pp. 174–253.

50. Cf. his *Aktuelle Fragen zur Eucharistie* (Munich, 1960), pp. 190–194.

51. *Kommunikation und Sakrament*, Quæstiones Disputatæ 8 (Freiburg im Breisgau, 1960).

52. *Das Geheimnis unseres Christus* (Munich, 1959), pp. 12–18; ET: *Meditations on the Sacraments* (New York, 1977).

53. Cf. Encyclical *Mysterium Fidei* in *Documents on the Liturgy 1963–1979: Conciliar, Papal, and Curial Texts*, ed. ICEL, (Collegeville, Minnesota, 1982), pp. 378–392. For a critique of E. H. Schillebeeckx by J. Ratzinger, cf. ThQ 147 (1967), pp. 129–158, esp. pp. 493–497; also Piet Schoonenberg, *Transubstantiation: How Far Is This Doctrine Historically Determined?* (New York, 1967) = *Concilium* 24:78–91.

54. Victor Warnach, "Symbol and Reality in the Eucharist," in: *The Breaking of Bread*, ed. Pierre Benoit, et al. (New York, 1968) = *Concilium* 40:82–105.

55. *Eucharistie als Symbolwirklichkeit* (Regensburg, 1969).

56. *Theologie der Eucharistie* (Munich, 1973).

57. Cf. Aristotle, *Met.* VII, 3: 1029 a 1.8; VIII, 3: 1043 b 30; *Cat.* 5: 2 a 10–12; 4 a 10–12.

58. On the concept of substance, see R. Eisler, *Wörterbuch der philosophischen Begriffe*, 4th ed. (Berlin, 1930), III, 177–190.

59. *Summa theol.* III, q.75, a.4.

60. *Ox.* IV, d 11 q 4 n 14: XVII, 457f.

61. Cf. LThK.

62. Cf. *Epitome*, c. 29: PL 178, 1743 C; likewise *Sententiæ divinitatis tr.*, V, 3, ed. B. Geyer (Münster, 1909), p. 134.

63. Thus E. Maignan, O.M. (d. 1676), and J. Perimezzi, O.M. (d. 1740).

64. Cf. commentaries on this passage.

65. Acts 20,7; cf. *Didache* 14.1:ed. Funk I (1901) 32f; Justin, *First Apology*, ch. 67: PG 6 429f.

66. Cyprian, *Ep.* 56, 1: PL 4, 350: *quotidie calicem sanguinis Christi bibere.*

67. Cf. Basil, *Ep.* 93: PG 32, 484f., written in 372.

68. H. Jedin, Seripando II, 185–192.

69. Cf. K. Prümm, RH (Freiburg, 1943), pp. 490–504.

70. See volumes 4 & 5 on the doctrine of redemption.

71. See volume 8 on the sacrament of priestly ordination.

72. Cf. F. Klostermann, *Das christliche Apostolat* (Vienna, 1962).

73. For an understanding of the "sacrificial action" in the Mass, see section (3.C), "The Theological (Metaphysical?) Nature of the Sacrifice of the Mass: Theories About the Mass."

74. Cf. the liturgies of Mark, of James, of Basil, of John Chrysostom, and the old Roman Liturgy as seen in the *Apostolic Constitutions*, VIII, 12.

75. "Do this in memory of me": 1 Cor 11,24;26; Luke 22, 19.

76. *Contra Marcionem* III, 22, 6; IV, 1, 8:*CChr* I, 539f., 546.

77. *Patres Apostolici,* ed. Funk, I (Tübingen, 1901), pp. 32f.

78. 28, 5; 41,2; 116,3; 117, 1ff.: PG 6, 536 C, 564 C, 746 A.

79. *IIOM.* 25, 3 *in Mt* 7,28–8.4: PG 57, 331; cf. PG 63 (Liturgy of St. John Chrysostom), 907, 912, 917, 921.

80. Cf. treading the winepress in Isa 63,3 and Rev 19,15.

81. *Augsburg Confession* (Apol.), a. 24.

82. *Schmalkaldic Articles* II, 2; *Thirty-Nine Articles,* 31; *Heidelberg Catechism.* question 80.

83. *Opera omnia*, II/1, 156f. (Gütersloh, 1952).

84. *Opera omnia*, II/2, 533f., 540 (Gütersloh, 1952).

85. Session 22, Sept. 1562; D 937 a–956–DS 1738–1759.

86. This question has already been explored in depth by Jacobus Bayus in his *De venerabili eucharistiæ sacramento et sacrificio* (Paris, 1626), III, c. 15, pp. 905f.

87. *Tractatus de missæ sacrificio,* disp. 75, sect. 6, n. 6; ed. Paris, 1856–1861, 675.

88. In his *De Eucharistia,* disp. 19,sect. 5, n. 67.

89. In his *Vita abscondita sub speciebus velata* (Rome, 1728).

90. *L'idée du sacerdoce et du sacrifice de Jésus-Christ* (Paris, 1677), P. 2, m. 2, pp. 54–58.

91. *Dogm. theol,* vol. 4, lib. 10, c. q,n. 13 (Paris, 1868), p. 320.

92. *Œuvres* (Versailles, 1816), vol. 18, pp. 128–130.

93. *Das Opfer des Alten und Neuen Bundes* (Munich, 1870).

94. *L'idée du sacrifice de la Messe d'après les théologiens depuis l'origine jusqu'à nos jours* (Paris, 1926), p. 754.

95. IV/1, 5th ed., p. 369.

96. The subtle but essential distinction here is between *Mahlopfer* ('sacrifice-as-meal' or 'sacrifice-reduced-to-a-meal') and *Opfermahl* ('meal-as-sacrifice' or 'meal-raised-to-be-a-sacrifice'). The more profound and genuine understanding, Auer here says, is the latter. [Translator's Note]

97. Part 2, III; DS 3854.

98. Encyclical *Mediator Dei,* 2nd part, I.

99. *Mediator Dei,* 2nd part, I; cf. 2 Cor 5,20.

100. 2nd part, II, quoting Robert Bellarmine.

101. *Mediator Dei,* 2nd part, I.

102. Cf. Gregory of Nazianzen, *Ep,* 171: PG 37, 282.

103. AAS 39 (1947), pp. 521–595.

104. AAS 39 (1947), pp. 549f.

105. *Apol.* I, 65: ed. Quasten I, 16.

106. *Apol.* 39, 2:CChr 1, 150.

107. *Ep.* 149, 16:CSEL 44, 362f.

108. *De dom. or.* 8:CSEL 3, 271.

109. *Trad. apost.* 22,5.

110. VIII, 6–11.

111. Cf. already the *Didache* 9,4; 10,5: ed. Quasten I, 10ff.

112. Cf. the apocryphal *Acts of John,* 85, 110: Hennecke-Schneemelcher, *Neutestamentliche Apokryphen,* 3rd ed., v. 2 (1966), pp. 172, 174.

113. BKV, 2nd ed., 6 (Syrian Writers), p. 99.

114. Ibid., pp. 305–315.

115. *Conf.* IX, 12, 32: PL 32, 777 (death of his mother in Ostia: *offerre pro ea sacrificium); De 8 Qq. Dulcitii,* q. 2: PL 40, 157f.; *De cura pro mort.* 18, 22: PL 40, 609.

116. Cf. J. Jungmann, *Missarum sollemnia,* II, 1st ed. (Freiburg im Breisgau, 1950), 52ff; J. M. Hanssens, *Institutiones liturgicæ de ritibus orientalibus,* v. II/III: *De missa* (Roma, 1930/32), II, pp. 282–300.

117. Cf. B. Kleinheyer, *Erneuerung des Hochgebetes* (Regensburg, 1969).

118. Cf. D 1530–DS 2630; in 1794 Pius VI expressly defends the practice of mass stipends.

119. Cf. LThK 7 (1962) 354f. (Mörsdorf); M. Kaiser, *Klerusblatt* 49 (1969), pp. 367–370.

120. Thomas, *Summa theol.* III, q. 79, a. 3; likewise the Council of Trent, D 940–DS 1743.

121. *Adv. Hær.* cap. 49 and 79; PG 41, 880 CD; 42, 741 and 744f.

122. *Schmalkaldic Articles*, part 2, art 2: Müller, *Symbolische Bücher*, 2nd ed. (1928), pp. 301–305; *Augsburg Confession*, art. 13 (ibid., p. 203); *Book of Concord*, II, 7 (ibid., 663).

123. *Inst. Christ. Rel.* IV, 19, 22–33: Weber, 2nd ed. (1963), 1021–1029.

124. D 938ff., 960, 961, 948–951–DS 1739–1743, 1767–1770, 1771, 1751–1754.

125. *1 Clement*, cap. 40–44: PG 1, 288–300.

126. 10, 7; 13, 3; 15, 1.

127. *Ad ux.* 2, 5: *CChr* 1, 389.

128. *Ep.* 93:PG 32, 483.

129. *Cat. myst.* 5, 21: PG 33, 123.

130. Cyprian, *De lapsis*, 25:PL 4, 484.

131. Cf. Tertullian, *ad ux.* 2, 5:*CChr* 1, 389; Augustine, *Ep.* 54, 6: PL 33, 203; *Synod of Hippo* (393), can. 29:Mansi 3, 885; *Corpus Iuris Canonici,* can. 858; LThK 7 (1962), pp. 1066f.

132. Possidius' *Vita*: PL 32.

133. Paulinus' *Vita*.

134. Cf. J. Haring, *Die Armensünderkommunion* (Graz, 1912).

135. *Ep.* 93: PG 32, 484f.

136. *Ep.* 71, 6: PL 22, 672.

137. Cf. P. Browe, *Die häufige Kommunion im Mittelalter* (Münster, 1938).

138. Mansi 8, 327.

139. Inst. IV, 17, 47.

140. "To receive from both species of the sacrament" (1522): WA 10/2, 11–41.

141. D 930–32, 934–36–DS 1726–1729, 1731–1733.

142. Mansi 29, 699–868.

143. AAS 59 (1967), p. 558.

144. On spiritual communion, see J. Auer, GuL 24 (1951) 113–132; R. Schnackenburg, ibid. 25 (1952), pp. 407–411; K. Rahner, ibid., pp. 412–429; H. R. Schlette, *Die Lehre von der geistichen Kommunion bei Bonaventura, Albert dem Grossen und Thomas von Aquin* (Munich, 1959); Schlette, *Kommunikation*

und Sakrament (Quæstiones disputatæ 8), (Freiburg im Breisgau, 1959).

145. On this point, see Gertrude the Great, *Herald of Divine Love*, III, 35.

146. See G. Baum, *That They May Be One: A Study of Papal Doctrine from Leo XIII to Pius XII* (Paris, 1961).

147. Cf. "Directory Concerning Ecumenical Matters: Part One (1967), Part Two (1969)," in *Doing the Truth in Charity*, eds. Thomas F. Stransky and John B. Sheerin, (New York, 1982), Ecumenical Documents I:41–74.

148. Cf. Declaration of the Secretariat for Promoting Christian Unity (dated January 7, 1970), "The Position of the Catholic Church Concerning a Common Eucharist Between Christians of Different Confessions," in: *Doing the Truth in Charity*, pp. 117–121.

149. Cf. Declaration of the Secretariat for Promoting Christian Unity (dated June 1, 1972), "Cases When Other Christians May Be Admitted to Eucharistic Communion in the Catholic Church," in: *Doing the Truth in Charity*, pp. 122–126.

150. *Osservatore Romano*, March 7, 1971.

151. Cf. J. Höfer, K. Lehmann, W. Pannenberg, and E. Schlink, *Evangelish-Katholische Abendmahlsgemeinschaft* (Regensburg, 1971). A. Kirchgäßner and H. Bühler, eds., *Interkommunion in Diskussion und Praxis: Eine Dokumentation* (Düsseldorf, 1971). *Okumenisches Pfingsttreffen Augsburg, 1971: Dokumente* (Berlin-Paderborn, 1971); *Catholica* 26 (1972) 2.

152. *Lutherische Monatshefte*, Oct./Nov. 1975, pp. 614ff.

153. Cf. the *Offizielle Gesamtausgabe* ("complete official edition"), pp. 212–216.

154. KNA, no. 3 (January 28, 1976).

155. *The Final Report* of the Anglican/Roman Catholic International Commission.

156. "Towards a Common Eucharistic Faith?" (Group of Les Dombes), in: *Modern Eucharistic Agreement* (London, 1973), pp. 51–78.

157. "The Eucharist" (Lutheran/Roman Catholic Dialogue in the USA) in: *Building Unity*, eds. J. A. Burgess and J. Gros (New York, 1989), pp. 91–101.

158. On this, see *Herder Korrespondenz* 32 (1978), pp. 193–199; ibid., p. 33 (1979), pp. 306–309. R. Frieling, *Ökumene in Deutschland: Ein Handbuch der interkonfessionellen Zusammenarbeit in der Bundesrepublik* (Göttingen, 1970).

159. Cf. Bonaventure, *Sent.* IV d 12 p 2 q 3.

160. *Salmanticenses*, vol. XI, p. 2 fol 335–348: Disp. 10; Suárez, *Op. om.* (Paris, 1866), vol. XX, pp. 381–391.

161. AAS 59 (1967), p. 541.

162. *Op. om.*, ed. J. Fèvre, vol. IV, c. 17 (Paris, 1873; Frankfurt, 1965), pp. 249–251.

163 See volume 5, *The Gospel of Grace.*

164. D 123–DS 262 (Council of Ephesus, canon 11).

165. Cf. Sent, IV, d 10 p 1 a 1 q 1.

166. Cf. Rudolf of Biberach (d. 1350), *De septem itineribus* VI, 6 (inter Opera Bonaventuræ, ed. Peltier, Paris, 1866, VIII, 469); Dorothea of Montau (d. 1394), *Septililium*. tr. 3 c. 7–8.

167. *Horologium sapientiæ*, II, c. 4; *Bibliotheca Mystica Ordinis Prædicatorum* (Munich, 1923), 383–434.

168. Cf. DSAM IV, 2 (1962) 1553–1653, esp. 1586–1621: Eucharist and the Mystical Experience, V; 1621–1648: Eucharistic Piety, V; K. Rahner, "The Doctrine of the 'Spiritual Senses' in the Middle Ages," in: *Theological Investigations* 16 (New York, 1979), pp. 104–134; E. Longpré, "L'Eucharistie et l'union mystique selon la spiritualité franciscaine," RAM 25 (1949), 306–333; J. Daniélou, "Eucharistie et Cantique des Cantiques," *Irénikon* 23 (1950), pp. 257–277.

169. *Cat. myst.* 22, 3: PG 33, 1100.

170. *Mysterium fidei*, 3rd edition (Paris, 1931), pp. 475–498.

171. D 882–DS 1649; Augustine, *In Joh.* 26, 13: PL 35, 1613.

172. See volume 9, *Eschatology: Death and Eternal Life.*

173. D 891–DS 1659; cf. *Corpus Iuris Canonici*, canons 859 and 863.

174. Cf. the capitulars of Charlemagne and the *Decretum Gratiani*: c. 131, D. 14, *de consec*r.

175. AAS 41 (1949), pp. 509f.; 59 (1967), p. 566.

176. Eusebius, *Hist. eccl.* V, 24: PG 20, 494.

177. AAS 59 (1967), p. 570.

178. AAS 59 (1967), p. 566.

179. Cf. LG 3, 11, 26, 50; UR 2: "the sacrament of the Eucharist, through which the unity of the Church is both symbolized and effected."

180. Especially in the Tübingen School (J. A. Möhler), in J. H. Newman's writings, and even more after the schemata drawn up by the Roman School of theologians for Vatican I, and in the general outlook of the Church since the encyclical *Mystici Corporis* (1943).

181. See volume 8, *The Church: The Universal Sacrament of Salvation.*

182. Cf. *Contra Cresc.* 2, 16, 19: PL 43, 477; K. Adam, "Zur Eucharistielehre des Heiligen Augustinus," in: ThQ 112 (1931) 494ff.

183. *Sermo* 272: PL 38, 1247f.; cf. *Sermo* 227:ibid. 1099ff.

184. K. Adam, *Die Eucharistielehre des heiligen Augustinus*

388   Notes

(Paderborn, 1908), p. 147; cf. J. Ratzinger, *Introduction to Christianity* (NewYork: Seabury, 1969), pp. 182–204; "Excursus: Christian Structures."
185. Luke 22,19; 1 Cor 11,26; D 430–DS 802.
186. In volume 8, *The Church: The Universal Sacrament of Salvation*.
187. Mozarabic collect: PL 96, 759B.
188. Leo the Great, *Sermons* 63, 7: PL 54, 357C; LG 26.
189. Pius XII, AAS 48 (1956), p. 212.
190. LThK 4 (1960) 631ff., "Gelassenheit" (Vorgrimler).

EPILOGUE

1. *Eccl. hier.*, chap. 3.
2. Ed. by E. von Ivanka (Klosterneuburg, 1958), pp. 101–144.
3. Cf. N. Liesel, *Die Liturgien der Ostkirche* (Frieburg im Breisgau, 1960); A. Kirchgässner, *Die Mächtigen Zeichen: Ursprung, Formen und Gesetze des Kultes* (Freiburg im Breisgau, 1958); T. Klauser, *A Short History of the Western Liturgy: An Account and Some Reflections*, 2d ed. (Oxford, 1979); Second Vatican Council, Documents on the Liturgy; *Ordo Missæ*, edited by the Sacred Congregation of Rites, April 6, 1969; F. Kolbe, *Die liturgische Bewegung* ("Der Christ in der Welt," IX, 4), Aschaffenburg, 1964.

APPENDICES TO THE TEXT

1. Critical edition of his works in Sources Chrétiennes: *Kephalaia* (no. 51, Paril, 1957) and *Hymns* (no. 174, Paris, 1971).
2. Cf. P. Scazzoso, *La teologia di S. Gregorio Palamas* (Milan, 1970).
3. Hotz, pp. 205–217. Cf. on this Vladimir Lossky, *The Mystical Theology of the Eastern Churches* (London, 1957); Lossky, *Schau Gottes* (Zürich, 1964); N. von Bubnoff, *Russische Religionsphilosophen: Dokumente* (Heidelberg, 1956); B. Schultze, *Russische Denker: Ihre Stellung zu Christus, Kirche und Papsttum* (Vienna, 1950); F. Schupp, *Glaube–Kult–Sumbol: Über den Symbolwert von Sakrament und Kult* (Düsseldorf, 1973).
4. *De cæl. hier.*, chaps. 6–7: PG 3, 529–565.
5. Cf. WNT 2 (1935) 623–631:Rengstorf.
6. Cf. P. N. Trembelas and C. Androutsos; Hotz, pp. 266–287.
7. Athanasius, *De incarn.* 8: PG 26, 996C.
8. Basil, *De Spiritu Sancto*. XIX, 49: PG 32, 157AB.
9. WNT III (1950) 498–501.
10. Cf. J. Jezlorowski, "Kinder als eucharistische Gäste: Zur

Diskussion über Kinderabendmahl in den reformatorischen Kirchen," in: *Klerusblatt* 56 (1976), pp. 91–94.

11. Acts 2,42.46; 20,7,11; *Didache* 14.1; Ignatius of Antioch, *To the Ephesians*, 20.2.

12. Cf. B. Reicke, *Diakonie, Festfreude und Zelos in Verbindung mit der altchristlichen Agape* (Uppsala-Vienna, 1951), pp. 1–229.

Select Bibliography

Prepared for the English translation by Michael A. Fahey, S.J.

A GENERAL DOCTRINE OF THE SACRAMENTS

Introduction

a. Sacraments in General

Amadio, Anselm M. "Sacrament of the Church." In *New Catholic Encyclopedia* [NCE], 12:786. Washington, 1967.

Béguerie, Philippe, and Claude Duchesneau. *How to Understand the Sacraments*. New York, 1991.

Beyer, Hermann W. "*eulogeo* [blessing]." In *Theological Dictionary of the New Testament* [TDNT], translated and edited by G. W. Bromily, 2:754–765. Grand Rapids, MI, 1964–1974.

Boff, Leonardo. *Sacraments of Life, Love of the Sacraments*. Washington, 1975.

Browning, Robert L. *Sacraments in Religious Education and Liturgy*. Birmingham, AL, 1985.

DeGidio, Sandra, *Sacraments Alive: Their History, Celebration and Significance*. Mystic, CT, 1991.

Eigo, Francis A., ed. *The Sacraments: God's Love and Mercy Actualized*. Villanova, 1979.

Feider, Paul. *The Sacraments: Encountering the Risen Lord*. Notre Dame, IN, 1986.

Fransen, Piet. *Faith and the Sacraments*. London, 1958.

Ganoczy, Alexander. *An Introduction to Catholic Sacramental Theology*. New York, 1984.

Halligan, Nicholas. *The Sacraments and Their Celebration*. New York, 1986.

Hanley, Philip L. "Sacraments, Conditional, Administration of." In NCE 12:801.

Howell, Clifford. *Of Sacraments and Sacrifice*. Collegeville, MN, 1953.

Irwin, Kevin W. "Sacrament." In *The New Dictionary of Theology*, ed. Joseph Komonchak, 910–22. Wilmington, DE, 1988.

Jounel, Pierre. "Blessings." In *The Church at Prayer*. gen. ed. Aimé Martimort. Vol. 3: *The Sacraments* 263–284. Collegeville, MN, 1986.

Komonchak, Joseph A., et al., eds. *The New Dictionary of Theology*. Wilmington, DE, 1987.

Kucharek, Casimir. *The Sacramental Mysteries: A Byzantine Approach*. Allendale, NJ, 1976.

Leeming, Bernard. *Principles of Sacramental Theology*. Westminster, MD, 1956.

Martos, Joseph. *Doors to the Sacred: A Historical Introduction to Sacraments in the Catholic Church*. Rev. ed. Tarrytown, 1991.

Martos, Joseph. "Sacraments in the 1980s: A Review of Books in Print." *Horizons: The Journal of the College Theology Society* 18 (1991):130–142.

Martos, Joseph. *The Catholic Sacraments*. Wilmington, DE, 1983.

Mick, Lawrence E. *Understanding the Sacraments Today*. Collegeville, MN, 1987.

O'Neill, Colman E. *Meeting Christ in the Sacraments*. Staten Island, NY, 1964.

Osborne, Kenan B. *Sacramental Theology: A General Introduction*. New York, 1988.

Piault, Bernard. *What Is a Sacrament?* New York, 1963.

Quinn, John Richard. "Sacramental Theology." In NCE 12:789–790.

Rahner, Karl. *The Church and the Sacraments*. Freiburg, 1963.

Rahner, Karl. "What Is a Sacrament?" *Theological Investigations* 14 (1976):135–148.

Roberts, William P. *Encounters with Christ: An Introduction to the Sacraments*. New York, 1985.

Roguet, Aimon Marie. *Christ Acts Through the Sacraments*. Collegeville, MN, 1954.

Schanz, John P. *The Sacraments of Life and Worship*. Milwaukee, 1966.

Schanz, John P. *Introduction to the Sacraments*. New York, 1983.

Scheeben, Matthias J. *The Mystery of the Church and the Sacraments*. St. Meinrad, IN, 1953.

Schillebeeckx, Edward, and Boniface Willems, eds. *The Sacraments in General*. New York, 1968. =*Concilium* 31.

Schulte, Raphael. "Sacraments." *Sacramentum Mundi* 5 (1970): 378–384.

Smith, Patricia. *Teaching Sacraments*. Wilmington, DE, 1987.

Sullivan, C. Stephen, ed. *Readings in Sacramental Theology*. Englewood Cliffs, NJ, 1964.

Taylor, Michael J. *The Sacraments as Encasement: Jesus Is with Us.* Collegeville, MN, 1986.

Vorgrimler, Herbert. *Sacramental Theology.* Collegeville, MN, 1992.

White, James F. *Sacraments as God's Self-Giving: Sacramental Practice and Faith.* Nashville, 1983.

b. Liturgy

Collins, Mary. "Liturgy." In *The New Dictionary of Theology,* ed. Joseph Komonchak, 591–601. Wilmington, DE, 1988.

Cullmann, Oscar. *Early Christian Worship.* London, 1953.

Dalmais, Irénée Henri. *Introduction to the Liturgy.* Baltimore, 1961.

Daniélou, Jean. *The Bible and the Liturgy.* Notre Dame, IN, 1956.

Davies, John Gordon, ed. *The New Westminster Dictionary of Liturgy and Worship.* Philadelphia, 1986; title in the UK: *A New Dictionary of Liturgy and Worship.* London, 1979.

Delling, Gerhard. *Worship in the New Testament.* London, 1962.

Diekmann, Godfrey. *Come, Let Us Worship.* Baltimore, 1961.

Dix, Gregory. *The Shape of the Liturgy.* 2d ed. London, 1945.

Ellard, Gerald. *Christian Life and Worship.* Rev. ed. Milwaukee, 1956.

Fink, Peter E., ed. *The New Dictionary of Sacramental Worship.* Collegeville, MN, 1990.

Grigassy, Daniel P. "The Liturgical Movement." In *The New Dictionary of Theology,* ed. Joseph Komonchak, 586–91. Wilmington, DE, 1988.

Hahn, Ferdinand. *The Worship of the Early Church.* Philadelphia, 1973.

Hoffman, Elizabeth, et al., eds. *The Liturgy Documents: A Parish Resource.* 3d ed. Chicago, 1991.

International Commission on English in the Liturgy (ICEL). *Documents on the Liturgy 1963–1979: Conciliar, Papal and Curial Texts.* Collegeville, MN, 1982.

Irwin, Kevin. *Liturgical Theology: A Primer.* Collegeville, MN, 1990.

Johnson, Lawrence J., ed. *The Church Gives Thanks and Remembers: Essays on the Liturgical Year.* Collegeville, MN, 1984.

Jones, Cheslyn, Geoffrey Wainwright, and Edward Yarnold, eds. *The Study of Liturgy.* London, 1978.

Jungmann, Josef A., and Angelus Häussling. "Liturgy." In *Sacramentum Mundi* 3:320–340. New York, 1969.

Kavanagh, Aidan. *On Liturgical Theology.* New York, 1984.

Kilmartin, Edward J. *Christian Liturgy*: Vol. I: *Theology.* Kansas City, 1988.

Kilmartin, Edward J. *Culture and the Praying Church: The Particular Liturgy of the Individual Church*. Rev. ed. Ottawa, 1990.

Klauser, Theodor. *A Short History of the Western Liturgy: An Account and Some Reflections*. 2d ed. Oxford, 1979.

Lee, Bernard J., ed. *Alternative Futures for Worship*. 7 vols. Collegeville, MN, 1987.

Martimort, Aimé Georges, gen. ed. *The Church at Prayer*, Vol. 1: *Principles of the Liturgy*, by Irénée Henri Dalmais, et al. Collegeville, MN, 1987; Vol. 2: *The Eucharist*, by Robert Cabié (1986); Vol. 3: *The Sacraments*, by Robert Cabié, et al. (1986); Vol. 4: Liturgy and Time, by A. G. Martimort, et al. (1986).

Moule, Charles F.D. *Worship in the New Testament*. London, 1962.

Newman, David R. *Worship as Praise and Empowerment*. New York, 1988.

Palmer, Paul F. *Sacraments and Worship: Liturgy and Doctrinal Development of Baptism, Confirmation and Eucharist*. Westminster, MD, 1955.

Pius XII, *Mediator Dei* [November 20, 1947]. In *The Papal Encyclicals 1939–1958*, ed. Claudia Carlen, 119–154. Wilmington, NC, 1981.

Ratzinger, Joseph. *Feast of Faith: Approaches to a Theology of the Liturgy*. San Francisco, 1986.

Reinhold, Hans A. *The American Parish and the Roman Liturgy*. New York, 1958.

Schultz, Hans-Joachim. *The Byzantine Liturgy: Symbolic Structure and Faith Expression*. New York, 1986.

Seasoltz, Kevin. *The New Liturgy: A Documentation, 1903–1965*. New York, 1966.

Simcoe, Mary Ann, ed. *The Liturgy Documents: A Parish Resource*. Rev. ed. Chicago, 1985.

Trethowan, Illtyd. *Christ in the Liturgy*. London, 1952.

Vagaggini, Cipriano. *Theological Dimensions of the Liturgy: A General Treatise on the Theology of the Liturgy*. Collegeville, 1976.

Verheul, Ambrosius. *Introduction to the Liturgy: Towards a Theology of Worship*. Collegeville, MN, 1968.

1. Concept and Nature of Sacrament

1. The Meaning of the Word "Sacrament"

Bornkamm, Günther. "*mysterion* [mystery]." In TDNT 4:802–827.

2. The Objective Meaning of Sacrament: Definition of Sacrament

Amaladoss, Michael. *Do Sacraments Change?* Bangalore, 1979.

Bausch, William J. *A New Look at the Sacraments.* Rev. ed. Mystic, CT, 1977.

Beeck, Frans Jozef van. *Grounded in Love: Sacramental Theology in an Ecumenical Perspective.* Washington, DC, 1981.

Cooke, Bernard J. *Sacraments and Sacramentality.* Mystic, CT, 1983.

Cooke, Bernard J. *Christian Sacraments and Christian Personality.* New York, 1965.

Hellwig, Monika. *The Meaning of the Sacraments.* New York, 1972.

Kilmartin, Edward J. "Theology of the Sacraments: Toward a New Understanding of the Chief Rites of the Church of Jesus Christ." In *Alternative Futures for Worship*, ed. Regis Duffy, 1:123–175. Collegeville, MN, 1987.

Martimort, Aimé Georges. *The Signs of the New Covenant.* Collegeville, MN, 1963.

O'Neill, Colman E. *Sacramental Realism: A General Theory of the Sacraments.* Wilmington, DE, 1983.

Schillebeeckx, Edward. *Christ the Sacrament of the Encounter with God.* 3rd rev. ed. New York, 1963.

Semmelroth, Otto. *Church and Sacrament.* Notre Dame, IN, 1965.

Taylor, Michael J., ed. *The Sacraments: Readings in Contemporary Sacramental Theology.* New York, 1981.

Vaillancourt, Raymond. *Toward a Renewal of Sacramental Theology.* Collegeville, MN, 1979.

Verdier, Philippe. "*Iconography of Sacraments.*" In NCE 12: 802–806.

Villette, Louis. "Sacraments as Signs of Faith." In NCE 12:813–816.

Wainwright, Geoffrey. *Doxology: The Praise of God in Worship, Doctrine and Life.* New York, 1980.

Worden, Thomas, ed. *Sacraments in Scripture: A Symposium.* London, 1966.

3. Pre-Christian and Non-Christian Sacramental Analogies

The Ancient Mysteries: A Sourcebook: Sacred Texts of the Mystery Religions. San Francisco, 1987.

Angus, Samuel. *The Mystery-Religions and Christianity: A Study in the Religious Background of Early Christianity.* New York, 1928.

Godwin, Joscelyn. *Mystery Religions in the Ancient World.* London, 1981.

Metzger, Bruce M. "Considerations of Methodology in the Study of the Mystery Religions and Early Christianity." *The Harvard Theological Review* 48 (1955):1–20.

Rahner, Hugo. *Greek Myths and Christian Mystery.* London, 1963.

4. Short History of General Sacramental Doctrine

Downey, Michael. *Clothed in Christ: The Sacraments and Christian Unity.* New York, 1987.

Hugh of Saint Victor. *On the Sacraments of the Christian Faith.* Mediaeval Academy of America Publication 58. Cambridge, MA, 1951.

Jungmann, Josef A. "Liturgy on the Eve of the Reformation." *Worship* 33 (1959):505–515.

Rahner, Karl. "Introductory Observations on Thomas Aquinas' Theology of the Sacraments in General." *Theological Investigations* 14 (1976):149–160.

Rogers, Elizabeth Frances. *Peter Lombard and the Sacramental System.* Merrick, NY, 1976.

II. The Essential Structure of the Sacramental Sign

1. The Synthetic Structure of the Sacramental Sign: Symbol

Bouyer, Louis. *Rite and Man: Natural Sacredness and Christian Liturgy.* Notre Dame, 1963.

Cassirer, Ernst. *The Philosophy of Symbolic Forms.* 3 vols. New Haven, 1953–57.

Chauvet, Louis-Marie. *Symbol and Sacrament: A Sacramental Rereading of Christian Existence.* Collegeville, MN, 1994.

Douglas, Mary. *Natural Symbols: Explorations in Cosmology.* 2d ed. London, 1973.

Eliade, Mircea. *Images and Symbols: Studies in Religious Symbolism.* New York, 1969.

Fawcett, Thomas. *The Symbolic Language of Religion: An Introductory Study.* Minneapolis, 1971.

Frazer, James George. *The Golden Bough: A Study in Magic and Religion.* 3 vols. London, 1900.

Gassmann, Günther. "The Church as Sacrament, Sign and Instrument: The Reception of This Ecclesiological Understanding in Ecumenical Debate." In *Church, Kingdom, World,* ed. Gennadios Limouris, 1–17. Geneva, 1986.

Guardini, Romano. *Sacred Signs.* St. Louis, 1956.

Happel, Stephen. "Symbol." In *The New Dictionary of Theology*, ed. Joseph Komonchak, 996–1002. Wilmington, DE, 1988.

Happel, Stephen. "Sacrament: Symbol of Conversion." In *Creativity and Method: Essays in Honor of Bernard Lonergan*, ed. Matthew Lamb, 275–290. Milwaukee, 1981.

Kelleher, Margaret Mary. "Ritual." In *The New Dictionary of Theology*, ed. Joseph Komonchak, 906–907. Wilmington, DE, 1988.

Langer, Susanne. *Philosophy in a New Key: A Study in the Symbolism of Reason, Rite and Art*. 3d ed. Cambridge, MA, 1976.

Lawler, Michael G. *Symbol and Sacrament: A Contemporary Sacramental Theology*. New York, 1987.

Leeuw, Gerardus van der. *Sacred and Profane Beauty: The Holy in Art*. Nashville, 1963.

McKenna, John J. "Symbol and Reality: Some Anthropological Considerations." *Worship* 65 (1991) :2–27.

Mitchell, Leonel L. *The Meaning of Ritual*. New York, 1977.

Pieper, Josef. *In Search of the Sacred*. San Francisco, 1991.

Power, David N. *Unsearchable Riches: The Symbolic Nature of Liturgy*. New York, 1984.

Rahner, Karl. "The Theology of Symbol." In *Theological Investigations* 4 (1966):221–252.

Richter, Klemens. *The Meaning of the Sacramental Symbols: Answers to Today's Questions*. Collegeville, MN, 1990.

Ricoeur, Paul. *The Rule of Metaphor: Multidisciplinary Studies of the Creation of Meaning in Language*. Toronto, 1977.

Shaughnessy, James D., ed. *The Roots of Ritual*. Grand Rapids, MI, 1973.

Thiselton, Anthony C. *Language, Liturgy and Meaning.* Bramcote, Notts, 1975.

Turner, Victor. *The Ritual Process: Ritual and Anti-Structure.*. Chicago, 1969.

Worgul, Goerge S., Jr. *From Magic to Metaphor: A Validation of Christian Sacraments*. New York, 1980.

III. The Sacraments' Saving Reality and Efficacy

1. The Principal Effects of the Sacraments

Foerster, Werner, and Georg Fohrer. "*sozo, soteria* [save, salvation]." In TDNT 7:965–1024.

Fourez, Gérard. *Sacraments and Passages: Celebrating the Tensions of Modern Life*. Notre Dame, 1983.

Häring, Bernard. *A Sacramental Spirituality*. London, 1965.

Huebsch, Bill. *Rethinking the Sacraments: Holy Moments in Daily Living*. Mystic, CT, 1989.

Taymans d'Epernon, Francis. *The Blessed Trinity and the Sacraments*. Westminster, MD, 1961.

2. *Conformity to Christ as Chief Effect of a Sacrament: Basic Theories of Mystery Theology*

a. Mystery Theology

Crehan, Joseph. "Mystery." *A Catholic Dictionary of Theology*, 3:316–319. London, 1971.

Dalmais, Irénée Henri. "The Liturgy as Celebration of the Mystery of Salvation." In *The Church at Prayer: An Introduction to the Liturgy*. Vol. 1: *The Principles of the Liturgy*, 253–272. Collegeville, MN, 1987.

Neunheuser, Burkhard. "The Mystery Presence." *The Downside Review* 76 (1958):266–274.

b. Dom Odo Casel (1886–1948)

Bridgehouse, Donald. "Dom Odo Casel." *The Downside Review* 75 (1957):140–148.

Casel, Odo. *The Mystery of Christian Worship*. Westminster, MD, 1962.

Neunheuser, Burkhard. "Odo Casel in Retrospect and Prospect." *Worship* 50 (1976):489–503.

Neunheuser, Burkhard. "Odo Casel and the Meaning of the Liturgical Year." *Studia Liturgica* 15 (1982–83):210–13.

Rossum, Joost van. "Dom Odo Casel OSB." *St. Vladimir's Theological Quarterly* 22 (1978):141–151.

3. *The Sacramental Character as Effect of the Sacrament*

Hanley, Philip L. "Sacramental Character." In NCE 12:786–789.

Ruffini, Eliseo. "Character as a Concrete Visible Element in Relation to the Church." In *The Sacraments in General*. eds. Edward Schillebeeckx and Boniface Willems. New York, 1968. = *Concilium* 31:101–114.

4. *The Sacraments' Objective Efficacy (ex opere operato)*

Dillenschneider, Clement. *The Dynamic Power of Our Sacraments*. St. Louis, 1966.

Pourrat, Pierre. *Theology of the Sacraments: A Study in Positive Theology*, 93–203. St. Louis, 1910.

5. *The Manner of the Sacraments' Effect*

Crehan, Joseph. "Causality of the Sacraments." *A Catholic Dictionary of Theology* 2:6–11. London, 1967.

Gallagher, John F. *Significando causant: A Study of Sacramental Efficiency*. Fribourg, Switzerland, 1965.

IV. Origin, Number, and Organic Structure of the Sacraments

1. The Historical Christ, Author of the Sacraments
Rahner, Karl. *The Church and the Sacraments*. Freiburg, 1963.

2. *Seven, the Number of the Sacraments*
Collins, Mary, and David Power, eds. *Blessing and Power.* New York, 1985. = *Concilium* 178.
Dournes, Jacques. "Why Are There Seven Sacraments?" In *The Sacraments in General*, eds. Edward Schillebeeckx and Boniface Willems. New York, 1968. = *Concilium* 31:67–86.

3. Order and Necessity of the Seven Sacraments
Roguet, Aimon Marie. "The Sacraments in General." In *Christ in His Sacraments*, ed. A. M. Henry, 3–46. Theology Library 6. Chicago, 1954.

V. The Minister of the Sacraments

1. The Person of the Minister
Rahner, Karl. "Considerations on the Active Role of the Person in the Sacramental Event." *Theological Investigations* 14 (1976): 161–184.

2. *Subjective Requirements in the Minister of the Sacraments*
Hughes, John Jay. *Absolutely Null and Utterly Void: The Papal Condemnation of Anglican Orders 1896.* New York, 1968.
Hughes, John Jay. *Stewards of the Lord: A Reappraisal of Anglican Orders*. London, 1970.
Pourrat, Pierre. *Theology of the Sacraments: A Study in Positive Theology*, 256–294. St. Louis, 1910.
Sedgwick, Timothy F. *Sacramental Ethics: Paschal Identity and the Christian Life.* Philadelphia, 1987.

VI. The Recipient of the Sacraments

1. The Person of the Recipient
Deiss, Lucien. *Persons in Liturgical Celebrations.* Chicago, 1978.

*2. Subjective Requirements for the Recipient of the
   Sacraments*

Bro, Bernard. *The Spirituality of the Sacraments: Doctrine and
   Practice for Today*. New York, 1968.
Rahner, Karl. "Personal and Sacramental Piety." *Theological In-
   vestigations* 2 (1963) :109–133.

vii. The Sacramentals

1. The World as Sacrament

a. Sacramentals

Brett, Laurence F.X. *Redeemed Creation: Sacramentals Today.*
   Wilmington, DE, 1984.
Champlin, Joseph. *Special Signs of Grace: The Sacraments and
   Sacramentals*. Collegeville, MN, 1986.
Chupungco, Anscar. *Liturgical Inculturation: Sacramentals, Reli-
   giosity, and Catechesis*. Collegeville, MN, 1992.
Groot, Jan. "The Church as Sacrament of the World." In *The
   Sacraments in General*. eds. Edward Schillebeeckx and Boni-
   face Willems. New York, 1968. = *Concilium* 31:51–66.
Häring, Bernard. *The Sacraments in a Secular Age*. Slough, 1976.
Löhrer, Magnus. "Sacramentals." *Sacramentum Mundi* 5(1970)
   :375–378.
Quinn, John Richard. "Sacramentals." In NCE 12:790–792.
Runyon, Theodore. "The World as the Original Sacrament." *Wor-
   ship* 54 (1980) :495–511.

b. Desacralization

Aubert, Roger, ed. *Sacralization and Secularization.* New York,
   1969. = *Concilium* 47.
Chereso, James C. *Here and Now: The Sacred Secular*. Dayton,
   OH, 1969.
Fenn, Richard K. *Towards a Theory of Secularization*. Storrs, CT,
   1978.
Lynch, William F. *Christ and Prometheus: A New Image of the
   Secular*. Notre Dame, IN, 1970.
McCauley, George. *Sacraments for Secular Man*. New York, 1969.
Panikkar, Raimundo. *Worship and Secular Man: An Essay on the
   Liturgical Nature of Man*. Maryknoll, NY, 1973.
Richard, Robert L. *Secularization Theology*. New York, 1967.
Schillebeeckx, Edward. *God, the Future of Man.* New York, 1968.
Skelley, Michael. *The Liturgy of the World: Karl Rahner's Theol-
   ogy of Worship*. Collegeville, MN, 1991.

Thils, Gustave. *A "Non-Religious" Christianity?* Staten Island, NY, 1970.

2. Human Sacramental Existence and the Sacramentals

Miller, John H. *Signs of Transformation in Christ.* Englewood Cliffs, NJ, 1963.

Murray, Donal. *Life and Sacrament: Reflections on the Catholic Vision.* Wilmington, DE, 1983.

Von Hildebrand, Dietrich. *Liturgy and Personality.* 2d rev. ed. Baltimore, 1960.

VIII. God's Word as Sacrament

1. Toward an Understanding of "Word"

Bouyer, Louis. *The Word, Church and Sacraments: In Protestantism and Catholicism.* New York, 1961.

Cooke, Bernard J. *Ministry to Word and Sacraments.* Philadelphia, 1976.

Debrunner, Albert. *"lego, logos* [speak, word]." In TDNT 4:69–136.

Ebeling, Gerhard. *Introduction to a Theological Theory of Language.* London, 1973.

Fischer, Balthasar. *Signs, Words and Gestures: Short Homilies on the Liturgy.* New York, 1981.

Grainger, Roger. *The Language of the Rite.* London, 1974.

Grasso, Domenico. *Proclaiming God's Message: A Study in the Theology of Preaching.* Notre Dame, 1965.

Jenson, Robert W. *Visible Words: The Interpretation and Practice of Christian Sacraments.* Philadelphia, 1978.

Ramshaw-Schmidt, Gail. *Christ in Sacred Speech: The Meaning of Liturgical Language.* Philadelphia, 1986.

Schmidt, Hermann, ed. *Liturgy: Self-Expression of the Church.* New York, 1972. = *Concilium* 72.

Semmelroth, Otto. *The Preaching Word: On the Theology of Preaching.* New York, 1965.

Zimmerman, Joyce Ann. *Liturgy as Language: A Liturgical Methodology in the Mode of Paul Ricoeur's Hermeneutics.* Lanham, MD, 1988.

2. The Sacramental Form the Word of God Assumes in the New Covenant

Eijk, A.H.C. van. "The Difference Between the Old and the New Testament Sacraments as an Ecumenical Issue." *Bijdragen* 52 (1991) :2–36.

THE MYSTERY OF THE EUCHARIST

Introduction

1. Toward an Understanding of the Eucharistic Mystery

Anglican/Roman Catholic, et al. *Modern Eucharistic Agreement.* London, 1975.

Anglican/Roman Catholic International Commission. *The Final Report.* London, 1982.

Balasuriya, Tissa. *The Eucharist and Human Liberation.* London, 1979.

Balthasar, Hans Urs von, ed. "The Eucharist." *Communio: International Catholic Review* 12 (1985) :115–157, 223–237.

Bernier, Paul. *Bread Broken and Shared: Broadening Our Vision of Eucharist.* Notre Dame, 1981.

Betz. Johannes. "Eucharist: Theological." *Sacramentum Mundi* 2 (1968) :257–67.

Bouyer, Louis. *Eucharist: Theology and Spirituality of the Eucharistic Prayer.* Notre Dame, 1966.

Cabié, Robert. Vol. 2: *The Eucharist.* In *The Church at Prayer,* gen. ed. Aimé Georges Martimort. Collegeville, MN, 1986.

Conzelmann, Hans. "*eucharisteo* [thanksgiving]." In TDNT 9: 407–415.

Crockett, William R. *Eucharist, Symbol of Transformation.* New York, 1989.

Dewan, Wilfrid F. "Eucharist as Sacrament." In NCE 5:599–609.

Echlin, Edward P. *The Anglican Eucharist in Ecumenical Perspective.* New York, 1968.

Emminghaus, Johannes H. *The Eucharist, Essence, Form, and Celebration.* Collegeville, MN, 1978.

Fahey, Michael A., ed. *Catholic Perspectives on Baptism, Eucharist, and Ministry.* Lanham, MD, 1986.

Grassi, Joseph A. *Broken Bread and Broken Bodies: The Lord's Supper and World Hunger.* Maryknoll, NY, 1985.

Hellwig, Monika. *The Eucharist and the Hunger of the World.* New York, 1976.

Jungmann, Josef A. "Eucharist: Liturgical." *Sacramentum Mundi* 2 (1968):267–273.

Kiesling, Christopher. "Roman Catholic and Reformed Understandings of the Eucharist." *Journal of Ecumenical Studies* 13 (1976) :268–274.

Kilmartin, Edward J. *Church, Eucharist, and Priesthood.* New York, 1981.

Kilpatrick, George Dunbar. *The Eucharist in Bible and Liturgy.* Cambridge, 1983.

Lash, Nicholas. *His Presence in the World: A Study of Eucharistic Worship and Theology.* Dayton, OH, 1968.

Lutheran/Roman Catholic Joint Commission. *The Eucharist.* Geneva, 1980.

Moloney, Raymond. "Eucharist." In *The New Dictionary of Theology,* ed. Joseph Komonchak, 342–355. Wilmington, DE, 1988.

O'Carroll, Michael. *Corpus Christi: An Encyclopedia of the Eucharist.* Wilmington, DE, 1988.

Orthodox Perspectives on Baptism, Eucharist and Ministry. Brookline, MA, 1985.

Osborne, Kenan B. *The Christian Sacraments of Initiation: Baptism, Confirmation, Eucharist.* New York, 1987.

Pennington, M. Basil. *The Eucharist Yesterday and Today.* New York, 1984.

Power, David. *Eucharistic Mystery: Revitalizing the Tradition.* New York, 1992.

Quinn, James. *The Theology of the Eucharist.* Dublin, 1973.

Rahner, Karl. "The Word and the Eucharist." *Theological Investigations* 4 (1966):253–286.

Rahner, Karl. *Meditations on the Sacraments,* 29–41. New York, 1977. Also published as: *The Eucharist: The Mystery of Our Christ.* Denville, NJ, 1970.

Schillebeeckx, Edward. *The Eucharist.* London, 1968.

Schmemann, Alexander. *The Eucharist: Sacrament of the Kingdom.* Crestwood, 1987.

Seasoltz, R. Kevin, ed. *Living Bread, Saving Cup: Readings on the Eucharist.* Collegeville, MN, 1982.

Sheppard, Lancelot, ed. *The New Liturgy: A Comprehensive Introduction to the New Liturgy,* 101–248. London, 1970.

Swidler, Leonard, ed. "Eucharist in Ecumenical Dialogue." *Journal of Ecumenical Studies* 13 (1976) :191–344. Essays by 16 theologians.

Thurian, Max. *The Eucharistic Memorial.* 2 vols. London, 1960–61.

United States Catholic Conference of Bishops. *The Body of Christ.* Washington, 1977.

Wainwright, Geoffrey. *Eucharist and Eschatology.* 2d ed. New York, 1978.

World Council of Churches, Commission on Faith and Order. *Baptism, Eucharist and Ministry,* Faith and Order Paper 111. Geneva, 1982.

2. Short History of the Eucharistic Doctrine

Ashworth, Henry. "Sacramentaries." In NCE 12:792–800.

Baldovin, John F. *The Urban Character of Christian Worship: The Origins, Development, and Meaning of Stational Liturgy.* Rome, 1987.

Courtenay, William J. "Sacrament, Symbol and Causality in Bernard of Clairvaux." In *Bernard of Clairvaux: Studies Presented to Dom Jean Leclerq,* eds Henri Rochais, et al. 111–122. Washington, 1973.

Elert, Werner. *Eucharist and Church Fellowship in the First Four Centuries.* St. Louis, 1966.

Foley, Edward. *From Age to Age: How Christians Celebrated the Eucharist.* Chicago, 1991.

Gy, Pierre-Marie. "Sacraments and Liturgy in Latin Christianity." In *Christian Spirituality: Origins to the Twelfth Century.* eds Bernard McGinn and John Meyendorff. World Spirituality: An Encyclopedic History of the Religious Quest 16:365–381. New York, 1985.

Hanson, Richard P.C. *Eucharistic Offering in the Early Church.* Bramcote, Notts, 1979.

Heron, Alasdair. *Table and Tradition: Toward an Understanding of the Eucharist.* Philadelphia, 1983.

Jasper, R.C.D., and G. J. Cuming, eds. *Prayers of the Eucharist: Early and Reformed.* 3d rev. ed. New York, 1987.

Jungmann, Joself A. *The Early Liturgy: To the Time of Gregory the Great.* Notre Dame, IN, 1959.

Macy, Gary. *The Theologies of the Eucharist in the Early Scholastic Period: Study of the Salvific Function of Sacrament According to the Theologians 1080–1220.* New York, 1984.

Mazza, Enrico. *Mystagogy: A Theology of Liturgy in the Patristic Age.* New York, 1989.

McDonnell, Kilian. *John Calvin: The Church and the Eucharist.* Princeton, 1967.

Megivern, James J. *Concomitance and Communion: A Study in Eucharistic Doctrine and Practice.* New York, 1963.

Milburn, Robert L.P. "Symbolism and Realism in Post-Nicene Representations of the Eucharist." *Journal of Ecclesiastical History* 8 (1957):1–16.

Powers, Joseph M. *Eucharistic Theology.* New York, 1967.

Rordorf, Willy, et al. *The Eucharist of the Early Christians.* New York, 1978.

Schepers, Maurice B. "Sacramentarians." In NCE 12:792.

Sheerin, Daniel J. *The Eucharist, Message of the Fathers of the Church* 7. Wilmington, DE, 1986.

Smith, Mahlon H. *And Taking Bread . . . : Cerularius and the Azyme Controversy of 1054.* Paris, 1978.

Taft, Robert. "The Frequency of the Eucharist Thoughout History." *Beyond East and West: Problems in Liturgical Understanding,* 61–80. Washington, DC, 1984.

Vogel, Cyrille. *Medieval Liturgy: An Introduction to the Sources.* Washington, DC, 1986.

Iconographic Resources

Boyer, Mark. *The Liturgical Environment: What the Documents Say.* Collegeville, MN, 1990.

Loerke, William. " 'Real Presence' in Early Christian Art." In *Monasticism and the Arts,* ed. Timothy Verdon, 29–51. Syracuse, NY, 1984.

Maldonado, Luis, and David Power, eds. *Symbol and Art in Worship.* New York, 1980. = *Concilium* 132.

Mauck, Marchita. *Shaping a House for the Church.* Chicago, 1990.

McNally, Dennis. *Sacred Space: An Aesthetic for the Liturgical Environment.* Bristol, IN, 1985.

Milburn, Robert. *Early Christian Art and Architecture.* Berkeley, CA, 1988.

National Conference of Catholic Bishops, Bishops' Committee on the Liturgy. *Environment and Art in Catholic Worship.* Washington, DC, 1978.

Seasoltz, Kevin. *The House of God: Sacred Art and Church Architecture.* New York, 1963.

White, Susan J. *Art, Architecture, and Liturgical Reform: The Liturgical Arts Society (1928–1972).* New York, 1990.

1. The Meaning of the Sacramental Sign in the Eucharistic Mystery

1. Toward an Understanding of the Words of Promise and Institution

Benoit, Pierre, et al., eds. *The Breaking of Bread.* New York, 1969. = *Concilium* 40.

Bernas, Casimir. "Eucharist, Biblical Data." In NCE 5:594–599.

Bernier, Paul J., ed. *Bread from Heaven.* New York, 1977.

Delorme, Jean, et al. *The Eucharist in the New Testament: A Symposium.* Baltimore, 1964.

Jeremias, Joachim. *The Eucharistic Words of Jesus.* New York, 1966.

Kilmartin, Edward J. *The Eucharist in the Primitive Church.* Englewood Cliffs, NJ, 1965.

Léon-Dufour, Xavier. *Sharing the Eucharistic Bread: The Witness of the New Testament.* New York, 1987.

Tillard, Jean M. R. *The Eucharist: Pasch of God's People.* Staten Island, NY, 1967.

2. The Particular Shape of the External Sign in the Eucharistic Sacrament; Concelebration.

Baldovin, John F. "Concelebration: A Problem of Symbolic Roles in the Church." *Worship* 59 (1985) :32–47.

Howell, Clifford W. "Concelebration." *Worship* 28 (1954) :89–93.

McGowan, Jean Carroll. *Concelebration: Sign of the Unity of the Church.* New York, 1964.

Ostdiek, Gilbert. "Concelebration Revisited." In *Shaping English Liturgy,* eds. Peter C. Finn and James M. Schellman, 139–171. Washington, DC, 1990.

Rahner, Karl, and Angelus Häussling. *The Celebration of the Eucharist.* New York, 1968.

Taft, Robert F. "Ex Oriente Lux: Some Reflections on Eucharistic Concelebration." *Worship* 54 (1980) :308–325.

3. The Unique Symbolic Meaning of the External Sign in the Eucharistic Sacrament

a. Real Presence

Burr, David. *Eucharistic Presence and Conversion in Late 13th Century Franciscan Thought.* Philadelphia, 1984.

Duffy, Regis. *Real Presence: Worship, Sacraments and Commitment.* San Francisco, 1982.

Fink, Peter E. "Perceiving the Presence of Christ." *Worship* 58 (1984) :17–28.

Gelpi, Donald L. "Ecumenical Reflections on Christ's Eucharistic Presence." In *Essays on Apostolic Themes: Studies in Honor of Howard Ervin,* ed. Paul Elbert, 193–207. Peabody, MA, 1985.

Liderbach, Daniel. "The Eucharistic Symbols of the Presence of the Lord." *Philosophy and Theology* 1 (1987) :225–241.

Rahner, Karl. "The Presence of Christ in the Sacrament of the Lord's Supper." *Theological Investigations* 4 (1974) :287–311.

Rahner, Karl. "On the Duration of the Presence of Christ after Communion." *Theological Investigations* 4 (1974) :312–320.

Sasse, Hermann. *This Is My Body: Luther's Contention for the Real Presence in the Sacrament of the Altar.* Minneapolis, 1959.

Sheets. John R. "The Real Presence." *Communio: International Catholic Review* 4 (1977) :292–305.

Stebbins, J. Michael. "The Eucharistic Presence of Christ: Mystery and Meaning." *Worship* 64 (1990) :225–236.

b. Epiclesis

Crehan, Joseph H. "Eucharistic Epiklesis: New Evidence and a New Theory." *Theological Studies* 41 (1980) :698–712.

Kilmartin, Edward J. "The Active Role of Christ and the Holy Spirit in the Sanctification of the Eucharistic Elements." *Theological Studies* 45 (1984) :225–253.

McKenna, John H. "Eucharist Epiclesis: Myopia or Microcosm?" *Theological Studies* 36 (1975) :265–284.

McKenna, John H. *Eucharist and Holy Spirit: The Eucharistic Epiclesis in Twentieth Century Theology (1900–1966)* London, 1975.

McKenna, John H. "The Epiclesis Revisited." In *New Eucharistic Prayers*, ed. Frank C. Senn, 169–194. New York, 1987. Also contained in *Ephemerides Liturgicae* 99 (1985):314–336.

Tillard, Jean-Marie. "Blessing, Sacramentality and Epiclesis." In *Blessing and Power*, eds. Mary Collins and David Power. New York, 1985. = *Concilium* 178:96–110.

c. Transubstantiation

Clark, Joseph T. "Physics, Philosophy, Transubstantiation, Theology." *Theological Studies* 12 (1951) :24–51.

McCue, James F. "The Doctrine of Transubstantiation from Berenger Through the Council of Trent." In *Lutherans and Catholics in Dialogue, 1–3*, ed. Paul Empie, 89–124. Minneapolis, 1974.

Vollert, Cyril. "The Eucharist: Controversy on Transubstantiation." *Theological Studies* 22 (1961) :391–425.

II. The Eucharist as Sacramental Sacrifice (The Meal-Sacrifice)

1. Sacrifice and Sacrament

Cooke, Bernard J. "Sacrifice in Christian Theology." In NCE 12:837–840.

Daly, Robert J. "The Power of Sacrifice in Ancient Judaism and Christianity." *Journal of Ritual Studies* 4 (1990) :181–198.

Daly, Robert J. *Christian Sacrifice: The Judeo-Christian Background Before Origen.* Washington, DC, 1978.

Gartner, Bertil E. "The Eucharist as Sacrifice in the New Testament; The Words of Institution." In *Lutherans and Catholics in Dialogue, 1–3.* ed. Paul Empie, 27–35, 75–79. Minneapolis, 1974.

Jungmann, Josef A. *The Sacrifice of the Church: The Meaning of the Mass.* Collegeville, MN, 1956.

Kiesling, Christopher. "Roman Catholic Doctrine and Reformed Theology of the Eucharist as Sacrifice." *Journal of Ecumenical Studies* 15 (1978) :416–426.

Kilpatrick, George D. "Eucharist as Sacrifice and Sacrament in the New Testament." In *Neues Testament und Kirche*, ed. Joachim Gnilka, 429–433. Freiburg, 1974.

La Taille, Maurice de. *The Mystery of Faith: Regarding the Most August Sacrament and Sacrifice of the Body and Blood of Christ*. 2 vols. London, 1941.

Mackenzie, Ross. "Reformed Theology and Roman Catholic Doctrine of the Eucharist as Sacrifice." *Journal of Ecumenical Studies* 15 (1978) :429–438.

Miller, John H. "Mass Roman." In NCE 9:414–26.

Power, David N. *The Sacrifice We Offer: The Tridentine Dogma*. New York, 1982.

Scheffczyk, Leo. "Sacrifice, Substitution, Representation." *Sacramentum Mundi* 5 (1970) :391–392.

Semmelroth, Otto. "Concept of Sacrifice." *Sacramentum Mundi* 5 (1970): 388–394.

Stevenson, Kenneth W. *Eucharist and Offering*. New York, 1986.

Thurian, Max. *The Mystery of the Eucharist*. London, 1983; Grand Rapids, 1984.

Vaux, Roland de. *Studies in Old Testament Sacrifice*. Cardiff, Wales, 1964.

Williams, Bruce A. "The Eucharist as Sacrifice: Old and New Conceptions." In *The Sacrament of Eucharist in Our Time*, ed. George A. Kelly, 33–49. Boston, 1978.

Williams, Rowan. *Eucharistic Sacrifice: The Roots of a Metaphor*. Bramcote, Notts, 1982.

Wisloff, Carl F. *The Gift of Communion: Luther's Controversy with Rome on Eucharistic Sacrifice*. Minneapolis, 1964.

Young, Frances Margaret. *The Use of Sacrificial Ideas in Greek Christian Writers from the New Testament to John Chrysostom*. Cambridge, MA, 1979.

2. *The Reality of the Sacrifice of the Mass*

Bugnini, Annibale. *The Reform of the Liturgy 1948–1975*. Collegeville, MN, 1990.

Byron, Brian. *A Theology of Eucharistic Sacrifice*. Dublin, 1974.

Clark, Francis. *Eucharistic Sacrifice and the Reformation*. Westminster, MD, 1960.

Collins, Mary, and David Power, eds. *Can We Always Celebrate the Eucharist?* New York, 1982. = *Concilium* 152.

Daly, Robert J. *The Origins of the Christian Doctrine of Sacrifice*. Philadelphia, 1978.

Jungmann, Josef A. *The Mass of the Roman Rite: Its Origins and Development (Missarum Solemnia)*. 2 vols. New York, 1951–55; new revised and abridged edition in one vol. *The Mass of the*

Roman Rite. New York, 1959; revised again as *The Mass: An Historical, Theological and Pastoral Survey.* Collegeville, MN, 1976.

Kilmartin, Edward J. "Eucharist as Sacrifice." In NCE 5:609–615.

Kilmartin, Edward J. "Money and the Ministry of the Sacraments." In *The Finances of the Church,* ed. William Bassett and Peter Huizing. New York, 1979 = *Concilium* 117:104–111.

Mannion, M. Francis. "Stipends and Eucharistic Praxis." *Worship* 57 (1983) :194–214.

Masure, Eugène. *The Christian Sacrifice, the Sacrifice of Christ Our Head.* London, 1944.

Masure, Eugène. *The Sacrifice of the Mystical Body.* London 1954.

Mazza, Enrico. *The Eucharistic Prayers of the Roman Rite.* New York, 1986.

Scheffczyk, Leo. "Eucharistic Sacrifice." *Sacramentum Mundi* 2 (1968) :273–276.

Tillard, Jean M. R. "Sacrificial Terminology and the Eucharist." *One in Christ* 17 (1981) :306–323.

3. The Nature of the Sacrifice of the Mass

Hildebrandt, Franz. *I Offered Christ: A Protestant Study of the Mass.* Philadelphia, 1967.

Rahner, Karl, and Angelus Häussling. *The Celebration of the Eucharist.* New York, 1968.

III. The Eucharist as Sacrificial Meal (Meal as Sacrament)

1. The Minister and the Recipient of the Holy Eucharist

Howell, Clifford W. "Completing the Sacrifice." *Worship* 26 (1951):17–25.

Leclercq, Jean, "Eucharistic Celebrations Without Priests in the Middle Ages." *Worship* 25 (1981) :160–168.

Legrand, Hervé-Marie. "The Presidency of the Eucharist According to the Ancient Tradition." *Worship* 53 (1979) :413–438.

Macy, Gary. "Reception of the Eucharist According to the Theologians: A Case of Theological Diversity in the Thirteenth and Fourteenth Centuries." in *Theology and the University,* ed. John V. Apczynski, 15–36. Lanham, MD, 1990.

Szafranski, Richard T. "The One Who Presides at Eucharist." *Worship* 63 (1989) :300–316.

Vogel, Arthur A. *Is the Last Supper Finished? Secular Light on a Sacred Meal.* New York, 1968.

2. Intercommunion and "Open Communion"

Dulles, Avery. "Eucharistic Sharing as an Ecumenical Problem." In *The Resilient Church*, 153–171. New York, 1977.

Fahey, Michael A. "Eucharistic Sharing (Intercommunion)." In NCE 17:215–217.

Falardeau, Ernest. *One Bread and Cup: Source of Communion*. Wilmington, DE, 1987.

Kent, John, and Robert Murray, eds. *Intercommunion and Church Membership*. London and Denville, NJ, 1973.

Pigault, Gerard, and Jean Schlick. *Eucharist and Eucharistic Hospitality*. RIC Supplements 10 and 17. Strasbourg, 1974–75.

Reardon, Ruth, and Melanie Finch, eds. *Sharing Communion: An Appeal to the Churches from Interchurch Families*. London, 1983.

3. The Effects of the Holy Eucharist

Pius XII, *Mediator Dei* [November 20, 1947]. In *The Papal Encyclicals 1939–1958*, ed. Claudia Carlen, 119–154. Wilmington, NC, 1981.

iv. The Eucharist as an Object Worthy of Adoration

1. Adoration and Veneration of the Blessed Sacrament

Burback, M. "Eucharist, Worship and Custody of." In NCE 5: 615–617.

Carroll, Michael P. *Catholic Cults and Devotions: A Psychological Inquiry*. Kingston, Ontario, 1989.

Drury, T. W. *Elevation in the Eucharist: Its History and Rationale*. Cambridge, 1907.

King, Archdale Arthur. *Eucharistic Reservation in the Western Church*. New York, 1965.

Mitchell, Nathan. *Cult and Controversy: The Worship of the Eucharist Outside Mass*. New York, 1982.

National Conference of Catholic Bishops. *Eucharistic Worship and Devotion Outside Mass*. Washington, 1987.

Rubin, Miri. *Corpus Christi: The Eucharist in Late Medieval Culture*. Cambridge, 1991.

v. The Eucharist and the Church

1. The Eucharistic Body and the Mystical Body of Christ

Bermejo, Luis M. *Body Broken and Blood Shed: The Eucharist of the Risen Christ*. Anand, India, 1986.

Martelet, Gustave. *The Risen Christ and the Eucharistic World*. London, 1976.

Mascall, Eric Lionel. *Corpus Christi: Essays on the Church and the Eucharist.* 2d rev. ed. London, 1965.

Mersch, Emile. *The Theology of the Mystical Body.* New York, 1951.

Pius XII. *Mystici Corporis Christi* [June 29, 1943]. In *The Papal Encyclicals 1939–1958*, ed. Claudia Carlen, 37–63. Wilmington, NC, 1981.

Rahner, Karl. *The Church and the Sacraments.* Freiburg, 1963.

2. Birth and Growth of the Church from the Eucharistic Mystery to the End of the World

Keifer, Ralph A. *Blessed and Broken: An Exploration of the Contemporary Experience of God in Eucharistic Celebration.* Wilmington, DE, 1982.

Index of Names

Index of Subjects

A General Doctrine of the Sacraments and *The Mystery of the Eucharist* was composed in 9/11 Trump Mediaeval by The Marathon Group, Inc., Durham, North Carolina; printed on 50-pound Glatfelter Supple Opaque Recycled and bound by Thomson-Shore, Inc., Dexter, Michigan; and designed and produced by Kachergis Book Design, Pittsboro, North Carolina.